KNOPPIX
HACKS™

Kyle Rankin
foreword by Klaus Knopper

O'REILLY®

Beijing · Cambridge · Farnham · Köln · Paris · Sebastopol · Taipei · Tokyo

Knoppix Hacks™
by Kyle Rankin

Published by O'Reilly Media, Inc., 1005 Gravenstein Highway North,
Sebastopol, CA 95472.

O'Reilly books may be purchased for educational, business, or sales promotional use. Online editions are also available for most titles (*safari.oreilly.com*). For more information, contact our corporate/institutional sales department: (800) 998-9938 or *corporate@oreilly.com*.

Editor:	David Brickner	**Production Editor:**	Sarah Sherman
Series Editor:	Rael Dornfest	**Cover Designer:**	Hanna Dyer
Executive Editor:	Dale Dougherty	**Interior Designer:**	David Futato

Printing History:

October 2004:   First Edition.

 This book uses RepKover™, a durable and flexible lay-flat binding.

ISBN: 0-596-00787-6
[C]   [12/04]

Contents

Foreword

Apart from its applicability for everyday work, GNU/Linux is a great way to learn about operating systems. The Free Software license allows you to take the software apart, see inside, and understand how it works. You can also change the software to fit your needs. It can make you feel like a child happily taking a colorful and complex toy apart into thousands of little gears and switches, just to see how it functions, disregarding the fact that it may be very difficult to ever reassemble that toy again. The difference with GNU/Linux, of course, is that you can work on a copy of the software source code and won't break the original. And sometimes, while reassembling, you can build something entirely different and colorful without even planning to.

The Past

When, in 1999, bootable business card–sized Linux "Rescue CDs" appeared as giveaways at computer expos, I was extremely curious about how they worked. And since they were free software, I was able to look inside and try to figure out how the software worked. After I successfully made a bootable CD, I decided to make a "personal rescue CD." That way, it would be possible to use the software that I needed from a CD, rather than carry around an expensive and fragile laptop. Computers are available everywhere anyway, so why not just have the software in your pocket instead? The idea was to put in the CD and start working right away, without having to worry about installation or configuration of any kind.

But hardware is evil. (Everyone knows this, even if he's not a computer expert.) Vendors seem to create their own standards on demand, which are not standardized at all, and don't even provide technical specifications. Compatibility in hardware depends more on luck or chance than on approved norms, so I had to decide among choosing a system that was so cheap in its hardware requirements that it would work on virtually every PC (which would probably mean that graphics worked only in vesa mode, at best), installing a manual hardware selector in order to load the necessary drivers, or scripting some kind of automatic configuration. For some reason, the last option seemed the most flexible and optimized solution, so I started writing scripts that would automatically install a Linux distribution on hardware components: identify hardware components, load the matching drivers, and create configuration files that are optimized for the hardware, yet tolerant enough to work around small glitches in the hardware specification. This is still an ongoing process, because hardware manufacturers nowadays seem to be in a semipermanent fight against common standardization of hardware specification. But to my own amazement, my solution still seems to work quite well on a great number of machines, despite the sheer unlimited number of hardware configurations and intricacies.

In 2000, my friends from the LinuxTag association talked me into publishing Knoppix as a publicly available and joinable project. They also provided hosting space. The idea was to get more feedback (and possibly workarounds or code contributions) applicable to different computers and exotic hardware components that I had no access to. As new versions with added features were released, the number of downloads and, naturally, feedback (as well as questions to answer) grew tremendously. (Had I known that so many people would find this very experimental project useful, and that there is now even an O'Reilly book being published about it, I would have probably given it a more elaborate name than "Knoppix." But now it's too late, of course.)

The Present

Today, with thousands of Knoppix downloads per day and with about a dozen derivatives, each with a special focus group, language, or supported architecture, it seems that my experiment has gotten a little out of hand. I'm trying my best to keep up with the technical development, and I provide regular updates of the download edition and add new features and gimmicks. And occasionally, there are "Special Editions" like the LinuxTag Conference DVD, which contains a maxi edition of Knoppix with a lot more software than the CD version.

By saying this, I'm probably fitting the cliché that says programmers are naturally lazy in writing documentation, but, lucky for me, it seems that others are now writing manuals and documentation for Knoppix, which means I can stay focused on development. It's really useful to have a book at hand that not only contains technical information about the structure of a system, but also explains some of its components in detail, and I have learned a lot from this book about Knoppix. (In particular, I've learned that some things are not really as complicated as I thought they were.) Had I read this book earlier, I probably would have created Knoppix differently!

There are so many things you can do with Knoppix. The primary design is to use Knoppix as a desktop system platform for tasks, such as office work (using OpenOffice.org, for example) and Internet connectivity; power users and system administrators may use it for rescue operations (grabbing data from a defective or nonbooting filesystem on a different OS), or ad-hoc installations of web, file, or print servers, with or without hard-disk installation. With the terminal server utility (which is just a shell script that creates configuration files for DHCP, NFS, and squid, and starts all of them), you can boot an entire classroom of PCs over a local network, using just a single CD-ROM, which comes in handy if you want to run an Internet cafe, for example. It's also a good tool for learning about operating systems or for functioning as a base if you want to customize your own bootable GNU/Linux CD.

The Future

Knoppix, the downloadable edition from LinuxTag, will continue being a public experiment with a snapshot of the current, most representative desktop programs, rescue tools, and some popular servers installed. The challenge of keeping hardware support up-to-date is always difficult. Some of the newer hardware components, especially hotpluggable devices, require that binary firmware files be uploaded to the device during activation. Unfortunately, the licenses of the firmware don't allow free redistribution in every case, so some hardware will never be supported in the download edition, even if drives are available for private use. One attempt to circumvent this nontechnical problem with proprietary licenses is the "live installer" that was added by Fabian Franz for Knoppix Version 3.4. Maybe a "Knoppix customizing toolkit" would allow you to individually create such personal editions with a collection of software and drives. But currently, it seems to be virtually impossible to automate every single step of the customization process, though Morphix has made some interesting progress in this direction.

The Book

This book takes Knoppix's boot process apart, explains how to do hardware autoconfiguration, describes some of the excellent GNU/Linux tools for recovery of data or system repair, and assists you in finding out more about operating systems in general. Perhaps some part of this book will encourage you to create your own live CD with your own toolkit collection installed. You can do this by using the included Knoppix CD as a base or by downloading a fresh version from the Internet. This book shows you how.

Happy hacking!

—Klaus Knopper
LinuxTag e.V./KNOPPER.NET

Credits

About the Author

Kyle Rankin is a system administrator who enjoys troubleshooting, problem solving, and system recovery. He has been using Linux in many different forms for over six years, and has used live CDs to demo Linux and trouble-shoot machines—from DemoLinux to the LinuxCare bootable toolbox to Knoppix. He watched too much *MacGyver* during his developmental years, and carries a Swiss Army knife and a Knoppix CD with him at all times. Kyle is currently the president of the North Bay Linux Users' Group in California (*http://nblug.org*).

Contributors

The following people contributed their writing, code, and inspiration to *Knoppix Hacks*:

- John Andrews **[Hack #84]** is the creator of Damn Small Linux. He has no formal IT or technical computer training. He likes to play with GNU tools and loves an efficient, open source desktop.

- Jacob Appelbaum **[Hacks #18, #44, and #45]** is a security professional who primarily works with nonprofits and is currently employed at the Rainforest Action Network. His interests include cryptography, covert channels of communication, tunneling, monitoring wireless devices, music, activism, and reading. He would also like to note that he went *warflying* with Knoppix, using *kismet* in the San Francisco bay area before the Tom's Hardware people did it in Southern California.

- Dirk Eddelbuettel, Ph.D., **[Hack #88]** is the creator of Quantian and has been a long-time participant in free software/open source development. He lives and works in Chicago.

- Hilaire Fernandes [Hack #83] is a member of OFSET (Organization for Free Software in Education and Teaching) and a developer for Freeduc.

- Fabian Franz [Hacks #27, #29, and #38] studies computer science at the University of Karlsruhe and has been an active member of the Knoppix project since 2003. Fabian is the author of the Knoppix live-software installation program and does research in several fields of live-CD technology. In 2004, Fabian created the FreeNX server as a full, free-terminal server application, which uses the open source core components of the NX X compression technology.

- Alex Garbutt [Hack #36] is a 20-year-old computer science and engineering major at the University of California, Davis. He currently works tech-support in the computer science labs on campus.

- Marco Ghirlanda [Hack #82], born in Milan in 1977, lives in Turin, Italy. After completing classical studies (Liceo Classico Parini) in Milan, he moved to Turin to earn a degree in communication studies in 2002. Marco works as the open source manager at the Virtual Reality & Multi Media Park of Turin, making Opensourcelab and Mediainlinux with a geographically distributed team.

- James Greenhalgh [Hack #88] is a partner and developer for Open Door Software Inc., a Linux service corporation in Aurora, Ontario, Canada. James manages varying tasks, ranging from bookkeeping to database administration and SQL programming. His first experience with Linux was in 1994 while attending York University in Toronto. He has been running Debian Unstable since 2000.

- Alex de Landgraaf [Hacks #80, #99, and #100] is an AI student at the Vrije Universiteit in Amsterdam and part-time code monkey at the web design company AddMissions. A relative newcomer to free software/open source software, Alex's motto is to be as lazy as possible, but not lazier than that. He started Morphix in early 2003 and he believes the production of flexible live CDs is the way toward solving annoying problems (and monopolies).

- Matthias Mikule [Hack #85] is the creator of INSERT. He finished his diploma thesis in theoretical physics, "Numerical analysis and simulation of a socio-dynamic group model," at the Universitat Stuttgart in 1996. He is the co-owner of Inside Security IT Consulting GmbH.

- Simon Peter [Hacks #30 and #31] has been using Knoppix for years and is the initial developer of *klik*. At the time of this writing, he is conducting research on economic and business implications of open source software and Nanocompetition, just after having completed his studies of economics and management at Witten/Herdecke (Germany), Purdue, and Harvard University. He can be reached at *http://www.simon-peter.de.*

- Karl Sigler (a.k.a. t1ck_t0ck) **[Hack #87]** has been teaching information security for nearly a decade and is currently a security instructor in Atlanta, GA. In his spare time, he is the creator/maintainer of the Knoppix-STD Linux distribution.

- Wim Vandersmissen **[Hack #88]** is a system/network administrator, and he has been using Linux for over eight years now and still likes to play with it. He is the creator of ClusterKnoppix.

- Jascha Wanger **[Hack #86]** has been a network and security consultant for the past eight years. At 22, Jascha began his security consultation in Texas as co-owner of a systems integration firm. Jascha currently works with Local Area Consulting, where he holds the position of VP of Security Solutions. With his work, Jascha has forged new ground designing security solutions and compliance tools for HIPAA and Sarbanes-Oxley legislation. In his free time, Jascha enjoys collecting records (the vinyl kind) and rock art posters. Most of his free time is dedicated to his LocalAreaSecurity.com project.

Acknowledgments

First of all, I want to thank my wife Joy, the *real* writer in the family, for supporting me through this process. It's not easy to take so much time away from someone you love for a project like this. Thanks for understanding and helping me manage my priorities.

Thanks also to Fabian, who has helped answer questions from the very beginning and who has been a major contributor to the book, both in content and in critique. And thanks to all the other contributing writers who have helped tell their particular part of the Knoppix story. In true community spirit, thanks to Eaden McKee and the rest of the Knoppix.net forum for their excellent documentation, in particular the remastering instructions.

Extra thanks to Greg for making this all possible and to Brick for helping me through this and keeping me on track (and taming that darn passive voice). Thanks to all my friends for your continued encouragement, especially Jorge, whom I thought of whenever I wrote a system-recovery hack.

And of course, who can forget Klaus Knopper, the guy who started it all. Thanks for Knoppix; it has certainly saved me more than once. It's a true testament to your ingenuity that Knoppix is so flexible and just plain useful that it has been used by so many other projects.

Preface

As with so many great open source projects, Knoppix started because Klaus Knopper had an itch to scratch. Klaus wanted to take many of his favorite open source tools with him so he could work wherever he went and on any computer he had access to. Because he didn't want the expense of a laptop or the worry of losing or damaging it, he created a bootable Linux CD distribution called Knoppix. With Knoppix, Klaus was able to go from computer to computer and get right to work with an operating system and environment he was familiar with, and without the need to install software on every computer he came in contact with. Many people only view Knoppix as a Linux demo disk, a job it does perform quite well, but even from the beginning, Knoppix was to be used to get real work done.

Klaus wanted to be able to work on any computer, regardless of the hardware in the system, so he continued to improve the hardware support for Knoppix until it was able to recognize and automatically configure much of the hardware it came in contact with. There are a lot of live Linux CDs, but Knoppix's excellent hardware support, combined with the general flexibility of the included software, has made Knoppix the most popular.

Over the years, I have used many different live CDs both as demonstration disks and for system recovery. I have never been a Boy Scout, but I have always liked the idea of being prepared for anything, and at any moment, I might have been carrying a DemoLinux CD or a LinuxCare Bootable Business Card with me, along with a number of other tools, including a Swiss Army knife. I've found that it's handy to have both a screwdriver and a knife in my pocket while crawling under a desk to fix a machine or running cabling through the ceiling, and the Swiss Army knife gives me those tools in a compact form. My use of the Swiss Army knife probably has a lot to do with all the *MacGyver* watching I did as a kid. I marveled at how he seemed to get out of just about any jam with a few simple tools that fit in his pocket.

Knoppix has quickly become my preferred software Swiss Army knife. I no longer have to carry around a lot of different CDs and floppies, because a single Knoppix CD provides everything I need. What's better, I can easily (and legally) make copies of it for my friends, or customize it to have the special tools only I need because it is an open source CD.

This book shows you how to use Knoppix to its full potential with steps to use it as your desktop distribution, your rescue CD, and a launching point for your own live CD. You will find ways to use Knoppix that you may have never considered, and you may even think of ways to use Knoppix beyond what this book covers. I started this book as a Knoppix fan, but once I starting writing down the sheer number of things it can do, I quickly became a Knoppix zealot. I hope you find this book and Knoppix itself as useful and indispensable as I have.

Why Knoppix Hacks?

The term *hacking* has a bad reputation in the press. They use it to refer to someone who breaks into systems or wreaks havoc with computers as their weapon. Among people who write code, though, the term *hack* refers to a "quick-and-dirty" solution to a problem, or a clever way to get something done. And the term *hacker* is taken very much as a compliment, referring to someone as being *creative*, having the technical chops to get things done. The Hacks series is an attempt to reclaim the word, document the good ways people are hacking, and pass the hacker ethic of creative participation on to the uninitiated. Seeing how others approach systems and problems is often the quickest way to learn about a new technology.

Knoppix Hacks provides the hacker with an excellent multi-purpose tool for all of their hacking needs. The sheer flexibility of Knoppix means the clever hacker can get all of her work done with a single CD. Rescue CDs often bring out the hacker in people since you must often find clever ways to get a system functional again or recover lost data. Knoppix gives you all the repair tools you need as you go from plan A to plan Z, and *Knoppix Hacks* shows you how to use those tools in ways you may never have considered.

How to Use This Book

You can read this book from cover to cover if you like, but each hack stands on its own, so feel free to browse and jump to the different sections that interest you most. If there's a prerequisite you need to know about, a cross-reference will guide you to the right hack.

It's important to note that while Knoppix can be installed directly to a hard disk, and indeed there is an entire chapter devoted to that in this book, that unless otherwise noted, the hacks in this book assume you are running Knoppix directly from CD. The first chapter is an introduction to Knoppix itself and the Knoppix live-CD boot process. Refer to this chapter if you have any problems getting the CD to boot on your particular hardware or if certain hardware doesn't function. If you are new to Linux itself, the next two chapters provide you with a guide to the Knoppix desktop and a primer for the major desktop software Knoppix includes. If you find you really like the Knoppix desktop and want to use it on a system permanently, go to Chapter 4 for steps to install Knoppix directly to your computer.

The middle chapters cover more advanced uses for Knoppix, particularly for system administration and recovery. Use these chapters as a quick reference when you need to repair a system or just as a simple way to do much of your daily work with a single CD.

Use the final chapters in the book if you are interested in creating your own Knoppix-based CD. There's a chance the features you need have already been included in another live CD based on Knoppix, so check out the other Knoppix-based distributions in Chapter 8 before you start through the remastering process. You can use the final chapter in the book as a step-by-step reference for the remastering of your own Knoppix CD with the software and features you want.

How This Book Is Organized

Knoppix is incredibly flexible and can be used for many tasks, but these tasks generally fall into a few different categories: desktop use, system administration, system recovery, and live-CD remastering. The first few chapters act as an introduction to Knoppix and help you boot Knoppix on your hardware and then use it as your Linux desktop. The middle chapters feature Knoppix as a system administrator multitool with tips on how to do many common system recovery tasks both on Linux and Windows. The final chapters focus on Knoppix as a platform to create other live CDs with an introduction to many popular Knoppix-based distributions and steps to create your own.

Chapter 1, *Boot Knoppix*
>   Before you can use Knoppix, you must get it booted on your system. This chapter guides you through the process of getting the latest version of Knoppix and booting it on your hardware. The main focus of the chapter is the use of special boot time parameters, called *cheat codes*, to tweak the settings Knoppix uses as it boots.

Chapter 2, *Use Your Knoppix Desktop*
>   Knoppix boots directly into a full KDE desktop environment. This chapter covers all of the features of the Knoppix desktop and introduces the

major desktop and Internet applications Knoppix includes, as well as how to connect to the Internet. Use this chapter to get up to speed on the Knoppix desktop.

Chapter 3, *Tweak Your Desktop*

This chapter covers how to tweak settings on the Knoppix desktop, including installing software directly to ramdisk. This chapter also covers the use of persistent storage, which saves all of your settings and data between reboots, so your data and configuration can be as portable as Knoppix itself.

Chapter 4, *Install Linux with Knoppix*

Knoppix makes it easy to install Linux on your own machine. This chapter walks you through the Knoppix installation process with a few common installation scenarios, including how to turn an install into a regular Debian system.

Chapter 5, *Put Knoppix in Your Toolbox*

Knoppix isn't just for desktop use. This chapter discusses how to use Knoppix as your system administration multitool with tips on how to replace a failed server with Knoppix in an emergency, clone systems, and perform security audits.

Chapter 6, *Repair Linux*

When your Linux system breaks and you need a rescue disc, look no further than Knoppix. This chapter helps you repair a system that won't boot, with tips on restoring the boot loader, repair filesystems, and recover from failing hard drives.

Chapter 7, *Rescue Windows*

The Windows Recovery CD isn't all it's cracked up to be, and when your Windows system breaks, you can use Knoppix to rescue it. This chapter helps you back up files and settings, reset passwords, hack the registry, and even scan for viruses.

Chapter 8, *Knoppix Reloaded*

There are a number of other live CDs that have been based on Knoppix. Each derivative has its own special focus, and this chapter covers some of the most popular Knoppix-based distributions and why you might want to try them in addition to Knoppix. Before you remaster your own CD, check out these distributions.

Chapter 9, *Knoppix Remastered*

Knoppix is very flexible, but if you have a special need or your favorite software is missing from it, you can easily remaster Knoppix to include the special features, or custom branding, you desire. This chapter walks you step by step through the remastering process and features special tricks and tweaks to make the most out of your personalized distribution.

Conventions Used in This Book

The following is a list of the typographical conventions used in this book:

Italics

> Used to indicate URLs, filenames, filename extensions, and directory/folder names. For example, a path in the filesystem will appear as */Developer/Applications*.

`Constant width`

> Used to show code examples, the contents of files, console output, as well as the names of variables, commands, and other code excerpts.

`Constant width bold`

> Used to highlight portions of code, typically new additions to old code.

`Constant width italic`

> Used in code examples and tables to show sample text to be replaced with your own values.

Color

> The second color is used to indicate a cross-reference within the text.

You should pay special attention to notes set apart from the text with the following icons:

 This is a tip, suggestion, or general note. It contains useful supplementary information about the topic at hand.

 This is a warning or note of caution, often indicating that your money or your privacy might be at risk.

The thermometer icons, found next to each hack, indicate the relative complexity of the hack:

 beginner   moderate   expert

Using Code Examples

This book is here to help you get your job done. In general, you may use the code in this book in your programs and documentation. You do not need to contact us for permission unless you're reproducing a significant portion of the code. For example, writing a program that uses several chunks of code from this book does not require permission. Selling or distributing a CD-ROM of examples from O'Reilly books *does* require permission. Answering a question by citing this book and quoting example code does not require permission. Incorporating a significant amount of example code from this book into your product's documentation *does* require permission.

We appreciate, but do not require, attribution. An attribution usually includes the title, author, publisher, and ISBN. For example: "*Knoppix Hacks* by Kyle Rankin. Copyright 2005 O'Reilly Media, Inc., 0-596-00787-6."

If you feel your use of code examples falls outside fair use or the permission given above, feel free to contact us at *permissions@oreilly.com*.

How to Contact Us

We have tested and verified the information in this book to the best of our ability, but you may find that features have changed (or even that we have made mistakes!). As a reader of this book, you can help us to improve future editions by sending us your feedback. Please let us know about any errors, inaccuracies, bugs, misleading or confusing statements, and typos that you find anywhere in this book.

Please also let us know what we can do to make this book more useful to you. We take your comments seriously and will try to incorporate reasonable suggestions into future editions. You can write to us at:

O'Reilly Media, Inc.
1005 Gravenstein Highway North
Sebastopol, CA 95472
(800) 998-9938 (in the U.S. or Canada)
(707) 829-0515 (international/local)
(707) 829-0104 (fax)

To ask technical questions or to comment on the book, send email to:

bookquestions@oreilly.com

The web site for *Knoppix Hacks* lists examples, errata, and plans for future editions. You can find this page at:

http://www.oreilly.com/catalog/knoppixhks

For more information about this book and others, see the O'Reilly web site:

http://www.oreilly.com

Got a Hack?

To explore Hacks books online or to contribute a hack for future titles, visit:

http://hacks.oreilly.com

## CHAPTER ONE

Boot Knoppix
Hacks 1–9

Throughout this book, Knoppix is ascribed as the system administrator's Swiss Army knife. Like a Swiss Army knife, Knoppix has many handy tools, both general-purpose (like a knife or a screwdriver) and special-purpose (like a corkscrew). Some of these tools are used for specific repairs, while others are used for routine maintenance.

You should not use a Swiss Army knife for the first time when you are locked in a room with a bomb that is just seconds away from exploding—we can't all be MacGyver. Likewise, you should familiarize yourself with Knoppix before you use it to attempt to rescue the company's failed accounting server. This chapter starts you on the path to Knoppix mastery by beginning at the beginning: booting Knoppix. By using the cheat codes and boot time options covered in this chapter, you should be able to get Knoppix to boot on almost any x86 computer.

The first hacks in this chapter highlight the basics for obtaining the latest version of Knoppix and getting to the boot: prompt. All new computers should support booting from the CD-ROM drive, and most computers attempt to boot directly from a CD rather than from the hard drives on the system. In case your computer doesn't support booting directly from a CD, I have included instructions for booting Knoppix from a floppy disk.

The second part of this chapter covers cheat codes—options you pass at the boot: prompt in Knoppix to change its behavior. When talking about cheat codes, I'm really talking about ways in which Knoppix's hardware detection and support might fail and how to work around such failures. By the end of this chapter, you should be comfortable with booting Knoppix on a variety of computers and be ready to use the desktop environment.

I remember introducing a friend of mine to Knoppix on a laptop. We were at the university library, and he couldn't get his wireless card to connect to the library's wireless network with his current Linux distribution. We decided to give Knoppix a chance. Without using any cheat codes, we found that Knoppix booted with full video and sound support, and his wireless card was not only detected, but Knoppix automatically connected it to the wireless network!

I certainly hope your experience with Knoppix is as straightforward as my friend's experience. If not, it will be good to know that these cheat codes are at your disposal. They are quite like the can opener on a Swiss Army knife—something you don't usually reach for day to day, but when you do need it, you *really* need it!

HACK #1 Boot Knoppix on a Desktop

The common PC desktop is a great place to begin experimenting with Knoppix.

For computers purchased in 2000 and after, booting Knoppix is as simple as putting the CD in the CD-ROM drive and restarting the computer. For some computers, however, booting Knoppix might require changing the boot order in the BIOS. The BIOS is the screen that appears when you first boot a machine, and it usually lists the amount of RAM and the hard drives it detects. Older systems that don't support booting from a CD require that you boot from a floppy.

Change the BIOS Boot Order

If your computer supports booting from a CD-ROM, but won't boot the Knoppix CD by default, your problem is probably the system boot order setting in the BIOS. To change the boot order and save it, you must enter the BIOS setup, which you can do at boot time by pressing a special key. Some BIOSes tell you at boot time the key to press to change BIOS settings; the common ones are Esc, F2, and Del.

Once in the BIOS, find the section that changes boot device order. On some BIOSes this setting is changed by selecting a tab along the top labeled Boot, while on others the option may be named "Boot device order" or something similar. Once you have found this setting, move the CD-ROM device so that it is listed before any hard drives. If you can't find or change this option, or you need other information specific to you system, refer to the BIOS manual that should have come with your computer or motherboard. Once you have changed the boot device order, save your settings, which should reboot the computer, and after detecting the Knoppix CD, you should be placed at the Knoppix boot prompt.

Boot Knoppix from a Floppy

Some older computers do not support booting directly from a CD-ROM. For these computers, you must first create a boot floppy that enables the system to boot off of the Knoppix CD-ROM. Fortunately, Knoppix has made this process easy. The boot floppy process has changed between Knoppix 3.3 and 3.4. Knoppix 3.4 uses a new boot process that requires two floppy disks. To create these floppies, first boot Knoppix from a machine with a floppy drive that is capable of booting from a CD-ROM. Once the machine has booted, insert a blank floppy into the drive and click K Menu → KNOPPIX → Utilities → Create boot floppies for Knoppix. This script automates creating boot floppies with a progress bar and a prompt that lets you know when to insert the next disk.

Once the floppies have been created, put the first floppy in the floppy drive, leave the CD in its drive, and reboot. The floppy contains a boot loader and kernel image that your system can use to boot far enough along that the CD-ROM can then be loaded.

The Knoppix Boot Prompt

Once you have booted from either a CD or a floppy, you are presented with the Knoppix boot screen, as shown in Figure 1-1.

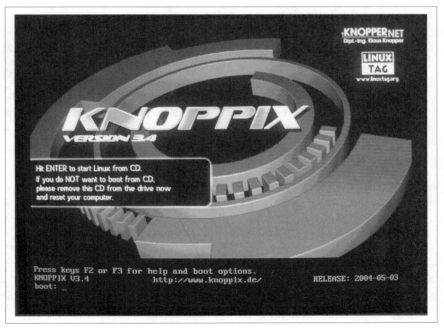

Figure 1-1. *The Knoppix boot screen*

To boot directly into Knoppix, either hit Enter or wait a few seconds, and Knoppix starts the boot process. At this boot prompt, you can enter special Knoppix cheat codes [Hack #3] to control the boot process. Press F2 and F3 at this prompt to display some of the cheat codes.

As Knoppix boots, it displays colorful output while it detects your hardware. Once it has detected and set up your hardware, it automatically launches into the desktop environment and finishes by opening a web browser showing Knoppix documentation. At this point, you can launch programs, browse the Web, and play games. When you log out of the desktop environment, Knoppix shuts down and ejects the CD for you. If you use a floppy to boot Knoppix, remember to eject it, or the next time you start your computer, it will try to boot into Knoppix again.

If Knoppix doesn't boot, refer to the different cheat code hacks, starting with "Use Knoppix Cheat Codes" [Hack #3], which provide Knoppix hardware-detection hints. The "Solve Knoppix Booting Problems" section of "Use Advanced Knoppix Cheat Codes" [Hack #7] offers specific tips.

HACK #2 Get Knoppix

Knoppix can be downloaded from the Knoppix mirrors or purchased from an online site.

This book includes a copy of Knoppix 3.4 from 2004-05-17 (KNOPPIX_V3. 4-2004-05-17-EN), which was the last release in the 3.4 series. All of the hacks have been tested and written in terms of this release, but most hacks should work fine across the new releases. At the time of this writing, the first version of 3.6 has been released; however, I felt it would be better to keep with 3.4 because it has had time to work out major bugs.

Get the Latest Version

Even though new, major versions of Knoppix are released every year or so, new, incremental releases occur as often as twice a month. These incremental CDs have the latest updates to all the software on the CD, the latest Linux kernels, and sometimes, new features. New software updates offer bug fixes and new-and-improved features. New kernel updates often mean better hardware support; if an older version of Knoppix doesn't boot on your computer, the latest release of Knoppix might give you better results. Sometimes new features are added in incremental releases in the form of improved hardware detection, extra Knoppix configuration tools, or new cheat codes. See "Use Knoppix Cheat Codes" [Hack #3] for more information. In general, if you need to address a problem on your Knoppix CD, the latest release might fix it.

Download Knoppix

To obtain the latest version of Knoppix, download the CD image from one of Knoppix's mirrors or send away for a CD. If you have an unmetered broadband Internet connection and a CDR/RW drive, simply download the CD image; it's the best way to get Knoppix. A collection of mirrors listed at *http://www.knopper.net/knoppix-mirrors/index-en.html* provides CD images in ISO form over http, ftp, or rsync. If you use Bittorrent (a peer-to-peer file-sharing application designed for sharing large files), you can use the Knoppix torrent link on this page. When you click on a mirror you are taken to a licensing agreement page. Have your lawyer read through the software license (your lawyer reviews all of your software licenses before you accept, right?), click Accept to proceed, and then choose a file from the list that is presented. In addition to the latest version of Knoppix, most mirrors host a few past CD images with their MD5sum.

When trying to decide which CD to choose, it helps to understand the scheme Knoppix uses for naming CD images. Here is an example ISO filename:

```
KNOPPIX_V3.4-2004-05-17-EN.iso
```

Deciphering the filename isn't tricky and can be quite informative. In the aforementioned example, KNOPPIX is followed by the current version, in this case 3.4. Following the version is a date stamp, which indicates the CD image's release date; in our example, the CD was released on May 17, 2004. These date stamps indicate the incremental version mentioned earlier. After the date stamp, there is a language code, in this case EN for English. Knoppix is a German project, and while the default language can be changed with cheat codes **[Hack #4]** at boot time, the Knoppix project releases both German and English CDs to save English-speaking users from having to enter a language cheat code at every boot. English-speaking users want to get images with the EN language code, and German-speaking users want to get images with the DE language code. Everyone else can choose either image and use a language cheat code at boot time.

Select the latest version of Knoppix by clicking on the filename. The 700 MB file can take anywhere from a few hours to a day to download, depending on the speed of your Broadband Internet connection and the current load of your mirror.

Once the image is downloaded, you might want to confirm that the full file has been downloaded correctly and is an exact copy of the original file. An *MD5sum* is a checksum created from a large stream of data using the MD5 algorithm and is often used to verify that large files downloaded correctly. Practically speaking, an MD5sum-generating program takes your Knoppix

ISO file and creates a fingerprint that only that one file is capable of making. Changing even a single bit affects the MD5sum; therefore, if any error occurs during the download process, the generated sum is different from the one listed on the mirror. If both MD5sums match, the file you have is exactly like the file on the mirror.

There are a number of utilities to create an MD5sum under Windows. One such tool can be found at *http://www.md5summer.org*. Once you install this program, run it and navigate to the Knoppix ISO you wish to verify, and click OK. On your Linux machine you will probably find that the md5sum utility is already installed. You'll need to install it if it is not. Once md5sum is installed, make sure the *.md5* file from the mirror is in the same directory as the image, and then type:

```
greenfly@clover:~$ md5sum –cv KNOPPIX_V3.4-2004-05-17-EN.iso.md5
KNOPPIX_V3.4-2004-05-17-EN.iso OK
greenfly@clover:~$
```

If the md5sums match, you are dropped back to a prompt; otherwise, you receive the following error:

```
greenfly@clover:~$ md5sum –cv KNOPPIX_V3.4-2004-05-17-EN.iso.md5
KNOPPIX_V3.4-2004-05-17-EN.iso FAILED
md5sum: 1 of 1 file(s) failed MD5 check
greenfly@clover:~$
```

You can also generate an MD5sum from the command line by typing:

```
greenfly@clover:~$ md5sum KNOPPIX_V3.4-2004-05-17-EN.iso
7ee0382655abf194aa300a98100cacde  KNOPPIX_V3.4-2004-05-17-EN.iso
```

Compare the MD5sum you generate to the corresponding *.md5* file from the mirror. If both match, you have a complete ISO and are ready to create a CD.

You can burn the Knoppix ISO to a CD using your favorite CD-burning software. It is important that you select the Burn Image or an equivalent option on your CD-burning software. Do not select the option to burn a data CD; you will end up with a CD containing a single ISO file, which will not boot.

Buy a Knoppix CD

If you don't have an unmetered broadband Internet connection, or you don't have a CD writer, or you simply don't want to bother with downloading and burning a CD, you can receive a Knoppix CD through the mail from a number of third-party vendors. There is a list of vendors to choose from at *http://www.knopper.net/knoppix-vendors/index-en.html*. These vendors are unaffiliated with the Knoppix project itself and also offer other Linux distributions on CD. When ordering, make sure that the version the vendor is offering is the latest version by comparing its release date with the latest release on one of the Knoppix mirrors. You can purchase a Knoppix CD for five dollars plus shipping, which is a small price to pay if you want to avoid the hassle of downloading and burning a CD.

HACK
#3

Use Knoppix Cheat Codes

Cheat codes are extra instructions you type at boot time that change many of Knoppix's settings. On some hardware, use of these codes may be necessary to get the most out of Knoppix.

Knoppix is good at automating many of the tasks that Linux users often conduct manually, such as hardware configuration, setting up the network, and logging into a desktop. If you want to customize options or change what Knoppix automatically runs, you can enter special commands at the boot prompt, which Knoppix refers to as *cheat codes*. Cheat codes are a reference to the secret passwords or key sequences entered in video games to get unlimited lives or other special items. Fortunately, cheat codes in Knoppix are simple words you type at the boot prompt, and not complicated joystick sequences like up, down, up, down, left, right, left, right, B, A. The cheat codes aren't secret either. Open the Knoppix CD under your current OS and browse to the *KNOPPIX* directory. The cheat codes file is called *knoppix-cheatcodex.txt*. You can also reference a list of the most frequently used cheat codes by pressing F2 at the boot prompt.

To use cheat codes at the boot prompt, type **knoppix** to select the default kernel, followed by the cheat codes you wish to use. For example, if your Knoppix CD doesn't work the way you expect, test for any physical errors on the disc; at the boot: prompt, type the following command:

```
knoppix testcd
```

The following table lists many of the settings and options you can change from the boot: prompt using cheat codes:

Cheat code	Purpose
knoppix testcd	Check CD data integrity and MD5sums
knoppix desktop=fluxbox|icewm|kde|larswm|twm|wmaker|xfce	Use specified window manager
knoppix 2	Runlevel 2, Textmode only
knoppix noeject	Do NOT eject CD after halt
knoppix noprompt	Do NOT prompt to remove the CD
knoppix splash	Boot with fancy background splashscreen

For example, if you want to use the fluxbox window manager instead of the default KDE desktop, at the boot: prompt type:

```
knoppix desktop=fluxbox
```

Look at the list of cheat codes to see a number of other window managers, including icewm, larswm, twm, wmaker, and xfce. Each of these window managers offers different features, and most of them offer a completely different environment from what a Windows user might be used to. In addition, these other desktop environments load faster and use less memory than the default KDE desktop.

The text mode cheat code (type **knoppix 2** at the boot: prompt) is useful in circumstances when you don't need a full graphical environment or your graphical environment does not work. This cheat code goes through the full hardware detection but leaves you at a simple prompt instead of launching a desktop environment. On machines with less than 64 MB of RAM (less than 82 MB if using KDE), this mode lets you boot into Knoppix and take advantage of all of Knoppix's command-line utilities—just without the desktop environment. This mode is also useful because it quickly boots into a full shell without the wait for X and a desktop environment to load. After you boot into text mode, you can switch into a full desktop environment by changing your runlevel; at a prompt, type the following command, and Knoppix will start up the default desktop environment:

```
root@tty1[/]# init 5
```

The splash cheat code adds some extra eye candy to the boot process. This cheat code replaces the colorized text output with a fancier graphical background as the system is booting, reminiscent of loading Windows. Hit the Esc key to drop back to the default text output.

The noeject and noprompt cheat codes are useful when, the next time you boot, you plan to use the Knoppix CD in the same system. By default, when Knoppix shuts down, it ejects the CD and prompts you to hit Enter to complete the shutdown. Use these cheat codes to disable these two convenience features, and when Knoppix shuts down, it leaves the CD in the drive for the next boot.

Experiment! Try out new desktops. Test different cheat code combinations. Remember that changes you make with cheat codes do not persist across reboots, and desired changes must be entered at the boot: prompt each time. To make settings persistent, save them on media, such as a USB drive, a floppy diskette, or an existing hard drive. (Saving persistent settings is covered in detail in "Create Persistent Knoppix Settings" [Hack #21].)

Speak Different Languages

HACK #4

One of the advantages of Linux is its native language support. Knoppix is provided in English and German versions, but other languages are supported.

Knoppix's popularity has spanned the globe, and as a result, it comes bundled with support for many different languages. While versions exist that default to German or English, Knoppix can easily boot into many different languages through the use of cheat codes. This hack covers the following language cheat codes:

Cheat code	Purpose
`knoppix lang=cn|de|da|es|fr|it|nl|pl|ru|sk|tr|tw|us`	Specify language/keyboard
`knoppix keyboard=us`	Use different console keyboard
`Knoppix xkeyboard=us`	Use a different X keyboard

When changing language options, the lang cheat code is the main cheat code to use. To change the default language to Spanish, for instance, simply pass the cheat code at the boot: prompt:

```
lang=es
```

This cheat code takes care of all of the locale options, so that all menus, prompts, the desktop environment, and the keyboard are set to the specified language.

> Many beta Knoppix CDs come only in German versions. The differences in the German and English keyboard layouts make themselves apparent when you try to enter the **lang=us** cheat code. The = key on the German keyboard can be entered with Shift-0, the / key is located at Shift-7, and the _ key can be typed with Shift-/. If you want to enter the keyboard or xkeyboard cheat code, keep in mind that the Z and Y keys on the German keyboard are swapped.

To change the keyboard mapping separately from the default locale, use the keyboard and xkeyboard cheat codes. These options change the keyboard language used on the console and graphical desktop respectively.

If you have forgotten to set the lang cheat code before booting up and find that your German is a bit rusty, you can change the language settings from the desktop without rebooting. The first step is to change KDE's language settings:

1. Click on the German flag at the bottom right of the desktop to the left of the clock. Each click will cycle through a list of flags corresponding to languages.

2. Click K Menu → Einstellungen → Kontrollzentrum to launch the KDE Control Center.

3. From the KDE Control Center, click on Regionaleinstellungen & Zugangshilfen → Land/Region & Sprache.

4. Pick out the appropriate country from the drop-down menu at the top, choose your language from the Languages list, and click Anwenden at the bottom to apply the changes.

While the Control Center is open, follow these steps to change your keyboard layout:

1. Click on Tastaturlayout in the Control Center sidebar.

2. Pick the appropriate language from the drop-down menu labeled Verfugbare Belegungen.

3. Click Hinzufugen to move that language to the list of active languages.

4. Click Anwenden to apply the changes. Changes to the language settings apply only to new programs, so anything that is currently open must be restarted if you want the menus to change.

This still does not change the language of any icons on the desktop. To do this, you must completely restart the desktop environment, so either click K Menu → KNOPPIX → Utilities → Choose/Restart KNOPPIX Desktop, or type this command in a shell to drop down to text mode:

```
knoppix@ttyp0[knoppix]$ sudo init 2
```

Then bring the desktop back up by typing this command:

```
root@tty1[/]# init 5
```

Some applications, such as Mozilla, still must have their language changed manually even after restarting the desktop. To change the Mozilla menus:

1. Click on Bearbeiten → Einstellungen to bring up the Mozilla settings.

2. Select Erscheinungsbild → Sprachen/Inhalt.

3. Choose your language under Installierte Sprachpakete and click OK. If your language isn't listed there, click the Weitere herunterladen button to download other language packs.

4. Restart Mozilla for the changes to take effect.

If you need to change many programs, it is simpler and faster to just reboot and use the correct cheat code.

Free Your CD to Make Knoppix Run Faster

Make Knoppix run faster by loading the Knoppix image to RAM or saving it to the hard drive. This also frees your CD-ROM drive for other uses.

Compared to other live-CD distributions, Knoppix runs surprisingly quickly, considering that it downloads data from a compressed image on the CD. If you want to speed things up, but aren't ready to install Knoppix on your hard drive just yet, there are cheat codes that allow you to copy the complete Knoppix CD image to either RAM or a partition on your hard drive, and run it completely from there. These cheat codes give you the added benefit of freeing up the CD-ROM drive for other uses—particularly handy if you have only a single CD-ROM drive in a system; you can play music or burn other CDs simultaneously while using Knoppix.

The toram cheat code instructs Knoppix, before it does anything else, to create a large ramdisk and copy the complete CD there. A *ramdisk* is a virtual hard disk that your operating system creates by setting aside a certain amount of your RAM. When you boot with this cheat code, Knoppix warns you that it might take some time to copy the full image and provides a progress bar while the image is copying. The Knoppix CD image is approximately 700 MB by itself, so this option is only for those of you with 1 GB or more RAM in your system, because even after copying the CD to RAM, Knoppix still needs a good portion of the RAM for loading applications and writing temporary files. If Knoppix runs out of space to copy, it alerts you that it ran out of space and cannot complete the copy and drops back to loading directly from the CD-ROM.

If you don't happen to have over a gigabyte of RAM in your system, you can still free up your CD-ROM drive by using the tohd cheat code. Similar to the toram cheat code, this cheat code copies the complete CD image to a partition on your hard drive. This partition can be almost any filesystem that the Knoppix supports, including Windows filesystems such as FAT and FAT32. NTFS (the default filesystem for Windows 2000 and Windows XP) cannot be written to directly, and it will not work with the tohd cheat code. This cheat code expects you to pick the partition using Linux device names, so if you want to use the first partition on your Primary IDE hard drive, type:

```
tohd=/dev/hda1
```

If you are unsure which device name to use, simply boot Knoppix from the CD and make note of the names on the hard-drive icons on your desktop. You can use any one of these devices that has enough available space. As with the toram cheat code, tohd requires you to have over 700 MB free on your partition. Knoppix copies its CD image into a directory called *knoppix* at the root of the partition that you specify.

One advantage to using the tohd cheat code is that the *knoppix* directory it copies is not deleted when you reboot. In subsequent boots, you can reference the already copied image by using the fromhd cheat code. So, if you have previously used the cheat code **tohd=/dev/hda1** on a computer, type this command to use the same image again:

    fromhd=/dev/hda1

You can even just type **fromhd** without any arguments, and Knoppix scans the hard-drive partitions for you.

Boot from a CD Image

A new feature in Knoppix 3.4 is the bootfrom cheat code. With this option, instead of a CD, you can choose an ISO image you currently have on your hard drive for Knoppix to run from. While similar to the fromhd cheat code, bootfrom uses an actual Knoppix ISO that you must already have on your hard drive. One stipulation for this cheat code is that the ISO you choose must have the same kernel version as the CD-ROM you are using to boot. There are different ways to check the kernel version, but probably one of the best ways is to go to a Knoppix mirror and download the *KNOPPIX-CHANGELOG.txt* file. This file lists all of the major changes in each Knoppix release and usually lists the kernel versions for each release. Otherwise, to quickly check the kernel version from within Knoppix itself, run the following command in a terminal:

    knoppix@ttyp0[knoppix]$ uname -r
    2.4.26

To boot from an ISO, type **bootfrom** followed by the full path to the ISO file. The bootfrom cheat code expects the same Linux paths as tohd and fromhd, so if you have *Knoppix.iso* in the root directory on your Primary IDE hard drive, type:

    bootfrom=/dev/hda1/Knoppix.iso

The bootfrom cheat code is particularly useful if you are customizing Knoppix [Hack #94], as you can have multiple ISOs in a single directory and choose between any of them at boot time. This cheat loads from an ISO and not directly from a CD, so you aren't restricted by the 700 MB capacity limit of a CD-ROM. If you are modifying your own Knoppix-based distribution and are having a difficult time squeezing it all within 700 MB, test your images directly from the ISO without having to worry about the CD size requirements.

After you boot off of the stored image, the Knoppix CD no longer needs to be mounted, so you can eject it and use the CD-ROM for other tasks. You can also use these cheat codes as an intermediate step before fully installing Knoppix to your hard drive; though most of the system files will be read-only, you still benefit from the speed of a full hard-drive install.

Straighten Out Your X Settings

HACK #6

Finely tune X to get the most out of your video hardware, and work around hardware detection mistakes.

Knoppix detects video card and monitor settings pretty well. If it can't detect any better settings, it tries to at least set up a generic environment for X. Even with its excellent hardware detection, sometimes Knoppix is unable to detect everything it needs to set up X the way you would like. If X won't start up correctly or at all, you might be able to get things working with the variety of cheat codes Knoppix provides for X:

Cheat code	Purpose
knoppix screen=1280x1024	Use specified screen resolution for X
knoppix depth=16	Use specified color depth for X
knoppix xvrefresh=60 (or vsync=60)	Use 60 Hz vertical refresh rate for X
knoppix xhrefresh=80 (or hsync=80)	Use 80 kHz horizontal refresh rate for X
knoppix xserver=XFree86|XF86_SVGA	Use specified X-Server
knoppix xmodule=ati|fbdev|mga|nv|radeon|savage|s3|svga|i810	Use specified XFree4-Module
knoppix wheelmouse	Enable IMPS/2 protocol for wheel mice
knoppix nowheelmouse	Force plain PS/2 protocol for PS/2 mouse
knoppix vga=normal	No-frame-buffer mode, but X
fb1280x1024	Use fixed frame-buffer graphics (1)
fb1024x768	Use fixed frame-buffer graphics (2)
fb800x600	Use fixed frame-buffer graphics (3)

Tweak the Monitor Settings

Knoppix attempts to automatically detect the highest resolution at the highest color depth your computer supports, and starts X at that resolution and depth. For some computers, these maximum settings might be hard on the eyes: screen flicker may occur when refresh rates are too low or tiny icons may occur when a resolution is too high. In these circumstances, you can usually fix the problem by using a few cheat codes to change your X server settings.

The screen cheat code lets you specify exactly at which resolution to run X. For instance, if your 15-inch monitor can support 1024×768, but 800×600 is more comfortable on your eyes, at the boot: prompt enter:

    screen=800x600

Similarly, the depth cheat code lets you configure how many bits per pixel for X to use to display color (for instance, the cheat code **depth=16** starts X with support for 65,536 colors). Set depth to 24, 16, 15, or 8 (256 colors). Use this cheat code when you want to use high resolutions with high refresh rates, but your video card can display them only at lower color depths.

If Knoppix can't automatically detect the appropriate horizontal and vertical refresh rates for your monitor, it might cause X to start up at a much lower resolution and refresh rate than your monitor is capable of. Alternatively, X might try to display the highest resolution possible, leaving you with screen flicker from the low refresh rate. In either case, you can force Knoppix to try X at a vertical and horizontal refresh rate of your choice with the xvrefresh and xhrefresh cheat codes. The documentation that came with your monitor should list in the technical specifications what range of vertical and horizontal refresh rates it supports. If you don't have your monitor documentation, you can usually find technical specifications by searching for your monitor's model number on the Internet. Also, some monitors actually list the horizontal and vertical refresh rates on a label on the back. Once you have a list of valid refresh rates your monitor supports, you can experiment with different values in the range until you find the optimal resolution, color depth, and vertical and horizontal refresh rates for your computer.

Video Card Cheats

Knoppix may not always detect the exact video card that is installed in your system. If you have two different video cards installed, it might detect one while you want to use the other, or you may have a cutting-edge video card that isn't yet supported fully in X. Whatever the problem is, you can tell Knoppix which video card module to try by using the xserver and xmodule cheat codes.

The xserver cheat code specifies video card settings to use for the XFree86 Version 3 server, while xmodule specifies video card settings for the XFree86 Version 4 server. To determine which module your video card uses, visit the driver status page on the XFree86 Project site. For instance, to check the driver status for an ATI card on X 4.3, go to *http://www.xfree86.org/4.3.0/ Status.html* and click on ATI to see a list of modules for each chipset.

To take advantage of the newer Xfree86 4 server, use xmodule instead of xserver. To tell Knoppix to use a specific video card module instead of what it auto-detects, pass the name of the module as an argument to the xmodule cheat code. For example, to have Knoppix use the radeon module you would type:

```
xmodule=radeon
```

Three of the XFree86 modules, svga, vesa, and fbdev, are particularly useful when the X module for your chipset doesn't work, because X doesn't support the chipset yet or X's support is buggy. These modules access the lower-level generic video support many cards provide. This lower-level support means you do not get hardware acceleration for your video card, but you should be able to get basic functionality. The svga and vesa modules should work with any SVGA- or VESA-compliant video card. The fbdev module works a bit differently, as it accesses the low-level framebuffer support in the Linux kernel; its operation level depends on the level of support the Linux kernel has for the framebuffer mode of your particular video card hardware.

If you have tried all of the above modules, and X still does not load, there is still hope! One of the older XFree86 Version 3 servers might still support your card. The Version 3 X servers included with Knoppix are: XF86_3DLabs, XF86_8514, XF86_AGX, XF86_I128, XF86_Mach32, XF86_Mach64, XF86_Mach8, XF86_ P9000, XF86_S3, XF86_S3V, XF86_SVGA, XF86_VGA16, and XF86_W32. To use one of these servers, pass its name to the xserver cheat code. For instance, to try the S3 server, type:

```
xserver=XF86_S3
```

Help, My Mouse Is Crazy!

You can also configure mouse settings with cheat codes. If the mouse is moving wildly around the screen or moving down to the bottom-left corner, no matter where you try to point it, Knoppix might be trying the wrong protocol for the mouse. The nowheelmouse cheat code forces X to use the generic PS/2 protocol for the mouse. Alternatively, if it's your wheel mouse that isn't being detected, the wheelmouse cheat code forces the IMPS/2 protocol, which provides support for the scrollwheel, to be used.

Console Cheats

Just as you can tell Knoppix to run X directly through the framebuffer with the **xmodule=*fbdev*** cheat code, you can tell the Linux console to run through the framebuffer by passing **fb** along with the resolution you want to use. The fb cheat code is a bit different from most of the cheat codes in that it actually is specifying a special set of predefined kernel parameters to run the console at a specific resolution. To boot Knoppix into a 1280×1024 framebuffer console, type:

```
fb1280x1024
```

Do not type the following command at the command line:

```
knoppix fb1280x1024
```

These parameters change the vga= setting for the kernel and set xmodule=fbdev, so if there is a different resolution you want to use, you can look up the correct vga= line to use in */usr/src/linux/Documentation/fb/vesafb.txt*.

Knoppix defaults to using a high-resolution console framebuffer when it boots. If it picks a resolution that's too high, or there is some other problem with framebuffer support on your machine, you see a blank screen and are not able to read any console output.

If you want to disable the framebuffer console completely, and use a regular 25 × 80 VGA console instead, add the following to the boot: prompt:

```
vga=normal
```

HACK #7   Use Advanced Knoppix Cheat Codes

Choose advanced options for system tweaking and booting on exotic systems.

Knoppix's cheat codes let you change many of its default behaviors from which desktop environment to use to whether or not to eject the CD at shutdown. While many of the cheat codes have been merely enhancements to the defaults, there is also a full set of advanced options. Many of these advanced cheat codes can help you work around bugs in your hardware or in Linux's support of your hardware, or disable default options that could prevent Knoppix from booting. Some of the more advanced cheat codes for Knoppix are listed here:

Cheat code	Purpose
knoppix26	Boot with the 2.6 Linux kernel
knoppix atapicd	Do not use SCSI emulation for IDE CD-ROMs
knoppix alsa (or alsa=*es1938*)	Use ALSA sound driver
knoppix no{acpi,apic,agp,apm,audio,ddc, firewire,isapnpbios,pcmcia,scsi,swap,usb}	Skip parts of hardware detection
failsafe	Boot with (almost) no hardware detection
knoppix pci=bios	Workaround for bad PCI controllers
knoppix mem=*128M*	Specify memory size in megabytes
knoppix dma	Enable DMA for all IDE drives

Kernel 2.6

The first advanced cheat code to mention, the ability to boot with the 2.6 kernel, is new with Knoppix 3.4. The 2.6 kernel has speed enhancements for desktop users, more features, and, in some cases, better hardware support, specifically for ACPI, which can be important for laptop users. If you are having trouble with your hardware with the default 2.4 kernel, 2.6 kernel might give you better results.

By default, Knoppix loads a kernel from the 2.4 series. To boot into 2.6 at the boot: prompt, type:

```
knoppix26
```

One new feature of the 2.6 Linux kernel is the ability to write CDs from IDE CD-ROM drives without having to use SCSI emulation (the ide-scsi module). By default, Knoppix loads all of your CD-ROM drives with SCSI emulation so that you can easily use the included CD-burning software out of the box. If you are using the 2.6 kernel and want to disable SCSI emulation for all of your IDE CD-ROM drives, use the atapicd cheat code. This lets you burn CDs while accessing the IDE CD-ROM directly.

Use ALSA

Sound cards have traditionally been a problematic piece of hardware for Linux systems. Some cards don't have a driver, or the driver only addresses a part of the features that card supports. Knoppix's excellent hardware detection has eliminated much of the work in finding the proper driver for a sound card, but it defaults to using OSS (Open Sound System) drivers, because, in many cases, OSS drivers have proven to be more stable than the newer Advanced Linux Sound Architecture (ALSA) drivers.

If you need the extra features that ALSA provides, or your sound card works only through ALSA, tell Knoppix to use ALSA drivers instead of OSS by using the alsa cheat code. The alsa cheat code without arguments probes for the desired driver, or you can pass the driver as an argument. You can look up the ALSA module corresponding to your sound card on ALSA's sound card matrix at *http://alsa-project.org/alsa-doc/*. Input the manufacturer of your sound card into the form to receive links to pages for each chipset from that vendor. For instance, the Vortex 2 card uses the snd_au8830 ALSA module, so for Knoppix to use that module, type:

```
alsa=au8830
```

Solve Knoppix Booting Problems

Sometimes you might need to skip parts or full sections of Knoppix's hardware detection so that it boots on a system. On some hardware, certain parts of Knoppix's hardware detection have been known to freeze a system. On other systems, you might want to disable certain pieces of hardware you know are unstable. Knoppix allows you to use all of the standard Linux kernel parameters to disable as much of the hardware as you want. To disable a particular part of the hardware, just type no followed by the type of hardware to disable, such as noaudio to disable sound card detection. If you aren't sure which phase of hardware detection is failing, the expert mode **[Hack #9]** walks you through each phase step by step so you can see how far along Knoppix gets before running into trouble.

> The complete list of kernel parameters is listed along with every kernel's documentation in the *Documentation/kernel-parameters.txt* file, which can be found at */usr/src/linux/Documentation/kernel-parameters.txt* on the Knoppix CD.

There are many different kernel parameters you can use to disable hardware, but a few of these are well-known for booting Linux on problematic machines. A commonly suggested fix for many Linux boot problems is to disable APIC support, which can be done with the noapic cheat code. Disable power management with noapm or acpi=off to help stabilize systems with buggy power management. Pass pci=bios to the kernel to work around problems with bad PCI controllers. Experiment with disabling different options or multiple options at once, as sometimes it is more than one piece of hardware that prevents Linux from booting. If all else fails, boot with failsafe to disable almost all of the hardware detection. The failsafe mode serves as a good sanity check to see if the Knoppix hardware detection is even the problem.

Enable Hardware

Knoppix by default makes heavy use of ramdisks for temporary file storage while it is booted. Because of this, it is important that Knoppix actually detects all of your available RAM; otherwise, you might not be able to start X or load many programs once X is started. Some BIOSes have been known to be problematic and fail to accurately report the available RAM to Linux, but you can bypass these problems and tell Linux how much RAM is in the system by using the mem boot parameter. For example, if Knoppix isn't detecting all 256 MB of your RAM, tell the Linux kernel to use 256 MB of RAM, despite what the BIOS might claim, by typing:

```
mem=256M
```

Linux typically detects the proper DMA settings for any IDE devices in your system, and Knoppix enables DMA by default. DMA on hard drives gives a noticeable performance boost, and on DVD drives, DMA prevents movies from skipping. Sometimes you must force Knoppix to enable DMA on devices that you know support it. Use the dma boot parameter to enable DMA.

As you can see, there are many advanced cheat codes to pass to Knoppix at boot time. To get Knoppix to boot on a difficult system, the best combination of cheat codes depends heavily on the hardware involved. Hardware forums and newsgroups are great resources to search when trying to get Linux working with a particular chipset. Often other people have already done much of the guesswork for you. Pay particular attention to threads involving Linux installation even if the thread isn't about Knoppix, as those threads often list kernel parameters that work around or fix problematic hardware.

HACK #8 Run Knoppix on a Laptop

With laptops sales on the rise, it is increasingly common that your desktop machine is actually a laptop. Knoppix provides cheat codes and other options so it can boot on laptop hardware.

If any type of hardware will make you resort to cheat codes and kernel-parameter voodoo to boot Knoppix, laptops will. Laptop manufacturers often resort to using special proprietary hardware that often has little to no support in the Linux kernel. Some laptops don't even include an internal IDE CD-ROM drive, and instead have an external PCMCIA, USB, or IEE1394 CD-ROM. On Knoppix, support for the CD-ROM after the BIOS boots is pretty important! Laptops also rely on power management features that can be iffy at times. None of these issues should scare you away from trying Knoppix on a laptop. Many of these problems can be solved or at least worked around using cheat codes.

> Knoppix is one of the best distributions when it comes to getting laptops working out of the box. I recommend taking a Knoppix CD with you when shopping for laptops; it is one of the best ways to see how well Linux will run on that machine. Convincing the clerk at Best Buy to let you boot with Knoppix will be your real challenge.

Laptop Display Tweaks

The specifics of tweaking display settings have been covered already in "Straighten Out Your X Settings" [Hack #6]. Some of those cheat codes are particularly useful when setting up a laptop or desktop LCD display. Laptops use LCDs that have an ideal resolution even if they can display other resolutions. The fb cheat code is useful in these cases, because on some displays, running the console below the maximum resolution results in the text still being displayed with black bands around it. To display a framebuffer console on a laptop that has an ideal resolution of 1024×768, boot Knoppix with:

```
fb1024x768
```

In some cases, Knoppix may not detect the laptop's video card or may detect it incorrectly. If forcing Knoppix to use a particular module with the xmodule cheat code doesn't work, but the console displays fine, boot with **xmodule=fbdev** to use the same framebuffer support for X that you use in the console.

Special-Purpose Cheat Codes

There are many other special-purpose cheat codes to boot Knoppix on difficult hardware. Here are some bits of voodoo that have worked for other laptops. For some notebooks that use proprietary PCMCIA CD-ROM drives, the cheat code ide2=0x180 nopcmcia has been known to work by bypassing PCMCIA support in favor of direct BIOS support for the drive. If the PS/2 mouse on the laptop does not work, boot with pci=irqmask=0x0e98 to specify a specific PCI address.

For the worst cases, you might have to disable parts of the hardware to get the laptop to at least be partially usable. The cheat codes outlined in "Use Advanced Knoppix Cheat Codes" **[Hack #7]** can help, particularly noapic, nofirewire, or noscsi. On some lines of Dell laptops, passing nosmp has made the difference in being able to boot. For a time on my Fujitsu laptop, I needed to boot Knoppix with ide0=ata66 ide1=ata66 to work around a bug in my IDE chipset. If the power management support for your laptop is unstable—for instance the laptop goes to sleep, but you can't wake it back up—you might want to disable power management completely with noapm and acpi=off.

HACK #9   Explore Expert Mode

Do-it-yourself types may not like all of the automatic configuration and hardware detection that Knoppix does. For people trying to troubleshoot and for the just plain curious, Knoppix provides an expert mode.

The goal of the Knoppix expert mode is to provide the user with complete control over the different steps that Knoppix performs when booting a system. Each step that Knoppix normally performs automatically behind the scenes is presented to the user with a prompt allowing you to configure exactly what Knoppix will do or won't do. This can be particularly useful if you have a system that gets halfway through the boot process, and then mysteriously restarts. With the expert mode, you can see exactly which step in the Knoppix boot process has caused the boot to fail so you can bypass that step next time.

Step Through the Expert Mode

To start into the Knoppix expert mode, simply type this cheat code at the boot: prompt, along with any other cheat codes you might want to use:

```
expert
```

A new feature in Knoppix 3.4 is the expert26 cheat code that, like the knoppix26 cheat code, lets you boot with a 2.6 kernel. When booting in expert mode, Knoppix appears to boot normally—you should see a picture of Tux in the corner of the screen and the Linux kernel starting to detect hardware. Once the kernel loads, however, Knoppix begins to ask you questions.

Knoppix starts by listing all of the SCSI modules available on the system followed by the question "Load SCSI Modules?" At the prompt you have the option of typing in the names of any SCSI modules you wish to load, or **n** for none. If you just hit Enter, Knoppix probes for which SCSI modules to load just like it does by default. After making your choice, you should notice that, in expert mode, Knoppix gives much more output, telling you which particular devices it is probing for and if modules load successfully or not.

Next, Knoppix asks, "Do you want to load additional modules from floppy disk? [Y/N]." This option gives added flexibility to Knoppix in the case that the default Knoppix kernel doesn't have a third-party module that you need for your hardware. After you answer this question, Knoppix enables DMA acceleration for IDE devices, creates the ramdisk, and starts the init process. Knoppix then notifies you that you have entered the interactive configuration's second stage.

The interactive second stage gives you the opportunity to reconfigure many of your hardware settings through a series of questions. The first question is: "Do you want to (re)configure your console keyboard? [Y/N]." If you forgot to set the console keyboard to match your locale, you can now configure it. Following that is an option to configure your sound card. Select "yes" to launch the *sndconfig* program, which tries to detect your current sound card and loads the appropriate module for it. After you configure the sound card, you can set up your mouse. Select "yes" to start a mouse configuration program that asks you questions, such as how your mouse is connected and which protocol it uses.

After the mouse is configured, Knoppix detects your graphics settings and displays which default X configurations it will use and gives you the option to change them. Select "yes" to launch a full ncurses-based X configuration tool with options to configure your mouse, keyboard, monitor, video card, screen, and layout. This option is great for systems needing some extra tweaking to get X working correctly as you get a finer level of control over options than cheat codes can provide. After X is configured, Knoppix finishes its configuration and launches into the graphical desktop environment.

## CHAPTER TWO

Use Your Knoppix Desktop
Hacks 10–20

Every Swiss Army knife comes with a diagram that lists the different tools of the knife and explains their function. At first, everything may seem clear, and you may believe you understand everything necessary about your new knife. But, as you use it, you realize that you don't really know why it has three different sized knife blades or what the different saws should be used for, and you find yourself wishing you had paid more attention to that diagram.

This chapter is that diagram for your Knoppix CD. The start of this chapter is particularly geared toward people who are new to the Linux desktop. This chapter explains some basics, such as what a KDE panel is and how to find applications to run. If you are already experienced with using a Linux desktop and programs, such as OpenOffice.org and Mozilla, you might want to skip ahead to the end of the chapter where I talk about connecting to the Internet [Hacks #17 and #19].

The first few hacks introduce you to the default Knoppix desktop environment and get you comfortable with the purpose of the different desktop items and the location of available programs.

Later in the chapter, hacks are devoted to different application categories— from office programs to Internet programs to games. These hacks cover the desktop tools Knoppix includes for these different categories and get you started using them.

Once you finish this chapter, you should be able to comfortably navigate through the Knoppix desktop, use all of the desktop applications Knoppix has, and connect to the Internet. At that point, you will be ready for the next few chapters, which cover specialized tools included with Knoppix and their more advanced uses. But for now, on to the desktop!

Explore the Desktop

After you have booted Knoppix, figure out what these windows, icons, and strange panels are for.

If you have successfully booted Knoppix, as mentioned in Chapter 1, you should now be looking at the default Knoppix desktop, as shown in Figure 2-1.

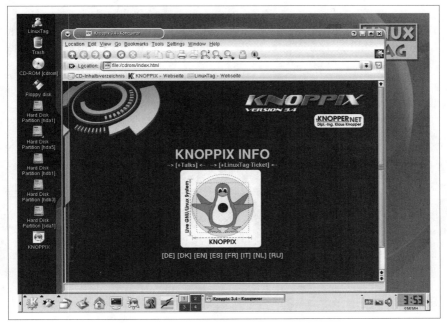

Figure 2-1. The default Knoppix desktop

The Desktop

Probably the first element that grabs your attention is the Konqueror web browser window that opens when K Desktop Environment (KDE) is started. KDE is one of the two most popular desktop environments for Linux (Gnome being the other). KDE's job is to manage your complete desktop environment. It draws your wallpaper, provides you with access to your programs through the menus and icons on the desktop, and manages the windows that appear once you launch an application. Once KDE starts, the first thing you see is the Knoppix help page. This web page contains information and help for Knoppix in many different languages, and includes links to sites to purchase Knoppix CDs, as well as get additional information. The help is available offline, which makes it very useful even when your network connection isn't working.

The desktop itself contains shortcuts to the hard drives, CD-ROMs, and floppy drives on your system (Figure 2-2). Click on any of the drive icons to automatically mount the drive as read-only and open up the mounted file-system in Konqueror. Under KDE, the default is set to open a directory or launch a file with a single click, which might take some adjustment if you are used to double-clicking icons on the desktop. As Knoppix defaults to mounting these filesystems read-only, you can view and open the files you see, but you can't edit, delete, or move any of the files on these filesystems. You can, however, copy the files to your desktop and edit them from there. To make these filesystems writable, right-click on the drive icon and select Actions → Change read/write mode.... The right-click menu also gives you options to unmount and, if the device is a CD-ROM, to eject the media.

Figure 2-2. Desktop icons

The K Menu

The KDE panel spans the entire bottom portion of your screen. On the left of the panel is the K Menu, represented by the K Gear icon. Click on this icon to display the K Menu, which contains most of the graphical applications and some of the command-line applications within Knoppix organized into categories such as Editors, Games, Internet, and Settings (Figure 2-3). If you are new to KDE, Linux, or Knoppix, you will want to explore each of the categories in this menu and get acquainted with how all of the applications on the CD are organized.

At the top of the K Menu is a section reserved for recently used applications. As you run programs from within the K Menu, their icons show up in this section to provide quick access if you wish to run them again. Below this section is the applications section with submenus for each of the following items:

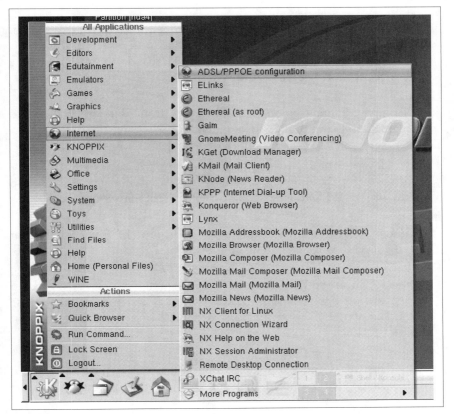

Figure 2-3. The K Menu

Development

Contains applications specifically useful for programming.

Editors

Lists a variety of text editors, including Vim, Emacs, Joe, and many others to satisfy most if not all of the text-editor zealots out there (myself included).

Edutainment

You'll find educational (and entertaining, get it?) applications here. The term "edutainment" is normally applied to children's games, but don't dismiss this category until you try the planetarium software, KStars.

Emulators

Contains the different computer emulators included with Knoppix, such as Bochs. Though this would seem to be a fitting place for the program *Wine*, which allows you to run Windows programs on Linux, you won't find it here. That is because technically, **W**ine **I**s **N**ot an **E**mulator.

Games

Who says Linux doesn't have games? Knoppix includes several—from arcade games to board games to card games. It is easy to get lost in this menu only to emerge hours later, but don't spend too much time here as there are more submenus to cover.

Graphics

Has many different graphics applications—from painting programs to scanning programs to image manipulation applications (such as Gimp).

Help

Provides some basic help applications that let you access info and manual pages for the different programs in Knoppix. For general desktop help, use the K Menu Help icon instead of the applications here.

Internet

Contains a slew of Internet applications—from web browsers to instant messengers to video conferencing applications.

KNOPPIX

Provides all of the Knoppix-specific applications that allow you to run particular configuration applications, start services, and special-purpose Knoppix utilities. This menu is also accessible from the penguin icon on the KDE panel.

Multimedia

Contains all of the multimedia applications—from players for CDs, MP3s, and videos to mixers and sound manipulation programs.

Office

Provides all of the applications useful in an office setting, including the complete OpenOffice.org suite.

Settings

Not to be confused with the System or Utilities menus, this menu contains applications specifically for changing KDE settings.

System

Contains many useful applications for different aspects of system administration from security scanners to backup utilities. Many of the programs in this menu require or give root privileges, so use these applications with caution.

Toys

Has a few fun applications that don't really qualify as games, including the famous Xeyes program, which creates two eyes on the desktop that follow the movement of your mouse.

Utilities
> Displays utilities that aren't necessarily geared toward system adminis-tration, such as calculators and clocks.

After Utilities, instead of more application submenus, you find icons that run specific KDE applications:

Find Files
> Runs the KDE find utility—a useful program for searching through your system for misplaced files.

Help
> Launches the KDE Help Center—a useful program for getting KDE-specific help and asking questions such as "How do I resize my panel?"

Home
> Opens your home directory in the Konqueror file manager.

Wine
> Loads Wine, a program that lets you run many Windows applications under Linux. The first time you click this icon it gives you the option to configure Wine.

Below the application section of the K Menu is the actions section, which organizes a few special-purpose menus for KDE:

Bookmarks
> Allows you to quickly access and edit bookmarks both in the Kon-queror and Mozilla web browsers.

Quick Browser
> Similar to the bookmark submenu, it provides quick access to your file-system in a menu form. Click on one of the directory icons to launch Konqueror in that directory.

Run Command...
> Opens a window that lets you type in a quick command you want to run without having to open a full shell. The keyboard shortcut Alt-F2 brings up the same dialog.

Lock Screen
> Locks your screen, requiring a password to get back in. Because Knop-pix doesn't use passwords by default, this feature has been disabled since Knoppix 3.2.

Logout...
> Launches the logout dialog, which lets you log out of the desktop, reboot, or halt the machine.

The K Menu is worth getting familiar with. Browse through the different categories and try out the huge library of programs Knoppix includes. Everything runs from CD, so you can't really harm anything with your experiments. Now that you are familiar with the K Menu, let's move on to the other parts of the Knoppix desktop.

The Panel

The panel is the gray bar along the bottom of the screen containing the K Menu and other items. The panel is like an extensible Windows taskbar. It allows for applets to be embedded in it; the default Knoppix panel (Figure 2-1) has several of these. To the immediate right of the K Menu are two other menus; the first has a penguin icon and is a shortcut to the KNOPPIX submenu. The next menu lists all of the applications open across all desktops. To lower all visible applications, click on the next icon, which looks a bit like a desk with a pencil on it. Click the icon again to raise all application windows. Next to those icons, you will find many shortcut icons for applications in the K Menu. These are meant to provide quick access to applications you commonly run. Right-click on any of these icons to display a context menu that gives you the option to move or delete the icons. Drag-and-drop icons from the K Menu to add them to the panel.

To the right of the application icons, you should see a box with the numbers 1, 2, 3, and 4 in it. This is known as a desktop pager, and it allows you to quickly switch desktops by clicking on the appropriate number, or if you prefer, Ctrl-Tab cycles through your applications and Ctrl-Shift-Tab cycles through the desktops. By default, Knoppix has four virtual desktops that allow you to reduce clutter by grouping open programs onto different desktops. The pager highlights the active desktop so that you don't get lost.

Next to the pager is the task list, which shows all of your open applications. Click on the program name to raise and lower the program window. Right-click on any of the windows in the task list to see a list of actions you can perform on that window, such as closing, maximizing, and moving the window to a different desktop.

After the task list are a few useful applets grouped in the system tray. Many applications that run in the background put an icon here to allow you quick access to the program's options. First, you see a flag to represent the KDE keyboard tool that lets you change which keyboard locale you are using on the desktop. Next, you see a screen display applet that is new to Knoppix 3.4. Click on this applet to change screen resolution and monitor frequency on the fly. The speaker icon represents the KDE mixer applet, which lets you change your volume settings. If Knoppix is unable to configure your sound card, you should notice that the mixer applet has a red slash through it. Finally, at the far right of the panel is a clock. Before you can adjust the date and time, you must create a root password. To do so, open a terminal window and type:

```
knoppix@ttyp0[knoppix]$ sudo passwd
Enter new UNIX password:
Retype new UNIX password:
Passwd: password updated successfully
```

Experiment with the panel. Click and drag icons to move them around on the panel. Drag the applet handles to move them. Right-click icons and applets to see a list of options for the applet, including removing it from the panel completely. Drag icons from the desktop or the K Menu and drop them on the panel to add them. To resize the panel, right-click on it and choose your size from the Size menu. Remember that all of the changes you make are not persistent unless you save your Knoppix configuration [Hack #21].

HACK #11 Customize the Desktop Look

The look of Knoppix's default desktop doesn't appeal to everyone. KDE has many tools to change the look and feel of the desktop.

Let's face it. People have different tastes. The themes, window borders, fonts, and colors that Klaus Knopper has chosen for himself might not appeal to you. If you don't like how Knoppix looks by default, you'll be pleased to find that Knoppix's flexibility extends to changing how it looks.

Appearance and Themes

Probably all of the changes you want to make in how the desktop looks and feels can be made from within the KDE Control Center. To start this program, click K Menu → Settings → Control Center. The KDE Control Center presents a listing of different configuration categories that let you change many different settings on the desktop. For our purposes, let's stick to the first category, "Appearance and Themes." Click on that category to expand the listing and display all of the different choices for changing the appearance. There are a number of different settings you can change:

Background
Change the wallpaper that appears on the desktop. You can choose many different images (look under /usr/share/wallpapers), pick a number of color gradients, or even configure a slide show.

Colors
Customize the color scheme for all of the buttons, menus, and text.

Fonts

Pick your favorite fonts to be used in the toolbar, the desktop, menus, etc.

Icons

Knoppix includes only a single icon theme, but you can download new icon themes from sites such as *http://www.kdelook.org*.

Launch Feedback

Control what KDE does when you launch applications. If that bouncy cursor is driving you nuts, disable it here.

Screen Saver

Enable and change the settings for the screen saver. Unfortunately, Knoppix does not include many screensavers by default.

Splash Screen

Choose from a list of graphical splash screens that show you the progress when KDE starts.

Style

Configure widget styles. If you don't like the rounded, three-dimensional buttons that Knoppix defaults to, change them here.

Window Decorations

Configure the look and placement if the title bar and buttons on all of your windows.

After you have changed the settings for any of those options, click Apply to commit them. If you apply new changes and don't like how things look, click Reset to take you back to how they were set before the change.

One of the fastest ways to customize the look of your desktop is to change the background image, or wallpaper. To do this, click on Background under "Appearance and Themes." To the right you should see all of your background options, as shown in Figure 2-4. You also have the option to set a different background for each of your virtual desktops. By default, each desktop shares the same background. Click on the drop-down menu to give you a list of other backgrounds. If you have an image somewhere else on your computer you would like to use, click the folder icon to the right to browse through the filesystem and find it. Both */usr/share/pixmaps* and */usr/share/wallpaper* have a number of images you can use. To use a background from one of your hard drives, click the drive icon on the desktop to open it, find the file you want to use, hold down the middle mouse button (push down the scroll wheel on a scroll mouse) or hold both the right and left mouse buttons (this is known as chording and it simulates a middle mouse button click) at the same time, drag the image onto the desktop, and choose "Set as Wallpaper" from the list of options that appears when you drop. If there are a series of images you would like to cycle through, select "Slide show" and click Setup. In this window, you can select a series of pictures to use in the slide show, and determine how often to cycle through them.

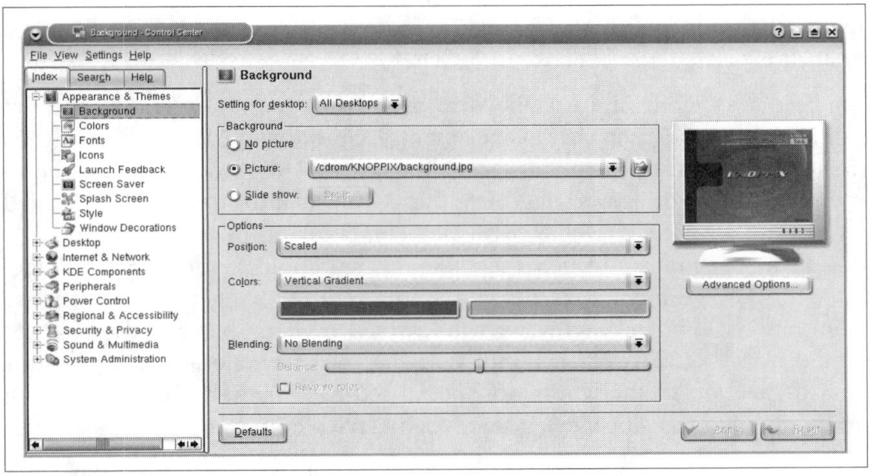

Figure 2-4. Background options

If you want to use a simple color for your background, select "No picture" and choose the desired color from the options below. You can choose from a series of gradient, pattern, and color options, which can create very unique backgrounds. After you have set up your background, click Apply to commit your changes. If you don't like the changes you've made and want to go back to the previous setup, click Reset.

You can change the color scheme to further customize the look of your desktop. Pick a scheme that blends well with your wallpaper or one that is just more pleasing to your eyes. To the left, click the Colors option in the listing to open the color configuration widget. There is a series of color schemes that have already been created for you, and each scheme changes how buttons, highlighted text, and fonts are colored. Above the selections is a preview window that lets you see how the color changes will look when you apply them. If you don't like any of the color scheme choices, create your own. Simply pick a color scheme to start from, and change individual widget colors from the Widget Color section to the right. Once you finish tweaking the color settings, click Save Scheme to save your changes.

Every user has his favorite fonts that he likes to use. Though Linux lacks many of the fonts available on Windows (most people don't know this, but fonts are copyrighted and cost money), it does have a large selection of community-created fonts, some of which you can find on Knoppix. The

Fonts option lets you change which fonts to use for different widgets and their sizes. This configuration window is especially useful for high-resolution laptop displays, because some fonts are too tiny to read. The font configuration window lets you turn on anti-aliasing for your fonts. Anti-aliasing makes the fonts look better by smoothing out the jagged edges on diagonal lines. It is particularly effective on LCDs.

Linux lets you control the shape, size, and representation of many common elements on your screen. The elements, collectively known as widgets, include the buttons, scrollbars, checkboxes, and drop-down menus common in all applications. KDE groups these widgets into configurations called *styles* to make it easy to change all elements at one time. Click on the Style option in the index to open the style configuration window. The Widget Style drop-down menu presents you with a series of widget styles to choose from, and below it is a preview window so you can see what the changes would look like. The Effects and Miscellaneous tabs along the top of this window let you further configure special settings for the widgets, including animation and translucency effects. Not all styles support these extra effects.

If that big, thick titlebar bothers you, or you want to move around the close, minimize, and maximize buttons, click Window Decorations in the index. This configuration window won't let you install Venetian blinds on your desktop, but you can change how the titlebar and borders on your windows look. Click on the drop-down menu to select among many different window border options. Look in the preview window below the options to watch your changes in action. To change the order buttons appear on the titlebar, check "Use custom titlebar button positions" and drag buttons around in the example window. How's that for customization?

Look Like That Other OS

Now that you are familiar with how to change the look of your desktop, let's practice changing settings. Here's a quick recipe for making your desktop look like that *other* operating system.

Versions of Windows prior to XP came with various solid-color default backgrounds. To duplicate the look of a Windows 2000 desktop, open the background configuration window, check "No picture," and select Single Color in the Colors drop-down menu. Then click on the first color (by default it should look blue) and make sure that it is set to the following: R=30, G=114, B=160 (a bit of red, a dab of green, and a dollop of blue give you the final desktop color). Then click Apply to commit the changes.

Windows 2000 has a very pleasing blue and gray color scheme. To use a very similar scheme in Knoppix, click on Colors in the index, select Redmond 2000 from the Color Scheme list, and click Apply.

The finishing touches are to give your Knoppix desktop a set of widgets and window decorations to mimic those found in Windows. First, click Style in the index, change the widget style to "MS Windows 9x," and click Apply. Things should look pretty familiar by this point except for the window borders. Click on Window Decorations and pick Redmond from the drop-down menu to take care of that. The last small step is to right-click on the K Gear on the panel and choose Panel Menu → Size → Small. Voila! It's not perfect, but then again, neither is Windows.

HACK #12 Get Office Work Done

You can't get much work done in an office these days without an office suite. Use OpenOffice.org and Kontact to turn any computer into your office workstation.

The inclusion of a complete suite of office tools, including all of OpenOffice.org, into Knoppix means that not only can you try out Linux with a full-featured desktop, but you can also get your work done while you're at it. This hack discusses how to use Knoppix to create and edit documents, spreadsheets, and presentations, as well as manage your contacts and appointments.

Microsoft Office has in many ways defined how people get work done in an office environment. To many people, there is no word processor other than Word, no spreadsheet program other than Excel, and no email client other than Outlook. For any new office suite to get any user interest at all these days, it must tout compatibility with the file formats Microsoft Office uses, and the office suites available under Linux are no exception. Knoppix provides the OpenOffice.org suite and the Kontact personal information manager. While these programs do take some getting used to if you are accustomed to Office, after a bit of adjustment you should find you can still get your office work done under Knoppix.

OpenOffice.org

When I introduce Linux to a Windows user, one question that often comes up is "Can I open all of my Word documents?" As a system administrator friend of mine (who likely dealt with the famous Word 95 and Word 97 compatibility issues) quipped, "OpenOffice.org's compatibility with Word is at least as good as Word's compatibility with Word."

OpenOffice.org is an open source office productivity suite that touts compatibility with many of the popular office file formats, including Microsoft Word, Excel, and PowerPoint, and runs on a variety of platforms, including Linux, Windows, and Solaris. The OpenOffice.org tools I discuss are the word processor Writer, the spreadsheet Calc, and the presentation software Impress.

Word processor. OpenOffice.org Writer is a full-featured word processor with support for spellchecking, macros, revision tracking, and most of the other features you expect to find in a word processor. It touts compatibility with many different versions of Microsoft Word and can even export a file to PDF. Writer, like all of the programs in the suite, saves files in an open XML-based format that takes up very little space.

To launch Writer, click K Menu → Office → OpenOffice.org → OpenOffice.org Writer. You can also browse through your filesystem and click on any documents with file formats that Writer supports, such as *.doc* and OpenOffice.org's own *.sxw* format, and Writer will launch and open them. Though OpenOffice. org's launch time is shorter than it used to be, it still takes some time to load, especially from a CD. Once loaded, you are presented with a blank document, as shown in Figure 2-5.

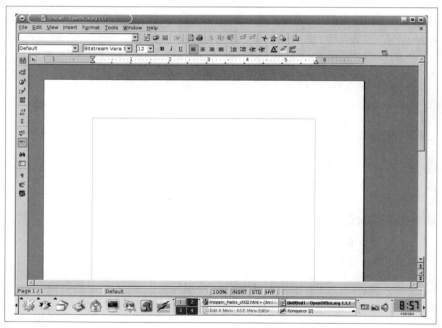

Figure 2-5. OpenOffice.org Writer

Surrounding the document, you can see multiple toolbars much like those in other word processors. These toolbars let you bold, italicize, colorize, and configure other aspects of the text; control alignment; insert figures; and insert bulleted lists. After you have created or edited a document, click File → Save As to select from a number of document formats, including multiple versions of Word, Rich Text Format, and OpenOffice.org's native document format.

To create a PDF of the current document, click the PDF icon on the toolbar, or select File → Export as PDF.... It is cheaper to create PDF documents this way than purchasing Adobe Acrobat.

> If you are saving a document that you have opened from a drive on your computer, remember that Knoppix by default mounts filesystems as read-only, so to save you must either right-click on the hard-drive icon corresponding to your partition and select Actions → Change read/write mode, or temporarily save to your desktop.

Spreadsheet. If you need to create or edit spreadsheets under Knoppix, start OpenOffice.org Calc by clicking K Menu → Office → OpenOffice.org → OpenOffice.org Calc. Calc is a full-featured spreadsheet program and supports editing Excel and comma-delimited files in addition to its own .sxc format. While Calc does not support Excel macros, it does provide its own macro language and recorder, and full support for Excel mathematical functions.

On opening Calc, you are presented with a blank spreadsheet surrounded by toolbars, and you are able to create macros and formulas. After you have entered your edits, click File → Save As to choose from a number of file formats, or you can export your spreadsheet to PDF using a word-processing program like Writer.

Presentation. For creating or editing your presentations, run OpenOffice.org Impress by clicking K Menu → Office → OpenOffice.org → OpenOffice.org Impress. Impress is OpenOffice.org's presentation program with support for many different animations and other slide effects.

On starting Impress, you are presented with the option of starting a blank presentation or using one of the predefined templates Impress includes. After you have made your decision, Impress loads the blank presentation with a layout and toolbars very similar to those in Writer and Calc.

With each slide, you can choose from many different layouts that have already been created. These layouts provide predefined bounding boxes for your text and graphics, making it easy to just drop in the data without worrying about lining up everything. You can make use of graphics, back-grounds, and animations much like with other presentation software.

Once your presentation is ready, start the slide show by pressing F9 or click-ing Slide Show → Slide Show from the menu. Click your mouse, hit the left arrow key, or hit the spacebar to move forward in the presentation; right-click your mouse, or hit the right arrow key to move backwards in the pre-sentation. To exit the slide show, hit Esc or the Backspace key. To save your presentation, click File → Save As, and select from either PowerPoint or OpenOffice.org's own Impress file format. You can also export the presenta-tion to a number of formats, including PDF, HTML, and even Flash.

If you find you like OpenOffice.org, you can also download it for your Win-dows desktop from the official site at, you guessed it, *http://www.openoffice.org*.

Calendar and Contact Management

Beyond the OpenOffice.org suite of tools, Knoppix has an application called Kontact that can manage your calendar, contacts, and email, and is very simi-lar to Outlook. Of course, for these applications to be useful, you must set up some sort of persistent home directory **[Hack #21]** so your calendar and contact settings don't get lost when you reboot.

To run Kontact, click K Menu → Office → Kontact. Kontact integrates many smaller KDE components, such as KOrganizer, KMail, and Knotes, into a single groupware application. You should see icons for the many different components on the left. Click on one of the program icons to load it into the window on the right, as shown in Figure 2-6.

KMail is KDE's primary email application and supports retrieving email from multiple POP and IMAP email accounts. Its integration into Kontact means that all the email addresses in the address book are easily accessible. To add new contacts directly from an open email, simply right-click on the email address and select "Add to Address Book." The address book itself has fields for all the different types of contact information you might wish to store, including a photo.

The Todo List and Calendar have all of the functionality you might be accustomed to in a Personal Information Manager (PIM), and they allow you to set appointments and integrate birthdays and anniversaries from your contacts.

The KAlarm applet runs in the taskbar and alerts you when an appointment draws near. This is very useful because you don't need to run the entire Kon-tact program just to receive notices of pending appointments or to-do items.

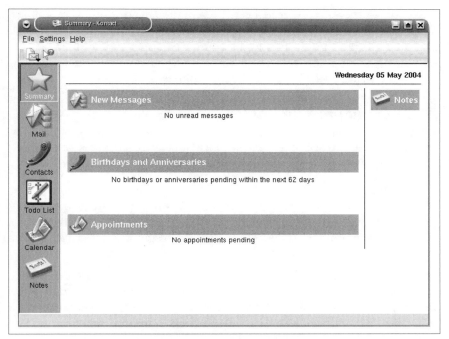

Figure 2-6. Kontact

The last application within Kontact is KNotes, which allows you to post bright yellow notes across your computer's desktop instead of your physical desktop. KNotes keeps track of all your notes and records the date that each note was made—something those paper notes won't automatically do for you.

If you happen to have a Palm PDA, you can also integrate its information with Kontact via the KPilot program. For Palm PDAs, the KPilot program (click K Menu → Utilities → KPilot) should support your USB or serial cradle without any extra configuration. If you want to change the hotsync speed or other settings, click Settings → Configure KPilot.

To sync a Palm PDA with Kontact, click Settings → Configure Conduits... and make sure that Addressbook, KNotes/Memos, KOrganizer Calendar, KOrganizer/Todo's, and Kroupware are checked. Apply your changes, and then hotsync with your Palm to populate your Kontact applications with all your data.

To perform a hotsync, click the hotsync button at the top left of the KPilot window, and then press the hotsync button on your cradle. The main KPilot window shows you the syncs progress.

With word-processing, spreadsheet, presentation, and groupware applications all on a single CD, Knoppix has all the common tools needed for getting office work done. Combine this with a persistent home directory and settings on a floppy or USB key **[Hack #21]**, and you can get your work done even while visiting Microsoft's Redmond campus.

HACK #13 Configure Your Printer

Even in an increasingly digital world, sometimes you still need a hardcopy of your files. The KDE printer manager has a lot of options, and this hack guides you through them.

If you have taken advantage of any of the office applications from "Get Office Work Done" **[Hack #12]**, you might find yourself wanting to print out some of the work that you have done. Knoppix's excellent hardware support extends to printers, and Knoppix provides a simple graphical configuration tool for setting up any printers you may need to use.

Click K Menu → KNOPPIX → Configure → Configure printer(s) to launch the KDE printer manager. In this application, you should find that a few special printers for faxing and printing PDFs have already been created for you. These default printers are provided by the Common Unix Printing System (CUPS) that is running on the Knoppix CD. CUPS is the standard printing system on most Linux distributions and is even the underlying print technology behind Apple's OS X operating system. To launch the new printer wizard to add a new local printer, click Add → Add Printer/Class....

The printer wizard has support for many types of printer connections, and this hack describes some of the more common ones. After the first few questions, the configuration is the same for both local and network printers; the first question the wizard asks is where the printer is located.

For printers that are physically connected to the computer with a parallel, serial, or USB cable, select Local Printer. You will be presented with a list of local devices your printer is connected to. If you use a parallel port, you most likely need to select Parallel Port #1, and if you use a USB connection, you should probably select USB Printer #1. These selections mean that the printer is connected to your first parallel or USB port.

For printers that are shared on the network with Windows printer sharing, select "SMB shared printer" instead of Local Printer. If this printer requires a special username or password to access it, the next window allows you to set those options. You are then asked to enter the workgroup, server name, and printer name to use (Figure 2-7). If you aren't sure what the correct printer name is, click Scan and the wizard scans the network for open printer shares.

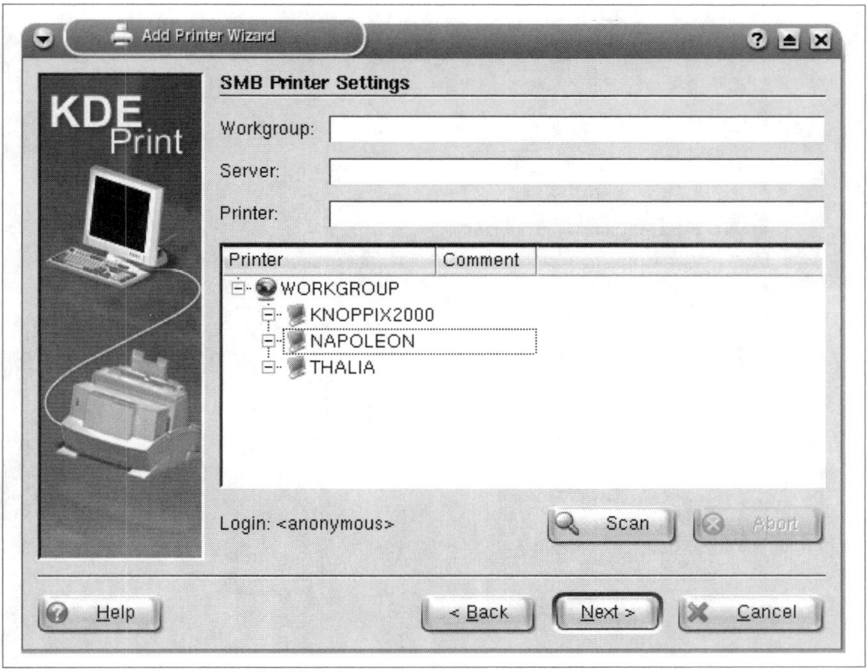

Figure 2-7. The SMB printer configuration window

If you have another CUPS server configured on the network, select "Remote CUPS server." The next window lets you define a username and password if the remote printer requires it, and afterwards you are prompted to enter the IP address or hostname for your CUPS server. The wizard then scans that server and presents you with any shared printers that it discovers.

The rest of the steps are common regardless of how your printer is connected. The next window (Figure 2-8) displays a full list of printer manufacturers. Find the manufacturer of your printer in the left panel and pick the specific model (or the model closest to yours if your exact model isn't present). If you can't find a printer resembling your own, but your printer supports a more generic printing protocol such as PCL or Postscript, then choose Generic from the list of manufacturers, and then choose the protocol your printer supports from the panel on the right.

The next few windows contain several default settings that rarely need to be changed. Modify these settings if you see fit; otherwise, just click through until you get to the General Information window. Enter a name for the new printer here and then click finish.

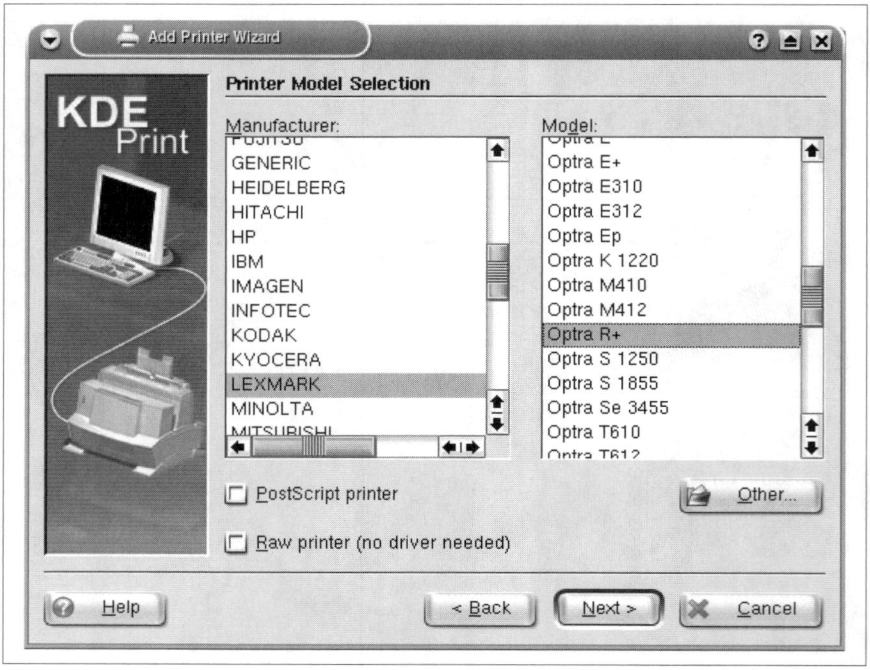

Figure 2-8. Select a printer model

Once you finish setting up a printer, a new icon appears for it in the print
manager. To set it as your default printer, right-click its icon and choose
"Set as User Default." If you prefer a paperless office, you can print directly
to a PDF, a Postscript file, or to a fax machine.

HACK #14   Use Peripheral Devices

Knoppix includes support for many popular scanners, cameras, PDAs, and
other peripherals—often with little to no extra configuration.

There is a common misconception that Linux has poor hardware support,
especially when it comes to peripherals. Actually, you might be surprised at
just how much hardware Linux supports out of the box without requiring
that you download any extra drivers. Knoppix goes a step further and automatically configures a lot of the peripherals you might use—just plug them in.

Scanners

Knoppix supports many popular scanners with little to no tweaking. I have
both SCSI and USB scanners, and Knoppix recognized and configured them
with no extra effort on my part. To start using your scanner, click K Menu
→ Graphics → Kooka to start Koka, KDE's scanning application.

When Kooka starts, it lists all of the scanners that Knoppix has detected and prompts you to choose one. After you select your scanner, Kooka's main window appears.

Kooka works like most other scanning applications. Click Preview Scan to perform a quick scan, then crop out the section of your scan you wish to use and click Final Scan to scan at full resolution. After completing a scan, Kooka will prompt you for the file format to save the image as.

Kooka can also perform some basic image manipulation, such as image rotation and mirroring, although for more advanced features you should probably use a complete image-editing program such as the Graphical Image Manipulation Program (GIMP), which is described in this section.

> Be aware of the image size when scanning at high resolutions, because the scanned image can easily become larger than your available ramdisk space, leaving you with an incomplete image file and a desktop with no extra free space (which might cause weird behavior or crashes in any applications that must write to the ramdisk afterwards).

Kooka includes Optical Character Recognition (OCR) capabilities as well, so you can convert a scanned document to text. To OCR scan an image, select it from the list of images in the top left of the main window and click Image → OCR Image…. The OCR window that pops up lets you configure gray levels, dust size, and spacing of your document. These settings can dramatically affect the results of the OCR scan, so it is worth you time to adjust them if you are getting poor results.

When the OCR scan finishes, the OCR window disappears and you are dropped back to the main window. You must save the results of the OCR scan so you can use it later in a text editor: click File → Save OCR Result Text…. Once you save the file, you can open it in your favorite text editor.

If you plan on doing a lot of image manipulation, you can scan an image directly from the GIMP. Load the GIMP by clicking K Menu → Graphics → The GIMP. From within the GIMP, select File → Acquire → xscanimage, and choose the scanner you wish to use from the resulting menu. Xscanimage does not provide as many scanning options as Kooka, but all image cropping and rotation can be handled directly in the GIMP itself. You can manipulate the image within the GIMP, and save it into one of the many file formats that the GIMP supports.

Digital Cameras

You can also manipulate images from your digital camera with little to no extra configuration in Knoppix. For digital cameras that work as a generic USB storage device (under Windows they show up as a removable drive), simply plug in and power on the camera, and a new hard-drive icon appears on your desktop, allowing you to view your images directly from the camera.

> Remember that Knoppix mounts filesystems as read-only by default, so to delete or edit any of these images directly from the camera, right-click on the hard-drive icon and select Actions → Change read/write mode.

You can open the images with the GIMP or one of the other image-editing applications included in Knoppix, crop or edit the images how you prefer, and save them back onto the camera or some other storage device. Remember to unmount the camera before unplugging it from the computer or powering it off by right-clicking on the hard-drive icon and selecting "Unmount." This ensures that all changed files have been completely written to the camera. Unplugging any USB drive while files are being written almost guarantees file damage.

To use cameras that don't work as generic USB storage devices, use *gtkam*, a program that uses the libgphoto libraries to provide basic access to the files on your digital camera. Before you run *gtkam*, depending on your camera, connect the camera to the computer by the USB or serial port. To run *gtkam*, click K Menu → Multimedia → Viewers → gtkam. The main window appears fairly blank by default, and the first step is to click Camera → Add Camera... to open a dialog that displays the full list of cameras *gtkam* supports (Figure 2-9).

Figure 2-9. Gtkam camera selection

Click Detect for *gtkam* to probe the USB ports for your camera, or select it from the list of camera models and click OK. You are dropped back to the main window, which then presents you with thumbnails of all of your photos. You can zoom in and out on your photos, and select some or all of them to save for later editing.

Removable USB and IEEE1394 Drives

Removable drives, especially small USB key chain drives, are useful in Knoppix, because they provide portable writable storage so your files can travel with you from computer to computer. "Create Persistent Knoppix Settings" **[Hack #21]** discusses how to use these devices to save configuration settings and create a persistent home directory that can follow you from machine to machine.

USB and IEEE1394 (also known as Firewire or iLink) drives work under Knoppix much like digital cameras. Plug in the drive—if necessary, power it on—and Knoppix will detect the device and create a new hard-drive icon on your desktop. USB and IEEE1394 drives are accessed as SCSI drives under Linux, so the first drive you plug into your system will probably be named *sda1*. These devices should work like any other hard drive installed in the system and will mount read-only by default. As with digital cameras, be sure to unmount the drive before unplugging it.

Other Devices

The *gqcam* program (click K Menu → Graphics → gqcam) lets you use many popular USB webcams and other video devices within Knoppix. Most popular USB joysticks should work out of the box, and joysticks that use the gameport on your sound card should work if the sound card is supported under Knoppix. There are many other types of devices that can work under Knoppix. In fact, booting Knoppix on a machine with a peripheral attached is a good way to gauge if there is Linux support for that device.

HACK #15 Have Fun and Play Some Games

While you can get a lot of work done with Knoppix, you can also have a lot of fun. Windows gives you Solitaire, Freecell, and Minesweeper. Knoppix gives you a virtual arcade full of games.

Primarily, you should use Knoppix to complete work, but sometimes it's good to have some fun too. Knoppix has something for everyone with its broad selection of games. Here's an overview of the game categories and descriptions of some of the games.

All of the games included in Knoppix are organized in the K Menu under Games. This submenu lists the different game categories, such as adventure, arcade, board games, card games, puzzles, strategy, and a special category for Tetris-like games.

You will find a lone title, Falcon's Eye, in the adventure category. This role-playing game is a graphical frontend to the console adventure game nethack. Nethack is a classic dungeon game that focuses on exploring the depths of the dungeon rather than simply killing everything in sight. Falcon's Eye takes the nethack engine and replaces the monotone ASCII symbols with colorized characters, monsters, and walls. To play the game, create a character, complete with attributes like strength and intelligence, just like in Dungeons & Dragons. Game play begins with your character in a dungeon with a trusty sidekick—a pet dog or cat. Use the mouse to move your character, attack monsters, and open doors. Icons along the bottom of the screen allow you to select items to use, spells to cast, or extended commands to perform. For nethack veterans, you'll find the key bindings familiar. Novices can click the question mark at the bottom righthand corner of the screen for help. Once you are done exploring the dungeons, quit by selecting [q] quit from the list of extended commands.

Many of the games in the arcade category revive classic arcade games from the 1980s, and most fall into two categories: games with spaceships and games with bouncing balls. Don't laugh; sometimes the simplest games are the most addictive. Galaga, Chromium, and KAsteroids are all space shoot-em-ups. Galaga is a Linux remake of the famous arcade game with more power-ups and a faster pace, KAsteroids provides all of the fun of the original Asteroids game but with three-dimensional asteroids, and Chromium is a fast-paced top-scrolling shooter with excellent graphics.

Chromium does require a 3D accelerated graphics card, so it won't play well on many systems, especially with new graphics cards. If you have an Nvidia card, you must install the binary Nvidia driver with the live installer **[Hack #28]** before 3D acceleration will work.

After shooting at things in space, try Xkoules, which makes me think of sumo wrestling in space with hi-bouncing balls; Xboing, a Super Breakout clone from Austrailia; and KBounce, a Qix-like game in which you attempt to isolate bouncing balls into a small percentage of the screen. Imaze is a multiplayer game that requires both a server and a client. Run the server to determine the size of the maze, and then connect the client to it to run through the maze firing bouncing balls at your opponents.

The board and card game categories provide computerized versions of many classic games: XBoard, KMahjongg, and KReversi are computerized counterparts to Chess, Mahjongg, and Go. The card game category contains many different card games, including Solitaire and Freecell. Many of these games also support playing against opponents over the Internet, adding a new dimension to old favorites.

For those who find brainteasers fun, the puzzles and strategy categories have plenty of programs to exercise your brain. The puzzle games range from Gtans, which has you rearranging and rotating shapes to match the given pattern, to Minesweeper, a requirement in any complete set of puzzle games.

In the strategy category, you find logic games such as KAtomic and KSokoban as well as battle strategy games as simple as KBattleship, a clone of the classic Battleship game. You will also find Xbattle, which lets you and an opponent set up many different battle scenarios with varying terrain, army size, and many other options, and then lets you control troop movements to see which team comes out as the victor.

A special category has been created for Tetris-style puzzle games containing Netris, a console-based Tetris clone, and Frozen-Bubble, a Bust-A-Move clone with a penguin motif (Figure 2-10).

Figure 2-10. Frozen-Bubble

With so many game choices, it is easy to find an escape from work that is suited to your tastes. With a few exceptions, most of these games run fine without having an advanced 3D graphics card, so you can have fun even on older systems. If you aren't familiar with some of the games, most of them come with a complete help section, which describes objectives and key bindings. Many of the programs allow multiplayer games over the Internet. You can even pass out Knoppix CDs to friends or coworkers and have a quick game over lunch.

HACK #16   Rock Out with Knoppix Multimedia

Knoppix comes with a full suite of tools to perform common multimedia tasks, such as listening to CDs or MP3s, editing audio, and burning CDs.

More people seem to be using their computers for multimedia applications, whether for listening to CDs, MP3s, or streaming radio and video. Combine Knoppix's excellent sound card support with its complete set of audio and video applications, and you get a platform for your multimedia needs that you can take anywhere. All of Knoppix's multimedia applications can be found under K Menu → Multimedia. This hack gives an overview of all the different programs you can use for your audio and video needs.

Before using any of the multimedia tools, make sure that Knoppix has identified your sound card. The first clue that Knoppix has detected your sound card is the "Initiating startup sequence" sound played by Knoppix as it loads your desktop. Another clue is the presence of a blue speaker icon near the bottom righthand corner of the screen near the clock. This icon belongs to KMixer and lets you adjust the volume just by clicking on the speaker. If the icon has a red slash through it, then Knoppix was not able to detect your sound card.

Use the *sndconfig* program to configure your sound card. *Sndconfig* is a fairly straightforward configuration tool that scans your system for any available sound cards and prompts you with any it detects. To load the *sndconfig* application, click K Menu → KNOPPIX → Configure → Sound card configuration. Other than selecting OK, the only interactive part of this tool is to listen for a sample sound once *sndconfig* configures your card and to answer "Yes" or "No," depending on whether you hear the sound. If your sound card still isn't working, there is a chance that there is no OSS sound module for your hardware. If this happens to you, try booting with the alsa cheat code [Hack #7] to use the ALSA drivers instead. Once your sound card is working, you are ready to try the multimedia applications.

Listening to Audio

The primary application used to play sound under Knoppix is XMMS (Figure 2-11). Click K Menu → Multimedia → Audio → XMMS to launch the program, or click on any *.mp3* or other sound file in your file manager. XMMS has an interface similar to Winamp under Windows, and can play most popular audio formats, including MP3, WAV, Ogg Vorbis, and audio CDs. To open the playlist editor, click the button labeled PL on the interface, right-click on XMMS and select Playlist Editor, or type Ctrl-E. Within the playlist editor, you can add, delete, arrange, and sort tracks. The audio settings are adjusted with the equalizer. Display the equalizer by clicking the EQ button next to the PL button on the interface, by right-clicking and selecting Graphical EQ, or by the keyboard shortcut Ctrl-G.

Figure 2-11. XMMS

Right-click XMMS and select Options → Preferences to access many additional XMMS plug-ins Knoppix includes. The shortcut is Ctrl-P. The preferences window has tabs organizing different XMMS plug-ins and options, and includes plug-ins for audio and visual effects that add extra stereo, makes the volume levels of all your tracks the same, or displays your music in interesting and colorful ways.

> Some people find the default look of XMMS too techno. Unfortunately, Knoppix doesn't include any extra skins for XMMS, but you can download new ones directly from XMMS's official site at *http://www.xmms.org* and save them in */home/knoppix/.xmms/Skins*. Right-click on XMMS and select Options → Skin Browser to choose one of the skins you have downloaded.

Editing Sounds

Knoppix also provides the capability to record and edit audio with the Audacity program (Figure 2-12). Audacity can record from microphone input or from a variety of audio formats, including WAV, MP3, and Ogg Vorbis. Once sound is loaded into Audacity, you can make basic edits, such as cropping and moving, to more advanced edits, such as noise removal and other effects. Once you are done with editing the sound, you can save it into any number of audio formats. When you save your sound as an Audacity project, it keeps track of any changes that you have made along with other aspects of the project. Audacity can be found under K Menu → Multimedia → Sound menu....

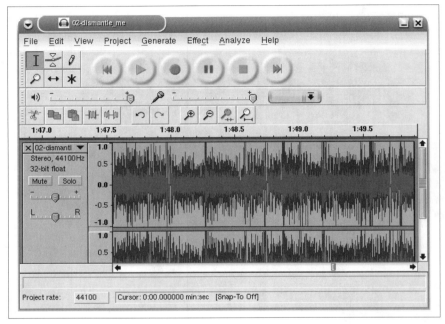

Figure 2-12. Audacity

Burn CDs and DVDs

Of course, Knoppix comes with a CD-burning application. If it didn't, how could you be expected to burn new Knoppix CDs, and distribute them to your friends, family, and fellow passengers on the subway? Knoppix includes the excellent K3b application, accessible by clicking K Menu → Multimedia → K3b. With K3b, you can create data and audio CDs and DVDs through an easy-to-use interface reminiscent of popular Windows alternatives like Nero. Of course, you can't burn to a CD if Knoppix is in your only CD drive; so use of this application does require that you either run Knoppix from a second optical drive, or if you have only a single CD-ROM drive, that you use one of the cheat codes that free up the CD-ROM drive [Hack #5].

After launching K3b, you can choose to create an audio CD, a data CD, a DVD, or copy an existing CD. K3b has a simple interface that lets you drag-and-drop files into the project that you would like to use. If you are creating audio CDs, you can drag-and-drop MP3s or other supported audio files onto a project, and K3b converts them to the proper format. Once you have selected all of the files you want to burn, click the Burn... button in the bottom righthand corner of the window to write the files to CD.

> Right about now, your fellow subway passenger is probably lusting after your Knoppix setup. Give them what they desire. Just click Tools → CD → Burn CD Image... and browse to a Knoppix ISO on a mounted filesystem to create another copy of Knoppix.

Watch Videos

Knoppix also allows you to view many different video files that you might have on your system. Unfortunately, DVDs and certain other proprietary video files like Quicktime *.mov* files cannot be fully played by default under Knoppix. This is because of legal issues surrounding distribution of the DeCSS program and the Windows media codecs, which decode these formats for playback. Despite these setbacks, you can still use *xine*, the default media player, to view MPEG1 and MPEG2 files, including VCDs and SVCDs, as well as other video formats, such as DivX 3, 4, and 5.

To start xine, click K Menu → Multimedia → Video → xine. Xine's interface resembles many common DVD-playing applications under Windows. To play a video file in xine, right-click and select Open → File... and browse to the file you wish to add to the play list. To play a VCD, insert the VCD into your CD-ROM drive, and click the VCD button on the interface. Xine allows you to control playback either through the GUI or through a complete set of key bindings. For instance, hit Enter to start playback, Space to pause, the arrow keys to move forward and backward within the video, and G to toggle the visibility of the GUI.

> If the default look does not appeal to you, other skins can be downloaded by right-clicking on xine and selecting Setup → Skin download....

Watching TV

If your computer has a working TV tuner card, you can watch TV under Knoppix using *xawtv*. To run xawtv, select K Menu → Multimedia → Video → xawtv. The first time it is launched, xawtv presents you with a configuration program so you can set up NTSC versus PAL mode for your tuner (United States residents should choose NTSC) and whether you receive TV through broadcast or cable, so that xawtv can correctly scan for all of your channels. Once the configuration process is completed, xawtv will load, and you will be able to watch television. If you want to turn a computer with a TV tuner card into your own personal TiVo, check out "TiVo Your Computer" **[Hack #92]**.

Whether you want to listen to or edit music, watch movies or TV, or create CDs, Knoppix comes with the multimedia tools you need along with the hardware detection to get you started. Remember that if you only want to listen to music files on your computer, you don't need to change to write mode on your hard drive; simply browse to the file you want to play and click it. Keeping your drives in read-only mode under Knoppix unless you must write to them adds an extra layer of protection in case you turn off your computer or lose power without properly shutting down. If you are really interested in multimedia under Knoppix, read "Pump Up the Volume with Mediainlinux" **[Hack #82]** to find out more about a multimedia-focused Knoppix-based CD.

HACK #17 Connect to the Internet

Knoppix comes with many different options to connect it to a network with dial-up, Ethernet, wireless, PPPoE, and other types of connections.

Before you can take advantage of the many Internet applications Knoppix has, you need to actually connect to the Internet. Knoppix comes with support for many different types of Internet and network connections, including dial-up, standard network connections you might find with DSL or Cable Internet services, ADSL/PPPOE connections, GPRS cell phone connections, ISDN, and wireless network connections. To configure these connection types, click K Menu → KNOPPIX → Network/Internet.

The most common type of Internet connection for broadband Internet users or computers inside a corporate network is through a standard network card. If this is the type of connection you use then you will find that when Knoppix boots, it automatically brings up the network and attempts to grab an IP address with DHCP.

If you do not automatically get an IP via DHCP, you must click K Menu → KNOPPIX → Network/Internet → Network card configuration to launch a program that will ask you questions about your network connection. This configuration program will also let you enter a static IP address and other network information if your network does not use DHCP.

If your ISP assigned a username and password to use when you connect to your broadband Internet connection, then you must set up PPPoE before you can connect to the Internet. Click K Menu → KNOPPIX → Network/Internet → ADSL/PPPOE configuration. This application will attempt to detect PPPoE use on your network, and then enter your username and password to connect to the ISP. Once you finish the configuration application, you will be connected to the Internet.

If you have an 802.11b wireless card connected to your computer, Knoppix will attempt to automatically configure the wireless card and connect to the first wireless access point it sees when you boot. This will not work if you need to enter special settings, such as a WEP key, to connect to your wireless network. To get around this, click K Menu → KNOPPIX → Network/Internet → Wavelan configuration to launch a program that lets you enter some information about your wireless network. It is safe to stick to the defaults if you are unsure of what to enter into the fields you see.

For ISDN connections, run the included Red Hat ISDN configuration program with K Menu → KNOPPIX → Network/Internet → ISDN Connection. With this program, you can configure the settings for your ISDN hardware for your provider, and then connect to the network.

To successfully use a modem under Knoppix, it must either be an internal or external hardware modem (a modem that performs all its logic on the hardware itself), a PCMCIA modem, or a cell phone or PDA with Internet connectivity. As software modems (commonly called WinModems) are generally incompatible with each other and require special drivers to be written to work correctly under Linux, you probably will not be able to easily connect to the Internet using a software modem under Linux.

To configure your modem under Knoppix, you must tell Knoppix which device to point /dev/modem to. Click K Menu → KNOPPIX → Network/Internet → /dev/modem connection setup to launch a configuration application, which asks you a series of questions about how your modem is connected to the computer. Next, click K Menu → KNOPPIX → Network/Internet → Modem Dialer to enter the phone number, username, and password for your dialup connection and connect.

If you are connecting with a GPRS connection on your cell phone, you must click K Menu → KNOPPIX → Network/Internet → GPRS Connection to configure the connection. This program asks you to choose the type of GPRS connection you are using, and then attempts to make a connection.

As you can see, Knoppix puts many different options at your disposal for connecting to the Internet. Now that you are connected, the next hack explains how to view web sites, access your email, and chat with friends through Knoppix applications.

Connect to the Internet with GPRS over Bluetooth

HACK #18

Attempt to get the impossible to happen: a GPRS data connection over Bluetooth with Knoppix.

Bluetooth is a Personal Area Networking (PAN) protocol with a very limited range (the most powerful consumer devices, Class 1, have a range of 100 meters). Bluetooth allows you to connect devices together into "pairs." GPRS, or General Packet Radio Service, is a packet-switched protocol that's layered on top of the circuit-switched GSM (or IS-136 TDMA) network. This permits the use of a packet-based data service (like TCP/IP). This hack pairs your cell phone with your computer's Bluetooth adapter and uses your cell phone as a pseudo-modem device. It's not your father's modem, that's for sure. No wires needed.

GPRS connections require either a terminal or cellular connection to your given provider. GPRS dynamically allocates bandwidth by the number of available timeslots (time period allocated to one call). In turn, it allocates timeslots based on need, and therefore, you will get extra timeslots only when it's necessary. This provides a very efficient use of the spectrum and has a major benefit over Circuit Switched Data, because it doesn't need to allocate a circuit for constant use. The theoretical bandwidth limit for GPRS is 172.2 Kbps; however, this is assuming that you are able to use all eight timeslots for a given cell. In reality, most providers only let you have two to four timeslots. For instance, T-Mobile gives four RX timeslots and two TX timeslots.

Parts List

You need more than just a Knoppix disc and a computer to get this connection to work. You must use the following parts:

A Bluetooth adapter
> I have the Belkin USB Class 1 Bluetooth adapter. I choose this because of its lack of an antenna (it's harder to break), its small form factor, and its range (advertised at 100 meters).

A cell phone
> I use the Nokia 3650 that has service with T-Mobile in San Francisco. The phone has the optional VPN Internet service for unlimited data. It's an extra $20 a month and it allows for unmetered GPRS data. This should work with other providers as long as they offer GPRS data.

Using GPRS data is useful for connecting to the Internet at low speed when there is no other reliable connection around. In nearly all cases, if you can make a cell phone call, you can get online. Be warned: GPRS data roaming is very expensive.

Configure the GPRS connection

First select K Menu → Knoppix → Network/Internet → GPRS connection.
Unless you have previously configured a modem, you will be prompted to
configure a device as a modem using the *gprsconnect* shell script. You can
also run the *gprsconnect* script from the command line to configure a
modem. Answer Yes at the prompt to move to the next window, which displays the different types of modem connections you can choose from.

The connection type window (Figure 2-13) gives you the choice between
Serial, USB, IRDA, and Bluetooth connections. Select Bluetooth.

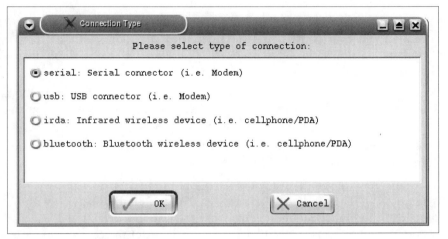

Figure 2-13. GPRS connection type window

After you select Bluetooth, the script scans for any Bluetooth devices in
range. It is entirely normal for this step to take 10 to 40 seconds. If the script
quickly flashes by without a progress bar and it doesn't find your phone, the
Bluetooth adapter didn't even attempt a scan. Make sure that you have a
working *hci0* device before you attempt to scan. You can test whether you
can see your Bluetooth device by issuing the **hciconfig –a** command:

```
knoppix@ttyp0[knoppix]$ hciconfig -a
hci0:   Type: USB
        BD Address: 00:0A:3A:52:3A:20 ACL MTU: 192:8   SCO MTU: 64:8
        UP RUNNING PSCAN ISCAN
        RX bytes:376 acl:0 sco:0 events:16 errors:0
        TX bytes:305 acl:0 sco:0 commands:15 errors:0
        Features: 0xff 0xff 0x0f 0x00 0x00 0x00 0x00 0x00
        Packet type: DM1 DM3 DM5 DH1 DH3 DH5 HV1 HV2 HV3
        Link policy: HOLD SNIFF PARK
        Link mode: SLAVE ACCEPT
        Name: 'Knoppix-0'
```

```
Class: 0x000100
Service Classes: Unspecified
Device Class: Computer, Uncategorized
HCI Ver: 1.1 (0x1) HCI Rev: 0x20d LMP Ver: 1.1 (0x1)
LMP Subver: 0x20d
Manufacturer: Cambridge Silicon Radio (10)
```

In the event that the script doesn't find a device (and it did actually scan), it prompts you for the address of the hidden Bluetooth device. Use the *hcitool* program to manually scan for discoverable Bluetooth devices:

```
knoppix@ttyp0[knoppix]$ sudo hcitool scan
Scanning ...
      00:0A:D9:7D:B8:93        Get Hacked :-)
      00:60:57:4F:49:98        Fonbot
```

After you find your device and its address, enter the address at the prompt. Assuming that the script finds your device, it will present you with a list of devices. Select your device (in my case, Fonbot) and click OK.

Next, you are prompted for your Bluetooth PIN. Nearly all phones and Bluetooth devices default to a PIN of 1234, just like my luggage combination—a *very* strong default password; it's clearly hard to guess.

The next screen asks you if you would like to set */dev/modem* to point to your newly configured device. Click "Yes."

You are now given a list of cell phone providers to choose from (Figure 2-14). This is the tricky part. My Nokia 3650 has service with T-mobile in San Francisco, but if you choose the Knoppix default of T-Mobile, it does not work. This means I have to manually enter the correct init string for my provider, so I select Other.

If you select Other, you are asked to enter the custom init string for GPRS. The init string for T-mobile in the USA is:

```
AT+CGDCONT=1,"IP","internet3.voicestream.com"
```

I suggest you call your service provider and ask for the correct custom init string. You may also find your answer by searching on the Internet.

The next window that appears warns you that GPRS use can cause high costs due to high traffic volume. This phone has the unlimited T-Mobile data service, so I won't worry about this.

Now that the Bluetooth connection between the phone and the computer is created, the Nokia brings up a prompt that asks for the passcode for knop-pix-0 (the default name for the Bluetooth device in Knoppix). Enter the passcode (in my case, 1234) and press OK on the phone.

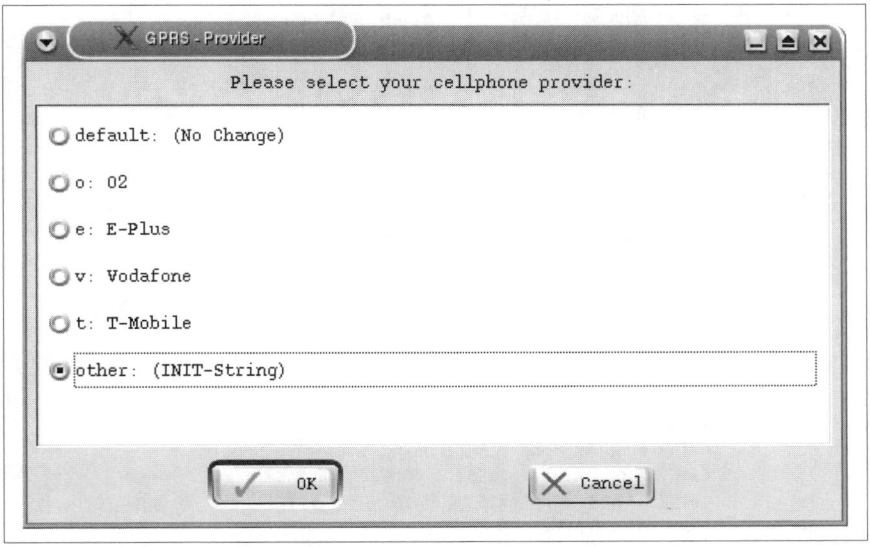

Figure 2-14. List of GPRS providers

You are then prompted on the computer for the outgoing Bluetooth PIN—in my case, 1234. The phone now asks you to "Accept connection request from Knoppix-0?" On the phone, select "Yes," and Knoppix attempts to create a GPRS connection and launches a terminal that displays the connection attempt. In this log, you are able to watch each step of the connection and tell whether the connection succeeded or failed.

Here is an example *ppp0* configuration after a successful connection:

```
knoppix@ttyp0[knoppix]$ sudo ifconfig ppp0
ppp0      Link encap:Point-to-Point Protocol
          inet addr:208.54.115.125  P-t-P:10.6.6.6  Mask:255.255.255.255
          UP POINTOPOINT RUNNING NOARP MULTICAST  MTU:1500  Metric:1
          RX packets:65 errors:0 dropped:0 overruns:0 frame:0
          TX packets:101 errors:0 dropped:0 overruns:0 carrier:0
          collisions:0 txqueuelen:3
          RX bytes:5282 (5.1 KiB)  TX bytes:8230 (8.0 KiB)
```

And here is the full output of *pppd* that you can see in the log window:

```
Jun 10 06:46:35 Knoppix pppd[2153]: pppd 2.4.2 started by root, uid 0
Jun 10 06:47:53 Knoppix chat[2244]: timeout set to 120 seconds
Jun 10 06:47:53 Knoppix chat[2244]: abort on (BUSY)
Jun 10 06:47:53 Knoppix chat[2244]: abort on (ERROR)
Jun 10 06:47:53 Knoppix chat[2244]: abort on (NO CARRIER)
Jun 10 06:47:53 Knoppix chat[2244]: send (ATE1^M)
Jun 10 06:47:54 Knoppix chat[2244]: expect (OK)
Jun 10 06:47:54 Knoppix chat[2244]: ATE1^M^M
Jun 10 06:47:54 Knoppix chat[2244]: OK
```

```
Jun 10 06:47:54 Knoppix chat[2244]:  -- got it
Jun 10 06:47:54 Knoppix chat[2244]: send (AT+CGDCONT=1,"IP",
"internet3.voicestream.com"^M)
Jun 10 06:47:55 Knoppix chat[2244]: expect (OK)
Jun 10 06:47:55 Knoppix chat[2244]: ^M
Jun 10 06:47:55 Knoppix chat[2244]: AT+CGDCONT=1,"IP",
"internet3 voicestream.com"^M^M
Jun 10 06:47:55 Knoppix chat[2244]: OK
Jun 10 06:47:55 Knoppix chat[2244]:  -- got it
Jun 10 06:47:55 Knoppix chat[2244]: send (ATD*99***1#^M)
Jun 10 06:47:55 Knoppix chat[2244]: expect (CONNECT)
Jun 10 06:47:55 Knoppix chat[2244]: ^M
Jun 10 06:47:55 Knoppix chat[2244]: ATD*99***1#^M^M
Jun 10 06:47:55 Knoppix chat[2244]: CONNECT
Jun 10 06:47:55 Knoppix chat[2244]:  -- got it
Jun 10 06:47:55 Knoppix chat[2244]: send (\d)
Jun 10 06:47:56 Knoppix pppd[2153]: Serial connection established.
Jun 10 06:47:56 Knoppix pppd[2153]: Using interface ppp0
Jun 10 06:47:56 Knoppix pppd[2153]: Connect: ppp0 <--> /dev/modem
Jun 10 06:47:57 Knoppix pppd[2153]: Warning - secret file /etc/ppp/pap-
secrets has world and/or group access
Jun 10 06:47:58 Knoppix pppd[2153]: Warning - secret file /etc/ppp/pap-
secrets has world and/or group access
Jun 10 06:47:58 Knoppix pppd[2153]: PAP authentication succeeded
Jun 10 06:48:13 Knoppix pppd[2153]: local  IP address 208.54.116.45
Jun 10 06:48:13 Knoppix pppd[2153]: remote IP address 10.6.6.6
Jun 10 06:48:13 Knoppix pppd[2153]: primary  DNS address 66.94.25.120
Jun 10 06:48:13 Knoppix pppd[2153]: secondary DNS address 66.94.9.120
```

Connection Errors

If the connection is successful, but then you get disconnected, you may notice an error in the *pppd* log that looks something like this:

```
Jun 10 06:49:58 Knoppix pppd[2153]: No response to 4 echo-requests
Jun 10 06:49:58 Knoppix pppd[2153]: Serial link appears to be disconnected.
Jun 10 06:49:59 Knoppix pppd[2153]: Connection terminated.
Jun 10 06:49:59 Knoppix pppd[2153]: Connect time 2.1 minutes.
Jun 10 06:49:59 Knoppix pppd[2153]: Sent 23896 bytes, received 93053 bytes.
```

To fix this error, you have to edit your PPP options. In the file */etc/ppp/options* are two options you need to change:

```
lcp-echo-interval 30
lcp-echo-failure 4
```

The lcp-echo-interval variable controls how many seconds between each echo request, and the lcp-echo-failure variable controls how many failed echo requests to allow before giving up. Experiment with changing lcp-echo-interval and lcp-echo-failure to higher values so you will not be disconnected as quickly. If you come across no carrier errors, such as after a forced disconnect, you will probably see the following log output:

```
Jun 10 06:53:19 Knoppix chat[2732]: timeout set to 120 seconds
Jun 10 06:53:19 Knoppix chat[2732]: abort on (BUSY)
Jun 10 06:53:19 Knoppix chat[2732]: abort on (ERROR)
Jun 10 06:53:19 Knoppix chat[2732]: abort on (NO CARRIER)
Jun 10 06:53:19 Knoppix chat[2732]: send (ATE1^M)
Jun 10 06:53:19 Knoppix chat[2732]: expect (OK)
Jun 10 06:53:19 Knoppix chat[2732]: ^M
Jun 10 06:53:19 Knoppix chat[2732]: NO CARRIER
Jun 10 06:53:19 Knoppix chat[2732]:  -- failed
Jun 10 06:53:19 Knoppix chat[2732]: Failed (NO CARRIER)
```

Wait until *pppd* tries to auto-reconnect, and the second time around, it should work. If this still fails, turn off the phone and start again.

Once you are connected, use the connection like any other Internet connection. On average, I can get between 1 and 3 Kbps, just enough for a shell connection or some web browsing. When you are finished, disconnect by pressing Ctrl-C in the GRPS connection terminal.

—Jake Appelbaum

HACK #19   Explore the Internet

Browse the web, check your email, and chat with your friends with Knoppix's Internet applications.

While Knoppix contains plenty of useful tools that don't require a network connection, with connectivity you can use Knoppix to browse the Web, check your email, send instant messages to friends, chat, and even set up a video conference. This hack covers many of the utilities located under the K Menu → Internet menu.

Web Browsers

Chances are the one thing you want to do most on the Internet is browse the web. Knoppix includes two web browsers, Konqueror and Mozilla, which should be adequate for all your web-browsing needs.

Konqueror is KDE's default web browser and is actually the web browser that greets you as you start the Knoppix desktop. If you want to immediately browse the Web, simply type the URL into the location bar at the top of the Konqueror window. Konqueror supports tabbed browsing. To open a new tab, hit Ctrl-Shift-N or middle-click on a link in the browser window. Konqueror is configured to support Java™ and JavaScript, but Flash support requires using Knoppix's live installer to install the Flash plug-in [Hack #27].

If you hate web pop-up ads, you're in luck; Konqueror supports blocking pop-up windows. To enable blocking, click Settings → Configure Konqueror…, select Java/JavaScript in the settings window that appears, select the JavaScript tab, and next to "Open new windows," check "Deny to block all pop-up windows" or "Smart" to intelligently block unrequested pop-up windows. If you really want to be annoyed, check "Ask," and your Internet browsing will be constantly interrupted by a dialog asking you if you want to allow a new pop-up. That's *almost* as annoying as using Internet Explorer.

Knoppix also comes with the complete Mozilla suite comprised of a web browser, mail and news clients, an HTML composer, and an address book. As a browser, Mozilla touts excellent standards compliance and supports tabbed browsing if you press Ctrl-T or middle-click a link. Mozilla also supports pop-up blocking. To configure this, click Edit → Preferences, select Privacy and Security → Popup Windows, then check "Block unrequested popup windows."

Email and News Readers

You can also use Mozilla as an email client. Run Mozilla Mail from the Internet menu or click the envelope icon on the bottom lefthand corner of the Mozilla browser window. Mozilla Mail fully supports POP and IMAP mail servers. The first time you start Mozilla Mail, you are presented with a wizard to configure your primary email account. First enter your name and the email address you wish to use in the wizard's window and click Next. The next window asks you whether you use a POP or IMAP server followed by your email account username. Your ISP or network administrator should have the information to fill out these fields. Mozilla Mail loads and checks for new email.

Mozilla Mail's interface is similar to most other basic email clients, with icons along the top to compose new mail, check for new messages, and delete messages. Mozilla Mail also comes with its own Bayesian spam filter. The Bayesian algorithm Mozilla uses learns from the spam you alert it to and gets better at identifying new spam as you continue to use it (Figure 2-15). To teach the filter, select any spam you receive and click the Junk icon along the top of the window.

Mozilla Mail and Mozilla News run from the same client and are configured much the same way. To add a news service, click Edit → Mail & Newsgroup Account Settings and click "Add Account..." to start the same account wizard you saw the first time you ran Mozilla Mail. Enter the news settings that your ISP has provided you, and a news account will show up on the left sidebar, allowing you to subscribe to and read newsgroups.

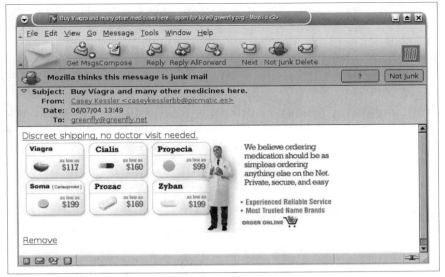

Figure 2-15. Mozilla Mail's junk mail filter in action

Instant Messaging and IRC

For all your instant-messaging needs, Knoppix has included Gaim. Gaim started as a Linux client for the AOL Instant Messaging service; extra plug-ins have now given it support for other instant-messaging networks, including ICQ, Jabber, MSN, Yahoo!, and even IRC. Through Gaim's simple interface, you can connect to different messaging networks and manage multiple instant-messaging accounts and buddy lists.

While Gaim's IRC support is excellent, Knoppix also includes a complete, standalone IRC client called XChat. To visit the official Knoppix IRC channel, for instance, click K Menu → Internet → XChat, fill out your choices for nicknames to use (chances are there will already be another *knoppix* user on this network), then select the FreeNode network and click Connect. After you connect to the Freenode server, join #knoppix by choosing it in the channel list you see when you click Window → Channel List, entering **knoppix** into the Regex Match: field and hit Apply, or simply typing in **/join #knoppix** in the text entry box next to your nickname in the main window.

Video Conferencing

If you want to chat in a more face-to-face fashion, Knoppix includes Gnome-Meeting for your video-conferencing needs. GnomeMeeting requires a sound card with a working microphone and a video camera if you want to do complete video conferencing. GnomeMeeting has full H.323 compliance, so it works with any other H.323-compliant hardware or software, including Microsoft NetMeeting. As with a lot of the programs I've covered, when you first launch GnomeMeeting it runs a configuration wizard to set up and test your hardware. After the wizard has finished, simply type in the H.323-compliant number you wish to talk to and hit Enter to connect.

With Knoppix you have a complete set of tools to browse the Web, check your email, and chat with your friends that you can take with you to any computer with a working Internet connection (although you might want to check first with the friendly folks at your local Internet café before using it on their machines).

Get Help

When you are lost or stuck, or you just have a question on Knoppix, there are a number of places you can go to get help.

Knoppix definitely makes it easy for a new user to get started on Linux, but even with all of the automated configuration tools and the easy-to-use desktop environment, you are bound to need help. Knoppix has a vibrant and multilingual community and a number of support outlets. Every Knoppix user is basically using the same exact software; if you are having a problem, someone else is probably having that problem too.

On the Disk

First of all, the Knoppix CD itself provides a good first line of support for any questions you might have. The Knoppix help page is actually the first page you see when the desktop environment loads. If you have closed your browser and want to get back to that page, click the icon labeled KNOPPIX on your desktop. Select your language along the bottom of the web page (for English, click EN) to see a basic help page that introduces Knoppix and provides some introductory information on the Knoppix project, and some links for getting further help.

If you need help with your desktop environment more than with Knoppix itself, click K Menu → Help to access KDE's full user manual. This help program also includes documentation for all of the main KDE applications, so you can use this resource if you have a question about the Konqueror web browser, for instance.

On the Web

There are a number of resources for getting help with Knoppix on the Internet. First of all, there is the official Knoppix site at *http://www.knoppix.org*, which maintains a FAQ you can view at *http://download.linuxtag.org/ knoppix/KNOPPIX-FAQ-EN.txt*. Corporate users of Knoppix might be interested in official commercial support provided by ed-media's Knoppix hotline located at *http://www.ed-media.org/knoppix/en/index.html*.

If you need more help, there are active online forums at *http://www.linuxtag. org/forum* (mostly a German-speaking forum) and at *http://www.knoppix.net/ forum* (mostly an English-speaking forum). Knoppix.net is an excellent all-around resource for Knoppix questions with an active community because it answers questions on the forum and writes and maintains documentation and HOWTOs at *http://www.knoppix.net/docs*. You can track reported bugs in different versions of Knoppix at *http://www.knoppix.net/bugs* and file a bug report yourself. There are also forums dedicated to supporting Knoppix in many other languages, including French, Japanese, Polish, Russian, and others. Visit *http://www.knopper.net/knoppix-links/index-en.html* for a full listing.

> When you ask for help, be sure to specify which version of Knoppix you are using and, if you have a hardware-related question, what hardware you are using with Knoppix and any cheat codes you have used.

If you would like more interactive support, you can also chat with other Knoppix users at the official IRC channel #knoppix on irc.freenode.net. For more information on how to connect to #knoppix with *xchat*, reference "Explore the Internet" [Hack #19].

## CHAPTER THREE

Tweak Your Desktop
Hacks 21–31

After you have become comfortable with the desktop and the different desktop applications that Knoppix includes, you might want to save documents or settings that you have worked on. This chapter contains hacks that cover methods to save your settings and documents so you can access them the next time you boot, along with how to utilize settings you might already have on the Linux or Windows system installed on your hard drive.

The next few hacks cover some specialized desktop uses for Knoppix, including using it as a kiosk or terminal server. With these hacks, you can turn a regular computer into a specialized kiosk for your business, and then use the terminal server to boot multiple computers all from the same Knoppix CD over the network. The final hacks cover different methods Knoppix includes so that you can install software "live" on the booted CD. You can use this to get that extra bit of software that Knoppix didn't happen to include without resorting to remastering the CD.

The ability to make your Knoppix settings persistent opens a whole world of possibilities for Knoppix as a portable desktop solution. With a USB key drive and a Knoppix CD, you can boot Knoppix on any machine available to you; load your settings from the USB drive and your desktop so your work can follow you wherever you go.

HACK #21 Create Persistent Knoppix Settings

Knoppix has the capability of saving changes you have made during your session to floppies, USB drives, or other removable media. Use this ability to create a Knoppix setup that you can take to any computer.

One of the great things about Knoppix is that it all resides on a single CD, so you can take the same desktop environment and programs with you to any accessible computer. One problem, however, is that a CD is read-only media, so any configuration changes you make or any special settings you might change to get Knoppix to work on your hardware are lost the moment you shut down the computer. If you have a USB drive, a floppy drive, or some other writable media, Knoppix has automated the process of keeping changes you make to Knoppix persistent across reboots. You even have the option of saving your entire /home directory if you want, which means you can take your data with you too.

Save Settings

To save all of your changes, click K Menu → KNOPPIX → Configure → Save Knoppix configuration or run /usr/sbin/saveconfig in a console. There are a number of settings that Knoppix can save. The different types of settings you can choose from are:

Personal configuration (desktop, programs)
Select this option to save the configuration files in your home directory. KDE and other Linux programs have standardized the saving of user settings in hidden files and directories, which begin with a period and are commonly referred to as dot files. So this option saves any theme or color changes you have made for your desktop, any settings changes made for any program (so, for instance, this would save your web browser bookmarks and your email settings), and any other configuration settings that are stored in these hidden files.

All files on the desktop
This option doesn't save settings per se but instead backs up the full /home/knoppix/Desktop directory, so any files you have saved on the desktop will still be there the next time you reboot if this option is checked. Use this option in lieu of saving the entire home directory, which is described below, if you just have a few files on the desktop that you wish to save and don't particularly care about keeping configuration changes.

Network settings (LAN, Modem ISDN, ADSL)
Select this option to save special network-specific directories and settings stored under /etc so they will be reloaded the next time the machine is booted. Choose this option if you had to make any special changes to your network settings, such as set up a wireless, PPPoE, or dial-up connection.

Graphics subsystem settings (XF86Config)
This option saves the configuration files under /etc/X11 and reloads them on reboot. Check this option to save direct edits you have made to your XF86Config file to get your graphics environment to load.

Other system configuration (printer, etc.)
This option saves some other miscellaneous configuration settings, including those for printers and other peripherals.

Saveconfig's default is to select all these options except for saving desktop files. If you plan to use Knoppix on many machines with different hardware and network configurations, you might want to just select the first option, "Personal configuration," so that desktop, data, and program settings will be saved, but network and graphics settings will be detected on each new machine you come to.

After you select which settings to save and click OK, Knoppix provides a list of all the available writable media you can store your settings to. This includes any hard drives on your system, floppy drives, and any USB or other removable storage currently connected. Select the device to save to, and Knoppix will back up your settings to that device.

Knoppix stores its configuration settings in the root directory of the device in a bzipped tar file called *configs.tbz*, along with a script that Knoppix runs to restore this configuration called *knoppix.sh*. To examine just which files Knoppix has saved, click on *configs.tbz* in a file manager (Konqueror automatically displays the contents of archives) or run the following command in a console:

```
knoppix@ttyp0[knoppix]$ tar tvfj configs.tbz
```

The size of the file varies depending on how many program settings are being saved and, if you are saving your desktop, the size of any files stored there.

Now that you have your settings and data saved, you need some way to use what you've saved in subsequent boots. This is where `myconfig` comes in. If you have saved your settings to a removable USB drive at */dev/sda1*, boot with the cheat code:

```
myconfig=/dev/sda1
```

If you don't know which device the settings are stored on, then boot with:

```
myconfig=scan
```

This command instructs Knoppix to scan for your settings on all devices it finds. In general, it is easier to just use the scan option unless you have saved settings at different times on different devices, in which case you may prefer to explicitly tell Knoppix which device to use.

After Knoppix boots, it then runs the *knoppix.sh* script it created when you backed up your settings and extracts the files from *configs.tgz*.

Remember that if you make any new changes that you would like to save, you must run the *saveconfig* script again.

Save Your Home Directory

Through the use of the *mkpersistenthome* script and the home cheat code, Knoppix also supports saving your entire home directory to an image that can be restored in later boots. The *mkpersistenthome* script backs up the complete */home/knoppix* directory with all of its hidden and unhidden files, including the desktop. This makes it different from the *saveconfig* script, which just backs up the hidden configuration files and the desktop. Another difference with this method is that creating a persistent home directory means that Knoppix mounts this new image as the home directory, so that as long as you pass the home cheat code at boot, any changes or new files in the home directory are still changed the next time you reboot without the need to run the script again.

To create the persistent home directory image, run K Menu → KNOPPIX → Configure → Create a persistent KNOPPIX home directory or from a console run:

```
knoppix@ttyp0[knoppix]$ /usr/sbin/mkpersistenthome
```

The execution of this script is similar to the *saveconfig* script. When run, it presents you with a list of detected drives on which to create the persistent home directory. One main difference is that after you choose your drive, you have the potentially dangerous option to format the drive and use the entire drive for the home directory. The safest choice is to tell Knoppix to create a *loopback file* on the device that it will save to. A loopback file is an entire filesystem contained within a single file, like a CD image. Loopback files can be formatted and mounted just as though they were full filesystems.

You must also choose a size for the loopback file. The size of your loopback file depends greatly on how many extra files you plan to store. See how much space you are currently using for your home directory by typing the following command:

```
knoppix@ttyp0[knoppix]$ du -sh ~
12M     /home/knoppix
```

Keep in mind that this loopback file does not grow even if there is more free space on the drive. Therefore, choose a file size based on how much space you think you will need in the future, not just how much you need now. Otherwise, when you need more space, you will have to create a brand-new persistent home directory and copy your files over. To resize the image to size megabytes, type:

```
knoppix@ttyp0[knoppix]$ resize2fs knoppix.img sizeM
```

After configuring the loopback file, Knoppix creates and formats the loopback file and then copies the full home directory to it.

When the script finishes, you should see a *knoppix.img* file on your storage device. To view the contents of the file, mount it with the following command:

```
knoppix@ttyp0[knoppix]$ mkdir ~/temp
knoppix@ttyp0[knoppix]$ sudo mount -o loop /mnt/sda1/knoppix.img ~/temp
```

Replace */mnt/sda1* with the path to your Knoppix image, then see the contents of the file at */home/knoppix/temp*.

To tell Knoppix to use the loopback file for your home directory at boot, use the home cheat code. This cheat code works just like the myconfig cheat code covered earlier in this hack. You can either pass it a specific device that contains *knoppix.img* or boot with home=scan for Knoppix to scan all available drives for *knoppix.img*. For example, to use a persistent home directory created in */mnt/sda1/knoppix.img*, boot with:

```
home=/mnt/sda1/knoppix.img
```

If you have a Linux partition available on your system and are willing to add the Knoppix home directory to it, you can also create a full Knoppix home directory without reformatting a drive or being limited by the space to which you have assigned an image. This method is particularly useful to add an extra directory to your desktop's home directory just for use by Knoppix. On the underlying Linux system, it looks just like a new user named *knoppix* has been added.

First, choose the partition you wish to use and make sure that it is writable—changing read/write mode is covered in "Explore the Desktop" [Hack #10]. For these examples, I use */mnt/hda3*, which contains my regular Linux home directories on this system. To create the new home directory and make sure that the *knoppix* user owns it, open a terminal and type:

```
knoppix@ttyp0[knoppix]$ sudo mkdir /mnt/hda3/knoppix
knoppix@ttyp0[knoppix]$ sudo chown knoppix:knoppix /mnt/hda3/knoppix
```

To copy your Knoppix home directory, run:

```
knoppix@ttyp0[knoppix]$ rsync -av /home/knoppix/ /mnt/hda3/knoppix/
```

To use this directory the next time you boot, use the home cheat code, but make sure to pass it the path to this new home directory. In this example, type:

```
home=/dev/hda3/knoppix
```

Now you can have a special Knoppix home directory along with all of your other user accounts. Similar to other persistent home directory methods, this method uses this directory in place of a ramdisk for */home/knoppix*, so any changes you make or files you create are always saved—without running any extra commands.

Knoppix's persistent cheat codes are especially handy if you use Knoppix frequently, as it bypasses many of the disadvantages of booting from a read-only media and allows you to save changes you have made. Combine these persistent settings with a small USB key drive, and your settings and files can follow you to any computer with a CD-ROM drive and a USB port.

Use Your Linux Desktop Settings

HACK #22

When you boot Knoppix on top of an existing Linux desktop, it is relatively easy for Knoppix to use files and settings on the system underneath.

If you've been a Linux user for some time and have your desktop application settings just right, you might be annoyed that the changes that you've already configured once (i.e., your bookmarks and email settings) must be redone under Knoppix. Trying to remember and recreate all your original tweaks and other settings can be a long, boring, and maybe impossible task, as anyone who has lost their home directory can attest to. However, if you boot Knoppix on top of your existing Linux desktop, you can easily import your application settings for use under Knoppix.

This hack covers how to copy settings from commonly used applications under Knoppix when you are booting on top of your normal Linux desktop.

There's No Place Like /home

The first step in exporting your desktop settings is to find your home directory. While the details vary depending on how your hard drive is partitioned, Linux installations generally have */home* as a directory under the root partition or on its own partition. If you're uncertain how your hard drive is partitioned, you should still be able to find your home directory without much trouble. To start, click each hard-drive icon on the desktop in turn and see which directories exist within. You're looking for a directory with the pattern */home/yourusername*. Once you find the partition that has your home directory, make a note of how the icon was labeled; this is the partition name and should be something like *hda3*.

Now that you have identified your home directory, the simplest method of importing your user's settings to Knoppix is to copy each application's hidden directory or configuration file. Most applications store their user-specific settings in hidden files in the home directory, and importing these settings is as simple as recursively copying the hidden directory to */home/knoppix/*. Details are provided below for some applications that require a bit of extra work to copy correctly. In all of these examples, I use */mnt/hda3/username* as the home directory, but you will need to change the path to correspond with the location of your user directory.

> While it might seem that it would be even easier to symlink */home/knoppix* or individual configuration directories to your home directory, your Knoppix user would not easily have write access to the drive, due to the differing user IDs.

KDE

To copy all of your KDE settings correctly, including all KDE application settings, you must make sure that KDE is shut down so that session files aren't written to after you restart KDE. *Session files* are records of window settings and open applications that KDE keeps stored in memory until it shuts down. To do this, close all running applications, then open up a terminal window. To switch to console-only mode, type:

```
knoppix@ttyp0[knoppix]$ sudo init 2
```

Once you are in the console, move your current Knoppix KDE settings out of the way temporarily and copy your Linux user's KDE settings:

```
root@tty1[/]# mv /home/knoppix/.kde /home/knoppix/.kde.bak
root@tty1[/]# su knoppix cp -a /mnt/hda3/username/.kde /home/knoppix/
```

If you make use of a *.kderc* file, copy that as well. Now restart KDE to be presented with your Linux user's normal KDE desktop:

```
root@tty1[/]# init 5
```

If you are content with the current settings, free up space by deleting the backup *.kde.bak* directory that you have created. If you want to switch back to how the KDE desktop was before, switch again to console-only mode:

```
knoppix@ttyp0[knoppix]$ sudo init 2
```

Then remove your new KDE settings, restore your old KDE settings, and start the KDE desktop back up:

```
root@tty1[/]# rm -rf /home/knoppix/.kde
root@tty1[/]# mv /home/knoppix/.kde.bak /home/knoppix/.kde
root@tty1[/]# init 5
```

All datafiles and directories on a KDE desktop are stored in the */home/username/Desktop* directory. If you want to just copy your Linux desktop over the top of the default Knoppix desktop, follow a similar procedure. First, drop to console-only mode by typing:

```
knoppix@ttyp0[knoppix]$ sudo init 2
```

Then back up your current desktop, copy the new desktop, and start KDE:

```
root@tty1[/]# mv /home/knoppix/Desktop /home/knoppix/Desktop.bak
root@tty1[/]# su knoppix cp -a /mnt/hda3/username/Desktop /home/knoppix/
root@tty1[/]# init 5
```

After KDE starts, your user's desktop icons and files are in place of the default Knoppix ones. Similar to the KDE settings, to restore your old desktop, drop to console-only mode again by typing:

```
knoppix@ttyp0[knoppix]$ sudo init 2
```

Then restore the settings, and start KDE:

```
root@tty1[/]# rm -rf /home/knoppix/Desktop
root@tty1[/]# mv /home/knoppix/Desktop.bak /home/knoppix/Desktop
root@tty1[/]# init 5
```

Other Applications

To copy the settings of most other applications, you don't need to drop to console-only mode. Simply make sure that the application itself is closed, which ensures there aren't any related temporary files open. Most program settings can be copied with a single, recursive copy of the configuration file or directory. For instance, to copy Gaim settings, run:

```
knoppix@ttyp0[knoppix]$ cp -a /mnt/hda3/username/.gaim /home/knoppix/
```

Or drag-and-drop the directory to */home/knoppix* from a file manager. The following table lists some other common applications and the commands to copy their settings:

OpenOffice.org	cp -a /mnt/hda3/username/.OpenOffice.org/* /home/knoppix/office/
The GIMP	cp -a /mnt/hda3/username/.gimp* /home/knoppix/
Xine	cp -a /mnt/hda3/username/.xine /home/knoppix/
XMMS	cp -a /mnt/hda3/username/.xmms /home/knoppix/
Xchat	cp -a /mnt/hda3/username/.xchat2 /home/knoppix/

By now you've probably noticed a pattern in the commands used to copy program settings. Most programs use the convention of naming their settings directory after the name of the program itself. If you are unsure of the name of the hidden directory that an application uses, before and after running an application for the first time, check the hidden files in your home directory by typing the following command:

```
knoppix@ttyp0[knoppix]$ ls -a /home/knoppix
```

Any new hidden directories that were created likely belong to that program.

One program that requires a bit of extra work to import settings from is Mozilla. While Mozilla does create a *.mozilla* directory when it is run, the directory containing the actual settings for a profile is inside the *.mozilla* directory and is given a random name that is unique to each user on each machine. This is a security measure that prevents a malicious script from easily target a known settings directory. If you simply copy the *.mozilla* directory to */home/knoppix*, you will discover Mozilla ignores your settings.

To copy the settings properly, identify the random directory name Mozilla used for your settings by running Mozilla at least once under Knoppix. After you run Mozilla, the settings directory appears under */home/knoppix/.mozilla/ knoppix/xxxxxxx.slt*, with *xxxxxxx* being replaced with random characters. Here is an example:

```
knoppix@ttyp0[knoppix]$ ls /home/knoppix/.mozilla/knoppix
ujixazk6.slt
```

Find the same directory for your Linux user under */mnt/hda3/username/.mozilla/ username/yyyyyyyy.slt* or, if you don't have a profile named after your user, check */mnt/hda3/username/.mozilla/* for a directory named *DefaultUser* or something along those lines. As an example, here is the output for my Linux user:

```
knoppix@ttyp0[knoppix]$ ls /mnt/hda3/greenfly/.mozilla/default/
3sd9n0b8.slt
```

Once you have identified both directories, copy your Mozilla settings with the command:

```
knoppix@ttyp0[knoppix]$ cp -a /mnt/hda3/username/.mozilla/username/yyyyyyyy.
slt/* /home/knoppix/.mozilla/knoppix/xxxxxx.slt/
```

Replace *yyyyyyyy* and *xxxxxxx* with the directory names you have found. Now you can start Mozilla, and your bookmarks, mail and news settings, and all other settings should appear.

> If the version of Mozilla installed on your machine differs from the version installed on Knoppix, you may find that your theme does not get moved. This is because most Mozilla themes depend on a specific version of Mozilla.

When copying your settings, be conscious of any major version differences between your local application and the application that ships with Knoppix, as sometimes configuration file formats change with major version releases. If you've spent all this time copying your settings and making the Knoppix desktop exactly how you like it, you should make use of "Create Persistent Knoppix Settings" **[Hack #21]** and make your settings persistent. Otherwise, all of your hard work will disappear the next time you reboot.

Use Your Windows Desktop Settings

Believe it or not, your underlying Windows system isn't completely useless while running Knoppix. You can leverage your underlying Windows system for settings and datafiles.

Quite a few of the applications included with Knoppix, such as Mozilla, OpenOffice.org, and Gaim, actually have Windows counterparts. If you have been using these open source applications under Windows and have them configured to your liking, you can copy the settings for use in Knoppix much like in "Use Your Linux Desktop Settings" [Hack #22]. The programs covered here typically use the same configuration files under Windows as they do in Linux. In fact, the only real difference is the location of the configuration files. This hack describes how to copy these settings and how to use some other common Windows file locations under Knoppix.

To use your Windows program settings, locate the Windows equivalent of the /home directory. For Windows 2000 and XP, this directory should be called *Documents and Settings* and is usually at the root of the C: drive. Click on each of the hard-drive icons on your Knoppix desktop and look for this directory, and find all the user directories that contain user-specific application configuration files. In my examples, the user is called *knoppix*, so all of the configuration files are stored under *C:\Documents and Settings\knoppix*.

Mozilla

Mozilla is probably the most likely application you would use both in Windows and under Knoppix. As I mentioned in "Use Your Linux Desktop Settings" [Hack #22], Mozilla stores its configuration settings under a directory with a randomly generated name, so you must first find that directory both in /home/knoppix and on your Windows partition. Make sure you run Mozilla under Knoppix at least once, and make note of the directory name under */home/knoppix/.mozilla/knoppix/*, which should resemble *xxxxxxxx.slt*, with each *x* replaced with a random character. Assuming your Windows partition is *hda1*, make sure the drive is mounted, open a terminal, and type:

```
knoppix@ttyp0[knoppix]$ cd /mnt/hda1/Documents\ and\ Settings/username/
Application\ Data/Mozilla/Profiles/default
```

If you have created special profiles for Mozilla, enter the name of the profile instead of **default** for this command. Type **ls** here to reveal a directory named *yyyyyyyy.slt*, where each *y* is replaced with a different random character. Now that you have both directories identified, copy the settings with the command:

```
knoppix@ttyp0[knoppix]$ cp -a yyyyyyyy.slt/* /home/knoppix/.mozilla/knoppix/
xxxxxxxx.slt/
```

If prompted whether you wish to overwrite any files, type **y**. Now when you start Mozilla you should see all of the same settings that you used under Windows. The *prefs.js* file, which contains many of your Mozilla preferences, stores a lot of Windows-specific directory paths for email, etc. If you don't mind your home directory being littered with a few oddly named directories, leave this as is. Otherwise, the following search-and-replace script should remedy most of the paths:

```
knoppix@ttyp0[knoppix]$ perl -pi -e 's|C:.*?Desktop|/home/knoppix/Desktop|;
s|\\\|/|g; s|C:/.*?slt|/home/knoppix/.mozilla/knoppix/xxxxxxxx.slt|'
/home/knoppix/.mozilla/knoppix/xxxxxxxx.slt/prefs.*
```

Be sure to replace each instance of *xxxxxxxx.slt* with the name of the random profile directory Mozilla created under Knoppix.

OpenOffice.org

OpenOffice.org is another application that you might use under both Windows and Knoppix. Under Windows, OpenOffice.org stores its configuration files along with the program under *C:\Program Files\OpenOffice.org1.1.1*, with the final part of the directory name differing, depending on which version of OpenOffice.org you have installed. To copy your OpenOffice.org settings to Knoppix, type:

```
knoppix@ttyp0[knoppix]$ cp -a --reply=yes /mnt/hda1/Program\ Files/
OpenOffice.org1.1.1/user /home/knoppix/office/
```

If you want to be prompted for each file that will be overwritten, remove the --reply=yes argument.

Instant Messaging and IRC

The multiprotocol instant-messenger program Gaim also has a client for Windows. You can share your Gaim configuration by typing:

```
knoppix@ttyp0[knoppix]$ cp -a /mnt/hda1/Documents\ and\ Settings/username/
Application\ Data/.gaim /home/knoppix/
```

The IRC client Xchat also has a Windows port. You can copy its settings with:

```
knoppix@ttyp0[knoppix]$ cp -a /mnt/hda1/Documents\ and\ Settings/username/
Application\ Data/X-Chat\ 2 /home/knoppix/.xchat2.
```

Use My Documents

Making use of your existing application settings is nice, but sometimes you really just want to listen to your music collection. I mean, fill out some TPS reports for work. To make your Windows data readily accessible, create a symlink to your Windows *My Documents* directory by typing:

```
knoppix@ttyp0[knoppix]$ ln -s /mnt/hda1/Documents\ and\ Settings/username/
My\ Documents /home/knoppix/Desktop/
```

Remember to change your Windows partition to have write access if you want to save the changes that you have made.

As you can see, it is pretty easy to make use of configuration files for the applications your Windows and Knoppix systems have in common, and to access your Windows datafiles for use under Knoppix.

Remember that all these settings will be deleted from the ramdisk the next time you reboot unless you set up persistent settings **[Hack #21]**.

HACK #24 Make a Kiosk

Turn a regular Knoppix disc and a computer into your own kiosk for a tradeshow, an Internet café, or even a basic web terminal.

A great way for a business to provide custom web applications to a customer or single-task employees is to set up a low-priced computer as a kiosk. A kiosk allows a user to perform a limited range of options, such as watch a demonstration, browse through a set of instructional pages, or search a company's intranet. In terms of software, these applications need only a web browser with most of its functions disabled and a web page for the browser to load. A few tweaks turn a vanilla Knoppix disc into your own personal kiosk.

Write the Kiosk JavaScript Code

To create a Knoppix kiosk, you must limit users to only browsing the Web. To do this, you must run Mozilla completely by itself so there are no other menus, panels, or other ways to run programs. Within Mozilla itself, you might want to limit the web sites that kiosk users can visit (unless you are fine with people browsing porn and checking their email with your tradeshow kiosk). You can limit widgets, such as the location bar and menu bar, by using the same technology annoying Internet advertisers use—pop ups! By setting your Mozilla's home page to a JavaScript file, you can boot into a minimal X environment and redirect the user to your kiosk pages in a pop-up window that has almost all of the widgets disabled.

First, boot your Knoppix CD into the default KDE environment. Open a text editor (such as K Menu → Editors → KWrite), create a file in your home directory called *.kiosk.html*, and add the following code:

```
<html>
<head>
<script language="javascript">
<!--
function StartKiosk(){
window.open("http://your.url.
here","","fullscreen,toolbar=yes,scrollbars=yes");
timeoutID=setTimeout("CloseLauncher()", 100);
}
function CloseLauncher(){
window.close();
}
-->
</script>
</head>
<body onLoad="StartKiosk()">
</body>
</html>
```

The dot (.) at the beginning of the filename is important because it ensures that the file is backed up automatically if you save your desktop settings **[Hack #21]**. When the file is opened, this basic JavaScript code opens a new pop-up browser window that loads the web page specified in the script with *http://your.url.here*. The extra options at the end define which functions the new window has. In this example, the window displays a full screen, has a toolbar (to provide back, forward, and stop buttons), and has scrollbars. Remove any of these three options to disable that function from the new window. After the window is launched, the browser window that loaded *.kiosk.html* times out and closes. The timeout is set very low, so the user shouldn't even see the launcher window.

Configure Mozilla

By default, Mozilla tries to aggressively stop pop ups, so you have to change some settings so that the kiosk JavaScript works. Click K Menu → Internet → Mozilla Browser to start Mozilla. In the location bar, type **about:config**. This page allows you to customize Mozilla's settings directly. Scroll down and find the preference titled *privacy.popups.first_popup*. To make searching easier, you can also enter keywords into the Filter: bar as shown in Figure 3-1. Using a filter allows you to see only the preferences that match your keywords. Once you find *privacy.popups.first_popup*, double-click it, and in the new dialog, make sure the value is set to "false." If this value is set to "true," Mozilla warns users that pop-up windows are not blocked when they first open the kiosk.

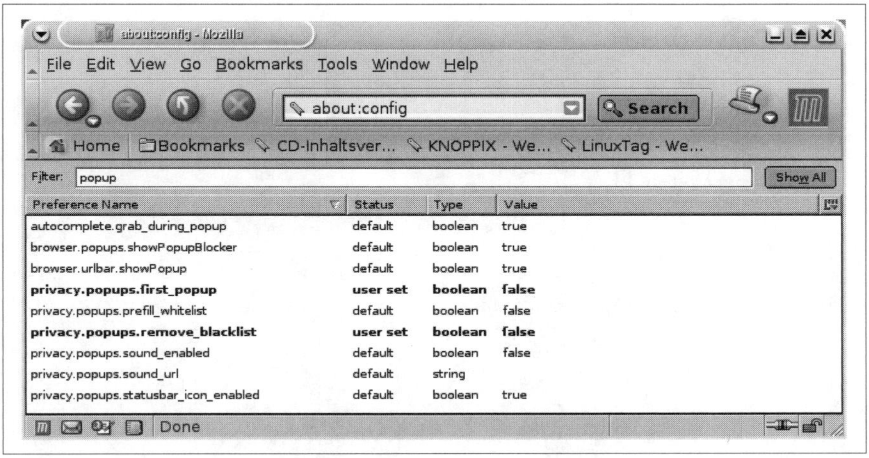

Figure 3-1. Mozilla preferences filtered

Next, find the *dom.allow_scripts_to_close_windows* preference, double-click on it, and make sure that it is set to "true." This preference setting allows JavaScript to close the launcher window, leaving only your kiosk application.

Now type `file:///home/knoppix/.kiosk.html` into the location bar to test the *.kiosk.html* page. The current browser window should close, and a new browser window should open to your kiosk page. Notice that the new window should have only a scrollbar and a toolbar with back, forward, up, and down buttons. Don't worry if the window does not yet open full-screen, as KDE is overriding the full-screen option. Just hit the F11 key to toggle full-screen mode and then close Mozilla, and it will remember the size for next time.

Once you are satisfied with your *.kiosk.html* page, set it to be Mozilla's default page. Close and reopen Mozilla if it is in kiosk mode, and then click Edit → Preferences and click Navigator in the sidebar. Make sure that "Home page" is checked on the righthand side, and that your "Home Page Location" is set to *file:///home/knoppix/.kiosk.html*, as in Figure 3-2. Now click OK and exit Mozilla.

Change the Default Desktop Environment

For the kiosk to work properly, you must change the default desktop environment so that only Mozilla loads. To do this, create an editable version of the */etc/X11/Xsession.d/45xsession* script, and then open it with root permissions in a text editor such as *kwrite*:

```
knoppix@ttyp0[knoppix]$ cd /etc/X11/Xsession.d/
knoppix@ttyp0[Xsession.d]$ sudo mv 45xsession 45xsession.bak
```

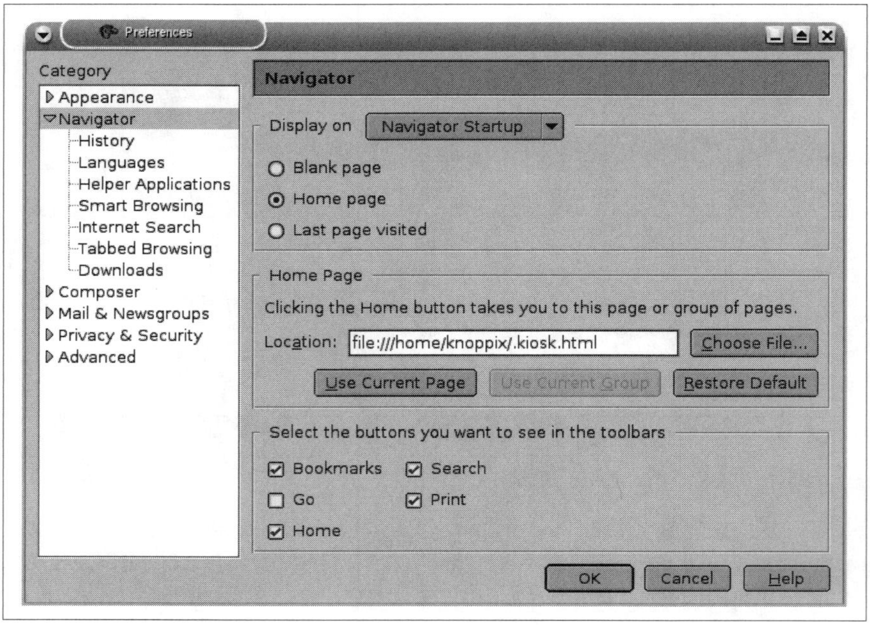

Figure 3-2. Mozilla home page settings

```
knoppix@ttyp0[Xsession.d]$ sudo cp 45xsession.bak 45xsession
knoppix@ttyp0[Xsession.d]$ sudo kwrite 45xsession
```

In the *45xsession* script, find the section of the file that has the startfluxbox function:

```
startfluxbox( ){
# Create automatic Desktop icons
mkdesktophdicons

playsound
GDK_USE_XFT=1 exec fluxbox
}
```

Under this function, add a new function called startkiosk:

```
startfluxbox( ){
# Create automatic Desktop icons
mkdesktophdicons

playsound
GDK_USE_XFT=1 exec fluxbox
}

startkiosk( ){

playsound
```

```
GDK_USE_XFT=1
while [ "$DESKTOP" = "kiosk" ]
do
  mozilla &
  wait
  [ -f /etc/sysconfig/desktop ]  && . /etc/sysconfig/desktop
done
}
```

This function creates a new desktop environment that infinitely loops *mozilla* as long as the $DESKTOP environment variable is set to kiosk. This loop ensures that if a user accidentally closes Mozilla or if Mozilla crashes, the kiosk application automatically restarts.

Scroll down to the bottom of the *45xsession* script and find a large case statement that looks like the following:

```
case "$DESKTOP" in
     kde|KDE) [ "$FREEMEM" -ge "60000" ] && startkde    || starttwm lowmem
82; ;;
     gnome|GNOME) [ "$FREEMEM" -ge "45000" ] && startgnome || starttwm
lowmem 67; ;;
     larswm|LARSWM) [ "$FREEMEM" -ge "35000" ] && startlarswm || starttwm
lowmem 64; ;;
     enlightenment|ENLIGHTENMENT) [ "$FREEMEM" -ge "35000" ] &&
startenlightenment || starttwm lowmem 64; ;;
     fluxbox|FLUXBOX) [ "$FREEMEM" -ge "35000" ] && startfluxbox || starttwm
lowmem 64; ;;
     xfce|xfce3|XFCE|XFCE3) [ "$FREEMEM" -ge "35000" ] && startxfce ||
starttwm lowmem 64; ;;
     xfce4|XFCE4) [ "$FREEMEM" -ge "35000" ] && startxfce4 || starttwm
lowmem 64; ;;
     windowmaker|wmaker|WINDOWMAKER|WMAKER) [ "$FREEMEM" -ge "35000" ] &&
startwindowmaker || starttwm lowmem 64; ;;
     icewm|ICEWM) [ "$FREEMEM" -ge "35000" ] && starticewm || starttwm
lowmem 64; ;;
     twm|TWM) starttwm;    ;;
             *) starttwm invalidwm;    ;;
esac
fi
```

To this statement, add the following line:

```
kiosk|KIOSK) [ "$FREEMEM" -ge "35000" ] && startkiosk || starttwm lowmem 64;
;;
```

Then it will start the kiosk mode if $DESKTOP is set to kiosk.

```
case "$DESKTOP" in
     kde|KDE) [ "$FREEMEM" -ge "60000" ] && startkde    || starttwm lowmem
82; ;;
     gnome|GNOME) [ "$FREEMEM" -ge "45000" ] && startgnome || starttwm
lowmem 67; ;;
     larswm|LARSWM) [ "$FREEMEM" -ge "35000" ] && startlarswm || starttwm
lowmem 64; ;;
```

```
    enlightenment|ENLIGHTENMENT) [ "$FREEMEM" -ge "35000" ] &&
startenlightenment || starttwm lowmem 64; ;;
    fluxbox|FLUXBOX) [ "$FREEMEM" -ge "35000" ] && startfluxbox || starttwm
lowmem 64; ;;
    xfce|xfce3|XFCE|XFCE3) [ "$FREEMEM" -ge "35000" ] && startxfce ||
starttwm lowmem 64; ;;
    xfce4|XFCE4) [ "$FREEMEM" -ge "35000" ] && startxfce4 || starttwm
lowmem 64; ;;
windowmaker|wmaker|WINDOWMAKER|WMAKER) [ "$FREEMEM" -ge "35000" ] &&
startwindowmaker || starttwm lowmem 64; ;;
    icewm|ICEWM) [ "$FREEMEM" -ge "35000" ] && starticewm || starttwm
lowmem 64; ;;kiosk|KIOSK) [ "$FREEMEM" -ge "35000" ] && startkiosk ||
starttwm lowmem 64; ;;
    twm|TWM) starttwm;   ;;
            *) starttwm invalidwm;   ;;
esac
fi
```

Save all of your changes and exit *kwrite*.

Now change the default desktop to be the kiosk mode, and use init to restart the X environment:

```
knoppix@ttyp0[knoppix] sudo sh -c "echo 'DESKTOP=\"kiosk\"' >
/etc/sysconfig/desktop"
knoppix@ttyp0[knoppix] sudo init 2 && sudo init 5
```

X restarts and launches *mozilla* with your kiosk page loaded. If for some reason the browser doesn't fill the screen, hit F11 and then close the browser. Each time the window opens afterwards, it should fill the screen.

If you decide you want to go back to KDE, hit Ctrl-Alt-F1 to get to the terminal, and type:

```
root@tty1[/]# echo 'DESKTOP="kde"' > /etc/sysconfig/desktop
root@tty1[/]# init 2 && init 5
```

Save Kiosk Settings

With the kiosk up and running, you will want to save all of your hard work to easily start in "kiosk mode" later. The easiest way to do this is to use the *saveconfig* script that is mentioned in "Create Persistent Knoppix Settings" [Hack #21]. The kiosk is probably loaded, so the easiest way to run this script is to hit Ctrl-Alt-F1 to get to a console, and then run the script as the *knoppix* user:

```
root@tty1[/]# su - knoppix saveconfig
```

Make sure that the "Personal configuration" and the "Graphics subsystem" settings are checked, and then select a floppy disk, or a USB drive (probably listed as */mnt/sda1*) for the script to save the settings to. Once the settings are saved, you can take the floppy disk or USB drive to any computer and add the cheat code below to the boot prompt:

```
myconfig=scan
```

Knoppix loads your kiosk settings and boots directly into the kiosk, and then you can take the floppy disk or USB drive to any other computer you want to use as a kiosk.

Remaster a Kiosk Disc

Now that you know how to set up a kiosk, you might want to create a remastered Knoppix CD so that your changes are permanent. Follow the steps from "Create a Customized Knoppix" [Hack #94] and *stop* before you get to the "Prepare the Source Filesystem" section. Now create the master directory, and then copy all of the files from the CD-ROM, including the compressed *KNOPPIX* filesystem:

```
root@ttyp1[hda1]# mkdir master
root@ttyp1[hda1]# rsync -a /cdrom/ master/
```

Now run the following command:

```
root@tty1[/]# su - knoppix saveconfig
```

Save the settings to the drive that contains your master directory—in this case, *hda1*. Then copy the *knoppix.sh* and *configs.tbz* files that the script creates to the *master/KNOPPIX* directory. If you prefer, you can skip this step and go straight to creating the new CD Image:

```
root@ttyp1[hda1]# mkisofs -pad -l -r -J -v -V "KNOPPIX" -no-emul-boot
-boot-load-size 4 -boot-info-table -b boot/isolinux/isolinux.bin -c
boot/isolinux/boot.cat -hide-rr-moved -o knoppix.iso master/
```

Once this command is completed, you should see a new *knoppix.iso* file in the root of your partition. You can burn this to a CD that boots directly into kiosk mode. Or if you prefer, you can boot into the default KDE desktop if you use the following cheat code at the boot prompt:

```
desktop=kde
```

You have an advantage if you create a remastered kiosk CD: you can follow the steps in "Network Boot Knoppix" [Hack #25] to run a network of kiosks from a single Knoppix CD. Just boot the first kiosk with the cheat code below so you can start the terminal server:

```
desktop=kde
```

Then if you want to turn that computer back to a kiosk, type:

```
knoppix@ttyp0[knoppix] sudo sh -c "echo 'DESKTOP=\"kiosk\"' >
/etc/sysconfig/desktop"
knoppix@ttyp0[knoppix] sudo init 2 && sudo init 5
```

HACK **Network Boot Knoppix**

#25 Use the Knoppix Terminal Server to boot multiple netboot-capable machines off of a single Knoppix CD.

Booting Knoppix off of a CD-ROM works fine for most normal uses. However, if you want to boot from a machine without a CD-ROM, or if you want to have Knoppix running on 20 different machines all at the same time, you might find it is easier to take advantage of the terminal server that is included with Knoppix.

With a terminal server started on a Knoppix CD, any netboot-capable machine can boot over the network from that original Knoppix machine, get the same desktop environment, and run the same applications as if it booted directly from the CD-ROM. As mentioned in detail in "Distribute the Load with ClusterKnoppix" **[Hack #89]**, a netboot-capable machine is a machine that supports either Pre-boot eXecution Environment (PXE) or etherboot, and can download bootstrapping code over the network from a properly configured server. Almost every new computer has support for PXE. To see if your machine supports PXE, look for "Booting from NIC" or PXE in the BIOS. On many modern computers, you can hit F12 at boot time to see a list of booting options, and if PXE is supported, you should see a reference to booting from the network card.

If you don't have a PXE-capable network card, read the section "Etherboot" in "Distribute the Load with ClusterKnoppix" **[Hack #89]** for instructions on downloading a floppy image to enable etherboot for your network card.

That's pretty much all you have to do for the clients. Most of the work for this hack occurs on the server.

To start, boot the machine that will be acting as the terminal server from the Knoppix CD. If Knoppix has automatically configured the network card from a DHCP server on the network, you do not need to further configure the network card for the server. However, a requirement of this terminal server setup is that Knoppix runs its own DHCP server. Because of this, you must turn off the existing DHCP. Failure to do so will cause problems when the clients attempt to boot from the network, as there will be no guarantee they will use the Knoppix DHCP server instead of the regular one.

 Ideally, your terminal server should be the machine with the most RAM and fastest CD drive and network connection. The clients use their own processor and RAM, but rely on the terminal server for all of the Knoppix files. Because Linux is an efficient multiuser OS, you can easily support a dozen or more terminals from a single well-configured workstation or server.

If there is no DHCP server on the network, click K Menu → KNOPPIX → Network/Internet → Network card configuration to configure your network card. Just add your IP address and netmask, and you're done.

Knoppix provides a Terminal Server Wizard that assists you in getting terminal services running. Several programs working together provide the actual terminal services. DHCP is used to configure the network connection and provide kernel images for clients using TFTP; files are shared using NFS.

Click K Menu → KNOPPIX → Services → Start KNOPPIX Terminal Server to start the Terminal Server Wizard. The configuration window gives you the options to set up, start, and stop the server. Choose "setup" and then choose your network card from the list of network devices that Knoppix detects. For machines with more than one network card, you must be aware of which network card is connected to the same network as the clients.

The next window asks you to enter the range of IP addresses for the terminal server to use. In general, the default is fine. In the next window (as shown in Figure 3-3), check all of the network card modules your clients are using. The most commonly used modules are preselected, so if you are unsure, go with the default. If you don't know the network modules used by a client, boot the Knoppix CD from the client and then run **lsmod** from a terminal to find the network card module in the list that Knoppix has loaded.

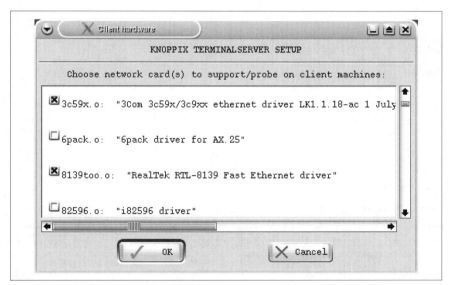

Figure 3-3. Configure NIC modules to support

Choose specific terminal services options from the next window. The default selections are secure (which disables root access on all of the clients), masq (IP masquerading and forwarding), and dns (nameserver cache and proxy). If you want to enable a transparent proxy for all web traffic, also check the squid option, although note that it uses an extra 40 MB of RAM on the server.

Next, choose any special cheat codes you want to use on the clients. Refer to "Use Knoppix Cheat Codes" **[Hack #3]** for more information about implementing cheat codes at boot time. By default, the wheelmouse cheat code is enabled, but that cheat code is deprecated, so just remove it. If you have a mixture of clients, some that need special cheat codes and some that don't, you can also enter cheat codes at the boot prompt of a client to use that cheat code on that client only.

Now that things are set up, the wizard lets you choose to start the terminal server. Once started, the wizard disappears. If you want to stop the terminal server later, rerun the wizard and choose "stop" instead of "setup" at the opening window.

For extra diagnostic information, click K Menu → KNOPPIX → Services → Start SYSLOG. Now you can boot each of your clients and see the default Knoppix boot screen. Simply hit Enter and boot the machines as you would normally. If a machine does not boot, reference the syslog window for any error messages that might appear.

H A C K #26 Develop Applications

Use Kdevelop with all of the languages Knoppix supports to rapidly create and manage software projects.

One of the great things about Linux, and open source in general, is that it isn't an exclusive club. Anyone who has the ability can contribute to his favorite projects or start a new open source project of his own. Basically, Knoppix is built from open source code, so it isn't surprising that Knoppix itself includes many of the programs you need to develop and build software of your own.

While Knoppix includes compilers and interpreters for many different languages, including C, C++, Perl, Python, Tcl/Tk, and others, it also includes a complete Integrated Development Environment (IDE), called Kdevelop, which combines all of the different tools, templates, programs, and scripts that developers frequently need into a single application. Kdevelop can handle your software development from picking a language to writing and debugging your code, reading documentation, compiling and running your program, and even keeping development in sync with applications, such as CVS and Subversion.

To start Kdevelop, click K Menu → Development → Kdevelop. The default window (Figure 3-4) has a number of toolbars that provide you with quick access to common functions so you can compile, execute, and debug your program with the push of a few buttons. On the toolbar are also shortcuts to all of the classes and functions in a program. Along the bottom of the window is a tab bar that lets you switch the bottom panel to show output from compiler messages, application output, CVS output, and a number of other programs.

Figure 3-4. The default Kdevelop window

This hack walks you through the steps of building a simple "Hello World" program in Kdevelop, so you can see just how easy it is to manage a program with Kdevelop.

To start a new project, click Project → New Project. In the project wizard that appears, select the language in which you wish to program to see a list of Kdevelop's predefined templates (Figure 3-5). For most languages, Kdevelop displays only basic "Hello World" templates, but for C, and C++ especially, Kdevelop provides templates for a basic Gnome application and a number of KDE applications, applets, and plug-ins. Select your language and template, and name your project. If you are using CVS or Subversion on your project for version control, select it in the next window. Then configure the header for your source code files. Here, you can put any licensing or contact information you want to include with your code.

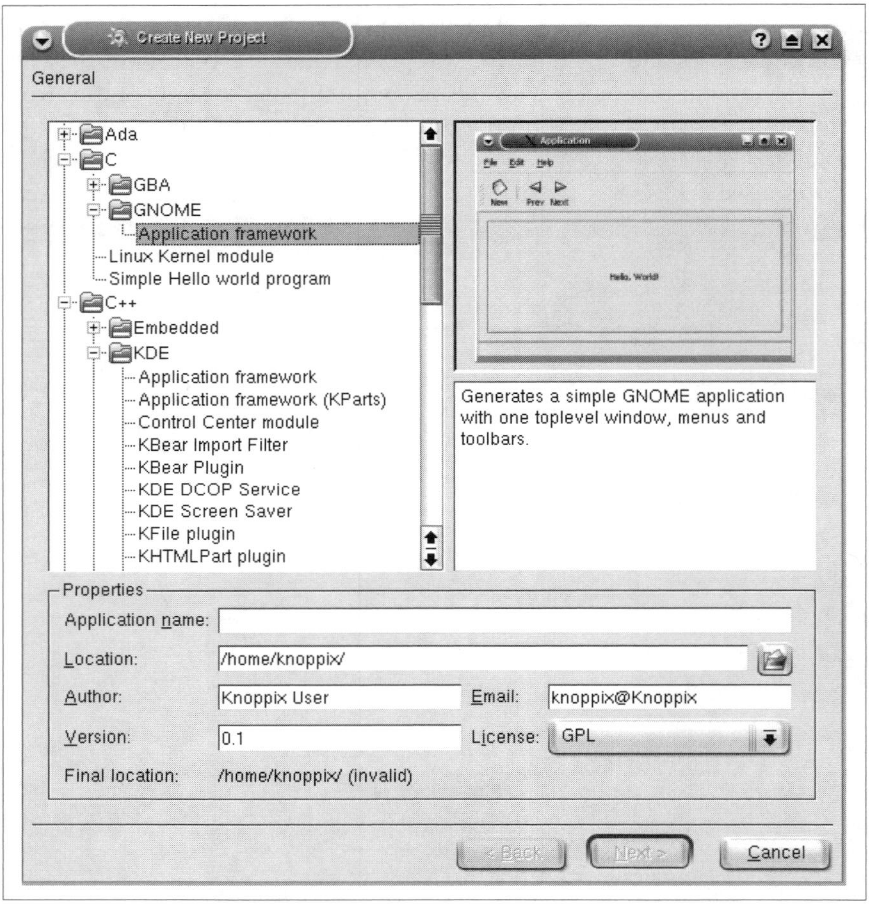

Figure 3-5. Kdevelop project templates

When the wizard completes, the main Kdevelop screen contains the skeleton code for your application (Figure 3-4). From this point, you can add functions and classes, and otherwise work on your project. When you are ready to test, click Build → Execute Program. The first time you compile and execute a program, Kdevelop automatically runs automake to create the *configure* script and Makefiles for your project. Even if you don't change any code, the default template should compile and run without any problems. In the case of a console application, the code execution takes place in a panel that opens along the bottom of the main window. Graphical applications open a new window. Even the default KDE template provides file open and file save dialogs and a number of features (Figure 3-6).

Figure 3-6. Kdevelop "Hello World" application

Kdevelop also comes with a nice debugging environment that lets you set breakpoints in your code, and then step through execution so you can test out specific parts of your program.

All of the project development can occur with your default user, which means you can easily save projects to removable media, such as a USB drive, and then boot Knoppix on a different machine and resume development. Even if Kdevelop isn't your style, you can still use one of the many text editors Knoppix provides and take your programming projects with you.

Use the Knoppix Live Installer

#27 While Knoppix includes a lot of great software, everything you need simply
won't fit on one CD, but with the live-software installer, you can install extra
packages directly to ramdisk.

Starting with Version 3.4, Knoppix has the ability to install new software
while running from a CD. If you need a virus scanner **[Hack #78]**, you can
install it directly to the home directory, and it works without touching your
hard drives.

Click K Menu → KNOPPIX → Utilities → "Install Software while running
from CD," or to launch the Live Installer, run:

```
knoppix@ttyp0[knoppix]$ knx-live-inst.sh
```

You should see a disclaimer that states that this is still an experimental feature (Figure 3-7). Don't worry. In my tests, the program doesn't have any
problems.

Figure 3-7. Live installer disclaimer

In the next window, you can choose from a variety of programs to install
(Figure 3-8).

The live installer automatically downloads the program you choose from the
Internet, installs it, and creates a menu entry under K Menu → KNOPPIX →
Extra-Software.

There are a number of programs you can install:

apt-get
> The live installer uses the famous *apt-get* program to deliver the most
> up-to-date software that is available in the Debian archive. This pro-
> gram is a needed dependency for most of the other live installer pro-
> grams and is automatically installed if needed.

Figure 3-8. The live installer supports a variety of programs from virus scanners to Flash plug-ins

f-prot

A nice virus scan program that can be used on the command line. Knoppix adds an easy-to-use GUI (Figure 3-9). "Scan for Viruses" **[Hack #78]** covers how to use this package.

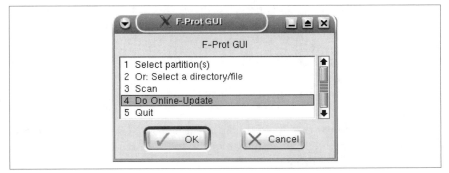

Figure 3-9. The Knoppix F-Prot GUI

Flash plug-in

Many web sites need Flash to be viewed correctly. While one could argue that this is bad design, arguing won't help you view the site. Knoppix does not ship the Flash plug-in due to legal reasons, but with just one click, the Flash plug-in is automatically downloaded from Macromedia and installed in all available browsers.

gkrellm

> A nice status monitor, it was one of the "I need it, but it's not on Knoppix" programs, so it was added to the live installer.

Kbabel

> *KBabel* is not useful to everyone. It is used to translate *.po* (portable object) files. The live installer itself uses this program for its language support, so it has been added mostly to support the live installer.

msttcorefonts

> If you have a Microsoft Word Document (*.doc*) and you view it with OpenOffice.org, but the fonts just don't look right, get the Microsoft True Type Core Fonts. Then restart OpenOffice.org; the document uses the native fonts you just installed, and they look exactly like they did on the Windows machine.

nvidia

> With this program, you can install the Nvidia graphics card drivers while running from the CD. It downloads, compiles and then installs the drivers automatically. Then you can enjoy the full power of 3D-accelerated graphics with the *tuxracer* and *tuxkart* games. This program is also covered in detail in "Install Nvidia 3D Drivers" **[Hack #28]**.

nvnet

> Before Knoppix had nforce2 support with native kernel drivers, many people complained about the lack of support for their network card. While one could argue that a live installer for such a driver is pretty useless, because you can't download a network card driver over a nonsupported network card, there are tricks to downloading it. (See "Caching and Reuse")

pingus

> You liked Lemmings? You'll love *pingus*. It's a very nice game with very sweet penguins. It just has one disadvantage: it is too quickly beaten because it doesn't have many levels.

quanta

> An HTML editor that has full support for management of big projects with syntax highlighting and many preformatted attributes that you can choose and drop into your code.

sim

> An ICQ client based on the QT Framework that features contact lists on the server, SMS, pictures, and most other ICQ features.

tuxkart

> A nice racing game. Unfortunately, it was never finished.

tuxracer

> A fun 3D racing game in which you guide a penguin down an ice track full of obstacles.

Caching and Reuse

If you've taken advantage of the installer, you've probably downloaded almost 30 MB of *apt-get* files and nearly 10 MB for *tuxracer*. The moment you reboot, everything is gone and must be downloaded again. There should be a way around it, and there is—caching.

All programs installed by the live installer are stored in a local cache in *~/.knx-live-inst/cache/*. Each program is stored in its own *AppDirs* (*~/Software/program_ name*), and wrappers to all binaries are stored in *~/.dist*. *AppDirs* is a concept taken from *klik* **[Hack #30]**. In *~/.dist/var/lib/apt/lists*, you can find huge lists of installable packages. To store the cache and the lists, back up the *~/.knx-live-inst* and *~/.dist/var/lib/apt/lists* directories and restore them at the next boot, or use a persistent home directory **[Hack #21]**. With either method, all programs are run after a reboot as if nothing has happened.

If you save your configuration **[Hack #21]**, you must reinstall those programs, but you won't have to download the programs again. Automatically reinstall programs from the cache with the noninteractive command-line mode for *knx-live-inst.sh*:

```
knoppix@ttyp0[knoppix]$ knx-live-inst.sh -ni
```

A short help page and a list of available programs appear.

To demonstrate the noninteractive mode, install *f-prot*:

```
knoppix@ttyp0[knoppix]$ knx-live-inst.sh -ni -s f-prot
```

To automatically (re)install all programs that are available from the cache, type the following command:

```
knoppix@ttyp0[knoppix]$ for i in ~/.knx-live-inst/cache/*; do
knx-live-inst.sh -ni -s $(basename $i); done;
```

History of Live Installation

Live-installation scripts are relatively new to Knoppix. The first live installation script was for the Flash plug-in, and it was published just last year in March of 2003. The post can still be found at *http://www.knoppix.net/forum/viewtopic.php?t=1495*.

Later, several other scripts were written that installed other programs. The similarities of these installers were analyzed and put into a command-line all-in-one program. Starting with Knoppix 3.4, this all-in-one program was enhanced by a GUI and is the live installer you can now use.

—Fabian Franz

HACK #28 Install Nvidia 3D Drivers

Get 3D acceleration under Knoppix for your Nvidia graphics card.

Linux has long had a bad reputation when it comes to 3D gaming. There are still many die-hard Linux users who dual-boot into Windows to play their favorite games. Some of this reputation has to do with poor 3D-driver support and performance from video card vendors. Other factors are to blame as well, including games that are programmed with 3D libraries and aren't easily ported to other platforms like Linux, and the fact that many Linux gamers buy Windows versions of games, even if a Linux alternative exists.

There is good news, however. Over the past few years, 3D-driver support in Linux has dramatically improved, particularly for Nvidia cards. Nvidia has released binary drivers that support their full TNT and Geforce line of video cards. In some benchmarks, games running under Linux even outperform their Windows counterparts. As the video support continues to improve, the application support improves as well, particularly in the first-person-shooter world. As an avid first-person-shooter fan myself, many of my favorite games, including the full Quake, Unreal Tournament, and Return to Castle Wolfenstein series, all have native Linux binaries.

You might not think of Knoppix as a 3D-gaming platform, and indeed there are only a few applications and games on the disk that take advantage of 3D acceleration. However, if you do want 3D acceleration for those programs and you have an Nvidia card, getting and using the Nvidia drivers is only a few mouse clicks away with the live installer [Hack #27].

To install the Nvidia drivers, click K Menu → KNOPPIX → Utilities → Install software. In the selection dialog that appears, click nvidia and then OK. Knoppix downloads and installs the files it needs, and prompts you to restart X. Close all running programs, and then click OK to tell the live installer to restart X.

After X restarts, open a console and test whether you have direct rendering enabled:

```
knoppix@ttyp0[knoppix]$ glxinfo | grep direct
direct rendering: Yes
```

You should see dramatic improvements in the performance of programs, such as *glxgears*, and 3D games, such as *Chromium*. If you have a fast Internet connection, you can even download the Quake 3 demo (45 MB) from *ftp://ftp.idsoftware.com/idstuff/quake3/linux/*, and install it locally (Figure 3-10), provided you have enough ramdisk space. Just tell the installer to install to */home/knoppix/* instead of */usr/local/games*, and run the installer as normal. The installer even adds an entry to your K Menu that you can use to launch the game.

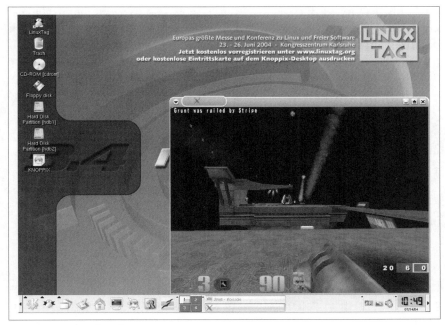

Figure 3-10. Quake3 demo

The Nvidia installer caches its files, so if you use a persistent home directory [Hack #21], you can rerun the installer at the next boot, and you won't have to download the files again.

HACK #29 Live Install Your Own Programs

Write your own live installer scripts to install programs you need that aren't on Knoppix by default.

As already briefly discussed in "Use the Knoppix Live Installer" [Hack #27], there are several techniques that allow live installation of software to the home directory. This hack discusses these techniques, shows you how you can create your own live installer modules, and gives an overview of possible future solutions.

The Problem

To understand how to write your own live installer scripts, you must understand the main problem with installing software to the home directory: most software expects to be installed in /. Most programs install their files in many different directories in Linux, with files in */usr*, */etc*, */usr/lib*, */var*, and other directories. Under Knoppix, the entire */usr* directory is part of the read-only CD-ROM filesystem. Even if you copy everything to */home/knoppix/usr*, */home/knoppix/etc*, */home/knoppix/var*, etc., it doesn't work because the program expects its files to be under the root directory. Even if that particular software does not need any other datafiles, most software depends on libraries, and these libraries are also searched for in */usr/lib*.

Use the Source Luke

One solution to this problem is to use the source. With the source code of a program, it is possible to install any program in the home directory.

The paths that determine where a program looks for its files are set during compile time. And most programs support setting the root to another prefix. With an *autotools*-compliant package, you can change the prefix by running the following command from the root of the source directory:

```
knoppix@ttyp0[knoppix]$ ./configure --prefix=/home/knoppix/.dist/
knoppix@ttyp0[knoppix]$ make
knoppix@ttyp0[knoppix]$ make install
```

Unfortunately, compiling is not a perfect solution. First, compiling a program is slow (depending, of course, on the speed of the computer). If I want to install a program, I want it now, not after a long coffee break. I'm not a Gentoo masochist!

Second, compiling a program often requires many dependencies, which must also be compiled, and these dependencies may have even more dependencies that you must also compile, and so on.

Dependency Hell

To install new software in Debian, use the *apt-get* utility. It not only installs the software you want, but also all dependencies this software needs and all dependencies of the dependencies. Unfortunately, *apt-get* isn't designed to be run from CD-ROM but from hard disk, and expects certain parts to be writable that are not writable under Knoppix. Despite this problem, the live installer uses wrappers that execute the original programs with special parameters to use *apt-get*.

Patch Me if You Can

After you download the *.deb* you need, use *dpkg* to extract the files into your local *~/.dist* directory:

```
knoppix@ttyp0[knoppix]$ dpkg -x file.deb ~/.dist/
```

To start the program, you must set up a library path so that you can install libraries in places other than the read-only /usr/lib directory. Fortunately, this is possible without the need for root rights. To modify the library path for a program, type:

```
knoppix@ttyp0[knoppix]$ export PATH=$HOME/.dist/usr/bin:$PATH
knoppix@ttyp0[knoppix]$ export LD_LIBRARY_PATH=$HOME/.dist/usr/lib:$LD_
LIBRARY_PATH
knoppix@ttyp0[knoppix]$ programname
```

Now the program searches for libraries and programs under your ~/.dist directory—at least most programs work this way. The live installer transparently writes a ~/.bashrc to set these paths so that starting **programname** in the shell also works. Games that need certain datafiles are still problematic. There isn't a set environment variable for these types of datafiles. Instead, you must determine which files the program is going to reference (**dpkg –L packagename** at least shows you which files the program includes). This is different for each program, and is one of the challenges that you must face when using live installs. Once you determine the paths that need to be changed, you must path the binary itself to change the hardcoded file paths. For example, *tuxracer* stores its datafiles in /usr/share/games/tuxracer. To change this path to a local path, run:

```
knoppix@ttyp0[knoppix]$ perl -pi -e \
's|/usr/share/games/tuxracer|./../share/games/tuxracer|' $DESTDIR/games/
tuxracer
```

This changes all occurrences of the global path /usr/share/games/tuxracer to the local path /share/games/tuxracer. If you start the program from /home/ knoppix/.dist/usr/bin/, it finds the datafiles in /home/knoppix/.dist/usr/share/ games/tuxracer.

Do It Yourself

OK, now you want to create your own live installer module. The best method is to find one of the existing modules and modify it for your program. To use your own live installer modules, make a directory called *modules* in your home directory, and run the live installer:

```
knoppix@ttyp0[knoppix]$ cp -a /usr/share/knx-live-inst/modules ./
knoppix@ttyp0[knoppix]$ cp -a modules/gkrellm modules/myprog
knoppix@ttyp0[knoppix]$ knx-live-inst.sh
```

This command makes a mirror copy of the Knoppix live installer modules in your home directory, and then copies the *gkrellm* modules to use as a base for your program. The files in *modules/myprog* allow you to change different settings for your module:

description
> Describes the live installer menu

exes
> Is the main executable for the program

files
> Shows which files to download and from where

install.sh
> Explains how to install the program

menu
> Is the name of the menu entry for the created Extra Software menu

While *description*, *exes*, and *menu* are simple, the one-line text file, *files*, has a special format, and *install.sh* is a shell script.

For a program that can be installed by apt, *files* is as simple as:

```
# Format of this is:
# basename location_to_download type md5sum
myprog          none    apt     none
```

And *install.sh* in most cases is as simple as:

```
#!/bin/bash
#
# File to actually install the software
# copy main prog

cp -fa myprog/usr/* $DESTDIR/
```

Sometimes (such as in the previous *tuxracer* example), you must add binary patches and wrappers that run when the program is installed to work around difficult file path issues. In these cases, use the *tuxracer* module as a base so that you can see how it handles patching and wrappers.

Advanced Techniques

Some programs, such as the Nvidia drivers, won't work with the previous techniques. The problem is usually that these programs must be in, and write to, */usr*. One option is to build a huge *symlink farm*. In a symlink farm, at boot every directory on the CD-ROM is copied as a new directory in the filesystem, and files in those directories are not copied but symlinked. This makes everything in */usr* writable. However, if you build a symlink farm when you create the live CD, you waste space; if you build it while you boot the live CD, it takes a very long time.

One solution to this problem is the dynamic creation of symlink farms. This is how the nvidia live installer works. The installer runs make -n install and checks the output of that program for files that need to be writable, and then builds the necessary symlink farm.

Another possible solution that isn't being implemented in the Knoppix live installer is to use *overlay filesystems*. The idea behind an overlay filesystem is simple. You can overlay */usr* with */ramdisk/usr*, and although you can read all files that lie in */usr*, all file writes go to */ramdisk/usr*. There are several of these filesystems, and they all have some problems:

Ovlfs
> Is the oldest and best working overlay filesystem (development started with kernel 2.0), but its source code is very complex and not portable to kernel 2.6.

Translucency
> Attempts to redirect files and directories if there is an open or readdir attempt. Translucency unfortunately still lacks support for symlinks, and directory entries that exist in both directories before the overlay are presented twice.

Linux User Space Filesystem (LUFS)
> Is slow because it uses user space tools as opposed to a kernel module.

Device Mapper
> Has a snapshot functionality that doesn't work reliably because it works on the so-called block-layer, which means the underlying filesystem does not know how much space is available.

What all of these solutions have in common is that they don't make use of the VFS Linux Virtual Filesystem Layer (VFS) very much, but reimplement it one way or another. It's possible that eventually a good overlay filesystem will be included in the main kernel tree.

—*Fabian Franz*

Point-and-Klik to Install Applications

HACK
#30

Install extra software on your Knoppix live CD just by clicking a link on a web site.

Knoppix offers a broad variety of software, but due to space limitations on the Knoppix CD and licensing issues, some software cannot be included with the Knoppix. There is an easy way to get additional software from the Web while using Knoppix from a CD. With the *klik* software store (a web interface for *klik* recipes), a plug-in for Konqueror allows you to execute the *klik* installer just by clicking on a URL that starts with "klik://".

Before you install software with *klik*, you must install the *klik* client itself. Go to *http://klik.sf.net* and follow the instructions. (I don't repeat them here, because by the time you have read this book, the installation of the client might have become even easier.) Once you have installed the *klik* client, a new window opens to *http://klik.sf.net*, and you can start installing software from the point-and-klik software store.

For example, to install KPlayer, the powerful KDE media player, click on the Kplayer link. Notice that the URL of the link is *klik://kplayer*. You can easily remember a *klik* link and also email it to friends or post it to discussion boards. Click on the link with Konqueror, and the *klik* client begins to download and install the KPlayer software along with any dependencies. You can also enter *klik* links into the Run Command window (Click K Menu → Run Command or press Alt-F2). Once the download is complete, *klik* automatically runs the software and places a new entry into the KDE start menu. Depending on the speed of your Internet connection, you should have KPlayer up and running in a few seconds or minutes.

When you install software with *klik*, the application and all additional software that it needs to run (libraries, help pages, icons, etc.) are placed within a single directory per application within your home directory. KPlayer, for example, is installed to *~/kplayer*. This concept makes it extremely easy for you to manage software. You always know what gets installed where, and if you want to uninstall an application, you simply delete its application directory, then remove that application's files under *~/.kde/share/applnk/klik/* to remove the application from the KDE menu. Every application is self-contained in its own directory (at least relative to the specific Knoppix base system). It is important to know that you can safely play around with *klik* and try as many applications as you want without the risk of breaking the system.

Klik installs all software into the current user's home directory by default. Knoppix uses a ramdisk for the home directory, so if you want to keep the software that you have installed with *klik* to stay across reboots, make your home directory persistent **[Hack #21]**.

—Simon Peter

HACK #31   Create Your Own Klik Recipe

Klik might be of interest to you even if the application you need is not on the Knoppix CD.

Originally, *klik* stood for "KDE-based Live Installer for Knoppix," but it is not really limited to KDE or to Knoppix. Currently, though, *klik* links work only in native KDE applications such as Konqueror.

The *klik* server tells a *klik* client where to download software from and how to install it using *klik recipes*. A *klik* recipe is required to install software using *klik*, and is essentially a shell script that tells the client where to obtain packages and what to do with them. So, to install your own software using *klik*, you must write your own recipe.

The best way to start writing *klik* recipes is to learn from existing recipes. You can view sample *klik* recipes in the point-and-klik software store at *http://klik.sf.net*. Test your shell script locally, and if it works, please contribute it to *klik*.

Most Linux software is designed to look for files in places such as */usr*, */var*, */bin*, */etc*, and so on. In order to make programs run in nonstandard locations, *klik* has to run the software using a wrapper script inside each application directory. Each *klik* recipe has to create its own wrapper script. Sometimes, application binaries even contain hardcoded paths. In these cases, the software must be patched by *klik* in order to change paths to point to the local application directory. Luckily, KDE applications generally do not use hardcoded paths.

Writing *klik* recipes by hand for every application is a bit tedious; there should be a better way to manage live-CD software installation. The idea behind *klik's serverside-apt* project is to automatically generate *klik* recipes for all software in the Debian distribution on the fly. There is a working development version you can try by pressing Alt-F2 and entering:

```
klik://packagename
```

Replace **packagename** with the name of any Debian package, such as **bidwatcher** (which is known to work). If you are a programmer interested in advancing *serverside-apt*, please contact the *klik* development team.

—Simon Peter

## CHAPTER FOUR

Install Linux with Knoppix
Hacks 32–36

Once you are comfortable using Knoppix for your desktop, you might find yourself booting onto the CD more often. While you can create persistent settings and a portable home directory to mount, at some point you might decide you would like to use Knoppix full-time by installing it to your hard drive.

The Debian GNU/Linux distribution, on which Knoppix is based, is becoming much more popular, but the Debian installer can be daunting even for the experienced Linux user. Some of the more complicated parts of the install ask questions that the new Debian user might not know the answers to. Knoppix handles all of the hardware and network configuration for you and comes with a great selection of applications, so it wasn't long before people began asking for a way to install Knoppix on their hard drives. As Knoppix's hard-drive installer has progressed, it has become known as the quickest and easiest way to obtain a Debian testing/unstable installation.

The Debian distribution has three main branches that are used to ensure high security and stability on one end, and rapid inclusion of new programs and updates on the other. These branches are:

Stable (currently nicknamed Woody)
> The Debian stable branch contains packages that have been rigorously tested with the other packages in the branch over a long period of time and is considered incredibly stable.

Testing (currently nicknamed Sarge)
> The Debian testing branch is a blend of the stable and unstable branches, and it consists of packages from the unstable branch that have been shown to be stable for some time. Once the packages in testing have been tested enough, Debian will declare the testing branch the new stable branch.

Unstable (nicknamed Sid)
> The Debian unstable branch contains newer packages in a more rapid state of flux that have only been moderately tested to work well together.

Some people mistakenly believe that the packages within the unstable branch are buggy. While packaging bugs and instability are more common in the unstable branch than in testing or stable branches, the packages in the unstable branch still undergo a fair amount of testing before release, particularly for large, popular packages such as desktop environments and X. It is commonly held that the packages in the unstable branch are as good as any you would find in other Linux distributions, if not more so.

You often hear Debian branches referred to as Woody, Sarge, and Sid. These nicknames refer to the stable, testing, and unstable branches, but change with each Debian release. For example, Woody is the name for the Debian 3.0 release. For as long as Debian is at 3.0, Woody will also be synonymous with the stable branch. However, with the next Debian release, Sarge (the current nickname for the testing release) will be declared stable, and will then become the nickname of the new stable branch. A new name will then be assigned to the testing branch. The advantages to this distinction are that you can choose to follow either a group of packages such as Sarge, which means you will eventually be running the stable release, or you can choose to follow a branch by its name. If you are using the testing branch, you can continue to use the testing branch even when the Sarge packages become stable.

The exception to this naming rule is the unstable branch. It will always have the nickname of Sid (after the boy in the movie *Toy Story* who broke all of the toys), and that name does not move up the list as packages stabilize.

This chapter discusses the state of the current Knoppix hard-drive installer, *knoppix-installer*, and provides a few installation scenarios that provide a complete guide to installing Knoppix on a single-boot setup and as a dual-boot setup with Windows. As you'll soon see, installing Knoppix is easy even for new Linux users.

HACK #32   Explore the Knoppix Installer

Learn the ins and outs of the Knoppix installer before installing.

Knoppix was originally intended to run just from the CD, but early on, users wanted to transfer the system to their hard drives once they discovered how well the CD recognized and worked with their computer. At first, this involved a complicated set of commands run from a shell to copy the CD to the hard drive and set up a boot loader. Eventually, this method was automated with a script that is currently maintained by Fabian Franz (*http://www.fabian-franz.de*).

The latest version of the hard-drive installer is pretty sophisticated and does much more than just copy the CD to the hard drive. Start the installer from the terminal by using:

```
knoppix@ttyp0[knoppix]$ sudo knoppix-installer
```

The first thing you should see is a disclaimer warning that this program is under heavy development. Don't worry. This just means that options might change in the future; it's safe to use.

The *knoppix-installer* script works both in a pure console environment and in X. If you run it from the console, navigate through the options with your keyboard, and hit the spacebar to select options and Enter to confirm them. If you run the script from X, you have a GUI that you can navigate with either a keyboard or a mouse.

Before you even get to the main menu, the installer checks to see that some minimum requirements are met. The first check is for the presence of any Linux partitions 2 GB or greater in size, including partitions containing other distributions. For systems with less than 512 MB of RAM, it also checks for a swap partition of at least 128 MB. If either of these conditions is not met, the installer presents you with the following informational warning and the option to partition the hard disk or quit:

```
The installer detected that the installation requirements are not fulfilled
yet.

Please make sure that you have a free partition with at least 2GB to install
Knoppix on.

Also we need a swap partition with at least 128MB if you don't have 512MB or
more.

If you really really know what you are doing start with: IGNORE_CHECK=1 sudo
knoppix-installer to avoid the menu.
```

You intend to install Knoppix, so the only choice is to select the Partition option. In X, *qtparted* runs, a graphical partitioning program somewhat similar to Partition Magic that you can use to create, delete, and resize partitions on your system. If you run the installer from the console, *cfdisk* launches instead. In either case, the goal is to create partitions to satisfy the installer requirements. Once you finish and close *qtparted* or *cfdisk*, the installer checks again for partitions it can use; if it finds them, the main installer menu appears (Figure 4-1).

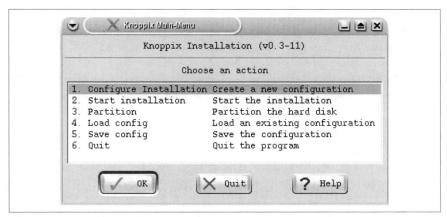

Figure 4-1. Knoppix installer main menu

The main menu presents you with six options:

Configure Installation
 Opens a new window that asks you which style of Knoppix install to use and where to install it.

Start installation
 Starts the installation process based on whichever configuration is currently loaded. If no configuration is loaded, it walks you through the configuration just as though you had selected Configure Installation.

Partition
 Starts *qtparted* in X or *cfdisk* in a console so you can partition your hard drive and presents you with the option to partition the hard disk, resize drives, etc., without having to exit the installer.

Load config
 Loads a configuration you have created beforehand from the home directory, floppies, USB drives, or any mountable storage device; this can be useful if you want to clone installations across multiple machines.

Save config
 Saves the installation settings currently loaded (either from selecting Configure Installation or Load config) to a file on the home directory or any mountable storage device so you can load it later.

Quit
 Exits the program without saving any settings.

If you are ready to install Knoppix and are familiar with the configuration options, or you have already configured the installer a previous time (if you configure and then exit the installer, Knoppix remembers the settings that you have chosen), skip right ahead and select Start installation. If you are new to installing Knoppix on your hard drive, you should probably select Configure Installation so you can see what kind of questions the installer asks before you commit to an install. When you choose Configure Installation, you are presented with a window that asks you to choose from one of the three types of systems:

Beginner

This is the preferred method for installing Knoppix to a hard drive. With this option, Knoppix sets up a multiuser Debian system, but also leaves all of the Knoppix hardware-detection scripts behind. You can still use most of the cheat codes at boot time and still have Knoppix run some of its hardware-configuration scripts. This type of installation is a blend of the best features of the following two system types.

Knoppix

This choice basically creates a copy of the live CD on your hard drive and allows you to boot from it. Just like the CD, this option installs only a single-user system with disabled passwords. Think of this option as running the Knoppix CD only without the read-only restriction, so you can install new software or updates, and more easily edit system files. Because passwords are disabled, this system type is potentially less secure than the other two.

Debian

This choice offers a multiuser Debian install without any extra Knoppix hardware-detection scripts. This means that the only cheat codes that still work are those that are actually options passed to the kernel (such as noapic, noscsi, etc.). Think of this as the beginner option without any of the hardware-detection scripts. Experienced Knoppix users may recognize this as being the same installation method provided by the old Knoppix installer scripts. Choose this option if you want to use Knoppix as an easy way to install a purer form of Debian.

Once you choose a system type, the installer shows you a list of potential partitions on which it can install. If you don't want to install on any of these partitions, click Previous until you can choose the Partition option, and then create a new partition.

Once you select a partition, Knoppix asks for personal information, such as your name, your username, your user and root password, and where you want to install the boot loader. You won't necessarily be asked all of these questions. It depends on the system type that you have chosen (for instance, the Knoppix system type uses the *knoppix* user just like the CD, so it won't ask you for a username). Once you answer all the questions, the configuration is complete and Knoppix drops back to the main menu, and allows you to start the installation with the options you have just configured, or to save the options so you can use them later.

Once you are satisfied with your configuration, click "Start installation." A report appears and displays the different options that Knoppix can use for the install with a final prompt before proceeding. Once you click Next, Knoppix begins the install process, so be certain everything is configured how you want it.

> Make sure that all of your hardware is working before proceeding with the install. If you need special cheat codes for your hardware to work properly (such as the alsa cheat code), make sure that you use them for this boot, because these are the hardware settings Knoppix uses for the install. This is especially important if you choose the Debian system type, which does not install the Knoppix hardware-detection scripts, because any hardware that isn't working when you install must be configured later without the benefit of Knoppix's scripts. (It is technically possible to reuse Knoppix's configuration scripts in this mode, but it requires a series of complicated steps.)

Now Knoppix formats the partition you chose and starts copying files to it. It does take some time to copy 2 GB from the CD-ROM to the hard drive, but unlike most other OS installers, you have a full set of applications you can use while the files are copying. Once all the files are copied, you have the option to create a boot floppy for rescue purposes in case the boot loader didn't install properly (or you accidentally delete or break the boot loader later). After the installer is finished, continue to use Knoppix from the CD or reboot into your newly installed Knoppix system. Remember to remove the CD-ROM when you reboot, and if everything goes well, you should see a new boot logo and options to boot from the 2.4 or 2.6 kernels.

HACK #33 Install Knoppix as a Single-Boot System

Ready to take the plunge and use Linux as the sole operating system on your computer? Then you need these instructions to know how to install Knoppix by itself on a computer.

While it isn't always possible to install Knoppix on its own empty hard drive, it certainly removes a lot of the complications that make installation tricky. These steps guide you through installing Knoppix on a drive that is unpartitioned and brand-new, or that you are willing to commit entirely to Knoppix.

From a terminal window, start the installer by typing:

```
knoppix@ttyp0[knoppix]$ sudo knoppix-installer
```

If this is an unpartitioned hard drive, you are prompted to create a root and swap partition for Knoppix. Choose the Partition option from the menu that appears to launch *qtparted*.

Once *qtparted* starts, select your hard drive from the list of disks on the left side of the window (*/dev/hdb* for our example). If you have any partitions that you need to delete before you can install Knoppix, select them and click Operations → Delete, then click on the gray free space labeled hda-1 and select Operations → Create.

The Knoppix installer requires that you create a swap partition, so select linux-swap from the Partition Type drop-down menu, and then choose a size for the swap as shown in Figure 4-2. The current rule of thumb is to pick a swap size, ranging from your amount of RAM to twice that amount, so for a system with 256 MB of RAM, you should choose a swap size between 256 MB and 512 MB. Click OK, and *qtparted* shows a new swap partition at the beginning of the disk.

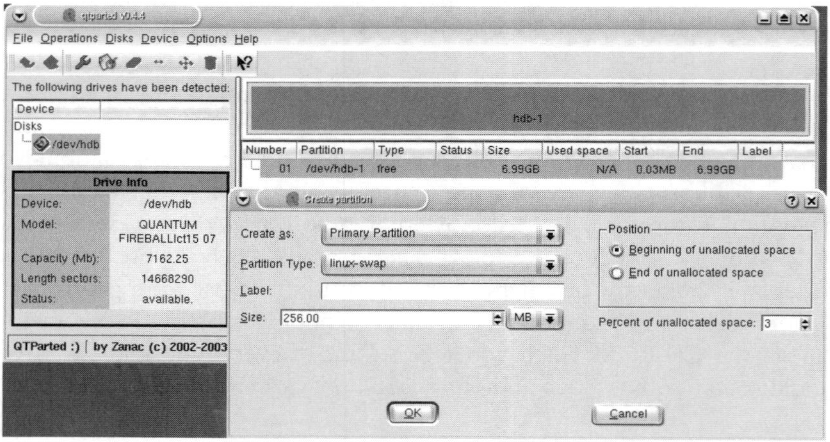

Figure 4-2. Create a swap partition with qtparted

To create your root partition, click on the gray free space after the swap partition, and select Operations → Create again. *Qtparted* defaults to creating an ext3 partition that spans the rest of the free space. Knoppix also supports installing to ReiserFS partitions, but only for the Debian install type. This example is for the beginner system, so click OK to create the partition. After you partition the drive (as shown in Figure 4-3), click File → Commit to save the changes to the disk. Once the changes are saved, close *qtparted* and the main installer menu should appear.

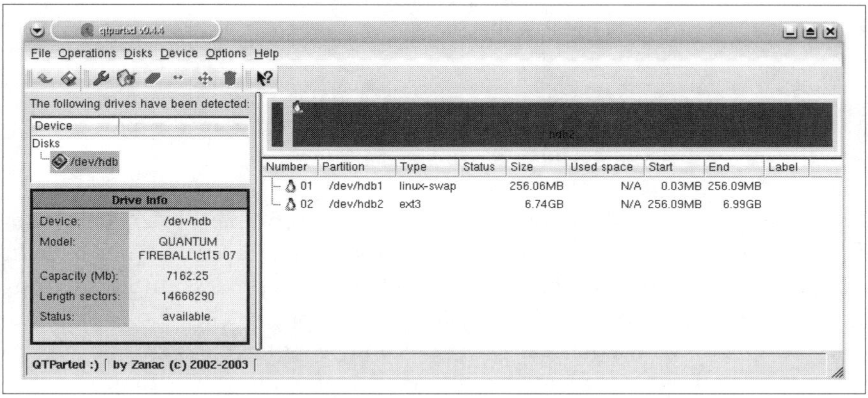

Figure 4-3. A partitioned hard drive ready to install

To start the configuration process, select Configure Installation and click OK. Select the beginner system type, and press Enter or click Next. The installer then asks you to choose the partition on which to install Knoppix. In our example, there is only one partition, so simply click Next.

At this stage of the install, set up user accounts. At the first window, enter your full name. The next window prompts you for a username; the default is your first initial and last name. If that is fine for you, then continue to the next window—otherwise, change the username. You are then asked to enter a password for your user. You can uncheck Hide typing if you're having trouble entering your password twice.

The next window looks like the previous, but this password is for the root account. The root account is a special account that has the ability to change and delete any file on the system, so choose a good password. You will use this account only when changing system settings, installing packages, or other potentially dangerous things.

Once your accounts are set up, it is time to enter a few system settings. The first setting is the hostname. This is the name your computer goes by on the network. You are asked to accept the default hostname or enter one of your choosing. Next, you choose where to install the boot loader. This is the only operating system on the disk, so choose MBR. This installs the boot loader on the boot sector of the Master Boot Record, the first 512 bytes on any hard drive that contains the boot code and the partition table. Now the configuration is done, and you are ready to install.

To install Knoppix on your hard drive based on this configuration, select Start installation and click OK. Read over the list of configuration options Knoppix presents you, and make sure everything is configured to your liking. Click Next to start the installation.

Knoppix formats your hard drive and then copies all the files to the system, but you can still play games or run other programs during this process to pass the time.

Once Knoppix is finished copying files, you are prompted to create a boot floppy. Boot floppies are important in case you accidentally delete your Linux kernel or otherwise damage parts of the boot process. Insert a floppy into your drive, and click Yes to create a boot floppy or click No to skip creating it. Once the installer exits, log out and reboot the system. Be sure to remove the CD-ROM when it ejects, and at reboot, you should be presented with the boot screen for your brand new Knoppix install.

HACK #34   Install Knoppix on a Multiboot System

A lot of people who use Linux also dual-boot their computer to Windows. The two most worrisome parts of such a setup are partitioning the drive and configuring the boot loader. Here's how to install Knoppix in a multiboot setup.

Installing Knoppix in a dual-boot configuration is a bit trickier than a clean install, as it requires you to resize partitions to make room for Knoppix and possibly requires you to configure your boot loader. This hack walks you through a typical Knoppix install that dual-boots with Windows. This walkthrough assumes that Knoppix is being installed on a computer with a single IDE hard drive containing a single Windows partition that fills the drive.

As in the single-boot system example [Hack #33], start the Knoppix installer with the following command:

```
knoppix@ttyp0[knoppix]$ sudo knoppix-installer
```

You are prompted to create partitions for Knoppix to install to. The entire hard drive is filled with a single Windows partition, so you have no free space to create a partition. Luckily, you can resize your Windows partition with *qtparted*, which can resize both FAT32 and NTFS partitions.

Resizing a partition can be risky, and there is always a potential for data loss. Before resizing any partition, defragment the hard drive completely from within Windows; otherwise, a file fragment near the end of the partition might be deleted when the partition is resized. Of course, it is always a good idea to back up any important data.

To resize your hard drive from within *qtparted*, select */dev/hda* from the list of disks on the left side of the *qtparted* window, then click on the */dev/hda1* partition listed on the right side and select Operations → Resize. In the resizing window that appears, you can decide how much free space to leave after the partition. In my experience, I've needed to create a root partition of 2.2 GB to have enough room for the Knoppix files. In our example, resize the partition so that 2.5 GB of free space is available, so you have enough room for the 2.2 GB root partition and a swap partition. After you click OK, *qtparted* displays the free space you have just created in the main window. Now click on the gray free space, and create a swap partition and a 2.2 GB root partition, as covered in "Install Knoppix as a Single-Boot System" **[Hack #33]**. Once you are finished resizing, click File → Commit to actually perform the resizing and partition creation. After you commit the changes, close *qtparted* to return to the main installer menu.

The next step is to configure the installation by selecting a username, password, and so on. Once you are finished, click Start installation to start copying the files to the partition. After this process, you are prompted to create an optional boot floppy, after which the installation is complete.

During the install process, Knoppix attempts to automatically detect any Windows partitions on the drive and will add them to the boot choices in */etc/lilo.conf*. If you are multibooting with another Linux system, be aware that Knoppix overwrites your boot loader with its version of lilo. To fix your *lilo.conf* file so you can boot both your new Knoppix install and your old Linux install, finish the Knoppix install, then mount the root partition for your new Knoppix install. Then edit the *etc/lilo.conf* file and update *lilo*, as in "Repair Lilo" **[Hack #52]**. Restart the computer and remove the CD-ROM from the drive, and you should see a new boot prompt with options for booting either Linux or Windows.

 If you would like to change the OS form which your system boots by default, boot into your new Knoppix install and edit the */etc/lilo.conf* file as root, changing the line that reads default="Linux" to default="Windows(hda1)" or whatever label your Windows partition is assigned at the bottom of the file. Once you have edited the file, run **/sbin/lilo** as root to apply the changes.

You should now be able to boot either into Knoppix or Windows. Similar to booting from the CD, the Knoppix hard-drive install has your Windows partition icons on the desktop so you are still able to access files in the same way you are accustomed.

Convert Knoppix to Debian Unstable

Even though Knoppix is based on Debian, and the installation instructions help you install Knoppix on your hard drive, what you have installed is a hybrid Debian system. Here's how to convert a Knoppix install to as close to a standard Debian unstable branch distribution as you can get.

Knoppix is based on the Debian GNU/Linux distribution, but Knoppix uses a unique mix of packages from the stable, testing, and unstable branches, as well as from other unofficial Debian repositories. As a result, even if you select the Debian system install type, you won't get the same system as if you had installed Debian unstable from scratch. There are some steps you can perform, however, to get closer to a Debian unstable system.

The installation process for this system is almost exactly the same as for "Install Knoppix as a Single-Boot System" [Hack #33]. The only exception is that you select the Debian system type during configuration instead of beginner. Remember, with the Debian system type, Knoppix does not include its hardware-detection scripts in the install, so make sure that you have all of your hardware detected and configured before you start the install. In order to convert the install to Debian, the real work begins after the files have been copied, and you boot into the new system.

Configure APT

Once you boot into your new Knoppix install, you must change your Advanced Package Tool (APT) settings. APT is a management system for software packages. Under Debian, it provides a series of tools to ease installing, removing, and updating packages. The most commonly used APT tool is *apt-get*, which automates downloading packages and their dependencies for installation. When you tell *apt-get* to install a package, it finds the newest version of the package from its list of package repositories. Then it checks its local cache of packages, and if it does not have the package you need, it downloads the package and any dependencies directly from the repository. All of the configuration files for APT are located in the */etc/apt* directory. The */etc/apt/sources.list* file contains a list of all of the repositories the APT tool uses to look for packages. The */etc/apt/apt.conf* file contains APT settings, such as which Debian branch to use by default.

The first step to convert Knoppix to Debian unstable is to edit */etc/apt/apt. conf* as root, changing:

```
APT::Default-Release "testing";
```

to:

```
APT::Default-Release "unstable";
```

This setting controls which branch Debian defaults to when installing and upgrading packages. By changing testing to unstable, you tell Debian to upgrade any packages from the testing or stable repositories it might have installed to unstable at the next upgrade, and to default to installing from the unstable branch in the future.

The next step is to update the list of repositories APT uses by editing */etc/apt/sources.list* as root. The default Knoppix *sources.list* file has sources for stable, testing, unstable, experimental, and a few other repositories. Comment all of the stable and testing repositories, which ensures that all our installs use the unstable packages. It is up to you if you wish to leave some of the other unofficial repositories in your *sources.list*. For a pure Debian Sid system, including *non-us* sources, delete all of the lines in your *sources.list* file, and edit it to look like this:

```
# Unstable
deb http://ftp.us.debian.org/debian unstable main contrib non-free
deb http://non-us.debian.org/debian-non-US unstable/non-US main contrib non-
free

# Unstable Sources
deb-src http://ftp.us.debian.org/debian unstable main contrib non-free
deb-src http://non-us.debian.org/debian-non-US unstable/non-US main contrib
non-free
```

Once you have edited your *sources.list*, update your system to unstable by running the following command as root:

```
root@ttyp0[knoppix]# apt-get update && apt-get dist-upgrade
```

This command downloads the latest list of packages from each source in your *sources.list* file, and then it upgrades the distribution to the very latest versions of each package. This ensures that old packages from stable or testing are replaced with packages from unstable.

As the packages install, you might be prompted that a configuration file for a package has been modified since installation. Chances are that Knoppix modified these configuration files to better suit your system, so it's safe to go with the default and keep the current version of the configuration file. Once this update has completed, your system should be up-to-date with the current Debian unstable.

As a final note, some packages on the Knoppix system come from other unofficial or experimental repositories, so there still might be a few packages on the system that can't be updated in this manner. Packages from the experimental repository, given time and testing, typically find their way into unstable. After using and updating your system, these packages should eventually sync up with unstable. In the case of packages from other sources (such as

Java), you must decide whether to keep these repositories in your *sources.list* file, so the packages can be updated, or you must decide whether to leave these packages at their installed version by leaving out the repository.

Install Gentoo with Knoppix

Installing Gentoo can be an overwhelming and uninviting task because you are limited to a shell interface, and the computer is unavailable for tasks during the installation. That is, of course, unless you use the Knoppix CD.

Knoppix makes installing Gentoo a much less painful experience. The Knoppix hardware detection seems to be more robust and is much more successful than the Gentoo system. A Gentoo install involves downloading packages from the Internet, so Knoppix provides you with much better support for your particular NIC. Furthermore, your computer is still fully functional while you compile the base Gentoo system, which provides you with some additional advantages. First, the compilation process for a Gentoo install can take hours, so with Knoppix, you can browse the Web, play games, and get work done while the system compiles in the background. Second, you can browse the Web with a graphical web browser, so if you run into a roadblock in the installation process, you can head straight to the Gentoo forums at *http://forums.gentoo.org* to ask a question. The installation instructions are also readily accessible (*http://www.gentoo.org/doc/en/ handbook/handbook-x86.xml*), so there is no need to print them out. The instructions are very thorough and explain not only what each step is, but also why it is necessary.

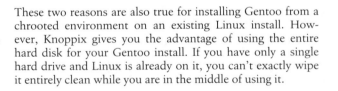

> These two reasons are also true for installing Gentoo from a chrooted environment on an existing Linux install. However, Knoppix gives you the advantage of using the entire hard disk for your Gentoo install. If you have only a single hard drive and Linux is already on it, you can't exactly wipe it entirely clean while you are in the middle of using it.

Installing Gentoo from Knoppix requires very few additional steps. First, boot your Knoppix CD with the noswap cheat code. This cheat code tells Knoppix not to automatically use any existing swap partitions it finds on the hard drive. This saves you extra steps of disabling the swap later if you need to delete the swap partition to create new partitions on your drive for the install. There is no need for a Gentoo Live CD, because the Knoppix CD is replacing it in your setup. When the desktop finishes loading, open a terminal window. At the prompt, type:

```
knoppix@ttyp0[knoppix]$ su -
```

This switches the current user to root and reloads the shell configuration. Next, type:

```
root@ttyp0[root]# mkdir /mnt/gentoo
```

While naming the mount point *gentoo* is not strictly necessary, it does make it easier to follow the install documentation that asks you to mount the root filesystem under */mnt/gentoo*. All Knoppix-specific steps have now been completed.

The first page of the *Gentoo Installation Handbook* has links to each chapter of the install. You are using a Knoppix CD for the install, so the first few chapters only provide information about the install process. You won't actually start performing any of the steps until Chapter 4.

Chapter 1 of the Gentoo Installation Handbook provides an overview of the entire installation process.

Chapter 2 describes the differences between the stages and how to boot the Gentoo CD. When you read Chapter 2, ignore the CD-booting steps, and instead focus on the differences between a Stage 1, Stage 2, and Stage 3 install. Each stage starts you at a different point in the compilation of the base system. The later the stage you choose, the less input you have into how the base system is configured. Which stage you choose is mostly a matter of personal preference and depends on the amount of time you have for this particular install.

Chapter 3 describes some additional steps that you may need if you are using the Gentoo CD, but since you are not, these steps can be safely ignored.

Once you have chosen a stage for the install, you are ready to start the Gentoo install process. First, partition and format your disk, as described in Chapter 4. Then simply follow the rest of the Gentoo Installation Handbook to complete the installation. Remember to retrieve your stage tarball from the Internet, as described in Chapter 5.b.

Now you have all the benefits of having a Gentoo system, such as the excellent portage package manager, but with a much less painful installation. If you enjoy puzzle games, I recommend playing Frozen Bubble while you wait for the system to compile.

—*Alex Garbutt*

## CHAPTER FIVE

Put Knoppix in Your Toolbox
Hacks 37–51

A system administrator's toolbox and desk tell you that his job requires that he wear many hats and use many tools. First, there are the hardware tools: screwdrivers, torx wrenches, CAT5 crimpers, duct and electrical tape, and of course, a hammer. Then there are the reference tools: books, manuals, CD-ROM documentation, and the secret phone number to upper-tier-vendor tech support. After these tools are the software tools: DOS boot floppies, driver CD-ROMs, BIOS flashing utilities, and a number of other special-purpose rescue disks. Lastly, there is the most important tool for a system administrator: caffeine.

Oftentimes, a system administrator doesn't know which of these tools he will be required to use in any given circumstance. "My computer is broken" or "the Internet is down" mean any number of things, so when an administrator goes to solve a problem, he often brings a number of different tools and is prepared for any problem.

Over time, a clever (or lazy, depending on how you want to look at it) administrator figures out how to consolidate all his most useful tools, just so there is less to carry. If you are this kind of administrator, Knoppix is for you. While a Knoppix disc is a great Linux demonstration tool for a new user and a great desktop environment for an average Linux user, in the hands of an experienced system administrator, it is the ultimate software toolbox for any number of auditing, troubleshooting, or emergency uses.

In this chapter, the hacks are roughly organized into two sections. The first section deals with tools that can help you administer a network. Knoppix not only comes with a lot of excellent tools to audit your servers over the network, but it can actually replace some of them in a pinch. The second section deals with tools that can help you administer local hardware. Here, you will find tools that help you clone, wipe, and scan hard drives, and probe hardware. The fact that all of these tools run directly from the CD means that you can take Knoppix to any computer on your network and turn it into a troubleshooting tool.

Knoppix might be worth considering as an option in a recovery plan. You could even create custom disks **[Hack #94]** that already contain any files and settings unique to your network, and any extra services or modules that Knoppix does not contain. Then, emergency failover from a crashed server would be as simple and as fast as booting a CD.

H A C K   Run Remote Desktops
#37

Use a computer running Knoppix as a base for remotely controlling other computers on the network via rdesktop or xvncviewer.

System administrators often need to be in two places at once. You might be on the phone walking a person through a technical problem when you realize that it would be much simpler if you could perform the problem-solving steps yourself. You might need to perform the same task on multiple computers, such as a manual virus or spyware scan or software update, that requires some initial setup and then a lot of waiting. If you could access all of the computers at the same time, you could start on the second computer once the first got going. In any of these cases, you might want to remotely control the computer, and with Knoppix, you can connect to both Remote Desktop Protocol (RDP) and any Virtual Network Computing (VNC) server using software on the CD. This hack explains the steps and software required to turn any machine on the network running Knoppix into a mobile command center for remotely controlling all of the computers on your network.

VNC

VNC is an open source remote access project created by AT&T Labs at Cambridge, U.K. VNC's original purpose was to enable remote access to computers running X from thin clients that could be disconnected and reconnected later from the same or another thin client. The fact that the software is open source and runs on a variety of different platforms (Windows, Linux, Solaris, and OS X among others) has made it rather popular to both system administrators, who want a single program to remotely control multiple platforms, and to programmers, who have improved the VNC protocol by adding encryption and compressions and incorporated it into their open source projects. The current open source version of VNC is maintained by the company RealVNC and can be downloaded for free from its site at *http://www.realvnc.com*.

Knoppix includes the Linux RealVNC client *xvncviewer* to connect to remote VNC servers. For system administrators who are familiar with that program, open a terminal, and type this command to connect to a remote VNC server:

```
knoppix@ttyp0[knoppix]$ xvncviewer server :display#
```

Now type the password for that server at the prompt. The *xvncviewer* program also has a large number of options to enable full-screen mode and control settings such as color depth. Use *xvncviewer* from the command line if you are already experienced with the program or your connection requires special options. If you're not comfortable with the command line or don't have one open, you can click on K Menu → Internet → More Programs → xvncviewer to launch a GUI that makes connecting to remote machines quick and easy.

If you are completely new to VNC or you plan on managing multiple connections at once, you might find the included KDE application *krdc* (for KDE Remote Desktop Connection) a better choice. *Krdc* allows you to manage multiple VNC and RDP sessions from a single easy-to-use program. To launch *krdc*, click K Menu → Internet → Remote Desktop Connection. When first run, you are presented with a simple window that prompts you to enter the address of the computer to which you wish to connect. For a VNC connection, this is as simple as typing the hostname or IP address for the remote computer, followed by a colon and the display name. Usually, the remote machine is running a single VNC session, so to connect to the machine at the IP address 192.168.0.1, type the following command and click Connect:

```
192.168.0.1:0
```

Krdc then prompts you for your connection type so it can choose the settings that best suit your connection (such as a lower color depth for low-speed connections). After configuring your connection, *krdc* next prompts you for the remote server's VNC password and, once it is provided, connects you. *Krdc* superimposes a small taskbar at the top of your VNC window that tells you which server this window belongs to and allows you to toggle full-screen mode and close or minimize the window. This taskbar is particularly useful if you are in full-screen mode and can't remember the key combination to escape it (Ctrl-Alt-Enter). If the taskbar bothers you, you can easily set it to hide by clicking the pushpin icon.

One nice feature of *krdc* is that it keeps track of servers to which you have already connected, and the next time you run the program you can quickly select your server from the drop-down menu. *Krdc* also saves session information, and you only have to enter settings, such as the resolution for the remote connection and the connection rate, once.

RDP

Knoppix also comes with tools to connect to servers accepting RDP connections. RDP is a protocol used by Microsoft for its Terminal Services software to allow mouse, keyboard, and even sound channels to be accessed remotely. The functionality to make at least a single RDP connection to a machine exists out of the box in Windows XP Professional, Windows Server 2000 and 2003, and NT Server 4.0 Terminal Server Edition. For instance, to enable RDP connections on a Windows XP Professional machine, click on System under the Control Panel and check "Allow users to connect remotely to this computer" under the Remote tab.

The primary client for RDP connections under Linux is the command-line program *rdesktop*. Like *xvncviewer*, *rdesktop* has a number of command-line arguments to tweak settings, such as color depth and desktop geometry, and even forward sound to your local machine. To reference all of these settings, run **man rdesktop** or visit the official site at *http://www.rdesktop.org*, but for most usage, simply type this command in a terminal:

```
knoppix@ttyp0[knoppix]$ rdesktop servername
```

If the remote computer accepts RDP connections, you are presented with a standard Windows login page. Once connected, you can toggle full-screen mode by pressing Ctrl-Alt-Enter in the *rdesktop* window or by passing the -f argument to *rdesktop* when you start it.

Similar to VNC connections, RDP connections are also managed within the *krdc* program in much the same way. The primary difference is the syntax used for the hostname. For VNC connections, the syntax is *hostname:display* or *vnc:/hostname:display*; with RDP connections, the syntax is *rdp:/ hostname*. To connect to a machine running at 192.168.0.1 at the prompt, type this command and click Connect:

```
rdp:/192.168.0.1
```

You are prompted for the resolution to use for the desktop and are then presented with the login screen. This presents a similar result as *rdesktop* only with the *krdc* taskbar appearing along the top of the screen, allowing you to toggle full-screen mode and a few other settings. These sessions are saved with any VNC sessions, making *krdc* an excellent choice for system administrators who are on a mixed network of VNC and RDP servers.

NX Server

Knoppix 3.4 has also introduced a suite of tools to connect to NoMachine's NX server. You can use the NX server to create encrypted and compressed remote connections to X, VNC, and RDP servers, which are responsive even over a dial-up connection. NoMachine's NX client and other software included on Knoppix are licensed under the GPL, but it is worth noting that the NX server does require that you purchase a license from NoMachine. Further information about the NX server can be found at *http://www.nomachine.com*.

If you have an NX server to which you wish to connect, start the NX Connection Wizard by clicking K Menu → Internet → NX Connection Wizard. The wizard asks you a series of questions about the server's IP address, your connection type, and the protocol the remote connection is using to share the desktop. Fill out the information in the wizard to see the NX Client login window, and the session for the server you have just configured is selected in the drop-down Session menu. Type in your NX server login and password, and click Login to connect to the remote NX server and start your remote desktop connection. For further help with using the included NX software, Knoppix has a direct link to NoMachine's support page that is accessible by clicking K Menu → Internet → NX Help on the Web.

Share the Local Desktop

Knoppix also supports sharing its own desktop with remote users by using the VNC protocol. This is useful when you find yourself talking someone through repairing a system that is unable to boot. The machine is unbootable so you can't take advantage of any remote control utilities the computer may already have. You know that with Knoppix, you can use some of the advanced system-recovery tools to fix the system, but it might be difficult to talk the user through all of the commands (not to mention that there is always a potential for typos that could cause further damage). If the user has a Knoppix disc (plan ahead and hide a copy under every user's machine), then she can boot and get network access. You can then walk her through the simple steps of sharing her desktop, and remotely connect and finish the system recovery.

Sharing the local Knoppix desktop is pretty simple. The user's first step is to run the Desktop Sharing applet by clicking K Menu → System → Desktop Sharing. Have the user click "Create Personal Invitation…" in the main window to create a personal invitation to share her desktop, which then displays a new window containing the address and the temporary password to use for the connection. This information can be entered into any VNC-compatible client on the remote end, causing a prompt to appear on the local user's screen and requesting the user to accept the remote desktop connection.

 The user can also click "Invite via Email…" to send an email containing connection information to the system administrator. This email provides a direct link to click on if the recipient is running a KDE desktop with *krdc* installed. The sender must have an email account set up on her Knoppix machine for this to work.

The randomly generated password expires after an hour, so any new connections after that point require creating a new invitation. To remove an invitation before it expires, click "Manage invitations" on the main Desktop Sharing Wizard screen to see all current invitations, along with options to delete them and create new invitations. The Desktop Sharing Wizard makes sharing your current KDE desktop pretty easy even for people new to VNC or Linux, and it is simple to explain to users over the phone or through email.

With all of the different remote desktop protocols Knoppix supports, along with the fact that it includes a simple method to share its own desktop, you might find it worthwhile to hand out an emergency Knoppix CD to friends or clients for those times when you need to do some quick technical support but are unable to physically be there. If a client has a network of machines that needs support, you can use the desktop-sharing feature of Knoppix to connect remotely to a machine on the network booted off of Knoppix, and then use that machine as a remote command center to connect to the rest of the machines within the network. This allows you to support all of the machines from a single remote connection.

Run X Remotely with FreeNX

#38 Use FreeNX to connect to a remote desktop that's responsive even over a slow dial-up connection.

Before exploring the technical details of NX, you should run the test drive first to see the performance NX offers; NX Client 1.3.2 is already included with Knoppix 3.4. To start NX Client, click K Menu → Internet → NX Client for Linux.

NX technology is new. It's actually so new that the newest developments are (at the writing of this book) not yet included in Knoppix. However, this hack gives you an overview of what to expect with the Knoppix Version 3.6.

The NX Connection Wizard starts and allows you to create a new session. It asks for a name for the session, *nxserver* host, and, optionally, a port, which in most cases is just the SSH port (22). You can also select the speed of your connection. Even if you have a very fast connection, it's worthwhile to try modem speed first.

If you don't have an NX Server to which to connect, visit NoMachine's web site at *http://www.nomachine.com/testdrive.php* and sign up for its test drive. You'll receive an email with details on how to connect to its test server.

You can select the type of the connection (Windows, Unix, VNC) and the preferred Desktop in the next step. NX can connect to other servers at the backend, so it's also useful as a secure and fast gateway to Windows or VNC machines.

You can use a full screen (in which case, you can click on the top-right pixel to minimize the session) or a specified size for the session window. You can also select "SSL encryption" to tunnel all traffic over SSH.

The advantages are clear:

- You don't have to open any port other than SSH, which, in most cases, is open for remote shell access anyway.
- Users don't have to fiddle with complicated SSH client and forwarding setups. Just installing NXClient is enough. NXClient is of course available for all major operating systems, such as Windows, Linux, and MacOS X.

As the last step, you can choose to create an icon on your desktop for that session automatically (which is recommended) and to configure advanced options.

Don't worry; you can always select the advanced options dialog from *nxclient* later.

As soon as you've finished, you should see the Login dialog of NX Client. Open up a web browser to *http://www.nomachine.com/testdrive.php*, and then enter your name and email address. Some minutes later, you'll receive an email with your test-account data to enter in a test drive's client.

Insert the account data and press Login. The NX Client then creates a connection, authenticates the user, and establishes the X-Server connection. Then a window appears and a normal KDE session is started—in Italy.

If the user authenticates, but it then times out, try to activate SSL encryption by checking "Enable SSL encryption of all traffic" on the Desktop screen of the NX Connection Wizard, and then reconnect.

The session should be very fast, and you should be able to browse the Web, write email, and do your office work on it. Indeed, I do this regularly. Wherever I am, I can connect to my PC at home and graphically read my email—even if it's just a modem uplink.

The NX Technology

How can NX achieve this speedup of X?

There are five major reasons:

Very efficient X Protocol compression

The X Protocol is highly compressible. Each X-Request or Confirmation has a fixed part and a variable part. With Differential X Protocol Compression (DXPC), you can transmit what has changed only on the display, instead of the complete desktop.

Caching of the protocol

The X Protocol compression makes it possible to cache the data to improve responsiveness. For example, in VNC it takes equally long to open the same menu multiple times while NX sessions get faster with time. For example, the first time the menu opens in NX it takes some time, but the second time, the menu just pops up as if it were opened locally. Also, due to a disk cache, this effect is also preserved if you start a new session.

Round-trip suppression

A *round trip* in the X11 protocol is a request plus the wait for confirmation. While you can increase bandwidth without problems, it's not possible to reduce latency (as the speed of light, and in this case electricity, has a maximum speed).

One round trip is tolerable, but imagine that you have to make 1000 round trips, and you have to wait each time for the answer over a link with high latency, which is very slow. This effect is especially bad with modern tool kits, such as QT or GTK, because they are typically programmed to run on the same machine—not over the network.

NX solves round-trip problems locally by usage of an *nxagent* that groups requests and then sends them chunked to the client.

Compression of X-Images

NX uses state-of-the-art compression techniques like PNG and JPEG to compress huge bitmaps. VNC uses this technique too, but VNC always compresses the entire screen along with fonts, because it cannot distinguish between the different elements on the desktop. With NX, just the X-Images are compressed, and the fonts and most other elements on the desktop are crystal clear.

Chunking of image data

Image data is the biggest part of a desktop to be transferred over the network. Even if it's possible to compress it, you still want to use the desktop while a huge image transfers. NX never uses all of the bandwidth and always has a small control channel so that it can stop the transfer of the chunked images to react to a mouse click or similar events. As a result, the desktop is more responsive.

Set Up NX Server

NoMachine sells a commercial server with support but has also put all core components under the GPL, which allows anyone to write a free server, which I did.

 The following instructive details were not programmed at the writing of this book, so it is possible that the actual program differs in some ways from what is described here.

To set up the NX server, click K Menu → KNOPPIX → Services → Manage NX Server. This informs you that you are starting a service that allows other users to access this computer. The server then creates a user called *nxfree* and starts the SSH service.

Then it starts an interface, and you can manage your server:

Add user
    Before users can use your NX terminal server, add them to your server.

Remove user
    If you no longer want a certain user to use your NX server, remove her.

Stop server
    Stop the NX server.

Quit
    Quit the management program but leave the server running.

As it is not currently clear how the NX server interface will handle these functions, the following shows you how to perform them from the command line.

User Management

To add a new user *joe* to Knoppix, open a console and type:

```
knoppix@ttyp0[knoppix]$ sudo adduser joe
```

You are then asked a number of questions about this user, including his full name. Fill in the fields, and then choose a password for the account. Joe can now log in to this server with *ssh*. However, if he wants to use NX, you must activate his account for the NX server. First, I add *joe* to the NX user database, then I give him a password:

```
knoppix@ttyp0[knoppix]$ sudo nxserver --useradd joe
knoppix@ttyp0[knoppix]$ sudo nxserver --passwd joe
```

Joe can now use the NX Client on his laptop to connect to this machine.

Server Management

The NX server has a number of command-line options:

--help
> Shows a small help page.

--useradd
> Adds a user.

--userdel
> Deletes a user.

--userlist
> Lists all configured users.

--passwd
> Sets a password for a user.

--start
> Starts NX server.

--stop
> Stops NX server. This option does not stop the SSH daemon.

--restart
> Restarts NX server.

--status
> Shows whether the server is currently running.

--list
> Each session that starts on the server receives a unique session ID. This
> option lists all running sessions.

--terminate
> Terminates all sessions for a user. Alternatively, you can terminate users
> based on the display number they use to connect.

--suspend
> Suspends a session to be reconnected later.

--send
> Sends a message to the specified user.

--broadcast
> Enables you to send a message to all connected users.

--lock
> Locks the display of a user.

--unlock
> Unlocks the display of a user.

NX can help you as a tool for remote administration. Knoppix offers the NX server so setting it up is very easy.

—Fabian Franz

HACK #39   Browse Windows Shares

Tweak a few settings for the lisa daemon so you can graphically browse Windows shares on your network.

Microsoft has made it easy to browse for and connect to network fileshares. If you are used to browsing network shares under Windows, learning how to browse network shares under KDE might seem like a black art. Under Knoppix, the issue is aggravated by the fact that Knoppix does not automatically configure *LISa* (KDE's LAN information server) to work beyond the local machine. Luckily, it takes only a few steps to get network browsing up and running.

First, reconfigure LISa so it scans for all fileshares on your network. To do this, you must move *lisarc*, LISa's read-only configuration file, out of the way, and then start *kcontrol* as root so that you can create a new configuration file:

```
knoppix@ttyp0[knoppix]$ sudo mv /etc/lisarc /etc/lisarc.bak
knoppix@ttyp0[knoppix]$ sudo kcontrol
```

When the KDE Control Center opens, click Internet & Network → Local Network Browsing, select the LISa Daemon tab, and click "Guided LISa Setup." If your network is already correctly configured, either by Knoppix automatically or by you manually, the guided setup should provide you with all of the correct defaults. Just click Next through all of the options, and then click Apply at the bottom of the screen to save the changes.

With the new settings in place, start the LISa daemon:

```
knoppix@ttyp0[knoppix]$ sudo /etc/init.d/lisa start
Starting LAN Information Server: lisa.
```

Now click K Menu → Home, type **lan://localhost** in the location bar, and press Enter. The machines on the network that LISa detects should appear, named according to their IP address, as in Figure 5-1.

Click on a machine to see the different filesharing services it offers (Figure 5-2). Click on any of the folders to access files that the services offering. To access Windows shares, click on the SMB folder.

There are a number of filesharing services LISa supports, including FISH (filesharing over SSH), FTP, NFS, and SMB.

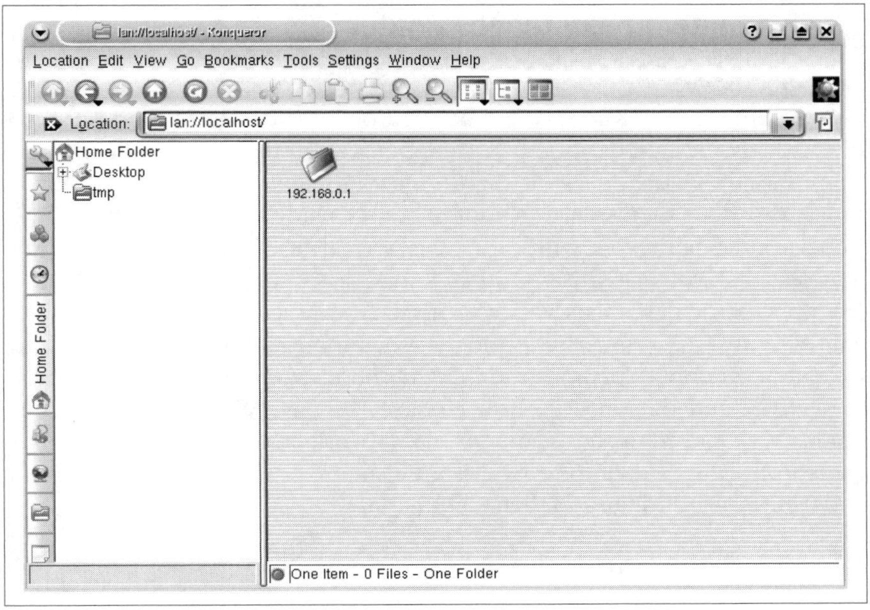

Figure 5-1. Networks detected by LISa

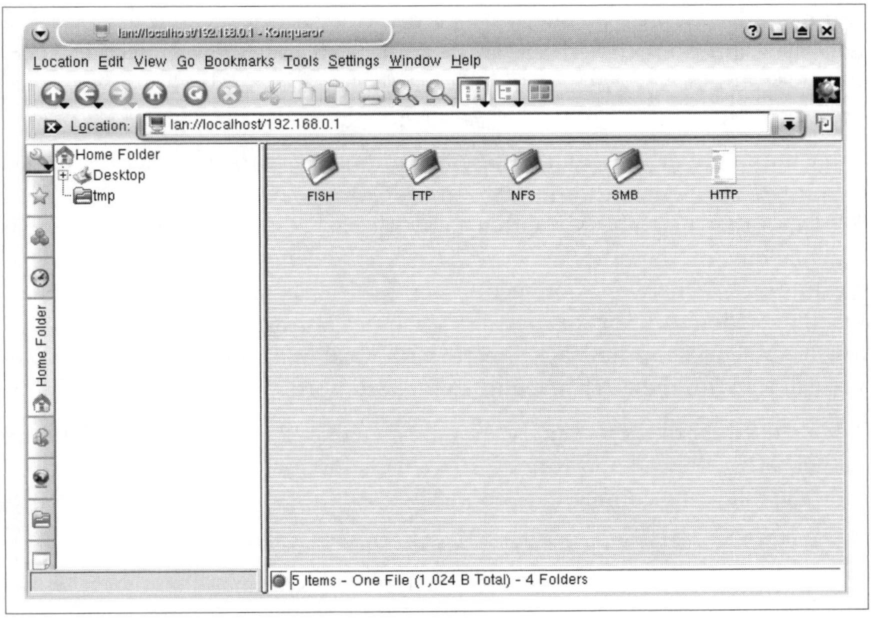

Figure 5-2. View filesharing services

Create an Emergency Router

HACK
#40

Turn Knoppix into a router or firewall.

Avoid thinking that Knoppix can be used only for demonstration purposes or is fit only for light desktop use. Knoppix is a full-fledged portable installation of Linux, which means it can do most anything an installed version of Linux can do. For instance, Knoppix comes ready to use as a fully functional router or firewall with all of the normal utilities, such as *route* and *iptables*, that you use on any other Linux distribution. These tools make Knoppix particularly handy if you need an emergency Network Address Translation (NAT) router or a bridge. When the router goes down, you can take your Knoppix "demonstration" CD, boot it on a spare machine with two NICs, and demonstrate how to save the day. With just a few commands, you can route across any of the network connections Knoppix supports from DSL to dial-up to wireless. This hack walks you through turning a machine into a bridge and then a NAT router.

Configure the Network

The machine you are using as the emergency router must have two different network connections that already work independently of each other. This can be satisfied with two network cards, a network card and a modem, a network card and a wireless card, or any two network connections that Knoppix supports. Configuring network connections under Knoppix is covered in "Connect to the Internet" **[Hack #17]**.

After both networks are working, you can link the two either with a bridge or with NAT. Generally, you want to use a bridge to connect two local networks so that machines on either network can communicate directly with any machine on the other network. Use NAT when you need to share a single Internet or network connection across a local network with the NAT machine acting as a sort of firewall. Machines on the other side of the NAT are not able to communicate directly with local machines unless you set up firewall rules on the NAT machine to forward ports.

To create either of these routers, you must enable IP forwarding in the Linux kernel. Most firewall and routing HOWTOs instruct you to do this by running the following command as root:

```
root@ttyp0[root]# echo 1 > /proc/sys/net/ipv4/ip_forward
```

However, under Knoppix, you must change that command so that it works under the *sudo* environment by typing:

```
knoppix@ttyp0[knoppix]$ sudo sh -c "echo 1 > /proc/sys/net/ipv4/ip_forward"
```

Now that IP forwarding is enabled, you can configure your bridge or NAT router.

 If you are dropping this Knoppix machine in the place of a broken router, save a lot of trouble by giving Knoppix the same IPs as the previous router. In the case of a bridge, once you provide Knoppix with the same IPs and enable IP forwarding, the bridge is ready to go.

For the purposes of these examples, assume that the Knoppix computer is connected to two networks—192.168.0.* on eth0 and 192.168.1.* on eth1. Run *ifconfig*, and you should get the following output:

```
knoppix@ttyp1[knoppix]$ /sbin/ifconfig
eth0      Link encap:Ethernet  HWaddr 00:DE:AD:BE:EF:00
          inet addr:192.168.0.5  Bcast:192.168.0.255  Mask:255.255.255.0
          UP BROADCAST RUNNING MULTICAST  MTU:1500  Metric:1
          RX packets:6918 errors:0 dropped:0 overruns:0 frame:0
          TX packets:4678 errors:0 dropped:0 overruns:0 carrier:0
          collisions:0 txqueuelen:1000
          RX bytes:675976 (660.1 KiB)  TX bytes:447963 (437.4 KiB)
          Interrupt:9 Base address:0xb800

eth1      Link encap:Ethernet  HWaddr 00:C0:FF:EE:00:00
          inet addr:192.168.1.5  Bcast:192.168.1.255  Mask:255.255.255.0
          UP BROADCAST RUNNING MULTICAST  MTU:1500  Metric:1
          RX packets:4933 errors:0 dropped:0 overruns:0 frame:0
          TX packets:4988 errors:1 dropped:0 overruns:0 carrier:0
          collisions:0 txqueuelen:1000
          RX bytes:496574 (484.9 KiB)  TX bytes:749568 (732.0 KiB)
          Interrupt:3 Base address:0x100

lo        Link encap:Local Loopback
          inet addr:127.0.0.1  Mask:255.0.0.0
          UP LOOPBACK RUNNING  MTU:16436  Metric:1
          RX packets:33 errors:0 dropped:0 overruns:0 frame:0
          TX packets:33 errors:0 dropped:0 overruns:0 carrier:0
          collisions:0 txqueuelen:0
          RX bytes:3016 (2.9 KiB)  TX bytes:3016 (2.9 KiB)
```

These networks already have a default route set up for each of these interfaces, which you can see by running the route command:

```
knoppix@ttyp1[knoppix]$ route
Kernel IP routing table
Destination     Gateway         Genmask         Flags Metric Ref    Use
Iface
192.168.0.0     *               255.255.255.0   U     0      0        0 eth0
192.168.1.0     *               255.255.255.0   U     0      0        0 eth1
default         192.168.1.1     0.0.0.0         UG    0      0        0 eth0
default         192.168.0.1     0.0.0.0         UG    0      0        0 eth1
```

Build a Bridge

Creating a bridge with *route* is pretty straightforward once you see the commands involved. In fact, if both networks are already configured to use this machine as the gateway, and you have already enabled IP forwarding, then congratulations—you are finished! Otherwise, read the following instructions to learn how to configure the routing for your bridge.

So far I haven't had to change anything in the networking. In my example, I set up static IPs ("Connect to the Internet" [Hack #17]), but if you had DHCP running on either or both sides of the network with different default gateways, the bridge would have worked fine too. At this point, the Knoppix machine should be able to ping machines on both the 192.168.0.* and the 192.168.1.* networks, but machines on 192.168.0.* shouldn't be able to ping 192.168.1.* and vice versa.

I want to make the Knoppix machine the link between my two networks. For this to happen, the machines on either network must use the Knoppix machine as the bridge to the other network. If one of the two networks is already configured to use this Knoppix machine as its default gateway, then all packets going outside of the subnet route through it by default, and you don't have to bother with any extra routing for that network. If both networks are already set to use this machine as the default gateway, then you are finished. Either of these scenarios might be the case if you drop in Knoppix to replace a bridge and assign it the same IP addresses as the previous bridge.

If a network does not use the Knoppix machine as its gateway, you must add a route to the actual gateway on that subnet. This route tells the gateway to route any traffic going to the other subnet, through the Knoppix bridge. To route through the Knoppix bridge requires root access to the network's default gateway, to add the new route. In our example, the default gateways are 192.168.0.1 and 192.168.1.1, respectively, so on 192.168.0.1, run the following command as root:

```
root@ttyp0[root]# route add -net 192.168.1.0 netmask 255.255.255.0
gw 192.168.0.5
```

On 192.168.1.1, run:

```
root@ttyp0[root]# route add -net 192.168.0.0 netmask 255.255.255.0
gw 192.168.1.5
```

Once you set up these new routes, machines on either side of the bridge can ping each other, and your bridge is complete.

Network with NAT

Performing IP masquerading or NAT with Knoppix is as simple as configuring it as a bridge, if not simpler. NAT is commonly used to share a single public IP address (like you might get from a DSL or cable provider) with a local network behind the NAT router.

For NAT to work, all of the machines on the local network must be configured to use the Knoppix machine as the default gateway. In our example, the 192.168.1.* network is behind this NAT "firewall" to access the 192.168.0.* network, so each of the machines on 192.168.1.* is using 192.168.1.5 (the IP address we assigned the NIC connected to the local network) as their default gateway.

The NAT works by taking all of the packets coming from 192.168.1.* (the local network) and going to 192.168.0.* (the external network) and making them appear as though they are from 192.168.0.5—the IP address we assigned the NIC connected to the external network. When a machine on the external network responds, it responds directly to 192.168.0.5. Then the Knoppix machine translates the address to refer to the 192.168.1.* machine that originally sent the packet. Then Knoppix forwards it to the local network. For all intents and purposes, the 192.168.0.* network doesn't know that the 192.168.1.* network exists.

To set up Knoppix as a NAT router, you really only need to type in a single *iptables* command. To create a NAT for our example network, type:

```
knoppix@ttyp0[knoppix]$ sudo iptables -t nat -A POSTROUTING -s
192.168.1.0/255.255.255.0 -o eth0 -j SNAT --to-source 192.168.0.5
```

This *iptables* command creates a rule to take all packets coming from the 192.168.1.* network and going from eth0 and makes them appear as though they are from 192.168.0.5. If you want to use IP masquerading instead of NAT (useful for forwarding over a dial-up connection that might drop while the computer is booted, which results in a different IP), type the following command instead:

```
knoppix@ttyp0[knoppix]$ sudo iptables -t nat -A POSTROUTING -o eth0 -j
MASQUERADE
```

Substitute ppp0 for eth0 if you are forwarding over a dial-up connection. At this point, you should be able access the outside 192.168.0.* network from any of the machines on the 192.168.1.* network.

The *iptables* command creates a NAT rule, but doesn't actually create a proper firewall. NAT does prevent people from easily accessing any local IPs behind the NAT router. However, if you are interested in setting up Knoppix with firewall rules suitable for your network, you can reference one of the many great HOWTOs and tutorials on using stateful packet filtering under Linux with *iptables*.

See Also

- The official netfilter page at *http://www.netfilter.org/documentation* (in particular, the packet-filtering HOWTO).
- The Advanced Routing HOWTO at *http://www.ibiblio.org/pub/Linux/ docs/HOWTO/other-formats/html_single/Adv-Routing-HOWTO.html*.

HACK #41 Create an Emergency File Server

When files need to be transferred quickly over the network, Knoppix can serve as a quick makeshift file server.

There are many different occasions that might call for creating an emergency file server. For instance, you might have a file server with multiple drives that has suffered hard-disk failure on the root drive. All of the hard disks that have shared data are fine, but you need to still serve files while waiting on the replacement drive. This is the perfect environment for anyone wanting to learn how to configure Samba or start up a quick temporary file server. For experienced systems administrators, this makes it easy to share all the drives on an infected system for a quick virus scan by a centralized corporate virus scanner while the infected OS is shut down. You can even connect a spare machine to a printer, boot Knoppix, and quickly configure a makeshift network printer server.

Knoppix includes a nice GUI configuration utility to configure Samba (the Linux SMB file server). You aren't required to use the Knoppix Samba utility to set up a file server. If you already know which kind of configuration you want, simply edit */etc/samba/smb.conf* directly, and then run this command to start the Samba process:

```
knoppix@ttyp0[knoppix]$ sudo /etc/init.d/samba start
```

To use the Knoppix-provided Samba configuration utility, click K Menu → KNOPPIX → Services → Start Samba Server. Each time you run this script, it wipes out the previous Samba configuration, so don't run this script if you have made changes to *smb.conf* that you want to keep. This program prompts you to choose a password to assign to the *knoppix* user if there isn't already one, because Knoppix's default behavior requires a username and password to access any shares it creates.

After it confirms your password, Knoppix asks you whether you want to export all your hard drives so that remote machines can access them. If you answer "no" to this question, the script creates an *smb.conf* file that shares your home directory and any printers that you have previously configured on the system. If you answer "yes" to this question, the script adds shares for all hard drives and CD-ROM drives that Knoppix has detected, and automatically mounts the devices for you as they are accessed. Once you click "yes" or "no," the script creates the *smb.conf* file and starts Samba.

If you only want to share all of the drives on your system as read-only over the network, then you are finished. By default, the share shows up in the WORKGROUP workgroup as a machine named KNOPPIX, and if you have shared all of the drives on your system, they appear with the same names they were previously assigned on your desktop, such as hda1. You can find the configuration for each drive at the bottom of the */etc/samba/smb.conf* :

```
[hda1]
    comment = /mnt/hda1
    browseable = yes
    path = /mnt/hda1
    writeable = yes
    preexec = /bin/mount /mnt/hda1
    postexec = /bin/umount /mnt/hda1
```

These shares all require that you log in with the username *knoppix* and the password you created for the *knoppix* account. Then Knoppix automatically mounts the drive when you access it and unmounts it when you are finished. Notice that by default, Samba is configured to allow writing to the drives, but Knoppix automatically mounts all drives read-only, so it overrides this, and you are still able to read from the drives. To allow write access to a drive, modify the preexec line in *smb.conf* to read:

```
preexec = sudo /bin/mount -o rw /mnt/hda1
```

and replace /mnt/hda1 with the drive you are configuring. To allow anyone to access the share without requiring a password, add the following line to the share's configuration:

```
guest ok = yes
```

In general, you do not need to restart Samba for share level changes to take effect; however, changes you make to the global configuration (under the [global] header) require you to restart Samba.

To share something entirely different from the hard drives, add new shares to the default configuration. It doesn't matter which script option you chose earlier, just add the new configuration to the end of the file. The following example creates a new directory called *share* under the home directory *knoppix* and configures it as a guest share under Samba. First, create the *share* directory:

```
knoppix@ttyp0[knoppix]$ mkdir /home/knoppix/share
```

Then edit *etc/samba/smb.conf* as root, and add the following lines:

```
[share]
    comment = Knoppix share
    browseable = yes
    path = /home/knoppix/share
    writeable = yes
    guest ok = yes
```

Once you save your changes, the new share immediately appears, and any-one is able to view, add, and delete files in that directory. Keep in mind that this share is running off of your home directory that is in a ramdisk by default. The size of files stored here are limited by RAM, so for storing large files, you want to configure a share on the system's hard drives.

> Remember that each time you run the Knoppix Samba con-figuration script, it creates a new *smb.conf*, and any manual changes are lost.

HACK #42   Create an Emergency Web Server

When the web server goes down, use Knoppix to pick up the slack.

On first glance, Knoppix may not seem like a distribution to use for web serving because of its colorful GUI, the desktop applications, and the games. But included in this huge bundle of software is the complete Apache 1.3 server and a large set of modules that give you many of the common tools you need to turn Knoppix into a replacement web server.

Before you set up Knoppix as a web server, make sure Knoppix has all the tools you need for your web site. Look in */usr/lib/apache/1.3/* to see if the modules you need are there. Knoppix includes quite a few modules, includ-ing support for CGI, server-side includes, PHP4, *mod_rewrite*, and SSL, and also comes with MySQL so you can run a database-driven site. If you need to use any Apache modules, check */etc/apache/modules.conf* and make sure they are listed in there. Not all modules Knoppix includes are automatically listed in that file, so, for instance, to add server-side include support, add this statement to your copy of */etc/apache/modules.conf*:

```
LoadModule includes_module /usr/lib/apache/1.3/mod_include.so
```

If Apache doesn't have the modules you need, you must remaster Knoppix with your custom Apache setup **[Hack #94]**. Otherwise, the next step is to actu-ally copy over the pages you want to serve, and configure Apache to use them.

If you choose, you can use your Apache configuration for your current server. This may mean restoring the configuration from tape backup if you cannot directly access it from its current hard drive. Simply copy your complete Apache configuration to a suitable spot, like */home/knoppix/ apache*, and use it by creating a symlink to it:

```
knoppix@ttyp0[knoppix]$ sudo mv /etc/apache /etc/apache.bak
knoppix@ttyp0[knoppix]$ sudo ln -s /home/knoppix/apache /etc/apache
```

Otherwise, you must edit Knoppix's Apache configuration. All of the Apache configuration in Knoppix can be found in a series of symlinks in */etc/apache/* that point to files on the CD-ROM, which are, of course, read-only. To make changes to these configuration files, you must first make them writable. The following step seems a little odd, but it breaks the symlink with the CD-ROM and gives you a writable *httpd.conf* on the ramdisk. You can repeat the process with other configuration files you need to modify.

```
knoppix@ttyp0[knoppix]$ sudo mv /etc/apache/httpd.conf /etc/apache/
httpd.conf.bak
knoppix@ttyp0[knoppix]$ sudo cp /etc/apache/httpd.conf.bak /etc/apache/
httpd.conf
```

With the configuration files now writable, you are able to modify */etc/ apache/httpd.conf* and add any special changes you need to make for your site, such as adding multiple virtual hosts or changing the location of the *DocumentRoot* directory. Remember that when copying over the configuration and the accompanying web content, you must change any paths in *httpd.conf* to point to the new content directories that you have created. Also, if you are adding virtual hosts, remember to change the IP addresses to match this machine if necessary.

Once you have your files and configuration copied over, running Apache is as simple as:

```
knoppix@ttyp0[knoppix]$ sudo /etc/init.d/apache start
```

You shouldn't notice much of a performance hit for running off of the CD, because most of the site is running from ramdisk, and Apache itself runs completely from memory once it is loaded. However, there is less RAM to use overall because of the ramdisk Knoppix creates.

With this functionality, you can easily turn some desktop machines into mirrors of your web site or possibly even emergency replacements for the site while you change out hardware or perform software upgrades. The nice thing about using Knoppix for your emergency web server is that you can run it on top of any PC regardless of OS installation. When you are done, you can just log out and reboot the machine, and no one will know the difference.

Run Other Emergency Services

#43   It is easy to set up Knoppix as a DHCP, DNS, or MySQL server. This ability could prove useful in an emergency.

There are a number of other services that Knoppix includes that require only a couple of steps to get running. Most of the principles behind starting these services are the same—copy over a configuration and start the service. However, some of these services require a few more steps to get fully functional. Most of the services log to */var/log/syslog*, which Knoppix disables by default. To start the *syslog* service, click K Menu → KNOPPIX → Services → Start SYSLOG, which launches a terminal that displays live output of */var/log/syslog*.

SSH

If you want to use Knoppix as a server for anything, you certainly want to be able to administer it remotely. Every administrator's favorite remote shell is openssh, and Knoppix includes it. It is incredibly simple to start the SSH service on Knoppix. Just click K Menu → KNOPPIX → Services → Start SSH Server. If you have not yet created a password for the *knoppix* user, the script prompts you to enter a new password so you can log in remotely. Alternatively, run:

```
knoppix@ttyp0[knoppix]$ sudo /etc/init.d/ssh start
```

DHCP

DHCP allows you to automatically assign IP addresses to other computers on the network along with other basic network information. It's quicker than manually entering the network information into each computer. The DHCP configuration file in Knoppix is */etc/dhcp3/dhcpd.conf* and, by default, it is not configured to run on any network interface. First, back up the following file:

```
knoppix@ttyp0[knoppix]$ sudo mv /etc/dhcp3/dhcpd.conf
/etc/dhcp3/dhcpd.conf.bak
```

If you use this machine to replace another DHCP server on the network, simply copy the other machine's *dhcpd.conf* file to */etc/dhcp3/*. If you do not have a preconfigured *dhcpd.conf* to use, here is a simple template you can use to get started. Create this file with your favorite text editor, then copy it to */etc/dhcp3/dhcpd.conf* as root. Change the IP addresses to match your local network.

```
# how long the DHCP lease lasts in seconds
default-lease-time 600;
# maximum length of lease in seconds
max-lease-time 7200;
```

```
# name servers for clients on all subnets to use
option domain-name-servers 192.168.0.1, 192.168.0.2

##### here we put specific per-subnet options #####
subnet 192.168.0.1 netmask 255.255.255.0 {
   # IPs will be assigned between these two ranges
   range 192.168.0.50 192.168.0.99;
   option subnet-mask 255.255.255.0;
   option broadcast-address 192.168.0.255;
   # the gateway for the network
   option routers 192.168.0.1;
}
```

Once you have configured *dhcpd.conf*, start *dhcpd*:

```
knoppix@ttyp0[knoppix]$ sudo /etc/init.d/dhcp3-server start
```

If *dhcpd* is unable to start, view the syslog for details, including possible errors you might have made in *dhcpd.conf*.

DNS

The name-resolution services provided by a DNS server are essential to any modern-day network. Knoppix comes with complete support for running your DNS server with the included BIND9 package. The simplest way to get your DNS server up and running is similar to the method used in "Create an Emergency Web Server" [Hack #42]. First, move */etc/bind/* out of the way with this command:

```
knoppix@ttyp0[knoppix]$ sudo mv /etc/bind/ /etc/bind.bak
```

Second, copy your complete BIND configuration (some distributions put it in */etc/bind/* while others put it in */etc/named/*) to your home directory, and symlink it so the system uses it instead:

```
knoppix@ttyp0[knoppix]$ sudo ln -s /home/knoppix/bind /etc/bind
```

Now start BIND by typing:

```
knoppix@ttyp0[knoppix]$ sudo /etc/init.d/bind9 start
```

Now your DNS server is up and running. If BIND does not start after this command, check the syslog for any errors it might have reported.

MySQL

Databases are vitally important to most businesses, and a rising star in the database world is the open source MySQL database. This database has proven to be especially popular as a backend to dynamic web sites because of its low cost and amazing speed. If you have a MySQL database server that is down and need to run something in its place, you may be able to use

Knoppix, which contains the MySQL database program. To configure MySQL under Knoppix, first start the MySQL server:

```
knoppix@ttyp0[knoppix]$ sudo /etc/init.d/mysql start
```

There are different methods to import and export a database, and this section highlights methods to import to and export from a database using *mysqldump*. Of course, if you are creating an emergency Knoppix server because your database server is down, your importing methods are tied to whatever backup method you have decided to use.

If you want to move a single database to Knoppix, first log in to your original database server, and export it with:

```
root@ttyp0[root]# mysqldump database > database.txt
```

Then copy over the resulting database file using *scp*, FTP, or whichever file transfer protocol you prefer. Once the database is copied, run *mysql* and create a corresponding database on Knoppix:

```
mysql > CREATE DATABASE database;
```

You can then import your data with:

```
knoppix@ttyp0[knoppix]$ sudo mysql < database.txt
```

To copy all of the databases from one server to Knoppix, the procedure is similar but requires an extra step. First, back up your */usr/lib/mysql* directory, and create an empty one:

```
knoppix@ttyp0[knoppix]$ sudo mv /usr/lib/mysql /usr/lib/mysql.bak
knoppix@ttyp0[knoppix]$ sudo mkdir /usr/lib/mysql
```

Then export your complete database from the remote machine:

```
knoppix@ttyp0[knoppix]$ mysqldump --all-databases > all_databases.txt
```

Finally, copy *all_databases.txt* to Knoppix, and import it:

```
knoppix@ttyp0[knoppix]$ sudo mysql < all_databases.txt
```

Inetd

Knoppix includes *inetd*, the Unix daemon that listens for incoming requests; when a request comes in, *inetd* starts the appropriate server daemon; *inetd* is disabled by default. Before you start *inetd*, check */etc/inetd.conf* and make sure that you don't mind if all the uncommented services are started. Even if you aren't sure, by default Knoppix allows only local connections to any of these services, so you are safe leaving them uncommented. This example shows you how to get FTP running with *inetd*.

Start *inetd* by typing the following command:

```
knoppix@ttyp0[knoppix]$ sudo /etc/init.d/inetd start
```

Now *inetd* listens on all of the ports configured in *inetd.conf* for connections. Once a connection is made, *inetd* starts the corresponding service.

At this point, if you attempt to connect to FTP on this server from another machine on the network, the connection is refused. One reason your attempt fails is because Knoppix disables anonymous FTP by default. A second reason might be because you haven't yet created a password for your *knoppix* user (with **passwd knoppix** in a terminal window). Most importantly, however, is that Knoppix uses *etc/hosts.deny* to disallow any remote connection to *inetd* services. You must edit */etc/hosts.allow* to allow remote connections.

Like most configuration files in */etc* under Knoppix, */etc/hosts.allow* is a symlink to a read-only file on the CD, so to edit it, you must move it to a backup file and then copy it back. In your */etc/hosts.allow* file, you see something like the following:

```
ALL : 127.0.0.1 LOCAL : ALLOW
ALL : ALL@ALL : DENY
```

The first field designates which service the rule is going to apply to. In both of these cases, the rule applies to all services. The second field is the list of hosts this rule applies to, in either IP address or hostname form. The third field determines whether this rule allows access or denies access. For example, if you want to allow your local subnet access to your FTP server, add a line reading:

```
in.ftpd : 192.168.0.* : ALLOW
```

Notice the use of the wildcard *. This tells *hosts.allow* to apply this rule to any host with an IP between 192.168.0.1 and 192.168.0.255. Any changes to this file affect any new connections, so you don't need to restart *inetd*.

NFS

Samba isn't the only filesharing method Knoppix supports. NFS (Network File System), the most commonly used Unix filesharing protocol, is also available. To configure NFS, you must first establish which directories you wish to share. If for instance, you wish to share a mounted filesystem, such as */mnt/hda1*, you must make sure that the filesystem is mounted *before* NFS is started. Also keep in mind that you are unable to unmount this filesystem as long as NFS is running. The */etc/exports* configuration file determines which directories are shared by NFS. Edit */etc/exports* as root, and add the directories you need to share. The syntax for this file is:

```
/share/path remote_host(options)
```

remote_host can be a particular hostname, IP, or an IP with wildcards, so if you want to share */mnt/hda1* with the entire 192.168.0.* subnet, add the following line to */etc/exports*:

```
/mnt/hda1 192.168.0.*(rw)
```

To mount an NFS share remotely, you must also allow the remote connections to *portmap* and *mountd* in */etc/hosts.allow*. (As discussed previously, Knoppix also uses */etc/hosts.allow* to allow remote connections to *inetd* services.) If you haven't already done so, back up */etc/hosts.allow* and copy a version back, and add the following two lines to enable NFS access for your local subnet:

```
portmap: 192.168.0.* : ALLOW
mountd: 192.168.0.* : ALLOW
```

Now that all of the configuration files are prepared, make sure that any filesystems that must be mounted are mounted, and start the *portmap* and NFS services:

```
knoppix@ttyp0[knoppix]$ sudo /etc/init.d/portmap start
knoppix@ttyp0[knoppix]$ sudo /etc/init.d/nfs-kernel-server start
```

If you want to monitor NFS-mount attempts, be sure to start the *syslog* daemon and read any error messages in case a connection request is refused.

HACK #44   Wardrive with Knoppix

Use Knoppix effectively as a wireless site survey tool that captures GPS coordinates along with data.

Kismet

Mike Kershaw, the author of Kismet, declares the following at *http://www.kismetwireless.net*:

> Kismet is an 802.11 layer2 wireless network detector, sniffer, and intrusion detection system. Kismet will work with any wireless card which supports raw monitoring (rfmon) mode, and can sniff 802.11b, 802.11a, and 802.11g traffic.

> Kismet identifies networks by passively collecting packets and detecting standard named networks, detecting (and given time, decloaking) hidden networks, and inferring the presence of nonbeaconing networks via data traffic.

Essentially, Kismet is your best friend from conducting a basic site survey to cracking Wired Equivalent Privacy (WEP).

Some people find it daunting to use the best wireless networking utility because of the setup. People are daunted not by Kismet per se, but by the correct drivers, the other needed patches to the kernel, and the needed userland tools. So imagine the ability to boot off of a CD-ROM and have all of your hardware—not only supported for use, but also already configured. That's the beauty of using Knoppix and Kismet together.

Required Wardriving Hardware

Wardriving normally requires just a wireless network card. However, with the addition of a GPS unit you can map your excursions:

Wireless card

Knoppix works with most wireless hardware. I've had good experiences with, and personally recommend, Orinoco, Cisco, and Senao/EnGenius cards.

USB-to-serial adapter

My laptop, like many new laptops, lacks a legacy serial port. This presents a problem when using serial devices, but luckily, there are USB-to-serial adapters readily available with support for Knoppix. I suggest the use of the Keyspan adapter series, because most of its adapters seem to be supported under Linux with the company's sponsorship. I use the Keyspan USA-19HS (how patriotic of them!). It's a single USB port to DB-9 and it's bus-powered.

GPS unit

If you want to combine GPS statistics with your wardriving, you need a GPS unit. I have one of those yellow Garmin eTrex units. It's a useful unit to have if you need a GPS unit for use without a computer. This unit supports interfacing with a DB-9 serial cable. These cables are available online for approximately $40, although it's possible to make your own. Basically, any GPS unit works if it's compatible with *gpsd*. According to */usr/share/gpsdrive/GPS-receivers*, the compatible modules are:

```
Magellan 310, 315, 320
Garmin GPS III
Garmin etrex
GPS 45
Crux II GPS PCMCIA card
Holux GM-200 serial version
Holux GM-200 USB (needs USB-to-serial support in kernel)
Holux GM-210 USB (needs USB-to-serial support in kernel)
Garmin eMap
Garmin GPSMAP 295
Garmin GNS 530
Garmin GPS 12MAP
EAGLE Expedition II
DeLorme Earthmate
Magellan Meridian Gold (works only with NMEA V2.1 GSA setting)
```

Set Up GPS

Plug in your USB-to-serial adapter; when Knoppix boots, the adapter is then automatically detected and its drivers are loaded. Plug the eTrex serial adapter into the USB adapter, then plug in your eTrex and turn it on.

For Kismet to use the GPS data, it must have a way to collect it. Kismet uses the *gpsd* program to read the data from this hardware.

To start *gpsd*, run:

```
knoppix@ttyp0[knoppix]$ sudo gpsd -K -p /dev/ttyUSB0
```

Replace */dev/ttyUSB0* with the address for your USB-to-serial adapter (check with the *dmesg* command). (With my setup, *gpsd* will die without the -K setting, so I suggest that you use -K if you have to use USB in your GPS setup.)

The *gpsd* command I use is a bit more complicated, because I like to keep a text log of all the output that *gpsd* generates. I keep a separate terminal tab open with the output of *gpsd* copied to the screen and to a log file. The screen output is helpful if *gpsd* crashes, and the log file preserves my data collection if the laptop loses power. Here's my command:

```
knoppix@ttypo0[knoppix]$ sudo gpsd -D 4 -K -p /dev/ttyUSB0 2>&1 |tee gpsd-
log
```

You can verify that *gpsd* is working with the following command:

```
knoppix@ttyp3[knoppix]$ sudo lsof -ni | grep gpsd
gpsd    6018 root   3u  IPv4   8922      TCP *:2947 (LISTEN)
```

To verify that *gpsd* is reporting correct values, connect to localhost:2947 with *netcat*:

```
knoppix@ttyp1[knoppix]$ nc localhost 2947
DATA
GPSD,D=,A=0.000000,A=0.000000
```

This output shows that the GPS unit isn't even plugged in, but it's clear that *gpsd* is keeping the device open and is ready for data. Even if you don't receive a signal for your GPS unit, Kismet still functions. This way, the GPS subsystem in Kismet knows that the GPS unit doesn't have a lock, but in the event that it does, Kismet receives that data without you starting up *gpsd* again.

Configure Kismet

The main configuration files for Kismet are in */etc/kismet/*. Most of the settings you are interested in changing are in *kismet.conf* and *kismet_ui.conf*. To make sure you have to set this up only once, you use a persistent home directory [Hack #21] and copy the configuration files to it:

```
knoppix@ttyp0[knoppix]$ mkdir ~/.kismet/
knoppix@ttyp0[knoppix]$ cp /etc/kismet/kismet.conf ~/.kismet/kismet.conf
knoppix@ttyp0[knoppix]$ cp /etc/kismet/kismet_ui.conf ~/.kismet/kismet_ui.
conf
```

 This hack works without the need to create a persistent home directory or copy the configuration files. You can edit the */etc/kismet* configuration files in place, but the changes you make will not be retained after a reboot.

At the very least, change the default card to match your hardware. Find this line:

```
source=orinoco,eth0,orinocosource
```

and change it to match your card type, card interface, and card name, respectively. The *kismet.conf* file contains example source lines for other cards to make changes easier. If you plan to use GPS when you are wardriving, also change:

```
gps=false
```

to:

```
gps=true
```

All of the other defaults are a matter of personal taste. After you get a feel for running Kismet, you will learn how to configure these defaults. Make your edits to the configuration files in your home directory, and save your changes. To launch Kismet with your alternate configuration files requires a -f option to specify the path to the *kismet.conf* file and a -u option to specify the path to the *kismet_ui.conf* file

```
knoppix@ttyp0[knoppix]$ sudo kismet -f ~/.kismet/kismet.conf -- -u
~/.kismet/kismet_ui.conf
```

When you start Kismet, you find that the wonderful world of wireless has a lot fewer secrets. If at any point you need help, hit H for a list of commands.

In Figure 5-3, you can see that I have 275 networks with a total packet capture of 13823. Ninety-two of those packets are encrypted, 81 are noise, and at the moment, I am capturing at a rate of 9 packets a second.

Notice that Kismet has Group filters and that Probe Networks has a number of elements. There is a default Linksys access point with factory settings (in red). In the bottom pane, there are various other alerts as they occur. In this case, I have a client that is probing networks.

Figure 5-4 shows the Network Details for a selected network. All of the fields are self-explanatory.

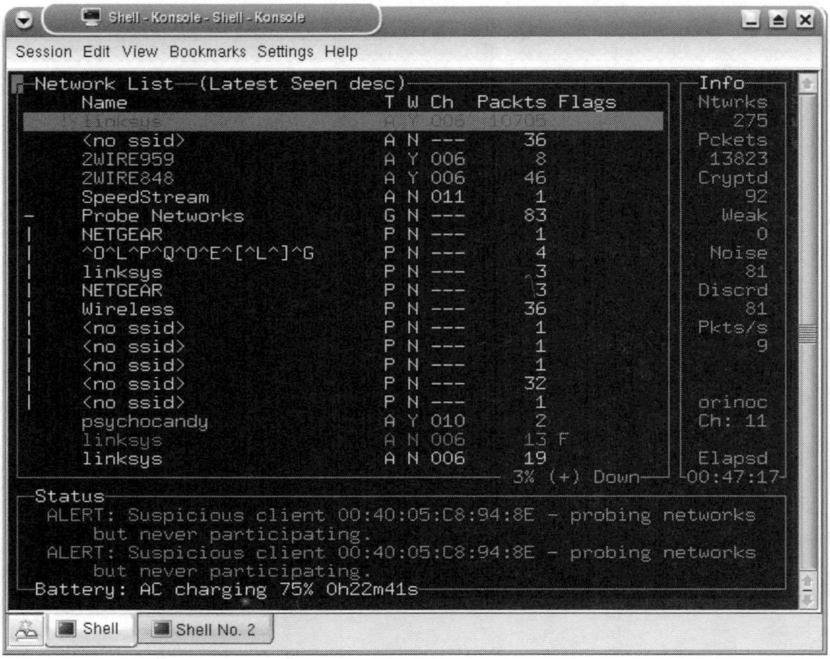

Figure 5-3. Kismet default screen

An interesting feature of Kismet is the ability to lock onto a network. Select a network, then hit the L key to lock on to stop the channel hopping and set monitoring only to the selected network's channel. To resume hopping, press H.

Once you finish running Kismet, you can close the program by hitting Ctrl-Q. By default, logs are written to the current working directory as Kismet runs. If you're in your persistent home directory, and it's a small USB storage drive, this directory may fill up quickly. In an example run, I have six log files in my home directory:

```
total 15912
-rwxrwxr-x  1 knoppix knoppix   346788 Jun 14 01:10 Kismet-Jun-13-2004-1.csv
-rwxrwxr-x  1 knoppix knoppix 13221727 Jun 14 01:10 Kismet-Jun-13-2004-1.
dump
-rwxrwxr-x  1 knoppix knoppix   574530 Jun 14 01:10 Kismet-Jun-13-2004-1.gps
-rwxrwxr-x  1 knoppix knoppix   639665 Jun 14 01:10 Kismet-Jun-13-2004-1.
network
-rwxrwxr-x  1 knoppix knoppix   100326 Jun 14 01:10 Kismet-Jun-13-2004-1.
weak
-rwxrwxr-x  1 knoppix knoppix  1398795 Jun 14 01:10 Kismet-Jun-13-2004-1.xml
```

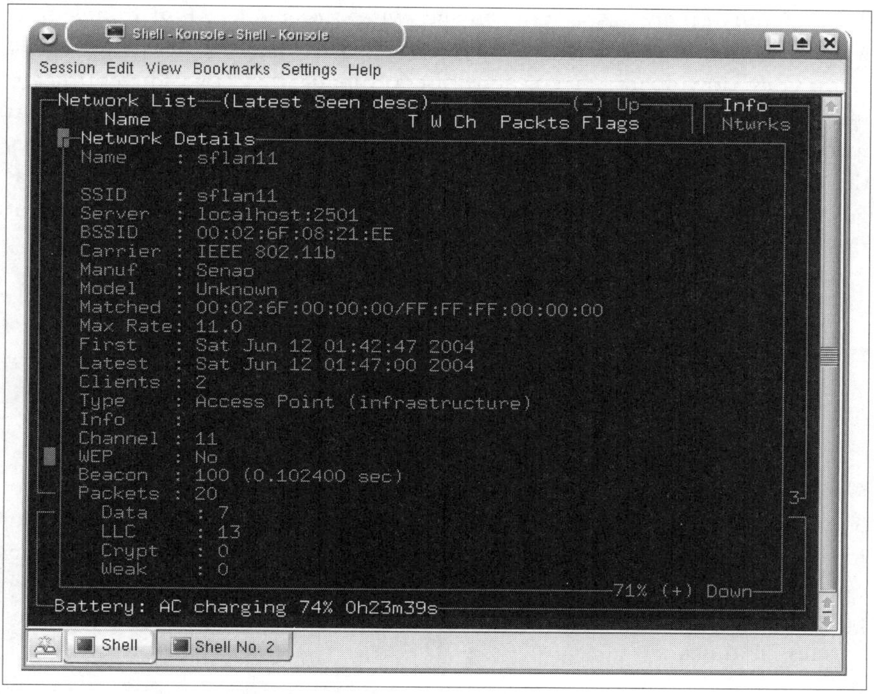

Figure 5-4. Kismet network details

You can look at the .csv, .xml, and .network with any text editor, and you can analyze the .dump file with ethereal. The .weak file is used for the capture of weak (otherwise known as "interesting") packets, and can be analyzed with airsnort or other programs that are used with cracking WEP. The storage of so-called "weak" packets in a separate file can come in handy if you're low on space, so you can delete the other files and keep just these to crack. The .gps file is an XML document that contains latitude, longitude, heading, speed, altitude, and time markers. When populated with correct information, this file makes your Kismet data useful on a large scale. You can overlay your network findings on a satellite map of the area or from other map sources.

Draw a Map of Your Wardriving Session

You can easily map the findings of your wardrive (or you can do this over GPRS while driving, as in "Connect to the Internet with GPRS over Bluetooth" [Hack #18]). To make a map with a Kismet log, connect to the Internet, then run:

```
knoppix@ttyp0[knoppix]$ gpsmap -v -o MapExample-test-Mapblast.gif
-S 0 -n 1 -G -t -b -r --feather-range -u -a -B 3 --feather-scatter
-p -q 0 -e -k Kismet-Jun-13-2004-1.gps
```

This command creates a GIF image with the name *MapExample-test-Mapblast.gif* in your current working directory. It uses the online Mapblast resource to download a given range of coordinates that cover the entire *.gps* file. *Gpsmap* color-codes networks based on their given WEP status and whether a given node is in a factory state. It makes a color map that displays the distance traveled and shows the range of networks based on strength at given points where the networks are still within range. Reference the key at the bottom of the map if the colors and symbols confuse you.

 Many city areas do not have positive GPS readings, and thus even if you find access points or probing clients, you do not have a precise reading of where it is. Without precise GPS readings, there are many networks that you won't be able to plot onto a map.

Gpsmap accepts a number of options so you should read the manpage. Some of the options, such as scaling, can take hours, but most of the time, it's a quick 30-second job. Experiment. By using filters, you can make interesting maps that show only access points that are open, that are owned by people you know, or that all have a given SSID, or you can make up other wireless settings.

If you find wardriving to be interesting, expand by exploring with *kismet_drone*. Using Knoppix, encryption, and a stealth computer, you can collect volumes of data (on your own network of course).

Join Networks

What's the purpose of wardriving if not to make use of the connections you find? Don't answer that. I prefer to assume you have harmless intent. To join a network you've discovered, you must either quit the *kismet* server or use a second wireless card for the connection.

I use a few short scripts to assist with joining networks. The first script, *cng_mac*, generates a random MAC address, which is useful for testing MAC filtering on a wireless network:

```
#!/usr/bin/perl
#
# GPL v2
#
# jake@appelbaum.net
#
# A quick script that generates a random variable
# It looks suprisingly like a MAC address
# Something like: 23:00:CO:FF:EE:00
```

```
# However it will take the first set of octets and set a vendor code
# Vendor codes are in /usr/share/ethereal/manuf
#

# /usr/share/ethereal/manuf

for (`cat /etc/kismet/client_manuf`){
push (@vendorcode, $1) if ($_ =~ /(^[^#]\S+)\s/);
}

srand(time( ) % 345);
printf("%s:%X%X:%X%X:%X%X",$vendorcode[rand(1) * $#vendorcode], \
rand(16),rand(16),rand(16),rand(16),rand(16),rand(16))
```

The *run_wardrive* script resets a PCMCIA wireless card and brings its interface back up with a random MAC address. If you are using an integrated
wireless card, you may comment out the first four lines of the script, leaving
only the *ifconfig* commands:

```
#!/bin/sh
# GPLv2
# jake@appelbaum.net
#
cardctl eject $1
sleep 1
cardctl insert $1
sleep 1
ifconfig $2 down
ifconfig $2 hw ether `~/bin/cng_mac`
ifconfig $2 up
```

Use *run_wardrive*, where *0* is the PCMCIA slot containing your wireless card
and *eth0* is the network interface:

```
knoppix@ttyp0[knoppix]$ sudo run_wardrive 0 eth0
```

Put both of those scripts in the ~/.dist/bin directory of your persistent home
directory (or create ~/.dist/bin with **mkdir ~/.dist/bin** if it doesn't already
exist) and give the scripts executable permissions:

```
knoppix@ttyp0[knoppix]$ chmod a+x ~/.dist/bin/cng_mac ~/.dist/bin/run_
wardrive
```

—Jake Appelbaum

H A C K   Audit Network Security
#45

Use the nessus tool under Knoppix to perform a security audit on your
network.

Being a systems administrator is 90% boredom and 10% absolute panic.
When a virus or worm infects your network, or a new exploit is announced,
you want to confirm that all of your machines are patched and that none of

your machines are vulnerable to any other known exploits. To reduce your stress during those panic times, put some of that 90% boredom to good use, and audit your network for vulnerabilities. To aid in network security audits, Knoppix includes the *nessus* tool, an excellent open source vulnerability scanner. With *nessus* on Knoppix, you can boot up on any machine on your network and perform an audit.

Nessus

The *nessus* tool is actually split into two parts: the *nessusd* server, which runs in the background and performs all of the actual scanning, and the *nessus* client, which provides an interface for *nessus* users to start network audits and view results.

Nessus allows for a detailed (and noisy) look at a given network or a given host. It probes each subnet, domain, and host that it finds in the ways that you direct it to.

To make *Nessus* as useful as possible, new plug-ins for *Nessus* are published frequently. You can get these plug-ins for your *Nessus* server by running the script *nessus-update-plugins*. While this script eliminates the time-consuming work of downloading plug-ins, it isn't without risk. The plug-ins are not signed, and it is possible for an attacker to hijack your updates and replace them with their own malware, so don't run this on an insecure network (such as HOPE or Defcon). This is a known risk; the manpage has more information on this subject.

To run the update script, you need root privileges, so click K Menu → KNOPPIX → Root Shell. The default */etc/nessus* configuration directory and the */usr/lib/nessus/plugins* directory are on read-only media, so you must move it out of the way, and copy it back to the ramdisk so you can download the new plug-ins to it:

```
root@ttyp0[knoppix]# mv /etc/nessus /etc/nessus.bak
root@ttyp0[knoppix]# mkdir /etc/nessus
root@ttyp0[knoppix]# cp -a /etc/nessus.bak/* /etc/nessus/
root@ttyp0[knoppix]# cp -a /usr/lib/nessus/plugins /etc/nessus/
```

Now edit */etc/nessus/nessusd.conf* and change:

```
plugins_folder = /usr/lib/nessus/plugins
```

to:

```
plugins_folder = /etc/nessus/plugins
```

Now run the *nessus-update-plugins* script and download all of the new plug-ins:

```
root@ttyp0[knoppix]# nessus-update-plugins -v
. . .
./osticket_view_attachments.nasl
./freebsd_php_438.nasl
./php_strip_tags_memory_limit_vuln.nasl
root@ttyp0[knoppix]#
```

With all of the latest plug-ins ready to use, click K Menu → System → Security → Nessus Security Tool to launch the Nessus client.

Nessusd Host

Knoppix has a modified version of *nessus* that is preconfigured and easy to use. The normal *nessus* setup requires setting up certificates and passwords to connect to the server. The Knoppix version of *nessus* has been modified to use a login and password that has already been set up for you, so you don't need to set up each time you use *nessus* with Knoppix. To connect to the *nessusd* server, make sure the host, port, login, and password fields under the Nessusd host tab are filled out with localhost, 1241, knoppix, and knoppix, respectively; then click Log In.

The new window that appears asks you to choose an SSL setup. It is OK to accept the default; click Yes to accept the certificate with which you are presented.

Plug-ins

Some plug-ins included with *nessus* have the ability to crash remote services or hosts. These plug-ins are disabled by default, and you should enable them only if you know what you are doing.

After you have logged in, the Plugins tab will be selected (Figure 5-5). It contains a list of all the categories of plug-ins on the *nessusd* that are available to you as a client.

You can select and deselect entire categories for a given target or network of targets. By clicking on each of the categories, a list of individual tests is shown in the space below.

The tests that have an icon of a triangle with an explanation point "!" next to them are tests that may result in damage or destruction of the system in question. By default, these tests are disabled, as noted previously.

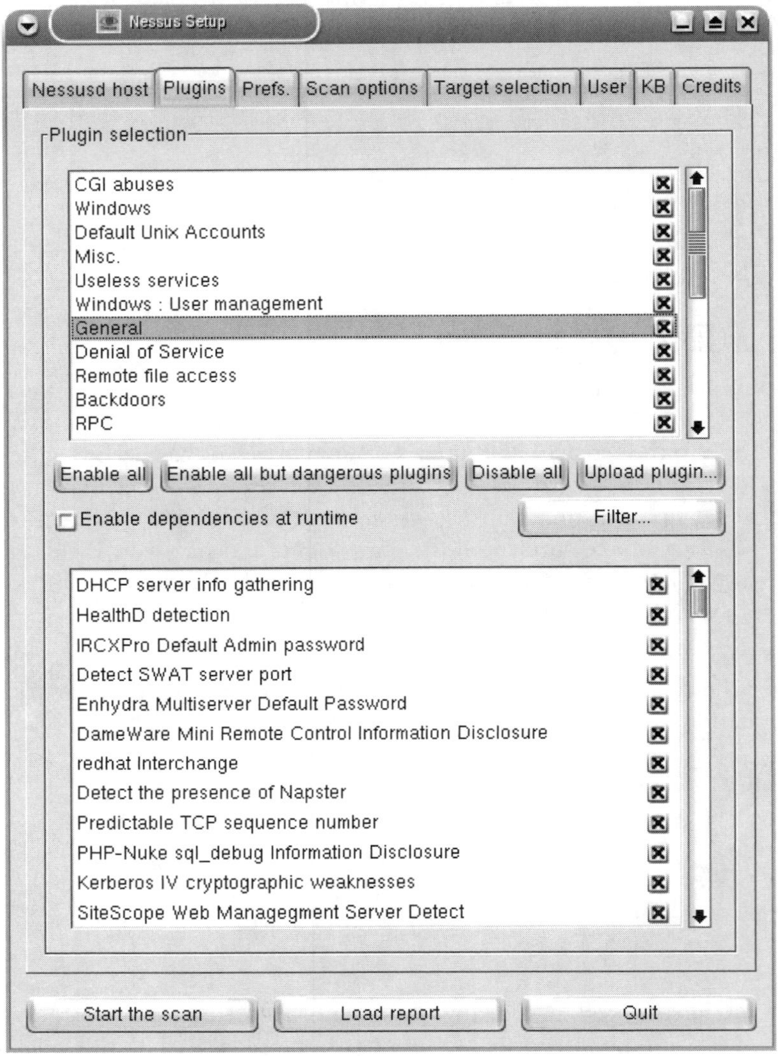

Figure 5-5. Nessus Plugin tab

For your first scan, it's best to click the "Enable all but dangerous plugins" button, then select only the relevant groups of plug-ins from what's now available. If you know the host you're going to scan isn't a Cisco router, you don't need to scan it with every Cisco plug-in. Choose your selection depending on your need. This increases the speed of your probing, as it's going to test only what you tell it to.

Prefs

After you select the desired plug-ins, click the Prefs tab.

Start at the top and work your way down, selecting the options that you want. Note that the differences in each preference can have a major impact on the type, length, and stealth of a given scan.

> *Nessus* uses *nmap* to perform port scans on targets. You can load a previous *nmap* port scan to speed up the scanning process. Scroll down in the Prefs tab and enter the *nmap* results in a field labeled "File containing nmap's results."

The *nessus* that comes with Knoppix has features that are disabled, because most of the other tools that *nessusd* uses are not on the CD. One example of this is *nessus*'s ability to force logins for various protocols. If your needs include some of these types of scans, you have outgrown the default Knoppix distribution and should give a security-focused distribution such as Knoppix STD [Hack #87] a try.

Scan

The Scan tab allows you to set the various scan options for the different methods of scanning. A number of plug-ins are listed at the bottom of the panel that can be disabled if they don't suit your need for scanning.

Target Selection

In the Target Selection tab, you can select your targets for scanning. You may enter multiple targets into the top field if you separate them with a comma, such as:

```
172.16.0.1,172.16.0.2,192.168.0.0/24,www.lostinthenoise.net
```

If the network's DNS server allows you to perform a zone transfer, you can enter that DNS server here. *Nessus* then automatically probes all the hosts that are returned by the zone transfer. It's worth noting that it's a bad idea to enter multiple hosts and enable zone transfers, because *nessus* attempts a zone transfer for each host, which can potentially generate a lot of network traffic and a lot of hosts to scan. Separate those scans from your general, random RFC 1918-address space scans unless you know better.

> Check the box for saving your session, because it is handy to have access to information that you have already created.

User Rules

The User Rules tab allows you to configure limitations on different users who access *nessus*. You can see the default rule sets in the file */etc/nessus/nessusd.rules*. By default, Knoppix allows everything.

Knowledge Base

If you wish to save your scans on the *nessusd* host for future reference, enable knowledge-base (KB) report-saving to rerun scans regularly, to stop and resume scans, and to probe conveniently. It's useful to use the difference scan options (check "Reuse the knowledge bases about the hosts for the test," and then check "Only show differences with the previous scan") to see what's changed since the last time you scanned a given host.

Credits

Who could forget the Credits tab?

Many thanks are attributed to the authors and contributors of this fine product. It's not the only one of its kind, but it's the best open source/free-software project of its type. It's easy to modify and even easier to extend with your own plug-ins.

Start the Scan

With all of the preferences configured (or not, if you have decided on defaults), click "Start the scan" option.

The current status of the scan is shown in a window. You can stop the scan at any point. Otherwise, take a coffee break or enjoy a movie, and then come back to read the report and its results. Depending on the probing depth that you have selected, this part of the process varies in completion time.

The Results

If you've made it this far, you're looking for results.

After the progress bars reach their end, the Nessus NG report is displayed with the familiar setup window.

For my sample scan, I choose to probe a local machine. The results are shown with a split screen view that makes it easy to asses the results for many hosts and subnets (Figure 5-6).

In this example, the results are broken into five main sections: Subnet, Host, Port, Severity, and Descriptions.

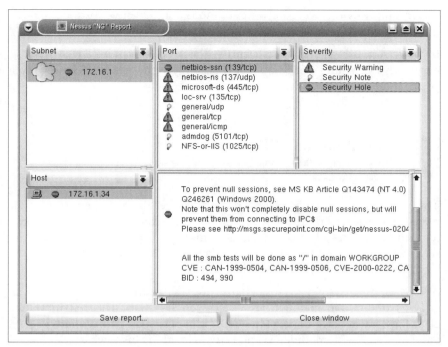

Figure 5-6. Results from a Nessus scan

You can see the number of open ports detected for each selected host, and for each port, you can see the severity of the potential security hole. This host has a number of security warnings, notes, and holes. Each different alert suggests fixes for the various problems that it has. It's quite obvious that this machine is running Windows 2000 and is lacking all of the needed updates available from Microsoft.

Save the Report

You can save the report in a variety of formats, including NBE, NSR, XML, HTML, LaTeX, ASCII text, or even HTML with pie charts and graphs. To revisit any past reports, click on the load report button.

Drawbacks to Using Nessus

The drawbacks to using *nessus* are mainly that it can be slow (if you're dealing with a large number of hosts), damaging (if you don't pay attention), and illegal (if you don't have permission). It can also give a false sense of security (no program catches everything), and it's quite noisy (HIDS/NIDS detects *nessus*). Remember that security is a process: it isn't a problem that can be solved simply by throwing software solutions at it. It's also worth noting that this is simply one part of a good security analysis of your network.

If you're seriously interested in security, check out Knoppix STD [Hack #87]. It has nearly everything that Knoppix is missing. It's the right tool for the job if you're interested in security.

—Jake Appelbaum

Check for Root Kits

Use your Knoppix CD as a safe "known good" system for scanning your Linux install for root kits.

The root user on a Unix system has always held a bit of mystique. The power to create and destroy user accounts on a whim has gone to many system administrators's heads. System administrators aren't the only ones who seek the power of root, however. Attackers have long sought to exploit the security holes in a system to illegally gain root access.

A *root kit* is a system of scripts that uses a security exploit to help an attacker obtain and maintain root access on a system. These scripts often clear logs and replace important system binaries, such and *ps*, *find*, and *su*, among others, with modified versions to further hide his tracks.

A single root kit is as damaging as a single lie. Just as Baltasar Gracian said, "A single lie destroys a whole reputation of integrity," a single root kit destroys a whole system's integrity. If an attacker has root access, he has free reign to your system. The result is that you can't trust the information in your system. Processes might be hidden, files might be hidden, and even kernel modules might be hidden. Programs like the *chkrootkit* can scan system binaries for root kits, but when *chkrootkit* is run from inside a rooted system, even it might be fooled.

Advantages to Scanning with Knoppix

If you are unsure whether your system is compromised, the solution is to scan for root kits from a system that is known to be clean. There are advantages to scanning a system for root kits with Knoppix:

- Knoppix runs from read-only media. As long as Klaus Knopper's system doesn't get rooted, once a CD image is known to be clean, there is no way it can be compromised later. This means that even if the version of *ps* and *find* are compromised on your system, Knoppix's versions are fine.

- Your OS is powered down. This means that any hidden kernel modules or hidden processes are no longer running, so you are able to scan the system when it is frozen in time. Also, this means that no processes are running that can potentially detect that you are scanning the system.

There are, however, a few limitations when using *chrootkit* with Knoppix. Knoppix is running *chkrootkit* from a system that has been rebooted, so *chkrootkit* can scan only files on the system, not anything in memory. Also, *chrootkit* is a signature-based scanner. That means that it looks for certain fingerprints popular root kits are known to have. If an attacker wants to evade detection, she could simply change the root kit so that its signature differs from the one on *chkrootkit*.

Got Root?

Using Knoppix to scan a system for root kits is pretty straightforward. Identify and mount the partitions you want to scan by clicking the hard-drive icons on your desktop. You don't need to mount the partitions as read/write for scanning. Once you have identified the partition to scan, open a terminal and type:

```
knoppix@ttyp0[knoppix]$ sudo chkrootkit -r /mnt/hda1
ROOTDIR is `/mnt/hda1/'
Checking `amd'... not found
Checking `basename'... not infected
Checking `biff'... not infected
Checking `chfn'... not infected
Checking `chsh'... not infected
Checking `cron'... not infected
Checking `date'... not infected
Checking `du'... not infected
Checking `dirname'... not infected
Checking `echo'... not infected
Checking `egrep'... not infected
Checking `env'... not infected
Checking `find'... not infected
. . .
Searching for suspicious files and dirs, it may take a while...
/mnt/hda2/usr/lib/j2re1.4.2/.systemPrefs
/mnt/hda2/usr/lib/j2re1.4.2/.systemPrefs/.system.lock
/mnt/hda2/usr/lib/j2re1.4.2/.systemPrefs/.systemRootModFile
Searching for LPD Worm files and dirs... nothing found
Searching for Ramen Worm files and dirs... nothing found
Searching for Maniac files and dirs... nothing found
Searching for RK17 files and dirs... nothing found
Searching for Ducoci rootkit... nothing found
. . .
Checking `scalper'... not infected
Checking `slapper'... not infected
Checking `z2'... nothing deleted
```

Replace */mnt/hda1* with the path to your mounted partition. Scan the output for any warnings, worms, or root kits. Be careful for false positives, particularly when *chkrootkit* is searching for suspicious files and directories. Files are considered suspicious if they have a large number of system calls. Certain files (in my experience, Java plug-ins in particular) trigger this scan. If you are unsure, simply double-check the suspicious files for any strange code.

If you do find a root kit on your system, consider all of the files on the system suspect. Back up important data and configuration files to audit later **[Hack #47]**, and reinstall your system. You can never fully trust a system that has had root compromised, so a reinstall is the safest option.

HACK #47 Collect Forensics Data

When your computer is broken into, use Knoppix to collect all of the forensics data for later analysis.

Possibly the worst sentence for a system administrator to hear is "The server has been hacked." If you take pride in the systems you run, finding out some vandal is having his way with your server makes you feel, well, violated. When your system gets hacked, and you want to track down the attacker, or at least how he hacked it, you must collect forensics data from the server.

An excellent tool for collecting forensics data is the Coroner's Toolkit (*http://www.porcupine.org/forensics/tct.html*). Two of the tools from this toolkit, *unrm* and *lazarus*, are covered in "Recover Deleted Files" **[Hack #58]**. The tool you should use to collect forensics data is called *grave-robber*. *Grave-robber* scans the system and collects as much useful information as it can (and it collects a lot) so that it can be pored through at a later date. You want to get as much data from the current state of the computer as possible; if you need to format and put the system back into service quickly, you can still see the state at which the machine was compromised.

 If you intend on collecting data stored on a swap drive, boot Knoppix with the noswap cheat code; otherwise, Knoppix automatically mounts any swap drives it finds and, as it uses the space, overwrites any data that was previously on there.

With a Knoppix disc, you can either boot onto the compromised server and scan the hard drives directly, or work with an image of the compromised server's hard drives. *Grave-robber* refers to this type of machine as a *corpse*, because (besides the TCT author's fondness for grave metaphors) the machine is no longer live. In fact, if you can, follow the steps in "Clone Hard Drives" **[Hack #48]** to create an image of your drive, so that you can leave the original alone and do all of your work from the copy. *Grave-robber* can potentially generate a few megabytes of output, depending on the size of the drive scanned and the data it collects. Keep this drive in as pristine a state as possible by finding some other media, such as another hard drive on the system, a USB drive, or a network share, to store the data. The default is to save all data in */var/cache/tct/data*, but as that directory is running from the ramdisk under Knoppix, not only does it not have enough room to store the data, the data is erased once Knoppix is shut down. So find a larger, more permanent place to store everything.

Mount both drives, and then start the *script* command as root, so that you can review the verbose output from *grave-robber* at a later date and follow the process of *grave-robber*:

```
knoppix@ttyp0[knoppix]$ sudo mount /dev/hda1 /mnt/hda1
knoppix@ttyp0[knoppix]$ sudo mount -o rw /dev/hdb1 /mnt/hdb1
knoppix@ttyp0[knoppix]$ sudo mkdir /mnt/hdb1/data
knoppix@ttyp0[knoppix]$ sudo script /mnt/hdb1/grave-robber-output
Script started on Tue Jul 13 21:53:20 2004
root@0[knoppix]#
```

Replace */dev/hda1* with the drive from which you want to collect data, and replace */dev/hdb1* with the drive to which you want to save data. The *script* command saves all input and output from the terminal into */mnt/hdb1/graverobber-output* so you can review your steps. If you run *script* with *sudo*, you should now have a root prompt to run the *grave-robber* command:

```
root@0[knoppix]# grave-robber -c /mnt/hda1 -o LINUX2 -d /mnt/hdb1/data -v
```

The -c argument tells *grave-robber* that instead of scanning the current machine (the default), to scan a corpse mounted at a specified directory, in this case */mnt/hda1*. The -o option tells *grave-robber* which OS the corpse was running and is required if you are scanning a corpse. This example was scanned on a Linux system, but *grave-robber* also supports FreeBSD, Open-BSD, and other OSes (view the manpage for the current list). The -d option specifies where to save the data *grave-robber* collects, and the -v option gives verbose output, so you can see each step *grave-robber* takes.

Once the command completes, type the following command to exit the screen and get back to a normal prompt:

```
root@0[knoppix]# exit
Script done, file is /mnt/hdb1/grave-robber-output
knoppix@ttyp0[knoppix]$
```

Most of files that *grave-robber* creates are readable only by root, so they are simpler to browse if you click K Menu → KNOPPIX → Root Shell to open a root terminal. Now change to the data directory that you have created to browse through the *grave-robber* output:

```
root@ttyp0[knoppix]# cd /mnt/hdb1/data
root@ttyp0[data]# ls
body body.S command_out conf_vault icat proc trust
```

If you understand how *grave-robber* organizes the output, you have a good point at which to start the analysis. Here are a few of the important files and directories:

body

Contains a database of information of all the files and directories on the drive, including md5sums of all of the files, permissions, user and group ownership, and size. Here is a sample from the file:

```
class|host|start_time
body|Knoppix|1089770144
md5|file|st_dev|st_ino|st_mode|st_ls|st_nlink|st_uid|st_gid|st_rdev|
st_size|st_atime|st_mtime|st_ctime|st_blksize|st_blocks
000|/mnt/hda1/var|61440|352722|16877|drwxr-xr-x
|16|0|0|0|2048|1084817810|1075129507|1076277991|4096|4
000|/mnt/hda1/var/yp|61440|32190110|16877|drwxr-xr-x
|3|0|0|0|2048|1084817810|1084660839|1084660839|4096|4
000|/mnt/hda1/var/yp/binding|61440|33599814|16877|drwxr-xr-x
|2|0|0|0|2048|1084817810|1005606373|1076277977|4096|4
c282385f892919eb4135dd333096fa06|/mnt/hda1/var/yp/Makefile|61440|33599692|
33188|-rw-r--r--|1|0|0|0|16868|1084660839|1084009530|1084660839|4096|33
e8407552a8b0c1447940b81fc1ad57a4|/mnt/hda1/var/yp/nicknames|61440|33599934|
33188|-rw-r--r--|1|0|0|0|185|1084722449|1003331481|1076277978|4096|1
```

body.S

Similar to *body*, this database contains only SUID files (file set to run as root) for quick reference.

command_out

As *grave-robber* runs, it executes certain system programs, such as *df*, *dpkg/rpm*, and *lsof* to grab extra information about the system. The output from these commands is stored in individual files in this directory.

conf_vault

Stores a copy of any files that *grave_robber* finds interesting, including configuration files and other critical files and directories. The *index.html* file in the root of this directory links to each of these files in an easy-to-view HTML format.

pcat/icat

Stores images of running processes recovered during the scan named by the ID process, and the date and time the image was made. When you scan a corpse, you receive images of your Knoppix processes.

proc
Similar to the *pcat/icat* directories, this directory contains images from running processes, but based on the proc filesystem. Again, this is not too useful when scanning from a corpse.

trust
Contains *.forward* and *.rhosts* files, and *crontab* and *at* output, along with other files related to trusted relationships.

user_vault
Stores copies of sensitive user files such as shell histories, ssh keys, etc.

Computer forensics is a complicated subject that requires a lot of time and experience and is outside the scope of this hack. For more information on forensics analysis, visit *http://www.cert.org*.

HACK #48 Clone Hard Drives

Use dd and partimage on Knoppix to clone hard drives even across the network.

Cloning entire partitions has long been a time-saver for system administrators. Instead of running through the same install process for tens or hundreds of machines, a system administrator can set up a single machine just how he wants it, then copy the hard-drive image to the next machine, saving hours of work. Plus, a broken machine can be reimaged and back to the "factory" state in minutes, reducing downtime. There are many different hard-drive-imaging programs you can purchase, but with a Knoppix disc, you can easily create partition images, partition-to-partition copies, and even disk-to-disk copies. This hack covers two programs: *dd*, which is commonly used to create and copy drive images, and *partimage*, which combines the power of *dd* with an easy-to-use interface and the capability to save images over the network.

Dd

Ask any Unix-system administrator about disk imaging, and, most likely, the first tool that she suggests is *dd*. *Dd* is a very powerful program that creates exact bit-for-bit copies of drives or partitions. You might have used this command previously if you had to create a boot floppy or an ISO from a CD-ROM.

While there are quite a few different arguments you can pass *dd* to change its behavior, the two basic options are if and of, which specify the input file and the output file for *dd* to use, respectively. As with Unix, in Linux "everything is a file," so the input file or the output file is an actual file on the system—for example, *drive.img*, a partition such as */dev/hda1*, or a complete drive such as */dev/hda*. When you use Knoppix for disk imaging, you run completely outside any disks on the system, so you don't have to worry about files changing or being modified by your login.

A direct disk-to-disk copy is a common use of *dd*. In this scenario, you have partitioned and configured one disk, hda, that you want to mirror—partition tables and all—to a second blank disk, hdb. It is important that hdb be the same size or greater than the size of hda when you copy the image; otherwise, only some of your files are copied, or, the worst case, the image does not mount. To perform the disk-to-disk copy, open a terminal and run the following command:

```
knoppix@ttyp0[knoppix]$ sudo dd if=/dev/hda of=/dev/hdb
```

This command takes some time depending on size and speed of your disks, and, unfortunately, *dd* does not provide a fancy progress meter.

If you don't want to copy a complete drive, but just copy a partition from one system to another, you add the particular partition number you want to use. Similar to copying a disk to another disk, make sure that the partition that you are copying to is the same size or larger than the partition you are copying from. This command copies the first partition from */dev/hda* to the first partition of */dev/hdb*:

```
knoppix@ttyp0[knoppix]$ sudo dd if=/dev/hda1 of=/dev/hdb1
```

Like with a disk-to-disk copy, this takes some time to complete, although, generally, cloning entire disks or partitions with *dd* is faster than doing file-for-file copies with *tar* or *cpio*.

You also have the option to store a complete disk image to a file. This enables you to create a complete snapshot of a hard drive that you can reimage back to the drive to restore it to a certain state. This can be particularly useful in the case of computer forensics [Hack #47], when you want to create a complete copy or multiple copies of a drive so that you can examine the drive without risking any data loss. To copy a disk image to a file, simply pass a filename instead of a device name to the of argument. Most likely, disks you want to image in this way are larger than your available Knoppix ramdisk, so you need to mount another disk to which to save the image. To create a complete image of the */dev/hda1* partition and save it in the root directory of a filesystem mounted at */mnt/hdb1*, use the following command:

```
knoppix@ttyp0[knoppix]$ sudo dd if=/dev/hda1 of=/mnt/hdb1/
hda1_drive_image.img
```

Many people make a point of adding an *.img* extension to their image files as a reminder that the file is a complete disk image, but you can name the file whatever you wish. Even though *dd* doesn't list progress, when you save to a file, you can monitor the size of the file to see how much time you have left.

The *watch* utility is particularly useful for this task because it performs a command every two seconds and shows you the output. To monitor the progress of this image, type the command:

```
knoppix@ttyp0[knoppix]$ watch ls -l /mnt/hdb1/hda1_drive_image.img
```

Once the operation completes, the complete contents of */dev/hda1* are stored in *hda1_drive_image.img*.

You can also utilize *ssh* to save the disk image over the network to a different machine. If you don't specify an output file, *dd* outputs the disk image to STDOUT, which can then be piped through *ssh* to the remote machine. So, if you have an account on 192.168.0.2 to which you want to save the file, issue the command:

```
knoppix@ttyp0[knoppix]$ sudo dd if=/dev/hda1 | ssh username@192.168.0.2
"cat > /home/username/hda1_drive_image.img"
```

After you enter your password, *dd* copies the complete encrypted drive image over the network and stores it in *hda1_drive_image.img*.

By storing a partition image in a file, you can use Linux's *loopback* mounting option to mount this file as though it were an actual partition and examine the files. For instance, if you have an image of an ext2 partition, you can create a new mountpoint in */mnt* and mount the file under Knoppix with the following command:

```
knoppix@ttyp0[knoppix]$ sudo mkdir /mnt/temp
knoppix@ttyp0[knoppix]$ sudo mount -o loop -t ext2 /mnt/hdb1/hda1_drive_
image.img /mnt/temp
```

Now you can browse through the filesystem at */mnt/temp* just as if it were the actual partition. This also works for browsing through ISO images, such as the Knoppix CD image, or any other CD images you might have.

To reimage */dev/hda1* with a file you have saved, simply issue the *dd* command in reverse:

```
knoppix@ttyp0[knoppix]$ sudo dd if=/mnt/hdb1/hda1_drive_image.img of=/dev/
hda1
```

If you have saved your image over the network, you can also reimage by reversing the command by typing:

```
knoppix@ttyp0[knoppix]$ ssh username@192.168.0.2
"cat /home/username/hda1_drive_image.img" | sudo dd of=/dev/hda1
```

With these commands, you can easily image and reimage machines just from *dd*, but if you want a more graphical experience, Knoppix has included a utility, *partimage*, that provides you with an easy-to-use GUI and still gives you many options without any command-line kung fu.

Partimage

While *partimage* can be run from the command line directly, this hack also covers *partimage*'s interactive mode, which it executes when you run *partimage* with no options. *Partimage* requires root privileges, so under Knoppix, type:

```
knoppix@ttyp0[knoppix]$ sudo partimage
```

When launched, the first option you see is to choose which partition you want to save or restore. Like its name alludes to, *partimage* is only for the purposes of saving and restoring partition images. *Partimage* also attempts to guess which filesystem the partition is currently using, which makes it easier to see which partitions you want to image on a multipartition, dual-boot system. After selecting the partition to save, move the cursor down to select the image file to save to. Knoppix has limited ramdisk space, so you must save the partition image to another partition on the system. Make sure that partition is already mounted and then type in the full path of the file you want to save—for instance, */mnt/hdb1/hda1_drive_image.img*. Once you enter the filename, if you are saving to the local machine, you can simply hit F5 to move to the next screen.

Partimage also provides an option to save the partition image over the network to another machine. This requires the other machine to be running the *partimaged* server, so you need either another machine running Linux with *partimaged* installed, or you can use another Knoppix disk booted on that machine to run the server. If you choose to run *partimaged* from Knoppix, you must create a password for the *root* user, because *partimage* prompts you for a username and password before connecting to *partimaged*. On the remote server, open a terminal and type **sudo passwd** to enter in a new password for root. Then you can run the *partimaged* server in interactive mode (which lets you see connections as they are created along with their progress):

```
knoppix@ttyp0[knoppix]$ sudo partimaged
```

Partimaged supports connections from multiple clients at the same time, so you could potentially image multiple systems at the same time over the network and save to a single file server.

After the server has been configured, on the *partimage* client, check "Connect to server" and enter the IP address or hostname of the *partimaged* server in the next field. Keep in mind that when you save to a remote server, the path and filename you enter are the path and filename you have used on the server, not on the local machine, so make sure that path exists and you have enough room for the image. When you hit F5 to continue, *partimage* attempts to connect to the remote machine and prompts you for a user-name and password. If the *partimaged* server is running on Knoppix as well, enter **root** for the username and the password you have set up, and then choose OK.

Once you've authenticated, you are presented with some compression and file-splitting options. *Partimage* can compress partition images using gzip and bzip2 algorithms, which are progressively slower but provide progressively smaller images. By default, *partimage* also splits images into files that are less than 2 GB. This is a safeguard in case you are saving to a filesystem that doesn't allow files to be larger than 2 GB. If you want to burn the images to a CD-ROM later, you can also modify this option to save the image to 650 MB or 700 MB files. Once you have changed these settings to suit your needs, hit F5 to move to the next screen, which allows you to type a description of the saved partition. By default, *partimage* presents you with information about the partition. Hit Enter to start the image-copying process.

One nice thing about using *partimage* over *dd* is that the progress bars tell you how far in the process you are, how much time has elapsed, how much time is remaining, and information about how large the image is and how much free space you have available. If you saved to a remote server, you can also monitor the progress from there. Once the process finishes, *partimage* displays how long the process has taken and then exits.

To restore an image using *partimage*, the process is quite similar: specify the partition to which you want to restore to, and specify the image file's path that has already been created. Check "Restore partition from an image file" instead of "Save partition into a new image file."

HACK #49   Wipe a Hard Drive

Securely wipe a hard drive of file traces before you get rid of it.

A paper shredder is a common tool in offices, particularly in offices that handle financial data. The shredder ensures that while it might still be possible to piece together a sensitive document, it takes a lot more time and effort than if the piece of paper were just crumpled up. Companies shred financial information; yet when many companies upgrade their computers, they don't bother to erase all of the sensitive data that every computer contains. Even if a company formats and reinstalls an operating system on a drive, that alone does not necessarily erase the files that were on the drive before, and with a little effort and some recovery software, an attacker could potentially recover sensitive data from the drive.

Knoppix contains a handy tool called *shred* that strives for the same goal as a paper shredder: to make file recovery difficult and not worth the effort. While a dedicated attacker might be able to recover a file you have shredded, it takes a lot of money and sophisticated equipment.

> If you are truly paranoid about your data, or the data on your drive is valuable enough to be worth the effort of an attacker to recover after a full shred, then the only way you can ensure that your data cannot be recovered is to take out the hard drive, hit it multiple times with a sledgehammer, and then burn it. Seriously.

Compare a hard-drive sector to a two-lane highway, with the data symbolizing the dotted, yellow stripe down the middle. When new data is written, the drive head paints a new, bright, dotted stripe somewhere on the road, but not necessarily covering the old stripe. Since hard drives work using magnetism, if you have sensitive equipment, you can pick up the faint magnetic fields from previous disk writes, even if new data is written over the top.

The only way to be sure that this faint magnetic field cannot be detected is to write over the entire drive many different times with random data. The idea is that the more times you write data to the drive, the more likely it is that the drive head actually writes over the top of a previous track. In effect, it is like painting many different stripes down the highway in which you hope to paint over the previous stripe at least once. The data being written is random, so it makes it much more difficult to piece together files than if the drive were written only with all ones or zeros.

To securely wipe your hard drive, boot into Knoppix and find the partition on your desktop that you want to shred. Then open a terminal and shred the drive:

```
knoppix@ttyp0[knoppix]$ sudo shred -n 2 -z -v /dev/hda1
```

Replace */dev/hda1* with the partition you intend to shred or with */dev/hda* if you also want to erase the partition table, and boot sector. The -n option tells *shred* how many times to write over the drive with random data. The default is to write over the drive 25 times. If time is not an issue or you are paranoid, feel free to stick with the default. The -z option tells *shred* to finish the wipe by overwriting the drive with zeros. This makes the partition look completely empty to a casual observer instead of filled with random ones and zeros. Finally, the -v option shows you *shred*'s progress, which is one of the main advantages to use *shred* to wipe drives instead of *dd*.

The time it takes *shred* to complete varies greatly, depending on the number of times you choose to overwrite the drive, and the size and the speed of the drive. The nice thing about using Knoppix for drive-wiping is that you have a lot of applications you can use to pass the time (check "Have Fun and Play Some Games" [Hack #15] for a good selection).

HACK #50 Test Hardware Compatibility

Knoppix's hardware detection has a reputation for being just about as good as Linux. Use your Knoppix disc to test the Linux-hardware compatibility of desktops, laptops, and peripherals.

Linux openly tells you what it knows about a system. From the moment Linux boots, you are presented with information about what Linux is doing and which hardware it is detecting. Through the /proc interface, you can also ask the kernel to display very detailed information about all of the hardware on the system. This is particularly useful to test hardware that you want to get working on another Linux distribution.

> You can also leverage this hardware detection when shopping for a new computer or laptop. Simply bring a Knoppix disc with you and get the clerk to agree to let you boot the CD-ROM for hardware compatibility testing. This sort of test is quick and much less painful than discovering that a major piece of hardware does not yet work under Linux after you have bought it.

This hack covers the major commands that provide you with hardware information under Linux. I can't possibly cover all of the different hardware that Linux can support and where it is configured, but after reading this hack, you should know where to look and what to do to check whether Linux has detected your hardware, and you should be able to check and copy the configuration for the major hardware on your system.

General Hardware Probing

When booting Knoppix, you can't help but notice a lot of information about your hardware scrolling by in the text output. Once the desktop starts loading, however, you can no longer see it (and what you could see might have scrolled by too fast for you to really read it). This text output is actually rather useful, because it shows which hardware the kernel has detected and gives you a good sense of which hardware should be working. You don't have to scribble down all of that information as it scrolls by or sit in front of your monitor with a camera taking snapshots, because Linux logs all of that information for you in /var/log/dmesg. Knoppix doesn't enable logging by default, so you might notice that /var/log/dmesg is empty under Knoppix.

You can still access the same information through the *dmesg* command. *Dmesg* outputs what is in */var/log/dmesg* to the screen, so if you want to reference it, redirect it to another file or pipe it to a pager such as *less*.

The first time you run *dmesg*, you might be overwhelmed by the amount of information you are presented with, because Knoppix probes for many different kinds of hardware that you probably don't have, and displays a lot of information about your motherboard and PCI devices. As you scroll through the output, you should start to see useful information about your hardware. For example, here's some sample *dmesg* output that gives me information about my IDE devices:

```
knoppix@ttyp0[knoppix]$ dmesg | less
. . .
AMD7411: 00:07.1 (rev 01) UDMA100 controller
    ide0: BM-DMA at 0xf000-0xf007, BIOS settings: hda:DMA, hdb:DMA
    ide1: BM-DMA at 0xf008-0xf00f, BIOS settings: hdc:pio, hdd:pio
hda: WDC WD1000BB-00CAA1, ATA DISK drive
hdb: WDC WD300BB-00AUA1, ATA DISK drive
hdc: SAMSUNG DVD-ROM SD-612, ATAPI CD/DVD-ROM drive
ide0 at 0x1f0-0x1f7,0x3f6 on irq 14
ide1 at 0x170-0x177,0x376 on irq 15
hda: attached ide-disk driver.
hda: host protected area => 1
hda: 195371568 sectors (100030 MB) w/2048KiB Cache, CHS=193821/16/63
hdb: attached ide-disk driver.
hdb: host protected area => 1
hdb: 58633344 sectors (30020 MB) w/2048KiB Cache, CHS=58168/16/63
Partition check:
 hda: hda1 hda2 hda3
 hdb: hdb1 hdb2 hdb3
. . .
usb.c: registered new driver hiddev
usb.c: registered new driver hid
input: USB HID v1.00 Mouse [Microsoft Microsoft IntelliMouse® Explorer] on
usb1:2.0
. . .
Linux Tulip driver version 0.9.15-pre12 (Aug 9, 2002)
eth0: Lite-On PNIC-II rev 37 at 0x1000, 00:A0:CC:32:BF:88, IRQ 5.
. . .
```

This output shows which IDE devices Linux has detected, whether DMA has been enabled in the BIOS, the size of any hard drives it has found, and which partitions it has found on those drives. Further down I can see that it has detected my USB mouse and my Ethernet card.

While this output can be useful, you might want more in-depth information about specific hardware on your system. In particular, you might want to find out which PCI devices Knoppix has found on the system. You could scan through the PCI bus by looking through the files under */proc/bus/pci*, but an easier way is to use the *lspci* tool. *Lspci* lists all of the PCI buses in a system with any devices connected to them. The standard output should give you some basic information about which devices Linux has detected on the system:

```
knoppix@ttyp0[knoppix]$ lspci
0000:00:00.0 Host bridge: Advanced Micro Devices [AMD] AMD-760 MP [IGD4-2P]
System Controller (rev 11)
0000:00:01.0 PCI bridge: Advanced Micro Devices [AMD] AMD-760 MP [IGD4-2P]
AGP Bridge
0000:00:07.0 ISA bridge: Advanced Micro Devices [AMD] AMD-766 [ViperPlus]
ISA (rev 02)
0000:00:07.1 IDE interface: Advanced Micro Devices [AMD] AMD-766 [ViperPlus]
IDE (rev 01)
0000:00:07.3 Bridge: Advanced Micro Devices [AMD] AMD-766 [ViperPlus] ACPI
(rev 01)
0000:00:07.4 USB Controller: Advanced Micro Devices [AMD] AMD-766
[ViperPlus]
USB (rev 07)
0000:00:0c.0 Ethernet controller: Lite-On Communications Inc LNE100TX
[Linksys
EtherFast 10/100] (rev 25)
0000:00:0d.0 Multimedia audio controller: Aureal Semiconductor Vortex 2
0000:01:05.0 VGA compatible controller: nVidia Corporation NV11 [GeForce2
MX/MX
400] (rev a1)
```

In this output, there are two basic columns. The first column lists the bus, slot, and function for a device in hexadecimal. The next column lists the type of device and any identification it can find for the device. The first few lines of output simply list information about different bridges on the motherboard, but the last few lines list a number of devices that are connected to the PCI bus, including an Ethernet card, a sound card, and a video card. If you want more information, pass the -v or -vv option to *lspci* to tell *lspci* to give progressively more information about the device. To see more information about the GeForce2 video card, just run **lspci -vv** and browse through the rather verbose output:

```
knoppix@ttyp0[knoppix]$ sudo lspci -vv
. . .
0000:01:05.0 VGA compatible controller: nVidia Corporation NV11 [GeForce2
MX/MX
400] (rev a1) (prog-if 00 [VGA])
    Subsystem: LeadTek Research Inc.: Unknown device 2830
    Control: I/O+ Mem+ BusMaster+ SpecCycle- MemWINV- VGASnoop- ParErr-
Stepping- SERR- FastB2B-
    Status: Cap+ 66MHz+ UDF- FastB2B+ ParErr- DEVSEL=medium >TAbort- SERR-
[disabled] [size=64K]
    Capabilities: [60] Power Management version 2
        Flags: PMEClk- DSI- D1- D2- AuxCurrent=0mA PME(D0-,D1-,D2-,D3hot-
,D3cold-)
        Status: D0 PME-Enable- DSel=0 DScale=0 PME-
```

```
        Capabilities: [44] AGP version 2.0
            Status: RQ=32 Iso- ArqSz=0 Cal=0 SBA- ITACoh- GART64- HTrans- 64bit-
    FW+ AGP3- Rate=x1,x2,x4
            Command: RQ=1 ArqSz=0 Cal=0 SBA- AGP- GART64- 64bit- FW- Rate=
```

Notice that this time I ran *lspci* with *sudo*. This is because *lspci* won't tell a regular user all of the information about a PCI device in the verbose output (most notably the capabilities lines), so to get verbose output, run *lspci* using *sudo*.

If you are new to Linux, reading through all this output to try to find out whether Linux sees your sound card is probably intimidating. Besides, just because *lspci* lists a device, it doesn't necessarily mean that modules are loaded and the device is up and running. If your desktop environment is running, Knoppix provides a tool, Info Center, that collects all of the hardware information for your system and displays it in a simple interface. When you run Info Center by clicking K Menu → System → Info Center, you are presented with a window, as shown in Figure 5-7.

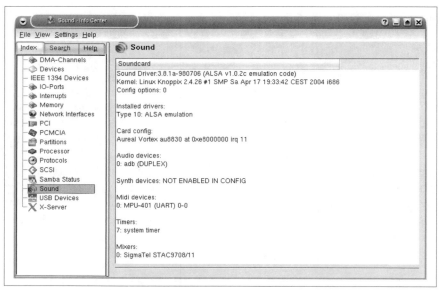

Figure 5-7. The KDE Info Center

On the lefthand side of the window are a number of hardware categories, and clicking on any of the categories displays information about that category on the righthand side of the window. Info Center is useful in that it not only lists the information that you might find by running *lspci*, but it also scans through other parts of the system and lists whether modules have been loaded for certain devices. To check whether your network card is running and has received an IP address, click on Network Interfaces in the sidebar to list all network devices, their IP addresses, and whether they are up. To check that a sound card is working, click on Sound in the sidebar to see which audio devices the Info Center has detected as well as their capabilities.

Specific Hardware Testing

Dmesg, lspci, and the Info Center provide you with a lot of information about hardware on your system, but these commands mostly tell you about hardware that has been detected, not necessarily hardware that is working. This section covers some common hardware and specific tests to confirm that it is working.

Sound card. "Rock Out with Knoppix Multimedia" **[Hack #16]** covers steps to test and configure your sound card, but the first clue that Knoppix has gotten your sound card to work is the "Initiating startup sequence" sound you hear when KDE starts.

Video cards. If Knoppix brings up a desktop environment, then obviously the video card and display work to some degree. Specific information about which video card features X was able to load, and which resolutions and color depths X accepted and rejected, can be found in */var/log/XFree86.0.log*. This file contains a lot of detailed information, much like *dmesg,* and like *dmesg,* much of it may not interest you. A lot of the interesting information (e.g., which resolutions were accepted and rejected, and which input devices were configured) can be found near the bottom of the file:

```
. . .
(--) NV(0): VideoRAM: 32768 kBytes
(==) NV(0): Using gamma correction (1.0, 1.0, 1.0)
(II) NV(0): Monitor0: Using hsync range of 30.00-70.00 kHz
(II) NV(0): Monitor0: Using vrefresh range of 50.00-120.00 Hz
(II) NV(0): Clock range:  12.00 to 350.00 MHz
(II) NV(0): Not using mode "1280x1024" (hsync out of range)
(II) NV(0): Not using mode "1024x768" (hsync out of range)
(II) NV(0): Not using mode "1152x864" (hsync out of range)
. . .
(**) Option "Protocol" "IMPS/2"
(**) USB Mouse: Protocol: "IMPS/2"
(**) Option "SendCoreEvents" "true"
(**) USB Mouse: always reports core events
(**) Option "CorePointer"
(**) USB Mouse: Core Pointer
(**) Option "Device" "/dev/input/mice"
(**) Option "Buttons" "5"
(**) USB Mouse: Emulate3Buttons, Emulate3Timeout: 50
(**) Option "ZAxisMapping" "4 5"
(**) USB Mouse: ZAxisMapping: buttons 4 and 5
```

```
(**) USB Mouse: Buttons: 5
(II) XINPUT: Adding extended input device "USB Mouse" (type: MOUSE)
. . .
```

X outputs warnings and errors in the files starting with (WW) and (EE), respectively. To see warnings and errors, type the following command:

```
knoppix@ttyp0[knoppix]$ egrep "^(\(WW|EE\))" /var/log/XFree86.0.log
```

Knoppix also attempts to enable hardware 3D acceleration, if possible, using Direct Rendering Interface (DRI). Knoppix falls back to software 3D acceleration if hardware acceleration isn't possible. Check the current status of DRI with the *glxinfo* command. This command outputs a lot of information about the GLX libraries on the system. You can use *grep* to display just the line showing whether DRI (and therefore 3D acceleration) is enabled:

```
knoppix@ttyp0[knoppix]$ glxinfo | grep "direct rendering"
direct rendering: No
```

Note that all recent Nvidia cards do not have 3D acceleration enabled by default. To enable 3D acceleration for these cards, you must install Nvidia's own kernel modules and X drivers with the Knoppix live-software installer **[Hack #28]**. Once the install finishes and X restarts, direct rendering is enabled.

Network cards. Testing network cards on the system is pretty simple—just browse the Web or the intranet. Obviously, if you can ping other hosts on the network or browse an external web site, then your network card works. However, view more detailed information about your network card configuration by using the *ifconfig* utility:

```
knoppix@ttyp0[knoppix]$ /sbin/ifconfig
eth0      Link encap:Ethernet  HWaddr 00:A0:CC:32:BF:88
          inet addr:192.168.0.2  Bcast:192.168.0.255  Mask:255.255.255.0
          UP BROADCAST RUNNING MULTICAST  MTU:1500  Metric:1
          RX packets:3927 errors:0 dropped:0 overruns:0 frame:0
          TX packets:3240 errors:1 dropped:0 overruns:0 carrier:2
          collisions:0 txqueuelen:1000
          RX bytes:5278944 (5.0 MiB)  TX bytes:1692461 (1.6 MiB)
          Interrupt:5 Base address:0x1000

lo        Link encap:Local Loopback
          inet addr:127.0.0.1  Mask:255.0.0.0
          UP LOOPBACK RUNNING  MTU:16436  Metric:1
          RX packets:16 errors:0 dropped:0 overruns:0 frame:0
          TX packets:16 errors:0 dropped:0 overruns:0 carrier:0
          collisions:0 txqueuelen:0
          RX bytes:896 (896.0 b)  TX bytes:896 (896.0 b)
```

This utility is standard on every major Linux distribution, and when run without any arguments, it lists all network devices on the system. In this example, it has found an Ethernet card, eth0, and displays its MAC address,

IP address, broadcast, and other networking information. In addition, it displays how many bytes have been received (RX bytes) and transmitted (TX bytes) across the interface.

For probing all the hardware on your system, use these commands. If you are probing the hardware to check for Linux compatibility but aren't planning on installing Knoppix itself to your hard drive, then check out the next hack for information on how to copy Knoppix configurations to other distributions.

HACK #51 Copy Settings to Other Distributions

Knoppix's intelligent hardware auto-detection can get all of a computer's hardware working out of the box. You can copy and reference the system files Knoppix creates to ease configuration of a new or existing installation.

With new hardware always coming out and with many vendors failing to list their Linux support (or lack thereof) on the box, it can sometimes be difficult to get all of your hardware working under Linux. While scanning the Web for HOWTOs, searching for the module that corresponds to your hardware, and configuring it by hand can be a good learning experience, some people might prefer to simply copy the information they need from a working system. This is where Knoppix comes in. Because of the excellent hardware detection and configuration Knoppix performs, there is a good chance that if the hardware is capable of working on your Linux distribution, it works in Knoppix. Many of the configuration files and modules are common across distributions; if hardware works in Knoppix, in many cases you can simply copy the configuration files and information you need to your distribution without any extra fuss.

Copy X Settings

Even with some of the automated tools that are available to configure X, it still seems to be one of the most problematic configuration files. After spending hours trying to get X to work, booting up Knoppix and having it work automatically might be a bit demoralizing. But you should be rejoicing. X's configuration file is pretty standard across Linux distributions, so you can copy Knoppix's configuration to your distribution almost directly.

Like pretty much every other Linux distribution, Knoppix stores X's configuration in */etc/X11/XF86Config-4*. Provided you have a similar version of X on your system, you can copy this file directly to your system and get the same exact configuration that you have in Knoppix. Knoppix does include quite a few fonts in the file, so X might give some warnings about missing font paths if your fonts aren't installed in the same location or aren't installed at all. If you are experienced with X configuration, you don't necessarily need to copy the complete file but can instead reference particular sections, such as the monitor section or input device sections.

For instance, to copy the complete monitor section that Knoppix uses, copy all of the text starting with Section "Monitor" and ending with EndSection to your *XF86Config-4* file. Then make sure that in your screen section (this section starts with Section "Screen") the Monitor line has the same monitor name as the name following Identifier in the monitor section you pasted in.

Copy Module Information

For much of the hardware on a system, there aren't many configuration files you need to bother with. You simply need to load the right module for the hardware to start working. Sometimes this means experimentation by loading multiple network card modules one at a time to see which module works best for your network card. Knoppix's kernel has most hardware built as a module so it can load only the modules it needs to work on a particular system. Most distributions by default have heavily modular kernels as well, so you can reference the modules that Knoppix loads and load the same modules on your system to get hardware working. This of course assumes that the same modules are built in your particular kernel.

The command *lsmod* shows all modules that are currently loaded in a system. Under Knoppix, many different modules are loaded by default, so it's best to have a general idea of which modules you might be considering for a device before digging through the output. For instance, if you are configuring ALSA, most of the relevant modules in the *lsmod* output are preceded by snd- or reference other modules preceded by snd- in the Used by column. If you are really lazy, you could simply copy the full list of modules and load them all, but it's better to try only the modules you need.

Copy Kernel Configuration

In addition to referencing the modules that Knoppix loads at boot, you can also reference the complete configuration Knoppix uses in its kernel when building your own kernel. Knoppix stores a copy of the configuration file for each kernel it includes in the */boot* directory in the format config-*kernel_version*. If you have a standard, unpatched kernel that's the same revision as the one Knoppix uses, then you can simply copy the configuration file to the root of your kernel source tree and name it *.config* to start using it. If your kernel source is located at */usr/src/linux-2.4.26*, for instance, copy Knoppix's configuration to */usr/src/linux-2.4.26/.config*. If your kernel revision is greater than the one Knoppix uses (for instance, you want to build 2.4.26 but the version of Knoppix you have uses a 2.4.25 kernel), then after you copy the configuration file to the kernel source tree and name it *.config*, you must run the following command from the root of the kernel tree to see new kernel options:

```
root@ttyp0[linux-2.4.26]# make oldconfig
```

Once the configuration is copied and ready, you can edit the configuration and build the kernel as you would normally. Do not use the kernel config for an older revision of the kernel (for instance, Knoppix uses 2.4.26 but you want to use 2.4.24) because, while it might work, problems may arise due to options that exist in the Knoppix kernel that don't exist in the kernel you are building. Also, do not use a configuration for a 2.4 kernel if you are building a 2.6 kernel and vice versa.

Copying some of these settings from Knoppix to your system can definitely save you time when trying to get hardware working. Unfortunately, many of the other configuration files in */etc*, such as network settings, are specific to either Debian or Knoppix, so you won't be able to reference those files without making some changes to suit your system, but at least you now have a good start in getting the hardware to work.

## CHAPTER SIX

Repair Linux
Hacks 52–70

Using Linux effectively is a learning process. One of the best ways to learn is to just dive in and try it. If you are new to Linux, you quickly discover another good way to learn is to fix something you accidentally broke. I consider myself an experienced Linux administrator; by "experienced," I mean that I have broken my system many times and have had to recover it.

The most frustrating mistake you can make under Linux is one that leaves your computer unbootable. Like with most things in Linux, there are a number of ways that you can do this, and once you do, you will need a rescue disk. Many distributions include special-purpose rescue disks, or the install CD itself doubles as a rescue disk. This works well enough when you need to recover some common mistakes on that particular distribution, but none of the distribution rescue disks come close to the flexibility and number of tools Knoppix includes to fix Linux. Besides, many distribution recovery CDs provide only a command prompt. Knoppix provides a full GUI and a number of very useful GUI tools for repairing mistakes. With Knoppix, it's easy to open a web browser or a chat client and search for help.

The first part of this chapter includes many different tips for repairing the Master Boot Record (MBR), including how to restore both *lilo* and *grub*, and how to back up and restore your entire MBR. The next part of the chapter is focused on overall disk repair, and covers how to undelete files you have accidentally removed, methods to back up and restore files, and even a complete set of hacks for software RAID. The final set of hacks focus on how to repair some important system files that can stop your system from booting, including the */etc/passwd* file and the kernel.

By the end of this chapter, you should be a master of Linux system recovery and be the "go to" guy your friends call when they break their machines.

HACK #52 Repair Lilo

Use Knoppix to restore lilo to the Master Boot Record (MBR).

A common tech-support problem you see on Linux forums is something along the lines of "Help I upgraded my kernel and didn't keep the old kernel in my *lilo.conf*, and the new kernel won't boot!", or "Help I installed Windows after Linux and now I can't get back to lilo." Whatever the reason, all of us have run into situations where we have needed to restore *lilo* on a system that won't boot. This is one situation where Knoppix can come to the rescue.

To restore *lilo* to the MBR, you must reference the */etc/lilo.conf* file that was used previously, as well as the original version of *lilo*. Knoppix comes with a version of *lilo* itself; however, it's best to use the same version of *lilo* that is installed on your system. The first step to restore *lilo* to your MBR is to find your root partition. Open the different partitions you see on your desktop until you find one that contains an */etc* directory with your *lilo.conf*, as well as an */sbin* directory that contains *lilo*. For these examples, the root Linux partition is */dev/hda1*.

> If you need to make changes to your *lilo.conf* (for instance, if you need to add an old kernel or change the default root partition), then now is the time to mount the partition read/write and edit the file.

To properly run your installation's version of *lilo*, you must make *lilo* think that */mnt/hda1* (or whatever your root partition is) is actually */*. You can do this with a *chroot* environment. By default, Knoppix mounts these partitions without the dev option, which means that none of the character or block special devices on the filesystem are interpreted. *Lilo* needs this option to work correctly, so if the filesystem is not yet mounted, mount it with:

```
knoppix@tty1[knoppix] $ sudo mount -o dev /mnt/hda1
```

If the filesystem is already mounted, then remount it with:

```
knoppix@tty1[knoppix] $ sudo mount -o remount,dev /mnt/hda1
```

Once the filesystem is mounted, restore *lilo* with the following command:

```
knoppix@tty1[hda1] $ sudo chroot /mnt/hda1 lilo
```

You should see output for the boot options that *lilo* has added and should be able to reboot with *lilo* fully restored.

Repair Grub

HACK
#53

Use Knoppix to restore grub to the Master Boot Record (MBR).

There are two popular bootloaders for Linux: *lilo* and *grub*. *Lilo* has been around longer, and many distributions default to installing it, but most also offer *grub* packages. *Grub* has many interesting features that have made it popular, including the ability to change kernels and basically any other *grub* options at boot time. *Grub* also reads from its configuration file at boot, so you can change options in the text file and don't have to reinstall *grub* to the MBR to make changes. Like *lilo*, *grub* sometimes gets overwritten by a Windows install or by an accidental installation of *lilo* to the MBR. The procedure to restore *grub* to the MBR is almost identical to restoring *lilo*.

First, identify your root partition as in the *lilo hack* [Hack #52]. In this example, the root partition is */dev/hda1*.

> If you want to make any changes to your *grub* configuration, now is the time to mount the partition read/write and edit the *boot/grub/menu.lst* file.

Next, mount the partition with the dev option enabled and with write permissions, so if the filesystem is not yet mounted, mount it with:

    knoppix@tty1[knoppix]$ sudo mount -o dev,rw /mnt/hda1

If the filesystem is already mounted, then remount it with:

    knoppix@tty1[knoppix]$ sudo mount -o remount,dev,rw /mnt/hda1

Once the filesystem is mounted, restore *grub* with the following command:

    knoppix@tty1[hda1]$ sudo chroot /mnt/hda1 grub-install /dev/hda

Of course, replace */mnt/hda1* and */dev/hda* with your mounted root partition and the device to which you wish to install *grub*, respectively.

> If you use *devfs*, or for some reason, the *chroot* environment doesn't work, mount the filesystem with write permissions, then run `sudo grub-install -root-directory=/mnt/hda1 /dev/hda`.

Install grub on a System Without grub

Once *grub* is installed on an MBR, all it needs is the contents of the */boot/ grub/* directory to boot your system. That means that you can actually use Knoppix to install *grub* to a system that doesn't actually have *grub* binaries on it. Obviously, once you have *grub* set up, you want to find and install the *grub* packages on your system, but with this next series of commands, you can use the *grub* tools from Knoppix to set up *grub* on your MBR.

To install *grub* directly from Knoppix, mount your root partition read/write and create a */boot/grub/menu.lst* file. If you are comfortable with *grub*, you can do this by hand with a text editor. You can also copy over */usr/share/ doc/grub/examples/menu.lst* from your Knoppix CD, and comment out the different operating systems it has already configured and use it as a reference. However, there is an easier way to configure *grub*: use the *update-grub* tool. This tool scans the */boot* partition for usable kernels and automatically creates a *menu.lst* file based on what it finds. This tool must be run from a *chroot* environment on the root partition, so assuming the root partition is mounted at */mnt/hda1*, you would run:

```
knoppix@tty1[knoppix]$ cd /mnt/hda1
knoppix@tty1[hda1]$ sudo mkdir boot/grub
knoppix@tty1[hda1]$ sudo cp /sbin/update-grub ./
knoppix@tty1[hda1]$ sudo chroot /mnt/hda1 /update-grub
```

The final command prompts you to create a *menu.lst* file. You want to do this, so answer "yes." It then scans your hard drive and adds new entries for all of the kernels it finds. The first time *update-grub* is run, it might not detect the correct root device to use. *Grub* uses special notation to define partitions, such as (hd0,0), which describes the first partition on the first hard drive in the system or translated to Linux */dev/hda1*. If your root partition is not at */dev/hda1*, but perhaps at */dev/hda5*, you must edit the *boot/ grub/menu.lst* file that was created, and find the following commented line:

```
# groot=(hd0,0)
```

Do not uncomment this line. This is a hint for the *update-grub* tool only, not for *grub* itself. Replace (hd0,0) with the correct root device for your Linux system. For example, if your root Linux partition is */dev/hda5*, change the line to:

```
# groot=(hd0,4)
```

Notice that *grub* counts partitions from zero instead of one. Rerun *update-grub* to update *menu.lst* with the correct values:

```
knoppix@tty1[knoppix]$ cd /mnt/hda5
knoppix@tty1[hda5]$ sudo chroot /mnt/hda5 /update-grub
```

This example uses */mnt/hda5*. You should of course change this, as well as the *grub* commands, to match your root partition.

Once the program has finished, you are ready to install *grub* to the boot sector. This doesn't require a *chroot* environment, but you must tell the *grub-install* program to use */mnt/hda1* as your root directory by typing the following command:

```
knoppix@tty1[knoppix]$ sudo grub-install --root-directory=/mnt/hda1 /dev/hda
```

Once again, change */mnt/hda1* and */dev/hda* to match your root partition and MBR. Now, you should be able to restart the computer and should be presented with your new *grub* prompt.

Kill and Resurrect the Master Boot Record
#54   How to (carefully) back up and restore the Master Boot Record (MBR).

The MBR is a 512-byte segment at the very beginning (the first sector) of a hard drive. This segment contains two major parts: the *boot code* in the first 446 bytes and the *partition table* (plus a 2-byte signature) in the remaining 66 bytes. When you run *lilo*, *grub-install*, or *fdisk /mbr* in DOS, it writes to these first 446 bytes. When you run *cfdisk* or some other disk-partition program, it writes to the remaining 66 bytes.

> Writing directly to your MBR can be dangerous. One typo or mistake can make your entire system unbootable or even erase your entire partition table. Make sure you have a complete backup of your MBR, if not your full hard drive, on other media (like a floppy or anything other than the hard drive itself) before you try any potentially destructive commands.

The MBR is very important and crucial for booting your system, and in the case of your partition table, crucial for accessing your data; however, many people never back up their MBR. Use Knoppix to easily create backups of your MBR, which you can later restore in case you ever accidentally overwrite your partition table or boot code. It is important to double-check each command you type, as typing 466 instead of 446 can mean the difference between blanking the boot code and partially destroying your partition table.

Save the MBR

First, before you attempt anything potentially destructive, back up the current MBR. Boot into Knoppix, and type the following command into a terminal:

```
knoppix@ttyp0[knoppix]$ sudo dd if=/dev/hda of=/home/knoppix/mbr_backup
bs=512 count=1
```

Change */dev/hda* to match the drive you wish to back up. In your home directory, you should now see a 512-byte file called *mbr_backup*. *Dd* is used to create images of entire hard drives **[Hack #48]**, and in this case, a similar command is used; however, it contains two new options: bs and count. The bs (byte size) option tells *dd* to input and output 512 bytes at a time, and the *count* option tells *dd* to do this only once. The result of the command is that the first 512 bytes of the drive (the MBR) are copied into the file. If for some reason you only want to back up the boot sector (although it's wise to always back up the partition table as well), replace 512 with 446. Now that you have backed up the MBR, copy it to a safe location, such as another computer or a CD-ROM.

> The full 512-byte copy of the MBR contains the partition table, so it gets out of sync whenever you change partitions on your drive. If you back up the full MBR, be sure to update your backup whenever you make partition changes.

Kill the MBR

Now that you know how to back up, you should know how to totally destroy the MBR. To do this, simply use the same command you use to back up an MBR, but replace the input file with */dev/zero* and the output file with the drive, overwriting each byte of the MBR with zero. If you only want to blank your boot code, type:

```
knoppix@ttyp0[knoppix]$ sudo dd if=/dev/zero of=/dev/hda bs=446 count=1
```

To clear the complete MBR, including the partition table, type:

```
knoppix@ttyp0[knoppix]$ sudo dd if=/dev/zero of=/dev/hda bs=512 count=1
```

While blanking the partition table in effect prevents you from accessing files on the drive, it isn't a replacement for proper wiping of the complete drive, because the files are still potentially retrievable from the drive. Even the partition table itself is recoverable with the right tools **[Hack #55]**.

Resurrect the MBR

If you deleted your boot sector in the last section, you probably want to restore it now. To do this, copy the backup you made earlier to your home directory in Knoppix and run:

```
knoppix@ttyp0[knoppix]$ sudo dd if=/home/knoppix/mbr_backup of=/dev/hda
bs=446 count=1
```

Because of the **bs=446** element, this command only restores the boot code in the MBR. I purposely left out the last 66 bytes of the file so the partition table would not be overwritten (just in case you have repartitioned or changed any partition sizes since your last MBR backup). If you have accidentally corrupted or deleted your partition table, restore the full 512 bytes to the MBR with:

```
knoppix@ttyp0[knoppix]$ sudo dd if=mbr_backup of=/dev/hda bs=512 count=1
```

How Do I fdisk/mbr?

Knoppix also provides a useful tool called *install-mbr* that allows you to manipulate the MBR in many ways. The most useful feature of this tool is that it can install a "default" master boot record on a drive, which is useful if you want to remove *lilo* or *grub* completely from the MBR so Windows can boot by itself, or so you can install Windows to a hard drive that previously used Linux. The results are the same as if you were to type **fdisk /mbr** in DOS. To remove the traces of *lilo* or *grub* from your MBR, run:

```
knoppix@ttyp0[knoppix]$ sudo install-mbr /dev/hda
```

Replace */dev/hda* with your drive.

See Also

- The *install-mbr* manpage by typing **man install-mbr** in a console.

 ## Find Lost Partitions

#55   If you have ever made a typo when deleting or restoring the MBR, you probably also have trashed your partition table. Use gpart, included on the Knoppix disc, to restore lost partition tables.

OK, so you had a little too much fun with the previous hack, ignored the warnings, accidentally typed 512 when you should have typed 446, and now your partition table is gone. Or maybe you accidentally ran *fdisk* on the wrong drive. No problem. Just restore from the backup you made before you started. You did back up your MBR, right? Don't worry; it happens to the best of us. The last time I trashed my partition table, I was trying to update *grub* on my laptop using *dd*. Like an idiot, I followed the instructions to create a *grub* boot floppy and applied them to install *grub* on my laptop's hard drive. Overwriting the first 512 bytes of a *floppy* with the *grub* boot sector is fine; overwriting the first 512 bytes of my *hard drive* is not. I was unable to boot and had no partition table. For many people, this might have been the time to reinstall, but I knew the files and partitions were there—I just couldn't get to them. If only I had a tool to figure out where the partitions began and ended, I could then recreate my partition table and everything would be back to normal.

Lucky for me, there is such a tool: *gpart* (short for "guess partition"). *Gpart* scans a hard drive for signs of a partition's start by comparing a list of filesystem-recognition modules it has with the sectors it is scanning, and then creates a partition table based on these guesses. Doubly lucky for me, *gpart* comes included with Knoppix, so I was able to restore my laptop's MBR without having to take apart the laptop and hook the drive to a desktop machine. I ran *gpart*, checked over its guesses, which matched my drive, and voila! My partitions were back.

Gpart is an incredibly useful tool, and I am grateful for it; however, it does have its limitations. *Gpart* works best when you are restoring a partition table of primary partitions. In the case of extended partitions, *gpart* tries its best to recover the partition information, but there is less of a chance of recovery.

To recover your partition table, run *gpart*, and then tell it to scan your drive:

```
knoppix@ttyp0[knoppix]$ sudo gpart /dev/hda
```

By default, *gpart* only scans the drive and outputs results; it does not actually write to the drive or overwrite your MBR. This is important because *gpart* may not correctly guess all of your partitions, so you should check its guesses before you actually write them to disk.

Gpart scans through the hard drive and outputs possible partition tables as it finds them. When it is finished scanning the drive, *gpart* outputs a complete list of partition tables it has found. Read through this list of partitions and make sure that it reflects the partitions you have created on the disk. It might be that *gpart* can recover only some of the partitions on the drive. Once you have reviewed the partitions that *gpart* has guessed, run *gpart* again but with the -W option to write the guessed partition table to the disk:

```
knoppix@ttyp0[knoppix]$ sudo gpart -W /dev/hda /dev/hda
```

This isn't a typo; you do actually put */dev/hda* twice in the command. You can potentially tell *gpart* to write the partition table to a second drive, based on what it detected on the first drive. Once the partition table has been written, reboot and attempt to access the drives again. If you get errors when mounting the drives, check the partitioning within Knoppix with a tool like *fdisk*, *cfdisk*, or *qtparted* to see whether *gpart* has incorrectly guessed where your partition ends. I've had to modify a partition that *gpart* ended 4 MB too early, but afterwards, the filesystem mounted correctly, and I was able to access all of my files.

It is scary to be in a position where you must think about partition-table recovery. At least with Knoppix and *gpart*, it's possible to recover the partition table without completely reinstalling the operating system.

HACK #56 Resize Linux Partitions

Use utilities, such as qtparted and parted, to resize ext2, ext3, linux-swap, ReiserFS, and XFS partitions.

Despite even the best planning, files sometimes fill up a partition. In the case of a drive with multiple partitions, you might end up moving one of the partitions to a second drive, back up the first drive, increase the size of the first partition, and restore. Of course, to back up and restore, you must have a spare drive large enough to store your important files, which may not always be the case. If you have a Knoppix CD handy, you can quickly and easily resize partitions without having to back up and restore.

> While resizing partitions does not require a backup and restore, resizing partitions is always a potentially dangerous activity that could result in data loss. Back up any important data on a partition, if possible, before you attempt to resize it.

Use the *QTParted* utility to resize partitions easily. This graphical tool lets you add, delete, move, and resize partitions with many filesystems, including ext2, ext3, ReiserFS, XFS, FAT, FAT32, and NTFS. To start *QTParted*, click K Menu → System → QTParted. The *QTParted* window that appears has two main sections: a left panel, which contains all the disks on the system, and a right panel, which displays partitions from the disk that you have selected on the left.

First, select the disk that has the partitions to be resized from the left panel. *QTParted* scans all of the partitions on that drive and displays them graphically along the top of the right panel. Below the graphical display is a table that lists all the drive's partitions with information, such as the partition's filesystem type, size, and used space. If you need to delete a different partition to make room to resize this partition, you must first delete the partition. To delete a partition, right-click on the partition in the right panel (either on the graphical representation or in the table) and choose the Delete option. The partition is not actually deleted until you commit your changes by clicking File → Commit.

To resize a partition, right-click on the partition you want to resize and select Resize. The window that appears allows you to drag the corners of the partition to increase its size, or you can enter the new size manually in a lower text box (see Figure 6-1). Once the partition is resized to your liking, click OK and then commit your changes. Once you commit your changes, the filesystem is officially resized. You might want to reboot your machine to make sure that the changes to the partition table have been applied universally.

Resize Without X

QTParted is an easy and useful program, but what if you don't have access to X? *Parted* is the command-line backend for *QTParted*. Start *parted* from a terminal by running:

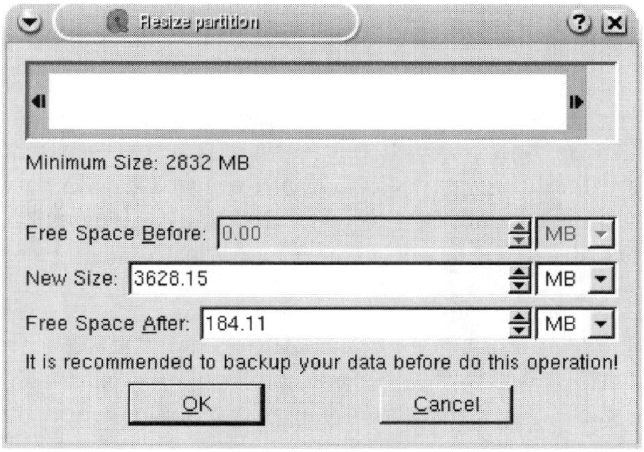

Figure 6-1. QTParted resize window

```
knoppix@ttyp0[knoppix]$ sudo parted /dev/hda
GNU Parted 1.6.9
Copyright (C) 1998, 1999, 2000, 2001, 2002, 2003 Free Software Foundation,
Inc.
This program is free software, covered by the GNU General Public License.

This program is distributed in the hope that it will be useful, but WITHOUT
ANY WARRANTY; without even the implied warranty of MERCHANTABILITY or
FITNESS FOR A PARTICULAR PURPOSE.  See the GNU General Public License for
more details.

Using /dev/hda
Information: The operating system thinks the geometry on /dev/hda is
4865/255/63.  Therefore, cylinder 1024 ends at 8032.499M.
(parted)
```

Replace */dev/hda* with the drive containing partitions you wish to resize. To
see a full list of *parted* commands and their syntax, type:

```
(parted) help
```

If you want help on a specific command, type:

```
(parted) help command
```

To list your drives partition table, type:

```
(parted) print
Disk geometry for /dev/hda: 0.000-38166.679 megabytes
Disk label type: msdos
Minor    Start        End      Type      Filesystem  Flags
1        0.031    38162.219  primary    fat32       boot, lba
(parted)
```

The partition table that *parted* outputs shows you the minor number, the start, the end, the partition type, the filesystem, and any flags the partition has. Reference this information as you use the resize command.

Once you have found the partition you want to resize, note its minor number, where it starts, and then where you want it to end. *Parted* displays the start and end values in megabytes, so if you want to grow a partition by 500 MB, add 500 to the end value. If you want to shrink the partition by 500 MB, simply subtract 500 from the end value. Once you are ready to resize, type:

> (parted) **resize 1 0.031 2000.000**

where *1* is the minor number for your partition, *0.031* is the starting point in megabytes, and *2000.000* is the ending point in megabytes. Of course, replace these values with the actual values of your partition. Once you are finished, exit by typing:

> (parted) **quit**

There are many other filesystem-specific tools on Knoppix that can resize partitions, such as *resize2fs*, *resize_reiserfs*, and *xfs_growfs*, but *QTParted* and *parted* take much of the work and risk out of resizing your partitions, and, if possible, I recommend trying these utilities before using filesystem-specific utilities.

Repair Damaged Filesystems

#57   Benefit from utilities included with Knoppix to repair corrupted filesystems, including ext2, ext3, ReiserFS, and XFS.

Whether it's due to a system that has lost power due to a UPS, a bad IDE cable, an IDE bus error, or some other bug, filesystems are sometimes damaged and must be repaired. Most filesystem-repair utilities require that the partition to be repaired is not mounted, and for repairs to the / partition, it is necessary to use a repair disc such as Knoppix. One advantage to using Knoppix for filesystem repair is that it includes tools to scan and repair all of the major filesystems under Linux on a single CD, in addition to tools to check MSDOS partitions for consistency. Besides, a filesystem check on a 100-GB ext2 partition can take quite some time, and Knoppix has a complete system full of other tools to pass the time while the filesystem check finishes.

The primary tool used to check and repair filesystems under Linux is *fsck* (short for FileSystem ChecK). If the power goes out while you are running a Linux system on an ext2 filesystem or a system freezes before you can unmount a filesystem, this tool comes up and checks the filesystem on the next boot. If an ext2 filesystem has a lot of corruption or is the root partition, you might be prompted to boot into single-user mode (or boot onto a rescue CD) and run a complete *fsck* from there on the unmounted filesystem. The *fsck* tool is actually a frontend to many filesystem-specific repair tools located in */sbin* named *fsck.filesystem*. When you run *fsck* on a filesystem, it attempts to guess the filesystem and run the appropriate tool. By default, most *fsck* programs scan through the filesystem for consistency errors, and if any are found, it prompts you before it attempts to repair them.

For all of the following examples, be sure that the filesystem you are scanning is not mounted. You must always run *fsck* under *sudo* in Knoppix, because the filesystems require root permissions to modify anything.

Ext2/Ext3

For ext2 and ext3 filesystems, the filesystem repair tool is *fsck.ext2* or *e2fsck*. To scan and repair a filesystem, simply run:

```
knoppix@ttyp0[knoppix]$ sudo fsck /dev/hda1
```

Replace */dev/hda1* with the partition you want to scan. If you want a nifty progress bar, add a -C option. If there are multiple filesystems you want to check, you can list them one after another on the command line.

ReiserFS

ReiserFS filesystems are repaired using the *fsck.reiserfs* or *reiserfsck* tools. *Reiserfsck* performs many levels of filesystem checking and repairing, and reports different error codes based on the problem at hand. First, check the filesystem for errors with the following command:

```
knoppix@ttyp0[knoppix]$ sudo reiserfsck --check /dev/hda1
```

Replace */dev/hda1* with the partition you want to scan. By default, *reiserfsck* outputs all progress to STDERR (you should see the output on the console), but if you want it to output to a file instead, use the --logfile option. If *reiserfsck* exits with a status of 0, then it hasn't discovered any errors. If it exits with a status of 1 and reports that there are fixable corruptions, then the next step is to fix those corruptions with the following command:

```
knoppix@ttyp0[knoppix]$ sudo reiserfsck --fix-fixable /dev/hda1
```

Otherwise, if *reiserfsck* reports fatal corruptions and exits with a status of 2, then you must make a backup of the complete partition, if possible, with *dd* or another tool **[Hack #48]**. Then cross your fingers, and attempt to rebuild the entire filesystem with this command:

```
knoppix@ttyp0[knoppix]$ sudo reiserfsck --rebuild-tree /dev/hda1
```

It is important that you do not interrupt the rebuild process. If you do interrupt it, the filesystem remains in an unmountable state until you finish rebuilding the tree.

XFS

Like ReiserFS, XFS comes with its own set of filesystem check and recovery tools. XFS uses *xfs_check* and *xfs_repair* for these tasks. To check an XFS filesystem for inconsistency, run:

    knoppix@ttyp0[knoppix]$ **sudo xfs_check /dev/hda1**

Replace */dev/hda1* with your partition. *Xfs_check* generates output that indicates that it has found inconsistencies on the filesystem that must be repaired. To repair the filesystem, run:

    knoppix@ttyp0[knoppix]$ **sudo xfs_repair /dev/hda1**

The *xfs_repair* utility outputs information about the repairs it is making, but does not prompt you to approve any of the changes, so be sure you have backed up any important files before running the repair, just in case. The *xfs_check* manpage also lists *xfsdump* and *xfsrestore* to move the filesystem to a newly created XFS partition in lieu of the in-place repair that *xfs_repair* performs.

While I have listed the primary methods you should use to check and repair a filesystem with Knoppix, there are also many other filesystem-specific options you can pass to these programs to suit a particular error your filesystem might have. Each of these programs has in-depth manpages accessible on the Knoppix CD. To list options and standard usage, run:

    knoppix@ttyp0[knoppix]$ **man *programname***

Some of the more sophisticated filesystems, particularly XFS, have many unique options that are worth referencing, as they differ from *fsck*.

See Also

* The *fsck* manpage by typing **man fsck** in a console.

HACK #58   Recover Deleted Files

Recover accidentally deleted files with unrm and lazarus.

When you use *rm* to remove a file in Linux, you generally consider that file completely gone. Unlike in the DOS days, you can't simply run through a list of undeleted filenames hoping your file hasn't been overwritten, because Linux unlinks a file when it is removed and no longer keeps track of it other than to note that the space is free. But if you have accidentally removed a very important file, there is still a chance you can recover the file, especially if the file is small, by using the *unrm* and *lazarus* utilities included as part of the Coroner's Toolkit (*http://www.porcupine.org/forensics/tct.html*).

If you have just deleted a file you want to recover, *turn off the machine now*! The *unrm* utility works by recovering files from the free space on your drive. When you delete a file, the system unlinks it and adds that space to the free space on the system, but it doesn't actually overwrite that segment of the hard drive with zeros. While you can't actually access the file any longer, the file still remains until a new file is written over it. The longer that system is running, the greater the chance that a new file that is written to the drive will be written over that space. Use Knoppix for file recovery to unmount the partition you intend to scan and eliminate the risk that new files will be written over the files that you are recovering.

Before you start, make sure you have an extra partition or drive available for *unrm* and *lazarus* to write its information to. The general rule of thumb is to allow at least 220% of the free space on the partition you are recovering from. Basically, *unrm* creates a copy of the entire free space into a file (~100%), and *lazarus* creates individual files based on the *unrm* file (~100%), with the HTML files and some other overhead it creates (~20%). Use the *df* command to figure out the free space on a drive:

```
knoppix@ttyp0[knoppix]$ df -h
Filesystem      Size  Used Avail Use% Mounted on
/dev/root       3.0M  1.1M  1.9M  38% /
/dev/scd0       690M  690M     0 100% /cdrom
/dev/cloop      1.9G  1.9G     0 100% /KNOPPIX
/ramdisk        396M  159M  238M  41% /ramdisk
/dev/hda1        93M   82M  6.4M  93% /mnt/hda1
/dev/hda2        38G   26G   12G  69% /mnt/hda2
```

The -h option passed to *df* displays the file sizes in megabytes and gigabytes where applicable, instead of just kilobytes. In this example, */dev/hda1* has 6.4 MB of free space, and */dev/hda2* has 12 GB. To recover a file from */dev/hda1*, you need at least 14 MB of free space. To recover a file from */dev/hda2*, you need at least 26.4 GB of free space.

It is important that you put your output on a different partition than the partition you recover, because otherwise, your *unrm* output has the potential to erase the very files you are trying to recover! Click on the icon for the partition on which you decide to store your output, then right-click on the icon and choose Actions → change read/write so you can write to it. You can also open a terminal and type:

```
knoppix@ttyp0[knoppix]$ sudo mount -o rw /dev/hda2 /mnt/hda2
```

Replace */dev/hda2* with your *recover to* partition. This example recovers the possible data from */dev/hda1* and stores the output on */mnt/hda2*. Create a directory to store the output, and then run *unrm* on your *recover from* partition:

```
knoppix@ttyp0[knoppix]$ sudo mkdir /mnt/hda2/unrm
knoppix@ttyp0[knoppix]$ sudo sh -c "unrm /dev/hda1 > /mnt/hda2/unrm/output"
```

A new file called *output* is created in the *unrm* directory that contains all of the free-space blocks on */dev/hda1*. Now use *lazarus* to analyze that file and split up the blocks into individual files. Create a *blocks* directory inside your *unrm* directory to store all of the files, just so they are separate from the rest of the output:

```
knoppix@ttyp0[knoppix]$ cd /mnt/hda2/unrm
knoppix@ttyp0[unrm]$ sudo mkdir blocks
knoppix@ttyp0[unrm]$ sudo lazarus -h -w . -D blocks output
```

The -h option tells *lazarus* to output results in the form of HTML files. The -w option defines where to store the HTML frames for each file—in this case, the current directory. The -D option tells *lazarus* where to store all of the files it recovers. The reason for all of these options is that by default *lazarus* stores all of its output under */var/cache/tct*. On Knoppix, this directory is part of the ram-disk and is limited in size, so you must tell *lazarus* to move the output to a directory with plenty of space.

Once *lazarus* completes, you should notice many *.html* files in the current directory, and many *.txt* files in the blocks directory. The *.txt* files in the *blocks* directory are all of the blocks that *lazarus* has recovered. The files are numbered, so you can't find the file you deleted just from the filename. If you have a lot of time on your hands, you can open each file, but if you can remember at least part of the contents of the file, you can use *grep* to search for it.

Try to think of some contents in the file that might be unique. For instance, to recover an email you have sent to sexy_chick4957@aol.com, go to the *blocks* directory and type:

```
knoppix@ttyp0[blocks]$ grep -i -l 'sexy_chick4957@aol.com'
```

The -l option lists only the filenames that contain that email address. Remove this option to output the filename and the matching line. The -i option performs a case-insensitive search. If you have sent a lot of emails to that address and are trying to narrow the search to a particular email about your birthday, run a second instance of *grep* that searches the files that the first *grep* has listed, by strings containing the word *birthday*:

```
knoppix@ttyp0[blocks]$ grep 'birthday' `grep -il 'sexy_chick4957@aol.com'`
```

If you can't seem to find the file you need with *grep*, or the file you are trying to recover is binary, go back to the *unrm* directory and open the HTML output page that *lazarus* has generated with this command:.

```
knoppix@ttyp0[unrm]$ mozilla file:///mnt/hda2/unrm/output.frame.html
```

This page (as shown in Figure 6-2) provides a view of the recovered blocks in the form of color-coded files. Along the top frame of the file is a key showing what all of the colors and letters represent.

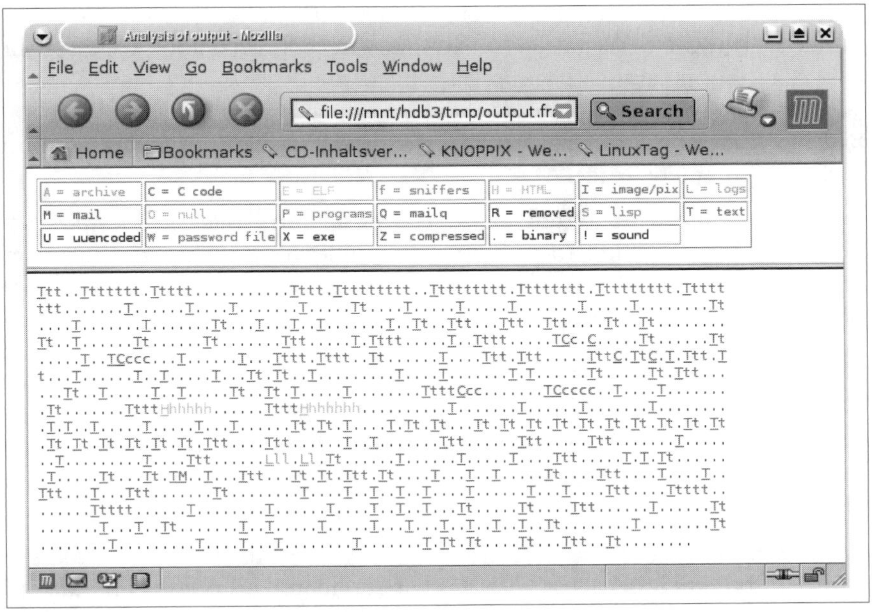

Figure 6-2. Lazarus HTML output

If you are looking for a lost email, look through the page for blue Ms. Click on any of the links to view that particular file. With luck, you should be able to recover at least a part of the deleted file this way.

HACK #59 Rescue Files from Damaged Hard Drives

When your hard drive is damaged or is on its last leg, use Knoppix to recover what's left on the drive and attempt to restore it.

Hard drives continue to get larger and more complicated, and at least in the desktop IDE market, hard drives seem to be getting less and less reliable. If you don't believe me, search the Internet for "IBM Deathstar" (referring to problems in the 60GXP and 75GXP series of hard drives). While a three-year warranty guarantees you a replacement drive, if your drive fails, there is no way to receive replacement data. When your hard drive starts to fail, you might notice that it becomes much louder than it used to be and makes a loud clicking noise that sounds a bit like your hard drive is crushing ice. Your drive has the click of death. In addition to general file-access failures, the click of death is the main indicator that your hard drive is dying and should be backed up immediately.

Unfortunately, most backup and imaging utilities operate on the assumption that they are running on fully functioning hardware. When a hard drive is dying, many backup utilities won't be able to handle the different access errors. If your drive has gotten so bad that you can't even boot from it, your best chance of creating a backup is to image the drive "Clone Hard Drives" **[Hack #48]**. But even the faithful *dd* program exits out with an error if it hits a bad block in a file, so if you try to image a failing hard drive, you end up with an incomplete image.

Knoppix comes with a tool called *dd_rescue* (*http://www.garloff.de/kurt/ linux/ddrescue*) that aims to pick up where *dd* leaves off when reading from questionable drives. When *dd_rescue* comes across a bad block, it simply skips it and moves on by default, or it can be set to move on after a certain number of failures. On a failing drive, this means you can create an image of a full partition with some holes here and there, and then use *fsck* to try to repair some of the damage on the filesystem. By using Knoppix for this recovery, you access the drives as little as possible, so you are only putting strain on the bad drive long enough to make a single copy, and then you can browse around the image from a fully functioning drive.

While you can do the complete drive rescue with the *dd_rescue* tool, there is a helper frontend tool called *dd_rhelp* that automates and speeds up much of the process. *Dd_rescue* doesn't stop when it hits bad sectors, but it does slow down significantly. If your drive has a number of bad blocks in a row, it can take *dd_rescue* a long time to move past them into recoverable data. If the drive is going to fail quickly, this means your drive can fail while *dd_rescue* is waiting on bad blocks. *Dd_rhelp* speeds up this process by assuming that bad blocks are generally in groups. When *dd_rhelp* sees that *dd_rescue* has hit a bad block, it skips ahead a number of blocks and reads from that point in reverse until it hits another bad block. It uses this method to map out sections of bad blocks on the drive and attempts to recover the good blocks first. Then, when it has recovered the good blocks, it goes back and tries to recover from the group of bad blocks.

Time is precious when a drive is failing, so *dd_rhelp* tries to spend more time recovering good data, and then goes back to recover questionable data if it can. There are other benefits to *dd_rhelp*, such as it can use the logs that *dd_rescue* generates to resume a rescue operation that you have stopped with Ctrl-C. Also, *dd_rhelp* generates nice ASCII output that shows you where it is on your drive and which bad blocks it has discovered.

So your drive has the click of death, and some files are missing. Don't panic. You should still be able to recover most or all of your data. First, you need something to store the disk image on. You are using Knoppix, so you can save the image to any drive that Knoppix supports, including locally mounted drives, USB drives, and remote file servers. This drive must be

large enough to hold a complete image of the failing disk partition, so even if
you have 7 GB free on a 10-GB drive, you still need 10 GB of space on a second drive to back up the image.

Boot Knoppix. Open a browser and go to *http://www.garloff.de/kurt/linux/
ddrescue/*. Knoppix includes *dd_rescue* v1.02, but *dd_rhelp* requires v1.03.
Download Version 1.03 or greater to your home directory, create a local *bin*
directory to hold the binaries (so the new *dd_rescue* is run instead of the one
shipped with Knoppix), and extract *dd_rescue* to that directory:

```
knoppix@ttyp0[knoppix]$ mkdir -p ~/.dist/bin
knoppix@ttyp0[knoppix]$ tar xzf dd_rescue-1.03.tar.gz dd_rescue
knoppix@ttyp0[knoppix]$ mv dd_rescue ~/.dist/bin
```

Now browse to *http://www.kalysto.ath.cx/utilities/dd_rhelp/index.en.html*
and download the latest version of the *dd_rhelp* tool to your home directory. Open a terminal, extract the files from the *dd_rhelp-version.tar.gz* file
that you have downloaded, and change to the directory it creates. Then
compile the program and copy the new *dd_rhelp* binary to your local *bin*
directory with *dd_rescue*:

```
knoppix@ttyp0[knoppix]$ tar xzf dd_rhelp-0.0.5.tar.gz
knoppix@ttyp0[knoppix]$ cd dd_rhelp-0.0.5/
knoppix@ttyp0[dd_rhelp-0.0.5]$ ./configure && make
checking for a BSD-compatible install... /usr/bin/install -c
checking whether build environment is sane... yes
checking for gawk... gawk
checking whether make sets $(MAKE)... yes
checking for a BSD-compatible install... /usr/bin/install -c
checking for bash... /bin/sh
configure: creating ./config.status
config.status: creating Makefile
config.status: creating src/include/begin-sh
config.status: creating src/include/copyright-sh
config.status: creating src/include/end-sh
config.status: creating src/include/vars-sh
rm -f dd_rhelp
echo "#!/bin/sh" > dd_rhelp
cat ./src/include/begin-sh >> dd_rhelp
cat ./src/include/copyright-sh >> dd_rhelp
cat ./src/include/GPL-sh >> dd_rhelp
echo "# TODO : " >> dd_rhelp
cat ./TODO | sed 's/^/# /g' >> dd_rhelp
cat ./src/include/vars-sh >> dd_rhelp
echo "# Including 'libcolor.sh'" >> dd_rhelp
cat ./src/include/libcolor.sh >> dd_rhelp
echo "# Including 'libcommon.sh'" >> dd_rhelp
cat ./src/include/libcommon.sh >> dd_rhelp
cat ./src/dd_rhelp-sh >> dd_rhelp
cat ./src/include/end-sh >> dd_rhelp
chmod ugo+x dd_rhelp
knoppix@ttyp0[dd_rhelp-0.0.5]$ cp dd_rhelp ~/.dist/bin/
```

Mount the drive to which you are saving the image with read/write access. You don't need to mount the problem drive (if the drive is far enough gone, you aren't able to mount it anyway). Then run *dd_rhelp*:

```
knoppix@ttyp0[knoppix]$ sudo mount -o rw /dev/hdb1 /mnt/hdb1
knoppix@ttyp0[knoppix]$ sudo dd_rhelp /dev/hda1 /mnt/hdb1/hda1_rescue.img
=== launched via 'dd_rhelp' at 0k, 0 >>> ===
dd_rescue: (info): ipos:   1048444.0k, opos:   1048444.0k, xferd:   1048444.
0k
                 *  errs:        0, errxfer:        0.0k, succxfer:   1048444.
0k
                  +curr.rate:    8339kB/s, avg.rate:     7564kB/s, avg.load:  7.
9%
dd_rescue: (warning): /dev/hda1 (1048444.0k): Input/output error!
dd_rescue: (info): ipos:   1048444.5k, opos:   1048444.5k, xferd:   1048444.
5k
                 *  errs:        1, errxfer:        0.5k, succxfer:   1048444.
0k
                  +curr.rate:     812kB/s, avg.rate:     7564kB/s, avg.load:  7.
9%
dd_rescue: (warning): /dev/hda1 (1048444.5k): Input/output error!
dd_rescue: (info): ipos:   1048445.0k, opos:   1048445.0k, xferd:   1048445.
0k
                 *  errs:        2, errxfer:        1.0k, succxfer:   1048444.
0k
                  +curr.rate:    1057kB/s, avg.rate:     7564kB/s, avg.load:  7.
9%
dd_rescue: (warning): /dev/hda1 (1048445.0k): Input/output error!
dd_rescue: (info): ipos:   1048445.5k, opos:   1048445.5k, xferd:   1048445.
5k
                 *  errs:        3, errxfer:        1.5k, succxfer:   1048444.
0k
                  +curr.rate:     994kB/s, avg.rate:     7564kB/s, avg.load:  7.
9%
dd_rescue: (warning): /dev/hda1 (1048445.5k): Input/output error!


dd_rescue: (info): /dev/hda1 (1048446.0k): EOF
Summary for /dev/hda1 -> /mnt/hdb1/hda1_rescue.img:
dd_rescue: (info): ipos:   1048446.0k, opos:   1048446.0k, xferd:   1048446.
0k
                    errs:        4, errxfer:        2.0k, succxfer:   1048444.
0k
                  +curr.rate:    1042kB/s, avg.rate:     7564kB/s, avg.load:  7.
9%
knoppix@ttyp0[knoppix]$
```

Replace */dev/hda1* with the partition that you are recovering, and */mnt/hdb1* with the mount point where you are saving the image. As *dd_rhelp* scans the drive, it prints out all of its progress, including any errors it finds. When it finishes, you should have two files in your recovery drive: the image and a log from *dd_rescue*, in case you want to audit its progress.

Now, run *fsck* on the image to attempt to repair any filesystem errors that might have occurred **[Hack #57]** by typing this command:

```
knoppix@ttyp0[knoppix]$ sudo fsck -y /mnt/hdb1/hda1_rescue.img
fsck 1.35 (28-Feb-2004)
e2fsck 1.35 (28-Feb-2004)
/mnt/hdb1/hda1_rescue.img: clean, 12/131072 files, 187767/262111 blocks
```

The -y option tells *fsck* to automatically repair any filesystem errors it finds. Mount the image with the -o loop option, and you should be able to access your files at that mount point as if it were a hard drive:

```
knoppix@ttyp0[knoppix]$ sudo mount -o loop /mnt/hdb1/hda1_rescue.img /mnt/
hda1
```

H A C K   Backup and Restore
#60
Use the classic tar command with Knoppix to quickly back up and restore important files.

If you have just gone through a filesystem repair unsuccessfully, then you probably have lost some files. No problem. You can just restore them from your backup. If you don't back up all of your important files, then there's no time like the present to start. Knoppix comes with the venerable *tar* command, which is used by system administrators to back up important files, and this hack covers using *tar* to back up and restore a system.

Generally, you want to run *tar* directly from the machine you are backing up, as opposed to using a rescue CD, so that you don't have to take down the server each time you need to refresh the backup. Although sometimes you might be in a situation where you want a complete backup of a system that has many files in a constant state of flux, you don't want any of the files to change while you are backing them up. You also usually run *tar* to restore lost files from the running machine itself, but in the situation that the missing files are preventing the machine from booting at all, you might need to make use of a rescue disk like Knoppix to restore the important files to the system so it can boot.

Back Up

Tar has many options, but the basics of creating a backup are pretty simple to remember. First, you should back up the */etc* directory. On most Linux systems, */etc* stores only text files, which compress to a very small size. If you have worked hard to configure a program and you delete or break that configuration, it can be upsetting and time-consuming to replace. To back up the */etc* directory from a root partition that you have mounted on */mnt/hda1*, you should change to the */mnt/hda1* directory and issue the following command:

```
knoppix@tty1[hda1]$ sudo tar cvzf /home/knoppix/etc.tar.gz etc/
```

Tar outputs the files it is backing up, and you should find a new file, *etc.tar.gz*, in your */home/knoppix* directory. Now, if you are backing up from Knoppix, you do not want to back up to your ramdisk, but instead want to back up to another mounted partition or over the network to another machine. As in "Clone Hard Drives" **[Hack #48]**, you can pipe *tar* to *ssh* to save to a remote file, as in:

```
knoppix@tty1[hda1]$ sudo tar cvzf - etc/ | ssh username@192.168.0.2
"cat > /home/username/etc.tar.gz"
```

Restore

To restore from this archive, replace the -c option with x in the previous command line; otherwise, the standard command is the same. Because the command is so similar, be careful that you restore when you want to restore and create when you want to create; otherwise, you might overwrite your backup instead of restoring to it. Mount the filesystem you want to restore to with read/write permissions, *cd* to the mounted directory, and run:

```
knoppix@tty1[hda1]$ sudo tar xvzf /home/knoppix/etc.tar.gz
```

Tar extracts the files into the current directory and overwrites any duplicate files it finds. If you pipe *tar* to *ssh* to save to a remote file, *cd* to the mounted directory and reverse the pipe:

```
knoppix@tty1[hda1]$ ssh username@192.168.0.2 "cat > /home/username/etc.tar.
gz" | sudo tar xvfz -
```

Back Up and Restore a Full Partition

You can also use *tar* to back up an entire partition to a remote location or another mounted filesystem. First, mount the filesystem, *cd* to it, and then use a dot (.) to specify the current directory instead of *etc/*. If you are backing up a large filesystem, you should be backing it up to another mounted filesystem, such as */mnt/hdb1*:

```
knoppix@tty1[hda1]$ sudo tar cvzf /mnt/hdb1/hda1.tar.gz ./
```

Replace */mnt/hdb1* with the mounted filesystem to which to save this archive. To save a backup over the network, you can pipe *tar* to *ssh* with this command:

```
knoppix@tty1[hda1]$ sudo tar cvzf - ./ | ssh username@192.168.0.2
"cat > /home/username/hda1.tar.gz"
```

To restore, mount the filesystem you wish to restore, *cd* to it, and run the same command used to restore from *etc.tar.gz*. If you only want to restore a particular directory—for instance, */home*—then specify that directory on the command line like so:

```
knoppix@tty1[hda1]$ sudo tar xvzf /mnt/hdb1/hda1.tar.gz home/
```

Tar is an old archival tool but still does a great job for back up and recovery in most circumstances. With these basic backup and recovery options, you can take a Knoppix CD to any machine, and back up or recover important files quickly with consistent results and without worrying about backed up or restored files being written to by other programs in the process.

HACK #61 Migrate to a New Hard Drive
Move your complete system to a new hard drive.

Not only do hard drives hold your programs and data, but they fill up and run out of free space sooner than you would like. When this happens, it's time to buy a larger hard drive and migrate the system. While there are many different ways to copy files from one hard drive to another, some work better than others when transferring the full / directory. This hack outlines a method to transfer full systems and partitions from one machine to another.

Why This Can Be Complicated

When you copy a full Linux system from one partition to another, there are a few issues you need to consider:

Preserve permissions
> If your files aren't owned by the same people and have the same permissions, your new system probably does not run as expected.

Properly handle special files
> Certain methods of copying a system don't properly handle the */dev* and */proc* filesystems. As a result, you boot on the new drive only to find you have no device entries listed.

Span filesystems
> When you copy one filesystem to another, especially the root filesystem, you don't want to span across filesystems. For example, if you have a new hard drive mounted at */mnt/temp* and you recursively copy / to */mnt/temp* and allow filesystem spanning, you could end up with */mnt/temp* copied into */mnt/temp/mnt/temp* and */mnt/temp/mnt/temp* copied to */mnt/temp/mnt/temp/mnt/temp* (not to mention the rest of the filesystem you have copied to */mnt/temp*). To avoid this, most copy programs have an option to copy only the mounted filesystem it is started from without continuing to other mounted filesystems.

Knoppix removes some of these complications. For instance, if you are booting on top of a system, you no longer have to worry about whether the copy method spans filesystems, because each filesystem is mounted under */mnt* only when you choose to mount it.

What to Do

The best method to copy the / filesystem combines *find* with *cpio* (both are utilities that are standard on any Linux distribution, including Knoppix). This example transfers a Linux installation from a single-root partition on */dev/hda1* to */dev/hdb1*, which is a freshly formatted partition that becomes the new root partition:

```
knoppix@tty0[knoppix] sudo mount /mnt/hda1
knoppix@tty0[knoppix] sudo mount -o rw /mnt/hdb1
knoppix@tty0[knoppix] cd /mnt/hda1
knoppix@tty0[hda1] sudo sh -c "find ./ -xdev -print0 | cpio -paoV /mnt/hdb1"
```

This example uses */mnt/hda1* and */mnt/hdb1*, but you should change those values to the two partitions you are using. When you run this command, it recursively copies everything on the */mnt/hda1* filesystem, without crossing over into other mounted partitions. It properly handles any special files, and it completely preserves permissions. For each file that is copied, this command prints out a single dot to the screen, so you get a sense of the progress. If you want more specific information on the progress, use the *watch* command in a different terminal:

```
knoppix@tty0[knoppix] watch df
```

The *watch* command runs *df* every two seconds and allows you to compare the used and available space on both the old and new partitions.

If you have other filesystems mounted on other partitions, you simply repeat the command and replace *hda1* and *hdb1* with the new partitions you want to copy from and migrate to, respectively.

After the partitions have been migrated, edit the */etc/fstab* file on the new partition if any partition numbers have changed. Remember to change */etc/fstab* entries to reflect the partition letters the new drive has once it is moved to its final bus location, not the partition letter it is currently assigned.

You must also restore the boot loader to the new partition. Follow the steps in "Repair Lilo" **[Hack #52]** or "Repair Grub" **[Hack #53]**, depending on your boot loader. Once the boot loader is restored, halt the machine, swap the old drive with the new drive, and boot the machine from the new partition and make sure everything has copied over correctly before wiping the old drive and using it for something else.

I have used this method to copy numerous systems from one drive to another, to transfer to a larger partition or a new filesystem, and even to move to software RAID5 (and back). While the options passed to *find* and *cpio* seem daunting at first, I have found this command so useful that it has become engrained in my memory. I usually run this command directly from the system being copied in single-user mode, but it's not necessary. When you use Knoppix, you also don't have to worry about whether files have changed since you started copying them. In addition, while the files are copying, you can browse the Web or play games if watching *df* output bores you.

HACK #62 Create Linux Software RAID
Use Knoppix to create and reconfigure software RAID 0, 1, and 5.

A rescue disk is very handy to configure and change a software RAID, particularly if the RAID is for a complete root partition. Knoppix comes with the major tools you need to create and modify Linux software RAID, and makes it very simple to create new software RAID drives. Linux software RAID supports many different styles of RAID, and this hack covers the three most popular configurations: RAID 0, RAID 1, and RAID 5. This hack assumes a basic familiarity with RAID principles, and a working knowledge of the differences between RAID 0, 1, and 5.

Configure /etc/raidtab

To create a RAID, first edit the */etc/raidtab* configuration file and add a new RAID device. This differs depending on which type of RAID you want to create, so I go over the configuration for each of the three types. I have provided default RAID configurations for each type, because usually */etc/raidtab* is empty or missing by default. Use these configurations as a starting point, and modify them to match your devices.

> When you create a RAID, you don't need to format the partitions beforehand, as they are reformatted after the RAID is created.

RAID 0. RAID 0, also known as striping, combines the storage and speed of two drives into a single larger drive. RAID 0 provides no redundancy, however, so if one drive fails, all of the data is lost. For this example, there are two regular Linux partitions, */dev/hda1* and */dev/hdb1*, of approximately the same size. To set up RAID 0, edit */etc/raidtab* and add any partitions you want to use in the RAID. Open */etc/raidtab* as root, and add the following lines to create a default RAID 0 config:

```
raiddev /dev/md0
  raid-level      0
  nr-raid-disks   2
  persistent-superblock 1
  chunk-size4
  device          /dev/hda1
```

```
raid-disk      0
device         /dev/hdb1
raid-disk      1
```

RAID 1. RAID 1, also known as mirroring, uses two or more partitions essentially as mirrors of each other, so every byte written to one partition is simultaneously written to the other partitions. RAID 1 provides protection from drive failure: if a single partition fails, any other partition on the array still contains all the data, and when the failed partition is replaced, all of the mirrored data is automatically written to the new partition by the RAID program. To create a RAID 1 array across */dev/hda1* and */dev/hdb1*, the configuration in */etc/raidtab* looks very similar to the one used for RAID 0:

```
raiddev /dev/md0
   raid-level      1
   nr-raid-disks   2
   nr-spare-disks  0
   chunk-size      4
   persistent-superblock 1
   device          /dev/hda1
   raid-disk       0
   device          /dev/hdb1
   raid-disk       1
```

Other than changing the raid-level variable from 0 to 1, the primary difference here is the addition of the nr-spare-disks option to configure automatic failover disks, which you can use to automatically replace any failed partitions. In this example, I do not create any spare disks, but I still include the variable set to zero.

RAID 5. RAID 5, also known as striping with parity, combines three or more similarly sized drives into a single larger drive. Any data written to the drive is striped across all drives in the array along with parity information. This parity information effectively uses up the space of a single drive, so if you combine three drives into a RAID 5 array, the array is only the size of two of the drives combined. With this parity information, if any drive fails, the remaining drives can continue running, and once a replacement drive is available, they can restore all of the data, including parity information, to the new drive. Unlike RAID 0 or RAID 1, RAID 5 requires at least three partitions, so this example creates a RAID 5 partition out of */dev/hda1*, */dev/hdb1*, and */dev/hdc1*. First create an */etc/raidtab* to describe your desired RAID:

```
raiddev /dev/md0
   raid-level      5
   nr-raid-disks   3
   nr-spare-disks  0
```

```
persistent-superblock 1
parity-algorithm        left-symmetric
chunk-size      32
device          /dev/hda1
raid-disk       0
device          /dev/hdb1
raid-disk       1
device          /dev/hdc1
raid-disk       2
```

Creating the RAID

Regardless of which RAID you configure, once you have edited */etc/raidtab*, creating the RAID is a simple matter of running:

```
knoppix@tty0[knoppix]$ sudo mkraid /dev/md0
```

At this point, you can read */proc/mdstat* to check the current status of the newly created RAID drive. For example, after you create a RAID 0 array, you see the following output:

```
knoppix@tty0[knoppix]$ cat /proc/mdstat
Personalities : [raid0]
read_ahead 1024 sectors
md0 : active raid0 hdb1[1] hda1[0]
      5242624 blocks 4k chunks

unused devices:
```

At this point, you can treat */dev/md0* like any other partition and format it, mount it, and copy files to it. If you have an existing Linux installation on a different partition and want it to use the RAID, make sure that its kernel supports software RAID and that it has the complete set of Linux software RAID tools like *mkraid*, *raidhotadd*, etc. Use the following command to mount the Linux installation read/write, then copy */etc/raidtab* to the */etc/* directory on that drive:

```
root@tty0[root]# mount -o rw /dev/hda1 /mnt/hda1
```

 Most vendor kernels support RAID by default. If you are building your own kernel, make sure that "Multiple devices driver support" is enabled as are the different RAID modes you want to use in the "Multi-device support" section.

Once you boot the Linux system without Knoppix, check */proc/mdstat* to see if an init script installed by your distribution has automatically started the RAID for you. If the RAID hasn't been started, run:

```
root@tty0[root]# raidstart /dev/md0
```

If your kernel supports software RAID autodetection (check the Multi-device support section in your kernel configuration), you can configure these partitions to be automatically detected by Linux as it boots. To do this, unmount the RAID and stop the array with:

```
root@tty0[root]# umount /dev/md0
root@tty0[root]# raidstop /dev/md0
```

Replace *md0* with the name of your array. Once the RAID is stopped, use *fdisk* or *cfdisk* as root to change the partition type for each partition in the RAID-to-RAID autodetection. By default, Linux partitions are of type 83, but there is a special partition type, fd, set aside for Linux RAID autodetection. Once you change the partition type for the partitions, write the changes and reboot. A Linux kernel that supports software RAID autodetection automatically starts the device during boot and stops the device during shutdown.

Configuration of software RAIDs under Linux is pretty straightforward, and with Knoppix, you can easily experiment with RAID configurations on a system full of blank disks. You can also modify an existing RAID and unmount, stop, and start the RAID even if you are configuring a root partition. In addition, you can also leverage most of the filesystem-and-partition copying methods referenced in other hacks to easily copy entire systems over the network to a newly created software RAID, even if your particular distribution doesn't necessarily support installing to RAID by default.

See Also

- "Clone Hard Drives" [Hack #48]
- "Migrate to a New Hard Drive" [Hack #61]

Migrate to Software RAID
#63

Move your entire root partition to RAID 1 or RAID 5 without a backup and restore.

Software RAID can ensure failover protection even on a low budget. If you want to migrate a system to software RAID, you might be faced with the prospect of doing a complete backup and restore. If you have a low budget, you might not have a spare drive to temporarily back up your data to in addition to the drives you are using for the RAID. With a Knoppix disc and the following instructions, you can migrate a system to RAID 1 or 5 with just the disks you are planning to use for the RAID.

RAID 1 and 5 provide failover, so you can run a system and access files even if a drive in the array has failed. You can leverage failover in RAID 1 and 5 to migrate a partition that is not yet software RAID to RAID 1 or 5 if you create the RAID with a failed drive (the current root partition), copy all of the data over to the newly created RAID, boot onto that RAID, and then add the root partition to the RAID. For this to work, all RAID utilities, such as *mkraid* and *raidhotadd*, should already be present on the system. Distribution package names vary, but two examples of package names are *raidtools* and *raidtools2* under Debian. The kernel should already have support for software RAID compiled in, so check the "Multi-device support" section of your kernel's configuration and make sure all the RAID types you wish to use are enabled. This hack covers migrating a complete root filesystem that is on */dev/hda1* to a RAID 1 spanning */dev/hda1* and */dev/hdb1*, or a RAID 5 spanning */dev/hda1*, */dev/hdb1*, and */dev/hdc1*.

First create the array; create */etc/raidtab* in Knoppix and add the following configuration for a RAID 1 array:

```
raiddev /dev/md0
  raid-level       1
  nr-raid-disks    2
  nr-spare-disks   0
  chunk-size       4
  persistent-superblock 1
  device           /dev/hdb1
  raid-disk        0
  device           /dev/hda1
  failed-disk      1
```

Or add the following configuration for a RAID 5 array:

```
raiddev /dev/md0
  raid-level       5
  nr-raid-disks    3
  nr-spare-disks   0
  persistent-superblock 1
  parity-algorithm         left-symmetric
  chunk-size       32
  device           /dev/hdb1
  raid-disk        0
  device           /dev/hdc1
  raid-disk        1
  device           /dev/hda1
  failed-disk       2
```

Notice that the main root partition, */dev/hda1*, is listed as a `failed-disk` for the moment. The RAID tools have problems starting the RAID when the first disk is a failed disk, so list */dev/hda1* last. Once you create this file, start the RAID with this command:

```
knoppix@tty0[knoppix]$ sudo mkraid /dev/md0
```

If you check */proc/mdstat*, it lists the RAID (in this example, a RAID 1):

```
knoppix@tty0[knoppix]$ cat /proc/mdstat
Personalities : [raid1]
read_ahead 1024 sectors
md0 : active raid1 hdb1[1]
      2621312 blocks [2/1] [U_]

unused devices:
```

Now the RAID is created, and you can format it with the filesystem of your choice with:

```
knoppix@tty0[knoppix]$ sudo mkfs -t xfs /dev/md0
```

 Since */dev/hda1* is marked *failed*, the RAID does not overwrite all of the files on that partition yet, and you are safe to format the new RAID partition and copy files to it.

Next, you must create a temporary directory to mount the new RAID, mount the RAID and the original partition read/write, and then copy the system over to the RAID using the same method covered in "Migrate to a New Hard Drive" **[Hack #61]**:

```
knoppix@tty0[knoppix]$ sudo mkdir /mnt/temp
knoppix@tty0[knoppix]$ sudo mount -o rw /dev/md0 /mnt/temp
knoppix@tty0[knoppix]$ sudo mount /dev/hda1 /mnt/hda1
knoppix@tty0[knoppix]$ cd /mnt/hda1
knoppix@tty0[hda1]$ sudo sh -c "find . -xdev -print0 | cpio -paoV /mnt/temp"
```

Once the copy process finishes, copy the */etc/raidtab* in Knoppix to */mnt/temp/etc/*. Then edit */mnt/temp/etc/fstab* and make sure the entry for */dev/hda1* is changed to */dev/md0*. You must also edit *lilo* or *grub* configuration files, and make sure that any root device configuration now references */dev/md0* instead of */dev/hda1*. Be sure to leave any boot device configuration alone so that it installs the boot code onto */dev/hda* instead of */dev/md0*. If you use *lilo* as your boot loader, you must also run *lilo* to update the MBR as covered in "Repair Lilo" **[Hack #52]**.

Once you update all of the configuration files, add the primary partition to the RAID by unmounting */dev/hda1*:

```
knoppix@tty0[knoppix]$ sudo umount /dev/hda1
```

 Note that the data on the partition has remained untouched. Once you add this drive to the array, it will be overwritten with whatever files are already in */dev/md0*, so be sure you are ready before continuing.

To add the drive to the array, edit */etc/raidtab* on the ramdisk, not the RAID, and replace failed-disk with raid-disk. Then, add the drive to the array with the following command:

```
knoppix@tty0[knoppix]$ sudo raidhotadd /dev/md0 /dev/hda1
```

Run the following command to monitor the RAID as it updates */dev/hda1* with all of the mirroring information:

```
knoppix@tty0[knoppix]$ watch cat /proc/mdstat
```

You can still use and write to the RAID while this is going on, so copy the new */etc/raidtab* to */mnt/temp/etc/*. You must wait for the mirror to be completely synced before moving to the next step (*/proc/mdstat* lets you know when you are in sync).

Now enable RAID autodetection for both of the partitions; unmount and stop the RAID:

```
knoppix@tty0[knoppix]$ sudo umount /dev/md0
knoppix@tty0[knoppix]$ sudo raidstop /dev/md0
```

Then run *fdisk* or *cfdisk*, and change the partition type for both */dev/hda1* and */dev/hdb1* from 83 to fd. Then write the changes to make sure that the Linux kernel autodetects this RAID as it boots (which is important because it is the root partition). After autodetection has been enabled, reboot into your new software RAID root partition.

See Also

- The Software RAID HOWTO: */usr/share/doc/raidtools2/Software-RAID. HOWTO* on your Knoppix disc.
- The *raidhotadd*, *mkraid*, *raidstop*, and other RAID tools manpages (type man *commandname* in a console).

Migrate Software RAID 1 to RAID 5

HACK #64

Move an existing software RAID 1 system to RAID 5 without a backup and restore.

After you use a RAID 1 array for some time, you might find that you need to increase the space on the array. Because of the way the RAID 1 array works, a two-disk array is expanded by buying two new larger hard drives. At this point, you might consider migrating over to RAID 5, because you can double your storage space by adding a single drive. A RAID 1 array with two 100-GB drives has only 100 GB of storage while a RAID 5 array with three 100-GB drives has 200 GB of space.

Switching RAID levels normally means a complete backup and restore for the server, which requires the temporary use of a fourth drive to store the system while you create the RAID 5 array. This, of course, defeats one of the reasons to consider RAID 5—doubling the storage of a RAID 1 array by purchasing a single drive. With a Knoppix disc, you can migrate from a software RAID 1 array to a software RAID 5 array without backing up the system to a fourth disc. This hack goes through this migration step by step.

Here is the hypothetical situation for this migration. The complete root partition exists on */dev/md0*, which is a 20 GB RAID 1 array that spans two 20-GB drives, which are */dev/hda1* and */dev/hdb1*. The */etc/raidtab* for this configuration is listed below:

```
raiddev /dev/md0
    raid-level      1
    nr-raid-disks   2
    nr-spare-disks  0
    chunk-size      4
    persistent-superblock 1
    device          /dev/hda1
    raid-disk       0
    device          /dev/hdb1
    raid-disk       1
```

To convert this array to a three-disk 40-GB RAID 5 array, add a third 20 GB partition at */dev/hdc1*. I have already used *cfdisk* (you could use *fdisk* or other programs as well) to create this partition and set it with the fd partition type (just like */dev/hda1* and */dev/hdb1*), and Linux automatically detects it as a RAID partition. The RAID 1 array can temporarily survive on a single drive, and a RAID 5 array can temporarily survive on two drives, so you can do something similar to what was done in "Migrate to Software RAID" [Hack #63] and disable drives from one array to add them to the other, then finally add the final drive once all the files have been copied. Sound scary? Well, it can be, so make sure that you already have tape backups of important data, just in case. Remember, RAID safeguards against a drive failure; it is not a substitute for backups.

First, create directories for the old and new RAID, mount the old RAID device, and copy its *raidtab* file to Knoppix:

```
knoppix@tty0[knoppix]$ sudo mkdir /mnt/md0 /mnt/md1
knoppix@tty0[knoppix]$ sudo mount /dev/md0 /mnt/md0
knoppix@tty0[knoppix]$ sudo cp /mnt/md0/etc/raidtab /etc/
```

Now edit */etc/raidtab* and change */dev/hdb1* from a *raid-disk* to a *failed-disk*:

```
    device          /dev/hdb1
    raid-disk       1
    device          /dev/hdb1
    failed-disk     1
```

Then remove it from the current array:

```
knoppix@tty0[knoppix]$ sudo raidsetfaulty /dev/md0 /dev/hdb1
knoppix@tty0[knoppix]$ sudo raidhotremove /dev/md0 /dev/hdb1
```

Now that */dev/hdb1* is removed from the RAID 1 array, you can create the RAID 5 array by using it and the new hard drive */dev/hdc1*. Make sure to set */dev/hda1* as a failed disk in this configuration, so it is not overwritten when you create the new RAID. The */etc/raidtab* file looks like this:

```
raiddev /dev/md0
  raid-level      1
  nr-raid-disks   2
  nr-spare-disks  0
  chunk-size      4
  persistent-superblock 1
  device          /dev/hda1
  raid-disk       0
  device          /dev/hdb1
  failed-disk     1
raiddev /dev/md1
  raid-level      5
  nr-raid-disks   3
  nr-spare-disks  0
  persistent-superblock 1
  parity-algorithm         left-symmetric
  chunk-size      32
  device          /dev/hdb1
  raid-disk       0
  device          /dev/hdc1
  raid-disk       1
  device          /dev/hda1
  failed-disk     2
```

Now you can create the new RAID 5 array with:

```
knoppix@tty0[knoppix]$ sudo mkraid --really-force /dev/md1
```

You must run *mkraid* with the --really-force option, because */dev/hdb1* already has RAID signatures from */dev/md0* (the RAID 1 array), and by default, *mkraid* does not overwrite an existing RAID with a new one. Since */dev/hda1* is listed as a failed drive, you can now format */dev/md1* (the RAID 5 array) and mount it without the risk of overwriting anything from */dev/md0* (the RAID 1 array). Then you can copy the entire system from *md0* to *md1* using the *find* command introduced in "Migrate to a New Hard Drive" [Hack #61]:

```
knoppix@tty0[knoppix]$ sudo mkfs -t xfs -f /dev/md1
knoppix@tty0[knoppix]$ sudo mount -o rw /dev/md1 /mnt/md1
knoppix@tty0[knoppix]$ cd /mnt/md0
knoppix@tty0[md0]$ sudo sh -c "find . -xdev -print0 | cpio -paoV /mnt/md1"
```

Once the filesystem is copied, unmount the RAID 1 array */dev/md0*, because you need it stopped before you can add its final drive */dev/hda1* to your new RAID 5 array, */dev/md1*:

```
knoppix@tty0[knoppix]$ sudo umount /dev/md0
knoppix@tty0[knoppix]$ sudo raidstop /dev/md0
```

With the RAID 1 array stopped, you no longer need the *md0* configuration in */etc/raidtab*; remove it and also change *md1* so that */dev/hda1* is no longer failed. Your new */etc/raidtab* should look like this:

```
raiddev /dev/md1
  raid-level        5
  nr-raid-disks     3
  nr-spare-disks    0
  persistent-superblock 1
  parity-algorithm        left-symmetric
  chunk-size        32
  device            /dev/hdb1
  raid-disk         0
  device            /dev/hdc1
  raid-disk         1
  device            /dev/hda1
  raid-disk         2
```

With the final disk restored, add it to the RAID 5 with this command:

```
knoppix@tty0[knoppix]$ sudo raidhotadd /dev/md1 /dev/hda1
```

You can watch it sync with the rest of the array by monitoring */proc/mdstat*:

```
knoppix@tty0[knoppix]$ watch cat /proc/mdstat
```

While the new partition is being restored, take this time to copy over the new */etc/raidtab* to */mnt/md1/etc/*, and edit your */etc/fstab* and *lilo* or *grub* configuration so that it references */dev/md1* instead of */dev/md0*. Once the RAID finishes recovering the new drive, you should be able to reboot into your new RAID 5 partition.

See Also

- The Software RAID HOWTO: */usr/share/doc/raidtools2/Software-RAID. HOWTO* on your Knoppix disc.
- The *raidhotadd*, *mkraid*, *raidstop*, and other RAID tools manpages (type **man *commandname*** in a console).

HACK
#65
Add an Extra Drive to a Software RAID 5 Array

Add a fourth drive to a three-drive software RAID 5 array without a backup and restore.

"Migrate Software RAID 1 to RAID 5" **[Hack #64]** explored a method of increasing the disk space in a RAID 1 array by adding a single drive and converting the array to RAID 5. With the ever-increasing storage needs in most businesses, you may find yourself needing to expand a RAID 5 array as well. You can replace all of the drives in the RAID with larger drives and copy all of the files over to the new, larger RAID. Of course, for a three-drive RAID 5 array, this means buying three new drives to use. A cheaper alternative is to back up the array, create a new array using four drives, and copy back the data. This method requires the four drives for the array and a medium to back up to, such as a hard drive large enough to hold the entire RAID or possibly tape. Although, backups and restores aren't as fun as watching a RAID 5 array grow in front of your very eyes.

Some expensive hardware RAID controllers support adding new drives to RAID 5 arrays without requiring a backup and restore. This feature did not exist in software RAID until the creation of *raidreconf*—a tool that can grow RAID 0 and RAID 5 drives. This hack is a step-by-step guide to adding a fourth disk to a three-disk RAID 5 array.

> Hot-adding a disk to a software RAID 5 array is serious RAID voodoo! Whenever you reconfigure a RAID array on the fly, you risk the loss of your data, so be sure that any important data is backed up and you say a little prayer before trying this. Also, *raidreconf* is designed primarily to allow you to grow drives. You can shrink a RAID using *raidreconf* only if the data on the old RAID fits on the new RAID; otherwise, *raidreconf* truncates the data.

Now that all the caveats are out of the way, let's talk about the example RAID used in this hack. It is a 20-GB three-disk RAID 5 array at */dev/md0* that contains the root partition for a filesystem that spans three hard drives: */dev/hda1*, */dev/hdb1*, and */dev/hdc1*, which are 10 GB each. You then add a fourth 10-GB drive to this array, located at */dev/hdd1*, which makes the final four-disk RAID 5 array 30 GB.

To add a drive to *md0*, mount the array and create two copies of the *raidtab* file: one to represent the original state of the RAID and one to modify to represent the new state of the array. Then unmount the array and stop it, so that *raidreconf* can change it:

```
knoppix@tty0[knoppix]$ sudo mkdir /mnt/md0
knoppix@tty0[knoppix]$ sudo mount /dev/md0 /mnt/md0
knoppix@tty0[knoppix]$ sudo cp /mnt/md0/etc/raidtab /etc/raidtabold
knoppix@tty0[knoppix]$ sudo cp /mnt/md0/etc/raidtab /etc/raidtabnew
knoppix@tty0[knoppix]$ sudo umount /dev/md0
knoppix@tty0[knoppix]$ sudo raidstop /dev/md0
```

Now you have two files, */etc/raidtabold* and */etc/raidtabnew*. You must modify */etc/raidtabnew* to reflect the configuration of the new RAID 5 array you want to create. First, here is *raidtabold*:

```
raiddev /dev/md0
    raid-level      5
    nr-raid-disks   3
    nr-spare-disks  0
    persistent-superblock 1
    parity-algorithm        left-symmetric
    chunk-size      32
    device          /dev/hda1
    raid-disk       0
    device          /dev/hdb1
    raid-disk       1
    device          /dev/hdc1
    raid-disk       2
```

Edit *raidtabnew* and add the new drive to the array:

```
raiddev /dev/md0
    raid-level      5
    nr-raid-disks   4
    nr-spare-disks  0
    persistent-superblock 1
    parity-algorithm        left-symmetric
    chunk-size      32
    device          /dev/hda1
    raid-disk       0
    device          /dev/hdb1
    raid-disk       1
    device          /dev/hdc1
    raid-disk       2
    device          /dev/hdd1
    raid-disk       3
```

Notice the increase to the nr-raid-disks variable and the addition of the fourth raid-disk. Once *raidtabnew* is modified, reconstruct the array with this command:

```
knoppix@tty0[knoppix]$ sudo raidreconf -o /etc/raidtabold -n /etc/raidtabnew
-m /dev/md0
```

As your array is reconstructed, *raidreconf* outputs a nice progress bar, which lets you know the completion rate.

> Do *not* interrupt *raidreconf* while it is in the middle of a reconstruction, or you lose your entire array.

Once *raidreconf* is finished, mount the new */dev/md0* and copy over the new *raidtab* file that you have created:

```
knoppix@tty0[knoppix]$ sudo mount /dev/md0 /mnt/md0
knoppix@tty0[knoppix]$ sudo cp /etc/raidtabnew /mnt/md0/etc/raidtab
```

While the drive is mounted, you might want to run *df* and confirm that the size of the array has in fact increased. Now you can reboot your machine into your new, larger array.

See Also

- The *raidreconf* documentation in */usr/share/doc/raidtools2/raidreconf-HOWTO.gz* on your Knoppix disc.

Reset Linux Passwords
#66
Use Knoppix to reset forgotten Linux passwords.

If you have forgotten a user's password under Linux and you have root access, you don't usually need a rescue disk because you can reset the password with the root account. Even if you have forgotten the root password, most Linux distributions let you log in to single-user mode (add the `single` or `init=1` argument to the kernel at the boot prompt) and change the password from the root account.

A paranoid system administrator might password-protect or disable single-user mode altogether in */etc/inittab*, but you can still get to a root prompt to reset the password if you pass `init=/bin/sh` to the kernel when you boot. However, if the boot loader itself is password-protected and you forgot the password, you must have some sort of rescue disk to reset the password both in the boot loader (reference "Repair Lilo" **[Hack #52]** or "Repair Grub" **[Hack #53]** for steps to reconfigure the boot loader) and in the */etc/passwd* file.

It is simple to reset a password in Linux, and to reset a password with Knoppix requires just one extra step. Boot the Knoppix CD and mount your Linux system with read/write permissions:

```
knoppix@tty0[knoppix]$ sudo mount -o rw /dev/hda1 /mnt/hda1
```

Replace *hda1* with your root partition. Now run *passwd* under *chroot*, so that the *passwd* command changes the root password for the mounted system, and not Knoppix:

```
knoppix@ttyp0[knoppix]$ sudo chroot /mnt/hda1 passwd
Enter new UNIX password:
Retype new UNIX password:
passwd: password updated successfully
knoppix@ttyp0[knoppix]$
```

To change the password for a user instead or root, invoke the same command but add the name of the user to the end:

```
knoppix@ttyp0[knoppix]$ sudo chroot /mnt/hda1 passwd username
Enter new UNIX password:
Retype new UNIX password:
passwd: password updated successfully
knoppix@ttyp0[knoppix]$
```

With the password set to a new value, reboot and get back into your system.

HACK #67 Fix Broken Init Services

Errors in init scripts may prevent a system from completely booting. Use Knoppix to disable the troublesome scripts.

Before you log in to a Linux system, a number of programs are automatically run to start various daemons and load services that the system needs. If your system uses a graphical login, then that program is also started at boot. If one of these programs stalls, then you might not be able to completely boot to fix it. Depending on the service, it might be tricky to even bypass it using single-user mode. Knoppix can mount all major Linux filesystems, so it is a great rescue disk to use to temporarily disable a broken startup service so you can boot the system. This hack covers a few different scenarios that might stop a system from booting and how to use Knoppix to disable bad services.

Some Init-ial Background

Before learning how to disable services, it's important to understand Linux's startup process and how Linux determines which programs to run when it starts. For most Linux distributions, System V init scripts govern which programs start at boot and which programs don't. All System V init scripts that could potentially be run at boot are typically located in the */etc/init.d/* directory, although some distributions place them elsewhere within */etc*. Not every script in */etc/init.d* is executed at boot however. Linux organizes which scripts to run for different circumstances into *runlevels*; most Linux systems have seven runlevels, ranging from zero to six. Think of a runlevel as a checklist of programs to start before it presents a login.

A few of these runlevels are set aside for special states in a Linux system:

Runlevel 0
> Halts the system.

Runlevel 1
> Sets up single-user mode.

Runlevels 2–5
> Sets up different multiuser modes. Although, typically, only one or two are used by a distribution.

Runlevel 6
> Reboots the system.

Each runlevel has a directory that stores symlinks to the init scripts in */etc/init.d*, which are started when that runlevel is selected and stopped when it is exited. While the location of these directories differs a bit across Linux distributions, they are often found at */etc/rcrunlevel.d*—for example, all runlevel 2 scripts are located in */etc/rc2.d/*.

If you look in one of these runlevel directories, you should notice that many of the symlinks to scripts in */etc/init.d* have odd names that begin with an S, K, or D, then a number, and finally the name of the script. The letter at the beginning of each filename tells init when to execute this script. If the script begins with an S, then init starts the script when it goes through the runlevel. If the script begins with an K, then init stops (or kills) the script when it changes to a different runlevel. If the script begins with an D, then that script is disabled for the time being and init ignores it. Init runs the scripts in alphabetical order, so the numbers in each script are just there to arrange the scripts in the order they are to be run. This is useful to ensure that dependent services start after the service they are dependent on.

When Linux boots and starts the init process, it reads its configuration from */etc/inittab*, which configures each available runlevel, the default runlevel to use, as well as some other settings. Next, init loads any system scripts from a special system runlevel directory often at */etc/rcS.d*. These scripts load daemons and services that are vital to the boot process. Lastly, init runs any startup scripts for the default runlevel in alphabetical order.

You can change the runlevel yourself on the command line with the *init* command. To switch to single-user mode from the command line, type:

```
knoppix@ttyp0[knoppix]$ sudo init 1
```

This command runs all of the shutdown scripts for your current runlevel and then any startup scripts for single-user mode. You can also start and stop scripts manually by running the script with the start or stop argument. For example, to start *samba* from the command line, run:

```
knoppix@ttyp0[knoppix]$ sudo /etc/init.d/samba start
```

Disable Broken Init Scripts

Now that you understand the basics of how services are started in Linux, it's time to learn how to disable a problem script. To disable a script, you must know your default runlevel. On Knoppix and Debian systems, the default runlevel is 2, but this varies across distributions—for example, Red Hat defaults to runlevel 5. All runlevels are defined in */etc/inittab*. To read this file, mount your root partition (for this example, */mnt/hda1*) and run:

```
knoppix@tty0[knoppix] grep initdefault /mnt/hda1/etc/inittab
id:2:initdefault:
```

Once you know your runlevel, you can disable the correct scripts. In general, to disable a script, change to the directory for that runlevel, identify the script name starting with an S, and then rename the file by changing the S to a D.

One common scenario that might prevent you from booting is a broken X configuration. Most Linux distributions today default to a desktop manager that lets you log in graphically. This desktop manager is typically set to run continuously so that even if X is stopped, it automatically restarts itself and presents you with another login screen. If X is broken, the desktop manager resets every five seconds or so, which makes it rather tricky to quickly switch to a virtual terminal, log in as root, and disable the program. Some desktop managers now set a maximum number of restarts before disabling the program for you, and you can also disable this script in a nongraphical or single-user runlevel, but for the purposes of demonstration, I explain how to disable the desktop manager.

In the previous example, the default runlevel for Knoppix is 2. Change to the directory for that runlevel on your root partition (in this example, */mnt/hda1/etc/rc2.d*). This directory has a number of scripts, but you want to disable the desktop manager, so you are interested only in scripts for *xdm*, *gdm*, or *kdm*—the three common desktop managers. In your system, you must determine which desktop manager is actually used, or otherwise, simply disable any of the three that you see for that runlevel. Typically, the desktop manager is one of the last scripts to be run, so it is often numbered 99. This is a script that is started at boot, so the symlink starts with an S; to disable *gdm*, the desktop manager for Gnome, look for a file named *S99gdm* or something similar. To disable this script, rename it by changing the S to a D:

```
knoppix@tty0[rc2.d] sudo mv S99gdm D99gdm
```

Of course, change the name of the script to *xdm* or *kdm* if you are disabling those services. After renaming the file, you should be able to reboot without the desktop manager starting, which gives you an opportunity to debug your X configuration.

Another scenario that might prevent you from booting is a stalled service that does not time out. Init runs each script in sequence, so if a script does not exit, any scripts after it do not run. I've had cases where an init script mounting networked filesystems stalled out and sat there for minutes without exiting, and I had to boot with a rescue disc to disable the service. In this case, the script was not part of my runlevel but was instead a system script, so I had to go to */etc/rcS.d/* to find and disable it. Avoid making changes to scripts in *rcS.d* unless you know what you are doing; these scripts are considered by the system to be important, if not essential, for booting.

Once you have disabled a service and booted the system, track down the cause of the problem. Remember that you can run a startup script after booting by running it from the command line with the start option. This allows you to test a broken script while still having it disabled should you need to reboot.

HACK #68 Repair Debian Packages

Knoppix is not only based on Debian; it also comes with a full set of tools to manage and change Debian packages.

Knoppix is over 90% pure Debian packages, and if you install Knoppix to your hard drive, you find that the programs and utilities are installed where they would be on a regular Debian system. It might not then surprise you to know that Knoppix comes with many of Debian's packaging tools and is an excellent rescue disk for fixing Debian-specific problems. This hack describes how to downgrade a broken package that is stopping you from booting, fix a broken *dpkg* package, and perform a few other Debian-specific fixes.

Knoppix includes the Debian *dpkg* tools: *dpkg*, *dpkg-buildpackage*, *dpkg-reconfigure*, and *dpkg-source*. With these tools, you can rescue a Debian system that might not boot because of a broken package or corrupted install.

For instance, if the *modutils* package (containing useful utilities such as *modprobe* and *insmod*) is corrupted, your system cannot load modules and probably won't boot. To correct this, boot Knoppix and mount the root Debian partition (in this example, */dev/hda1*) as read/write:

```
knoppix@ttyp0[knoppix]$ sudo mount -o rw /dev/hda1 /mnt/hda1
```

Check to see if you have a previous version of *modutils* under */var/cache/apt/archives/*. If not, open up a browser and use the search feature on *http://packages.debian.org* to locate your package from one of Debian's mirrors. In this case, *modutils* is located at *http://http.us.debian.org/debian/pool/main/m/modutils/*. This mirror contains packages for the architectures that Debian supports, so make sure to grab the package corresponding to your architecture (likely, the package ending in "i386.deb").

Once you have obtained the package that corresponds to your architecture, run *dpkg* in its *chroot* mode to install the package to the mounted Debian system. In this example, the Debian root directory is mounted at */mnt/hda1*, so the command is:

```
knoppix@tty0[knoppix]$ sudo dpkg --root /mnt/hda1 -i modutils_version_i386.
deb
```

Of course, replace the mount point to match where your Debian root partition is mounted, and change the package to whichever package you need to install. *Dpkg* runs through the full downgrade with any reconfiguration you might need to perform, and once *dpkg* is finished, you should be able to reboot into the system with a fixed package.

You can also use this method to fix a broken or corrupted *dpkg* package. Obviously, if your package installation program is broken, you can't use it to fix itself. But you can use Knoppix's working *dpkg* to install a new package manager in a *chroot* environment. After you download the appropriate package from *http://http.us.debian.org/debian/pool/main/d/dpkg/*, run this command:

```
knoppix@tty0[knoppix]$ sudo dpkg --root /mnt/hda1 -i dpkg_version_i386.deb
```

You can also download the replacement package, convert it to a *tar* file, and then untar it in the mounted root directory. Here are the steps to use *tar* and *alien* to install the package. *Alien* is a handy tool that acts as a translator between *.tgz*, *.rpm*, and *.deb* packages, and can convert a file in one format to any of the others. Use *alien* to convert the package to a *tar* file before unpacking:

```
knoppix@tty0[knoppix]$ sudo alien --to-tgz dpkg_version_i386.deb
knoppix@tty0[knoppix]$ sudo mv dpkg_version_i386.tgz /mnt/hda1
knoppix@tty0[knoppix]$ cd /mnt/hda1
knoppix@tty0[hda1]$ tar xzvf dpkg_version_i386.tgz
```

While there are many other packages you can leverage on Knoppix to fix broken Debian systems, generally it's best to fix the Debian system while you are booted into the system itself. Use Knoppix to repair those packages that prevent you from booting, then boot Debian and repair the rest from there.

Repair RPM Packages

Knoppix not only comes with Debian packaging tools; it also comes complete
with support for creating and installing RPMs.

While it might not be news to you that Knoppix comes with Debian packaging tools, it might surprise you to know that Knoppix also comes with many
corresponding RPM packaging tools, including *rpm*, *rpmbuild*, *rpmquery*,
and *rpmverify*. With these tools, you can actually use Knoppix to repair
packages on an RPM-based system that is preventing it from booting.

This hack is actually very similar to "Repair Debian Packages" [Hack #68], as it
makes use of the --root option of *rpm*, which allows it to install packages
from within a *chrooted* environment. This example uses the same scenario as
the previous hack—a broken *modutils* package that prevents the system
from booting correctly.

To fix this problem, go to the package repository for your distribution, find
the previous version of the *modutils* package, and copy it to your home
directory. Then mount the root directory for your distribution read/write (in
this example, */dev/hda1*). Once the partition is mounted, install the *modutils*
package with:

```
knoppix@tty0[knoppix]$ sudo rpm --root /mnt/hda1 -i modutils-version.i386.
rpm
```

You can also use the same method to repair *rpm* itself if it is broken or corrupted, because you wouldn't be able to use *rpm* on the system to fix itself.
Download the replacement *rpm* package from your distribution package
repository, and then run:

```
knoppix@tty0[knoppix]$ sudo rpm --root /mnt/hda1 -i rpm-version.i386.rpm
```

Or use *tar* and *alien* to fix *rpm* with:

```
knoppix@tty0[knoppix]$ sudo alien --to-tgz rpm-version.i386.rpm
knoppix@tty0[knoppix]$ sudo mv rpm-version.tgz /mnt/hda1
knoppix@tty0[knoppix]$ cd /mnt/hda1
knoppix@tty0[knoppix]$ tar xzvf rpm-version.tgz
```

With all of the included *rpm* tools, you definitely want access to a Knoppix
disc for system rescue even if you don't run Debian. Similar to Debian
repair, do most of your repairs from within the system itself if you can, and
use Knoppix to repair those packages that are preventing you from booting
or any other packages you can't fix within the system itself.

HACK
#70

Copy a Working Kernel

Use Knoppix to restore a working kernel to a system that has had its kernel either deleted or overwritten.

By default, most Linux distributions include only a single kernel. These kernels are generally very modular, which is fine, because it makes boot loader configuration simple—you have to configure only a single kernel. Unfortunately, if that kernel somehow gets deleted or corrupted, you have no way of booting, because it is the only kernel on the system. However, you can use a rescue disk like Knoppix to restore a working kernel to the system. This hack covers a number of methods that restore a working kernel to a system, including how to use Knoppix's own kernel on a system.

Before you can restore a kernel, you must determine which kernel needs to be restored and find another copy of it. If you have been using the default kernel for your distribution, this step is simple; just grab the installation CD and find the kernel package, or download the package from the distribution's package repository. To restore the kernel, simply use the appropriate package manager under Knoppix. If you have a Deb-based system, refer to "Repair Debian Packages" [Hack #68] for instructions on how to use *dpkg* within a *chrooted* environment. If you have an RPM-based system, refer to "Repair RPM Packages" [Hack #69] for instructions on how to use *rpm* within a *chrooted* environment.

If you have built your own kernel, you might still have a copy of the kernel on your system you can use. Unless you ran a make clean since you have built your kernel, a copy of the kernel might still be sitting in */usr/src/linux/arch/i386/boot/*. If you built a bzipped kernel image with make bzImage, then the file should be named *bzImage*. After mounting the drive read/write (type mount -rw /dev/hda1 /mnt/hda1 in a terminal), simply copy the *bzImage* file to *boot*, and name it after the corrupted or deleted kernel.

If you wish, you can also use Knoppix's own kernel on your system. The Knoppix kernels are in the */boot* directory on the Knoppix root filesystem. Copy the kernel image you want to use to the *boot* directory on your read/write mounted root partition. Finally, copy your chosen kernel's modules directory located in */lib/modules* on the Knoppix root filesystem to *lib/modules* on your root partition. For a root partition mounted at */mnt/hda1*, type:

```
knoppix@tty0[knoppix] sudo cp /boot/vmlinuz-`uname -r` /mnt/hda1/boot/
knoppix@tty0[knoppix] sudo cp -a /lib/modules/`uname -r` /mnt/hda1/lib/
modules/
```

These commands use the shell command uname -r to return the currently booted Knoppix kernel. This method should work identically for you. If you want to copy a kernel other than the one you are currently using, simply replace `uname -r` with the kernel version you are using.

Whichever method you use to copy a working kernel to your system, once it is copied, make sure that your boot loader's configuration file references the new kernel. If you simply installed the default kernel package for your distribution, you should not need to perform any additional configuration. If you use *lilo* as a boot loader, you also must update *lilo* in your boot sector (covered in "Repair Lilo" **[Hack #52]**) before you can reboot your system to the restored kernel.

Keep in mind that you aren't required to use a kernel included with your system. If there is another kernel image you wish to boot from that you know will work with your hardware, simply perform the same steps used to copy Knoppix's kernel to the system to use your kernel. If you do this, be sure to update your boot loader and, preferably, keep a backup distribution kernel just in case. Otherwise, if the new kernel doesn't boot, just try this hack again.

CHAPTER SEVEN

Rescue Windows
Hacks 71–79

Whenever I have to use the Windows Recovery CD, I cringe. It isn't because my Windows system needs to be rescued; I've come to expect that. What I dislike is the actual recovery CD itself, and I don't think I'm the only one who feels that way. While the Windows Recovery CD does an adequate job with a few tasks (i.e., resetting an MBR, replacing a *boot.ini* file, or restoring default system files), expect to come up empty-handed and frustrated if you try to complete a task that Microsoft hasn't explicitly created a tool for. Here are just a few things the Windows Recovery CD *should* be able to do but can't:

Edit text files
> While Microsoft has shied further and further away from allowing you to configure anything with a text file, there are still plenty of reasons why you might need to, including fixes to the *boot.ini* files beyond the abilities of the recovery CD.

Copy to a floppy
> You can't edit a text file in the Recovery Console, so you may think "I'll just copy the file to a floppy disk, edit it on another computer, and copy it back." However, the Recovery Console only allows you to copy *from* CD-ROMs or floppies and not *to* them.

Browse your full hard disk
> With the recovery CD, you are only allowed to browse the root directory (*C:*, for instance) or the *%systemroot%* directory (the *WINNT* or *WINDOWS* directory). If you stray from those two directories to access your *My Documents* directory, you get the "Access Denied" error message.

Fortunately, Knoppix makes up for the Windows Recovery CD's shortcomings. This chapter covers how to repair many of the common problems that plague Windows systems, including how to fix the *boot.ini* file, scan for viruses, reset lost passwords, and even edit the Windows registry. After you read this chapter, you"ll see how Knoppix can trump Windows on its home turf.

Many of these hacks aren't too complicated. Not too long ago, a friend of mine had a problem with her Windows machine. Her daughter had come home from college and accidentally infected the machine with a virus, and the machine refused to boot. My friend was pretty upset, because there were some important files on the drive, including tax receipts and, more importantly, some irreplaceable photos. While she could just attempt to reinstall Windows over the top and hope that it fixed things, she was nervous about risking the loss of those files. If she accidentally installed with the wrong option, she could format the drive and lose everything.

I had my laptop handy, so I burned a Knoppix CD for her and explained how it worked. She would boot up, click on the hard drive icons on the desktop, and locate her important files. She happened to have a USB key drive, so I explained how she could simply drag-and-drop files from the hard drive to the key drive, and then back them up to another machine.

The next time I saw her, she met me with a big grin. The CD had worked perfectly, and she was able to recover everything. She even gave me a USB key drive as a token of her appreciation—something I currently carry with me and use all the time.

HACK #71 Fix the Windows Boot Selector

If a Windows boot.ini file gets corrupted, you might find yourself unable to boot back into Windows. While the Windows Recovery CD can restore a default boot file, unlike Knoppix, it won't let you edit it directly.

Back in the old days of Windows, you could change many different startup settings by editing *.ini* files that were in the root of your hard drive. Over the years, Microsoft has moved most of the settings that control configuration to the registry, but there is one important file that remains, *boot.ini*. In this file, you can find information that the Windows boot loader uses to determine booting options and, in the case of more than one Windows OS on a system, which OS to boot. For example, this is a *boot.ini* file that allows you to boot between Windows 2000 and Windows XP Professional:

```
[boot loader]
timeout=30
default=multi(0)disk(0)rdisk(0)partition(1)\WINNT
[operating systems]
multi(0)disk(0)rdisk(0)partition(1)\WINNT="Windows 2000" /fastdetect
multi(0)disk(0)rdisk(0)partition(2)\WINDOWS="Windows XP Professional"
/fastdetect
```

This file is split into two parts: the part that contains settings for the boot loader that starts with [boot loader] and the part that containing the different operating systems available for booting that starts with [operating systems]. The first option, timeout, controls how many seconds the boot loader waits before booting the default operating system. The default option tells the boot loader which operating system to boot if the timeout has passed.

In and below the default option for each operating system, notice the syntax that looks like multi(0)disk(0)rdisk(0)partition(1). This syntax describes which partition the operating system is on. Each section of that partition description has a special meaning, regarding which IDE adapter the partition is on, which disk is on that adapter, etc., but the section that is probably of most interest is rdisk(0)partition(1). The rdisk(0) section denotes which disk on an adapter to boot from numbered from 0, and partition(1) lists which partition on the drive to boot from numbered from 1.

In the example, the second section of the operating systems line tells the boot loader where to find the Windows system files on that partition. Typically, this is either the *WINNT* or *WINDOWS* directory. The next part of the line (in quotes) controls which text the user sees in the boot loader menu. You can change this setting to label the operating system of your choice. As an example, assume that you have a system like the *boot.ini* describes: a Windows 2000 installation on the first partition of an IDE drive and Windows XP Professional installed on the second partition. You can resize the Windows 2000 partition and create a second partition from the empty space from within Knoppix, which makes Windows XP Professional the third partition. After you resize, change your settings to boot into Windows XP by default. Either use a tool like *bootcfg* and boot into Windows 2000, or edit the *boot.ini* with Notepad. Instead of rebooting, you can mount the new Windows 2000 partition read/write, click on the drive icon on the desktop to open it, then right-click on the icon and select Actions → Change Read/Write Mode. If the partition is NTFS, follow the steps in "Write to NTFS" **[Hack #73]**. Next, open up the *boot.ini* file with a text editor from Knoppix, and change it to the following:

```
[boot loader]
timeout=30
default=multi(0)disk(0)rdisk(0)partition(3)\WINDOWS
[operating systems]
multi(0)disk(0)rdisk(0)partition(1)\WINNT="Windows 2000" /fastdetect
multi(0)disk(0)rdisk(0)partition(3)\WINDOWS="Windows XP Professional"
/fastdetect
```

You have changed the partition information for the XP boot to read partition(3). Now when you reboot, the system loads Windows XP by default.

You can also use this ability to create a *boot.ini* file from scratch in case your file was has been corrupted and the Windows Recovery CD is nowhere in sight. Here is a sample *boot.ini* file that should work for most default single-OS Windows installations. This sample assumes that you have installed Windows on the first partition on the first IDE drive (the default for most home desktops) and that all of the system files are located in the *WINDOWS* directory on that partition.

```
[boot loader]
timeout=30
default=multi(0)disk(0)rdisk(0)partition(1)\WINDOWS
[operating systems]
multi(0)disk(0)rdisk(0)partition(1)\WINDOWS="Boot Windows" /fastdetect
```

Enter this configuration into a blank *boot.ini* file, and when you reboot, you should find that the boot selector is back with your default Windows settings.

HACK #72 Back Up Files and Settings

With all of the viruses, worms, and malware running loose on the Internet, it is not uncommon for a Windows user to find that her system has become unusable (some people argue that Windows systems are unusable by default). Use Knoppix's Windows filesystem support to back up important files and settings when Windows can't boot.

There are many utilities on the market designed for backing up and restoring files on Windows systems. Windows even comes with its own backup software preinstalled. These utilities are good only if you can actually use them. It is not uncommon for a virus or file corruption to leave you unable to use Windows or to boot into Windows Safe Mode. Even using Microsoft's Windows Update can leave your system in an unusable state. If you have not maintained your backups, you find yourself mournfully tallying up all the files you are about to lose. The Windows Recovery CD doesn't provide you with much help in this circumstance either, because you can't navigate outside the Windows *systemroot* folder (usually *WINDOWS* or *WINNT*), and even if you could, you don't have many options for backing up your important data. Don't worry. You can use Knoppix to back up your important files even when Windows no longer boots.

Knoppix picks up where the Windows Recovery CD leaves off, with the ability to navigate through your entire filesystem and back up important files to many different kinds of media from other connected hard drives, floppies, USB key drives, writable CD-ROMs, and even other computers on the network. Besides, you can browse through your filesystem graphically and open up files along the way, so you can tell if *P0311231923.jpg* is that important baby picture, and whether *Untitled1.doc* is a blank document or your graduate thesis.

Back That Thing Up

To back up your important data, determine what you need to back up and where you want to put it. First, find your Windows partition. If Windows is the only operating system installed on your computer, this should be easy—just click on the single hard drive icon that should appear on your Knoppix desktop; it is usually labeled */dev/hda1*. If you have more than one operating system installed, or more than one partition on your hard drive, you may need to search for it. Click on each hard-drive icon. Check for directories named *Documents and Settings* and *Program Files* to help you identify your Windows partition.

Open your Windows partition with the Konqueror file manager, and browse through your directories to decide which files you need to back up. To back up all of the user's files and settings on Windows 2000 or newer systems, you must back up the entire *Documents and Settings* directory. This directory contains settings for your applications, the *My Documents* directory, where you keep your important data, and the files on your desktop. You can back up your programs by backing up the *Program Files* directory, but realize that this does not back up registry settings your programs might have created when they were installed. For most programs, simply copying the directories to a clean system does not restore them—you must reinstall.

> If you are having difficulty finding all of your files, you can use Konqueror's find utility by clicking Tools → Find File in the menu bar.

Find the files you need to back up, and then decide where to back them up, depending on the availability of hardware and the number of files you need to back up. If only a few documents need to be backed up, simply use a single-floppy drive. If you are backing up your entire family album, you need more space. USB key drives can be handy for large backups, because you can quickly copy your important files to the drive, carry it over to another system, empty the drive, and repeat. If you have two CD-ROM drives in the system (or you free up your CD-ROM drive with "Free Your CD to Make Knoppix Run Faster" [Hack #5]), one of which can write to CDs, boot Knoppix on the regular drive, and click K Menu → Multimedia → K3b to launch K3b, KDE's easy-to-use CD-writing application, to back up the files to CD-ROM.

You can also back up files to shared directories on your network. Follow the steps in "Browse Windows Shares" [Hack #39] to mount the remote network filesystem to your Knoppix system. Then you can simply drag-and-drop files from your local hard drive to the remote network share.

Here's the worst-case scenario: if you need to back up only a few small files and you have no other way of transporting them, email the files to yourself. Just follow the steps in "Explore the Internet" **[Hack #19]** to set up an email client, and send the important files as attachments. If you do this, however, keep in mind that most mail servers have a limit to how large file attachments can be.

Write to NTFS

#73

One thing that has been missing from Knoppix (and Linux in general) is the ability to safely write to NTFS partitions. Now with Knoppix 3.4, you can edit, delete, and move files on your NTFS partition—jobs that are difficult with the Windows Recovery CD!

While the Linux kernel has been able to read NTFS partitions for some time, writing to them has always been considered very dangerous. The NTFS spec is a closed spec that requires kernel hackers to reverse engineer it to make a driver that supports it. However, this can be very problematic: if a programmer reverse engineers NTFS 3.0, she must repeat the process when NTFS 4.0 is released. Writing to NTFS has been so dangerous that instead of just warning users, some kernels go as far as disabling write support in the NTFS driver itself. Recently, a solution to write to NTFS partitions has appeared with Captive NTFS. This solution actually uses the NTFS drivers that Windows itself uses, and is included in Knoppix 3.4.

> Captive NTFS is still somewhat experimental, and while it has worked for many people, there is a chance for data loss, so be sure to back up any important files on filesystems you mount this way.

Configure Captive NTFS

The Knoppix Captive NTFS wizard makes it easy to configure and use the Captive NTFS system. When you run the wizard, it scans all the drives on your computer for the Microsoft-provided NTFS drivers it needs to safely write to your NTFS filesystems. Click K Menu → KNOPPIX → Utilities → Captive NTFS to launch the program. The wizard that appears automates the process of finding and using the NTFS *.dlls*. Click Forward to see a listing of the system files that Captive NTFS has already found on your Knoppix system. Click Forward again, and the wizard mounts and scans your hard drives for the essential files it needs.

Once Captive NTFS has the modules it needs to mount NTFS, it enables the OK button even though it continues to scan other directories and partitions for drivers. If you are in a hurry, you can click OK to immediately mount NTFS partitions. If you wait for the scan to finish, you are presented with an option to list specific locations for drivers (which could be on a USB key drive, for instance), or you can click Forward to get the option to download the files from the Windows XP Service Pack 1.

> In some countries, you must have a valid XP license to legally download Service Pack 1, so if you are unsure of the legality of downloading this publicly available file, consult with your lawyer and with Microsoft's lawyers, and then click "Yes, start the download."

If you have the time, Captive NTFS recommends downloading the latest version of the drivers, which is available in the Windows XP Service Pack 1. However, I have successfully written to NTFS partitions with Windows's standard drivers.

Mount NTFS Partitions

Once you are finished with the wizard, you are ready to mount an NTFS partition.

> Do not mount the partition by clicking on it on the desktop, because the standard Linux kernel NTFS module is used— not Captive NTFS.

Open a terminal and mount the drive manually using this command:

```
knoppix@ttyp0[knoppix]$ sudo mount -t captive-ntfs -o
uid=knoppix,gid=knoppix /dev/hda1 /mnt/hda1
```

Replace *hda1* with the name of your partition. The -t argument is used to specify a filesystem type. Use captive-ntfs to use the NTFS drivers that the Captive NTFS wizard previously found. The -o argument passes other general options to mount. In this case, tell mount to assign the user and group *knoppix* to the files on this drive. I recommend that you mount the drive at */mnt/hda1*, because this directory is created by Knoppix at boot time for this partition, but you can actually use any directory you wish. This drive is now writable by your regular *knoppix* user; you now possess the power to do good and evil to your drive. Once the drive is mounted, you can treat it like any other mounted filesystem, although I have noticed that write speed is substantially slower with Captive NTFS than with other filesystems.

Once you are finished with the partition, unmount it to ensure that any changes are synced. This is an important step, because normally, when you change a file on a drive, changes are cached to RAM to be written to the drive later. This is performance-enhancing behavior, because it allows writes to occur at an optimal time. Unmount the disk to synchronize any changes in RAM that haven't yet been written to disk.

```
knoppix@ttyp0[knoppix]$ sudo umount /mnt/hda1
```

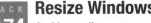

Resize Windows Partitions

Avoid spending money on Partition Magic or other commercial partitioning tools by using Knoppix to easily resize FAT, FAT32, and even NTFS partitions.

There are two methods for resizing Windows partitions with Knoppix: use *QTParted* for all filesystems or *ntfsresize* for NTFS partitions. *QTParted* gained the capability of resizing NTFS only recently, so if you use an older Knoppix CD, you might need to use *ntfsresize*, which requires more work and is more error-prone. *QTParted* is a GUI frontend for the command-line program *parted*.

 Before resizing any Windows partition, it is very important that you defragment the drive from within Windows. These resizing utilities work by basically truncating the partition and recreating it, and if you don't defragment, you lose the file fragments at the end of the drive. Be sure that all of the filesystems on the disk are not mounted before resizing, even if the partition that is mounted is not the partition that you plan to resize. Also, whenever you resize a partition, you risk data loss, so back up important files.

Once you defragment the filesystem that you wish to resize, boot into Knoppix and resize it with *QTParted* using the same steps outlined in "Resize Linux Partitions" [Hack #56]. To run *QTParted*, click K Menu → System → QTParted, choose the drive to resize, right-click on it and select resize, and then drag the corners of the partition, as shown in Figure 7-1, until it is the size you want. Finally, commit your changes to resize your filesystem.

If you want to resize an NTFS partition and your version of *QTParted* does not support NTFS resizing, you can also use the *ntfsresize* tool. There are two slightly different methods for using *ntfsresize*, depending on whether you want to enlarge or shrink a partition.

Enlarge NTFS Partitions

Before using *ntfsresize* to enlarge a partition, you must use a tool such as *fdisk* or *cfdisk* to delete the partition, and then recreate it in the new larger size. If you want a safeguard against mistakes, you should back up the

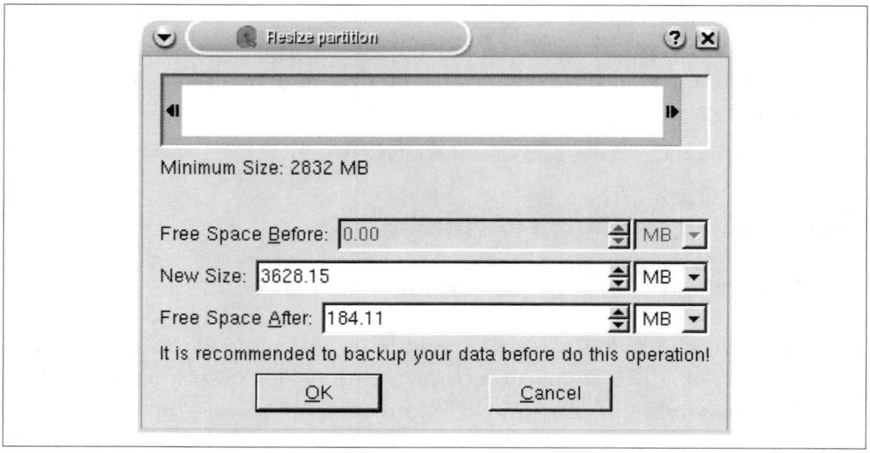

Figure 7-1. *Resize a partition with QTParted*

partition table with the steps outlined in "Kill and Resurrect the Master Boot
Record" **[Hack #54]** before making any changes. You can use *fdisk* or *cfdisk*
(*cfdisk* is considered to be more user-friendly) from the command line:

```
knoppix@ttyp0[knoppix]$ sudo fdisk /dev/hda
```

Change *hda* to the name of the drive you wish to edit. It is important that
you recreate the partition with the same starting block and partition type as
the old partition.

> *Ntfsresize* requires that the starting block remains the same,
> or you risk losing your files when you resize.

If you have any free space before the existing partition, you might find that
fdisk makes it easier to specify the starting block than *cfdisk*. Either way,
once you delete the old partition, recreate it at the same starting block and
with the same partition type. Write down the exact size of the new partition, because this information is necessary to use *ntfsresize*. Then write your
changes to the disk. Don't worry. This does not actually delete any data on
the partition, it only changes the partition table itself—a table describing
where partitions begin and end located at the beginning of your hard drive.
If you decide not to resize the partition, you can still turn back. Just use
cfdisk or *fdisk* to change the partition size back to normal. If you leave the
partition table at its new size, do not try to reboot to Windows until you finish the steps, or you could lose or damage your files.

Once you resize your NTFS partition, you might need to reboot before the kernel uses the new partition table. *Fdisk* or *cfdisk* should notify you if this is the case, once you write the changes. Once the new partition table is written and ready, you can resize the partition with the following command:

```
knoppix@ttyp0[knoppix]$ sudo ntfsresize -s size /dev/hda1
```

Replace *size* with the new size of the partition that you wrote down earlier, and replace *hda1* with the partition you want to resize. By default, the size parameter is in bytes, but you can specify kilobytes, megabytes, or gigabytes by appending K, M, or G, respectively.

 Make sure that the size you specify is the exact new size of the partition; otherwise, you risk losing the files on the partition.

When *ntfsresize* is finished, it sets the partition so that it requires a filesystem check at next boot. So, when you next boot to Windows, it checks the filesystem with *chkdsk* before it allows you to load Windows. It is important that you do not mount the new disk under Knoppix until you have allowed *chkdsk* to run on the new partition.

Shrink NTFS Partitions

The method for shrinking an NTFS partition with *ntfsresize* is the reverse for the method used to enlarge it. You must run *ntfsresize* on the drive, and specify the drive's new size:

```
knoppix@ttyp0[knoppix]$ sudo ntfsresize -s size /dev/hda1
```

The *ntfsresize* program then attempts to shrink the partition to the specified size. If it encounters file fragments, or you give it a size that is too small, *ntfsresize* exits with an error that states that the partition size is too small, and provides an acceptable size.

After you resize the filesystem itself, you must shrink the partition. Use *fdisk* or *cfdisk* to delete and recreate the new partition, making sure to start the partition on the same block with the same partition type as before:

```
knoppix@ttyp0[knoppix]$ sudo fdisk /dev/hda
```

Fdisk accepts a partition size in kilobytes, megabytes, or gigabytes just like *ntfsresize*, so just make a note of the new partition size. Once you have resized the partition itself, it is necessary to reboot the machine into Windows and allow it to run *chkdsk* before you attempt to mount or otherwise change the partition under Knoppix.

Reset Lost NT Passwords

HACK #75

If you forget a password for your user on your Windows system (especially if the user is administrator), your computer immediately becomes a paperweight. It's like being locked out of your car without a spare set of keys and without a way to contact a locksmith. Use Knoppix as your locksmith to reset the password to a new value or even completely erase it.

User accounts have an interesting history in Windows. The Windows 9x series did offer usernames and passwords, but every user could overwrite every other user's files, and the system did not offer any real security. If you forget your password in Windows 9x, resetting it is as simple as deleting a *.pwd* file with a DOS disk. With Windows NT, 2000, and XP, Microsoft has increased its user security by creating different user accounts on the same system and passwords that protect them. However, unlike in Windows 9x, if you forget your Administrator password, your only recourse is to purchase a tool to reset your Windows password or to reinstall Windows to create a new administrator account. If you have a Knoppix disc, you can download and use the *chntpw* tool, which is a small program that lets you reset the local passwords on a Windows system, and return to your system.

Get chntpw

The *chntpw* tool is part of the *ntpasswd* package, which can be downloaded in boot floppy form from its web site at *http://home.eunet.no/~pnordahl/ntpasswd/*. However, this gives you a floppy image and requires that you mount multiple loopback entries to extract the utility from the floppy image to use under Knoppix. While you can simply create an *ntpasswd* boot floppy, this means yet another rescue disk to carry with you, and the beauty of Knoppix is that you have access to all of your recovery tools in a single disc. Luckily, the *chntpw* tool is now part of Debian unstable, which means that you can grab it directly from Debian's repository.

You could use the *apt-get* wrapper, which is included for Knoppix, to download *chntpw*. However, to be certain you retrieve the latest version of *chntpw*, you must run the *apt-get* update, which downloads about 10 times as much data per repository as the 85-KB *chntpw* package. It saves bandwidth and time to download the package directly.

You can get the latest *chntpw* package from *http://packages.debian.org/unstable/admin/chntpw*. Download the *.deb* to your */home/knoppix* directory. Most of the Knoppix system is read-only, so you can't directly install this package. Instead, you must convert it to a *tar* file, and then extract out the *chntpw* utility. Open up a terminal, and run the following commands:

```
knoppix@ttyp1[config]$ alien --to-tgz chntpw_0.99.2-1_i386.deb
knoppix@ttyp1[config]$ tar xvzf chntpw-0.99.2.tgz ./usr/sbin/chntpw
knoppix@ttyp1[config]$ mv ./usr/sbin/chntpw ./
```

Change the *.deb* and *.tgz* filenames to match the version of *chntpw* that you downloaded. This command makes use of the *alien* utility, which has the ability to convert files between *.rpm*, *.deb*, and *.tgz*. This conversion is necessary to extract only the *chntpw* executable file. Once you are finished with these commands, the *chntpw* utility is in */home/knoppix* and ready to use.

Reset the Password

To reset the password, you must have write permissions on the Windows partition. If you have a FAT or FAT32 Windows partition, click on the drive on the desktop to mount it, then right-click on the hard-drive icon and choose Actions → Change read/write mode, or on the command line, type:

```
knoppix@ttyp1[config]$ sudo mount -o rw /dev/hda1 /mnt/hda1
```

Replace *hda1* with your Windows partition. If you have an NTFS partition, follow the steps in "Write to NTFS" [Hack #73] to mount the NTFS partition with write permissions.

Once the partition is mounted, you must locate the directory containing the *SAM* file. For Windows 2000 and XP systems, this directory should be located under *windows/system32/config* or *winnt/system32/config*. In this example, navigate to the */mnt/hda1/windows/system32/config* directory, and notice a number of files, including ones called *SAM*, *SYSTEM*, and *SECURITY*, that may or may not be in all caps. Once you have navigated to this directory on the command line, reset the Windows Administrator password by running:

```
knoppix@ttyp1[config]$ /home/knoppix/chntpw SAM
```

Remember that SAM is the name of the *SAM* file in the directory, and may or may not be all in caps. The default for this utility is to edit the Administrator password, so there is no need to specify an account. While you have the option to change the password to a different value, it is recommended to just reset the password and then change it when you get back into Windows. You can reset the password by typing * instead of a password when prompted.

```
knoppix@ttyp1[config]$ /home/knoppix/chntpw SAM
chntpw version 0.99.2 040105, (c) Petter N Hagen
openHive(sam) failed: Read-only file system, trying read-only
```

```
Hive's name (from header): <\SystemRoot\System32\Config\SAM>
ROOT KEY at offset: 0x001020
...output supressed...

* = blank the password (This may work better than setting a new password!)
Enter nothing to leave it unchanged
Please enter new password: *
```

If you want to reset the password for a user other than Administrator, list the users in the *SAM* file with the -l option:

```
knoppix@ttyp1[config]$ /home/knoppix/chntpw -l SAM
chntpw version 0.99.2 040105, (c) Petter N Hagen
Hive's name (from header): <\SystemRoot\System32\Config\SAM>
ROOT KEY at offset: 0x001020
Page at 0x6000 is not 'hbin', assuming file contains garbage at end
File size 262144 [40000] bytes, containing 5 pages (+ 1 headerpage)
Used for data: 218/16928 blocks/bytes, unused: 4/3392 blocks/bytes.

* SAM policy limits:
Failed logins before lockout is: 0
Minimum password length     : 0
Password history count      : 0
RID: 01f4, Username: <Administrator>, *BLANK password*
RID: 01f5, Username: <Guest>, *disabled or locked*
RID: 03e8, Username: <HelpAssistant>
RID: 03ea, Username: <SUPPORT_388945a0>, *disabled or locked*

Hives that have changed:
 #  Name
None!
```

This example has four users: Administrator, Guest, HelpAssistant, and SUPPORT_388945a0. Pick the user you want to edit, and then run *chntpw* with the -u option:

```
knoppix@ttyp1[config]$ /home/knoppix/chntpw -u username SAM
```

Once you change the password and save your changes, unmount the filesystem and reboot:

```
knoppix@ttyp1[config]$ cd
knoppix@ttyp1[knoppix]$ sudo umount /mnt/hda1
```

When you boot back to Windows, the password should be blank, so you can log in and change the password with the regular Windows tools.

Edit the Windows Registry

The chntpw tool not only resets an Administrator password, but it also comes with a full-fledged registry editor. This makes it a useful tool for solving other types of Windows problems (e.g., deleting the registry keys put in place by a virus or worm) without booting into Windows.

The *chntpw* tool mentioned in "Reset Lost NT Passwords" **[Hack #75]** works by changing the values in the Windows registry. This tool uses the same ability that allow you to navigate through the Windows registry, much like you would navigate through a Linux filesystem, and edit values. While this tool can be useful in a pinch, it is recommended to edit your registry using the tools included in Windows, such as *regedit.exe*. This example assumes that you are using *chntpw* to edit a registry value that is preventing you from booting Windows.

> Directly editing your Windows registry can be very risky and should be left to seasoned Windows administrators. One bad change could render your machine unbootable. Always back up your complete registry, and make sure you know what you are doing before attempting to change things.

Prepare to Edit the Registry

First, obtain the *chntpw tool* **[Hack #75]** to edit the registry. This example assumes that you are editing the registry of a Windows partition on */dev/hda1*. If */dev/hda1* is a FAT or FAT32 partition, click on the hard-drive icon to mount it, and then right-click on the icon and choose Actions → Change Read/Write Mode. You can also type the following command:

```
knoppix@ttyp1[knoppix]$ mount /dev/hda1
```

If the partition is NTFS, follow the steps in "Write to NTFS" **[Hack #73]**, and then mount it with:

```
knoppix@ttyp1[knoppix]$ sudo mount -t captive-ntfs -o
uid=knoppix,gid=knoppix /dev/hda1 /mnt/hda1
```

Getting to Know Your Registry

After you mount the filesystem, you must find where Windows is storing the registry. This is actually more difficult than just finding some *Registry.reg* file tucked away in a corner of your filesystem. Windows stores sections of the registry in different files called hives, located in different directories on the drive. (I like to think they are called "hives" because it's easy to get stung while you are poking around in them!) Most of the important hives (DEFAULT, SAM, SECURITY, SOFTWARE, and SYSTEM) are stored under *systemroot\System32\Config*, where *systemroot* is usually *WINNT* or *Windows* on Windows 2000 or newer systems. The remaining hive is located in the *NTuser.dat* file, which is located in *Documents and Settings\username* or in *systemroot\Profiles\username*. These files correspond to specific hives in the registry, as listed in the following table:

Registry key name	Hive filename
HKEY_CURRENT_CONFIG	SYSTEM
HKEY_CURRENT_USER	NTuser.dat
HKEY_LOCAL_MACHINE\SAM	SAM
HKEY_LOCAL_MACHINE\SECURITY	SECURITY
HKEY_LOCAL_MACHINE\SOFTWARE	SOFTWARE
HKEY_USERS\DEFAULT	DEFAULT

Edit the Registry

Once you decide which registry keys you need to edit and which hive they are in, open a terminal and change to the directory containing that hive's file. For this example, I change the value of my `SystemRoot` registry key to point to *E:\WINDOWS* instead of *D:\WINDOWS* because I have changed my partitioning scheme, and I must move my *WINDOWS* directory to a different partition. To find the location of your registry keys, browse in *chntpw*, browse *regedit* under Windows, or search the Web for information about the location of your key. In my case, the key is located under the following directory:

```
HKEY_LOCAL_MACHINE\SOFTWARE\Microsoft\Windows NT\CurrentVersion\
```

I must open the corresponding hive file, *SOFTWARE*, with *chntpw*:

```
knoppix@ttyp1[config]$ /home/knoppix/chntpw -e SOFTWARE
chntpw version 0.99.2 040105, (c) Petter N Hagen
Hive's name (from header): <emRoot\System32\Config\SOFTWARE>
ROOT KEY at offset: 0x001020
Page at 0x7f2000 is not 'hbin', assuming file contains garbage at end
File size 8388608 [800000] bytes, containing 1967 pages (+ 1 headerpage)
Used for data: 166446/8253944 blocks/bytes, unused: 1069/10280 blocks/bytes.
Simple registry editor. ? for help.

[1020] >
```

The last line is a command prompt that accepts a limited number of shell-like commands to browse through the registry structure and to edit values. Type a question mark (**?**) and hit Enter. The following list of commands and their syntax appears:

```
[1020] > ?
Simple registry editor:
```

```
hive [<n>] - list loaded hives or switch to hive numer n'
cd <key> - change key
ls | dir [<key>] - show subkeys & values,
cat | type <value> - show key value
st [<hexaddr>] - show struct info
nk <keyname> - add key
dk <keyname> - delete key (must be empty. recursion not supported yet)
ed <value>              - Edit value
nv <type> <valuename> - Add value
dv <valuename>          - Delete value
delallv                 - Delete all values in current key
debug - enter buffer hexeditor
q - quit
```

The main commands that you use are *ls* and *cd*, much in the same way as on
the command line. However, instead of directories, you list the contents of
registry keys. Type **ls** to see a list of keys in this hash and **cd** to go inside a
specific key:

```
[1020] > ls
ls of node at offset 0x1024
Node has 12 subkeys and 0 values
offs         key name
[  11b8]    <Aureal>
[  1958]    <CO7ft5Y>
[  1a30]    <Classes>
[637248]    <Clients>
[63bbc8]    <Gemplus>
[63bde0]    <Microsoft>
[7c9978]    <ODBC>
[7ccc80]    <Policies>
[7d8750]    <Program Groups>
[7d87d8]    <Schlumberger>
[7da6c8]    <Secure>
[7e5528]    <Windows 3.1 Migration Status>

[1020] > cd Mi

[63bde0] \Microsoft>
```

Notice that you don't have to type out Microsoft to go to that key. This
command shell does not support tab completion, but if you type the first
few characters of a key's name, it automatically fills it in with the first key
that matches those characters when you press Enter. Also, if you know the
full path of the key you want to change to, you can type it all at once, such
as **cd Microsoft\Windows NT\CurrentVersion**. Once you get to the directory
containing the key you wish to change, type **ls** and confirm that the key
exists, and then you can use the *cat* command to show the value of the key:

```
[791488] \Microsoft\Windows NT\CurrentVersion> cat SystemRoot
Value <SystemRoot> of type REG_SZ, data length 22 [0x16]
D:\WINDOWS
[791488] \Microsoft\Windows NT\CurrentVersion>
```

If you want to delete this key, simply type **dk SystemRoot** at the prompt.

Use the *ed* command to change the value:

```
[791488] \Microsoft\Windows NT\CurrentVersion> ed SystemRoot
EDIT: <SystemRoot> of type REG_SZ with length 22 [0x16]
[ 0]: D:\WINDOWS

Now enter new strings, one by one.
Enter nothing to keep old.
[ 0]: D:\WINDOWS
-> E:\WINDOWS

[791488] \Microsoft\Windows NT\CurrentVersion> cat SystemRoot
Value <SystemRoot> of type REG_SZ, data length 24 [0x18]
E:\WINDOWS
```

If you hit Enter, *chntpw* lets you leave the key as is. You can also type in the new value and hit Enter to make the change. After you make your changes, hit **q** to quit the registry editor. If you have changed any keys, *chntpw* prompts you to save your changes. Until now, *chntpw* has not actually written the changes you have made to the file; saying "yes" here writes any changes to the registry. Once the changes are written, you can exit *chntpw*, unmount your partition, and then reboot your computer back to Windows to observe the changes.

Restore Corrupted System Files
HACK #77

Extract important drivers and other system files from .cab files on your Windows system from within Knoppix.

One of the functions of the Windows Recovery CD is to restore system files that have been corrupted. Basically, the CD extracts the default versions of these drivers from *.cab* files stored on the CD and overwrites the versions on your system. If you have applied service packs since you have installed Windows, drivers updated by the service package are overwritten with these old ones. If you don't have a Windows Recovery CD handy or you want to use files from a service pack, restore important system files by using the *.cab* files that are already on your system with Knoppix. If you don't have the necessary *.cab* files, download the security patches from Microsoft's site, and extract the files you need [Hack #79].

Call a Cab

Before you can restore a system file, you have to locate the *.cab* file that stores it. Don't worry. It's much easier and faster to find a *.cab* with Knoppix than to find one in New York City.

In this example, the goal is to replace a corrupted *ntdll.dll* file, a very important Windows system file. First, find which *.cab* files on your system it is in. Mount the Windows partition under Knoppix (in this example, the partition is mounted under */mnt/hda1*), and then use the Linux *find* command combined with *cabextract* (a Linux utility that can extract files from *.cab* files):

```
knoppix@ttyp0[knoppix]$ find /mnt/hda1/ -name *.cab -exec sh -c
"if cabextract -l \"{}\" 2>/dev/null | grep ntdll.dll;
then echo \"{}\"; fi; " \;
    481040 | 27.10.1999 12:06:10 | ntdll.dll
/mnt/hda1/winnt/Driver Cache/i386/driver.cab
    491792 | 19.06.2003 12:05:04 | ntdll.dll
/mnt/hda1/winnt/ServicePackFiles/i386/sp4.cab
```

Basically, the script finds all *.cab* files on your Windows partition, and then searches through the files they contain for the file you are looking for. In this example, I found two *.cab* files that contain *ntdll.dll*: */mnt/hda1/winnt/Driver Cache/i386/driver.cab* and */mnt/hda1/winnt/ServicePackFiles/i386/sp4.cab*. Notice that the files have different sizes and different dates. A good rule of thumb is to use the most current version of the file; in this case, it is in *sp4.cab*.

> While this magic spell might seem complicated, you only need to focus on the *grep* command. Reuse this command to find other files by simply replacing *ntdll.dll* with the filename you are searching for.

If you can't seem to find a *.cab* file on your system with the files you need, you can also use *cabextract* to extract files directly from Microsoft's official Service Packs. As "Download Windows Patches Securely" **[Hack #79]** mentions, Microsoft's TechNet page (*http://www.microsoft.com/technet*) allows you to download full standalone executable patches for your system, including Service Packs. Use the search engine on TechNet's page to find Service Packs for your version of Windows. For instance, if you type "Windows 2000 Service Pack," the first few links direct you to the latest Service Packs. Even though these files end in ".exe," these Service Packs are actually self-extracting *.cab* files, and *cabextract* works with them the same way.

If you are given a choice between the Express Install version and the Network Install version, choose the Network Install. The Express Install does not actually contain all the system files and instead runs a program that downloads the ones your particular system needs. You want to extract specific files, so download the Network Install, which includes all the system files.

If you have not yet mounted your system with write permissions, right-click on the icon on the desktop and click Actions → Change Read/Write Mode, or in the case of an NTFS partition, follow the steps in "Write to NTFS" [Hack #73].

Once you choose the *.cab* file to use, change to the directory that contains your corrupted file. If you aren't sure where it is, type:

```
knoppix@ttyp0[knoppix]$ find /mnt/hda1 -name ntdll.dll -print
/mnt/hda1/winnt/system32/ntdll.dll
```

After you change to that directory, use *cabextract* to extract the file and overwrite the corrupted version:

```
knoppix@ttyp0[knoppix]$ cd /mnt/hda1/winnt/system32/
knoppix@ttyp0[system32]$ sudo cabextract -F ntdll.dll
"/mnt/hda1/winnt/ServicePackFiles/i386/sp4.cab"
Extracting cabinet: /mnt/hda1/winnt/ServicePackFiles/i386/sp4.cab
  Extracting ntdll.dll

All done, no errors.
knoppix@ttyp0[system32]$
```

Now change to a directory outside of your windows partition, unmount it, and then reboot.

```
knoppix@ttyp0[system32]$ cd
knoppix@ttyp0[system32]$ sudo umount /mnt/hda1
```

HACK #78   Scan for Viruses

Ridding a network of Windows computers of a virus or worm can seem impossible. Viruses may cause computers to reboot and infect new machines while you are in the process of removing them. Through the use of the live-software installer, Knoppix provides a solution to this catch-22.

Viruses and worms are a common problem in the computing world today. It seems every other day a new virus or worm comes out, and anti-virus vendors must quickly update their signatures to block the new outbreak. Unfortunately not everyone has a virus scanner installed on his system, or if he does, it might not be kept up to date. When the worst happens, you must make sure that the virus doesn't spread to other computers on the network or damage your files. If you install a virus scanner, you must be sure that the virus can't find a way to infect, disable, or hide from it.

There are several advantages to using Knoppix as a virus scanner over the alternatives:

You are booting off of read-only media. While the home directory in Knoppix is writable from a ramdisk, all the system files are on read-only media. Even if a virus can somehow infect Knoppix, it isn't able to modify any of the system files, and any files it can infect are deleted at the next reboot. Also, all the underlying partitions are mounted read-only by default. Unless you purposely mount a partition read/write, it is not possible for an infection to spread to your partitions.

The possibly infected system is not running. Knoppix is running outside of your underlying system, so any viruses that might have been loaded into memory have been erased, and the hard drive itself is, in effect, frozen in time, so you don't have to worry about a virus evading deletion. This also means you don't have to worry about the virus spreading, so you can connect the machine to the network while it is running Knoppix to read any advisories or download any files you might need.

You are booting off of a completely different operating system. While viruses have been written for Linux in the past and more will be written in the future, it is still rather uncommon. Let's face it; you are probably scanning a Windows system for a virus or worm that runs only on Windows, and Knoppix runs off of a completely different operating system, so even if you accidentally click on a virus-infected file, it doesn't launch the virus. If the virus has infected other machines on the network and is scanning systems to infect, you don't have to worry about reinfection while you are running off of Knoppix.

It's free. While it is still advisable to have virus protection running on a Windows system at all times, virus protection can be expensive—not only due to the initial cost, but also to the annual subscription fees to get virus-definition updates. If you can't afford virus-protection software, you can at least scan your system periodically with Knoppix for free.

F-Prot is a free virus scanner that you can run under Linux. You can install F-Prot with Knoppix's live-software installer, covered in "Use the Knoppix Live Installer" [Hack #27]. The live installer needs a working Internet connection to download the program, and the program itself needs to be able to download updates as well.

Click K Menu → KNOPPIX → Utilities → Install software, select f-prot, and click OK to start the installation. Once the installation finishes, click K Menu → KNOPPIX → Extra Software → f-prot to start the F-Prot GUI.

After you launch F-Prot, immediately select option 4, "Do Online Update," to make sure that you have the latest list of virus definitions (see Figure 7-2). Once the update is finished, choose "Select partition(s)" from the F-Prot GUI, or if you have already mounted the partition, you can choose "Select a directory/file" to pick the directory to scan. Once you choose a directory, you are dropped back to the main menu where you can then choose Scan to start the scanning process. A progress meter appears, and the length of the virus scan varies, depending on the size of the directory you are scanning.

Figure 7-2. The F-Prot GUI

Once the process is finished, F-Prot displays a report that lists the different files it has scanned. The information you are probably most interested in, whether you are infected or not, is listed at the very bottom of the file. There, you should see how many files F-Prot has scanned, and under that, you should see whether F-Prot has found any viruses. If you are clean, you should see "No viruses or suspicious files/boot sectors were found."

> If you do have an infection, it can be time-consuming to filter through the output to find which files are infected. To make this easier, run *grep* to search for the word Infection on the F-Prot output file that is in your home directory by typing the following command in a terminal: **grep Infection ~/report-2004-05-17-0.txt**.

Once you have a list of suspicious or infected files, you can mount the partition read/write and delete or rename the files. If you are a Windows expert who is comfortable with registry edits, you can follow the steps in "Edit the Windows Registry" **[Hack #76]** to remove any registry keys the virus might have left behind. You might also want to view advisories on the viruses that F-Prot finds on *http://www.cert.org* or other security sites, and see if perhaps there is a patch you can download to protect your system from this virus or worm in the future. Now is a good time to save any patches you might need to your hard drive, so you can boot back to your computer without having to connect to the network, and install the patch as covered in "Download Windows Patches Securely" **[Hack #79]**.

HACK #79 Download Windows Patches Securely

Use Knoppix to download Microsoft Windows patches onto a vulnerable Windows machine. Then boot to Windows, and apply the patch while disconnected from the network.

It seems like new vulnerabilities for Windows, or software running on Windows, appear every few weeks. The worst vulnerabilities are remote exploits that give the attacker full Administrative privileges on a machine. Worms that exploit these vulnerabilities are written rather quickly and are soon scanning the Internet looking for machines to infect. The common remedy for these exploits is to download a patch from the Internet with a service like Windows Update. The problem is that your machine is at risk of being exploited every moment it is on the Internet downloading the latest patches. It's like running across the battlefield to get your bulletproof vest! Use Knoppix to provide cover for you. Boot to Knoppix, grab the patches you need, and then apply them from within Windows with the computer disconnected from the network.

In addition to Windows Update, Microsoft also provides patches as individual downloads so that system administrators can download them once and apply them across the network, saving bandwidth and time. This service is provided at *http://www.microsoft.com/technet*, where you can browse for downloads and security bulletins for all of the software Microsoft supports.

To get the Windows patches, boot to Knoppix and visit *http://www.microsoft.com/technet*. Then click on the Security link or the Downloads link on the left side of the page. The security page provides links to the latest security bulletins and virus alerts, and the downloads page lists new security patches and bug fixes for Microsoft software. If you have the Knowledge Base ID (KB followed by six numbers) or the Security Bulletin ID (MS followed by two numbers, a dash, and three more numbers), then you can search by that ID under TechNet, and quickly get a link to the download you need.

You can register with Microsoft's Security Notification Service at *http://www.microsoft.com/technet/security/bulletin/notify.mspx* to get security bulletins emailed to you as they are announced. This makes searching by the Security Bulletin ID much simpler.

Once you find the appropriate download, mount your Windows partition with read/write permissions by clicking on the drive icon to mount it, and then right-clicking on the drive icon and selecting Actions → Change read/write mode, or for NTFS partitions, follow the steps in "Write to NTFS" [Hack #73]. Then you can save the download directly to your Windows partition.

Once the download is complete, temporarily disconnect your network cable from the computer (or otherwise disable your Internet connection), and boot to Windows to apply the patch following any instructions that Microsoft provides.

## CHAPTER EIGHT

Knoppix Reloaded
Hacks 80–93

If imitation is the sincerest form of flattery, Klaus Knopper should be blushing. According to Distrowatch, Knoppix is used as a base for 45 other live CDs—and those are just the CDs that Distrowatch knows about! It is difficult to include all the necessary software with only 2 GB of uncompressed space at your disposal. Knoppix variants have appeared because people who wanted to create their own live CDs discovered just how easy it is to remaster Knoppix—something you too will discover in "Create a Customized Knoppix" [Hack #94]. With Knoppix as a base, these developers benefit from the hardware support and the configuration that Knoppix uses, and can spend their energy on making specialized tweaks for their needs instead. Some of these Knoppix-based CDs, such as Morphix, are used as a base themselves to create other distributions.

Knoppix-based distributions run the full spectrum in terms of what they can do and what can be changed. Some distributions have kept most of Knoppix intact, and have added only extra special-purpose software here and there. Others have almost redone Knoppix from the ground up. Distribution sizes vary dramatically as well, ranging from 50 MB for business-card CD variants, to a gigabyte or more for some of the DVD-based variants. Think about it; each of these live CDs is a hack of Knoppix itself.

This chapter highlights just a few of the better-known or interesting Knoppix variants. If you plan to create your own Knoppix-based CD, it is worth it to check out some of the work that has already been done. You might find your needs are already met in one of these distributions.

In true community spirit, many of the following descriptions are from the developers themselves. Grab a stack of blank CDs and a magic marker, because after you read about some of these great distributions, you will want to try them yourself.

Master Morphix

#80   Morphix is a Knoppix-based distribution that takes a modular approach to CD creation.

Given the popularity of Knoppix and the vast amount of people working on derivative versions of Knoppix, it doesn't come as a surprise that people have been working to make Knoppix easier to modify and more flexible to use. In early 2003, people who used Knoppix as a base on which to build live CDs (which used Debian GNU/Linux) developed Morphix (*http://www.morphix.org*)—a remastered version of Knoppix.

What Makes Morphix So Special

As you have seen in this book, there are a number of ways to change Knoppix to your liking, particularly with remastering, which is covered in the next chapter. However, these possibilities have always been, and probably will always be, fairly limited. Knoppix was made for different goals: to detect your hardware as quickly and correctly as possible, to be a good demonstration of Linux, and to include as much commonly used Linux software as possible.

Morphix, on the other hand, is built on the idea of modules: you have one module that boots your live CD and detects your hardware, another that contains your live-CD filesystem, and zero or more extra modules that can contain minor or major changes and additions to the system. This way, Morphix promotes the reusing of smaller, existing modules instead of one large */KNOPPIX/KNOPPIX* file. If it seems complicated, a look at a typical Morphix live CD might help. This is the structure of Morphix 0.4-1 Light-GUI, one Morphix flavor:

```
/base
/base/boot.img
/base/morphix
/mainmod
/mainmod/MorphixMain-Light.mod
/minimod
/deb
/copy
/exec
```

While it seems quite empty, this is how typical versions of Morphix are released. They are quite bare, but offer users (or *morphers*, as we call ourselves) more possibilities to change the resulting live CD.

Morphix currently has four ready-to-burn *combined ISOs* available for download and a list of extra modules available for whoever needs them. All combined ISOs contain the Morphix installer, a graphical tool for installing

Morphix to your hard disk, and a number of other graphical and command-line Morphix tools for various purposes. Each of these live CDs has a targeted audience—morphers have always believed that we should offer limited choices to users and unlimited (as much as possible) choices to developers:

Morphix LightGUI
> Aimed at lower-end PCs, LightGUI features the XFCE4 desktop and contains a reasonable amount of lighter tools. It was the initial version of Morphix, and the aim has been to keep LightGUI small enough to fit on 210 MB mini CDR (W). LightGUI includes Abiword, Gnumeric, Dillo, and Firefox. For communication, Gaim and Xchat are included, and for photo processing, the GIMP has been added.

Morphix Gnome
> Formerly named Morphix HeavyGUI, this flavor was for some time the only counterpart of LightGUI. Morphix Gnome includes Gnome, OpenOffice.org, Mozilla. It was aimed at office users with more recent machines. Even so, a normal Morphix Gnome ISO still doesn't fill up the whole (650 MB) CD-ROM, and recent versions weigh in at around 500 MB.

Morphix KDE
> Although primarily focused on GTK/Gnome, the Morphix crew acknowledges that users might prefer KDE instead (and looking at the number of derivatives, a lot of users do!). Morphix KDE contains the whole KDE suite of programs, as well as Mozilla and other applications. Morphix KDE sits in between LightGUI and Gnome when it comes to size, and fills up approximately 400 MB of space on your CD-ROM.

Morphix Game
> An oddball in Morphix, this flavor contains the very light IceWM and a very large number of open source games. BZflag, Frozen Bubble, Freecraft, and many, many others are sure to entertain the kids (or entertain the kid in you) for quite a few hours. Normally, Morphix Game also includes one or more demo versions or free full versions of commercial Linux games, adding to the fun. Gaming on Linux a rarity? This hasn't been the case for many years, no matter which kind of games you enjoy!

All the official Morphix live CDs contain the Morphix installer. This tool allows users to easily install their Morphix (or derivative) live CD to a hard disk. The difference between a live CD and a hard disk install is very small indeed. The Morphix installer is also built in a flexible manner so that derivatives can even rebrand the Morphix installer, although the source itself is licensed under the GNU GPL. A graphical partition tool and a series of configuration tools have been under development, and are likely to be part of Morphix by the time this book comes off the press.

To find out more about the structure of Morphix and how to use Morphix to create your own CDs, check out "Morph Morphix" **[Hack #99]**.

See Also

- The official Morphix page at *http://www.morphix.org*.

—Alex de Landgraaf

 ## Gnoppix Gnome Gnirvana

Like Knoppix but dislike KDE? Before you remaster Knoppix, try Gnoppix, a Knoppix-based distribution that replaces the default KDE desktop with a Gnome desktop.

One of the great things about open source software is that it generally encourages choice. Indeed, even on Knoppix, you are given different choices for web browsers, email clients, text editors, and window managers.

But sometimes choice breeds contention. There are a few ongoing holy wars in the open source community. Some, like VI versus Emacs and GPL versus BSDL, have been going on for decades. Some, like KDE versus Gnome, are still relatively fresh. Without adding any fuel to the fire, it is sufficient to say that some people prefer the Gnome desktop to the KDE desktop. If you are one of these people, Gnoppix (*http://www.gnoppix.org*) is for you.

As the name indicates, the Gnoppix project's focus is to provide a Knoppix-like live CD with a complete Gnome desktop in place of KDE. From the moment you boot Gnoppix, you can see quite a difference from the default Knoppix desktop (see Figure 8-1). You even start programs differently. In Knoppix, icons on the desktop are single-clicked to run; in Gnoppix, they are double-clicked. In Knoppix, the application menu (K Menu) is located on the bottom panel; in Gnoppix, it is along the top panel.

For basically every KDE/QT application that Knoppix includes, Gnoppix offers the Gnome/GTK alternative. The following table illustrates some of the primary applications that Gnoppix offers as alternatives:

Function	Knoppix	Gnoppix
Email	Kmail	Evolution
File Management	Konqueror	Nautilus
Terminal	Konsole	Gnome-terminal
Address book	Kontact	GnomeCard
Programming IDE	Kdevelop	Glade

Boy, that's a lot of Ks and Gs. Really, even with all of the differences that a Gnome desktop and a KDE desktop have, Gnoppix and Knoppix share a lot of the same applications. Both offer Mozilla (Gnoppix defaults to it); both use OpenOffice.org; and both have the Gimp, Xchat, and Gaim.

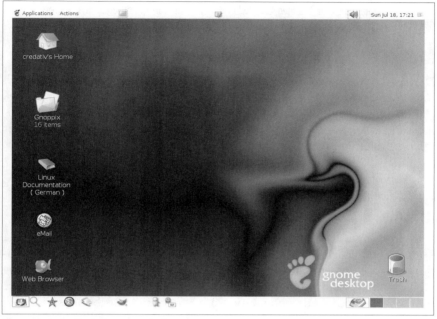

Figure 8-1. Default Gnoppix desktop

What might attract you to use Gnoppix, especially if you are a fan of Gnome, is the almost exclusive use of Gnome alternatives on the CD. This results in a desktop environment that is more tightly integrated, particularly in look and feel, because all major applications use the GTK toolkit for widgets.

The use of only Gnome alternatives also results in a desktop that is easier to use in many respects. In areas where only the Gnome alternatives are offered, the applications are given functional labels instead of program names. For instance, Mozilla is labeled Web Browser, Evolution is labeled eMail, and GnomeCard is labeled Address Book. For a user that is new to Linux who doesn't know one application from another, this kind of labeling might make it easier to identify which program to use for which function.

Gnoppix also offers the option to install the CD directly to a hard drive, which makes this distribution a great choice if you want to quickly and easily install Debian with Gnome. In short, if you are looking for a great live CD, but have avoided Knoppix due to the KDE desktop, give Gnoppix a try.

See Also

- The official Gnoppix home page at *http://www.gnoppix.org*.

Pump Up the Volume with Mediainlinux

HACK #82   Mediainlinux is the live-CD Swiss Army knife for multimedia. It's a free
ready-to-go kit for the multimedia professional to carry with him at all times.

Birth of Mediainlinux

During 2003, I was working at the Virtual Reality & Multi Media Park
(*http://www.vrmmp.it*) help desk. Some students attending the school
(*http://edu.vrmmp.it*) wanted to know how to configure and use the multimedia free software (basically Gimp, Blender, and OpenOffice.org) under
the proprietary operating system in use on their computers.

They were already conscious that those applications had real advantages
over their commercial counterparts, and at the same time, they had a strong
interest in the GNU/Linux operating system, its possibilities, its politics, and
its social implications.

The problem was they had neither the time nor the will to try and test
Linux. They had made some very early attempts with homemade installations or other experiments with the help of friends who were already using
GNU/Linux, but they obtained very poor results. I gave them some advice
on the installation and configuration of some major distributions, like Red
Hat and Mandrake, and later Debian. However, they still couldn't use
Linux, because they didn't want to install the new operating system. They
were afraid that they would lose all or a major part of their data stored on
their hard drive (often never backed up).

Besides the installation, there was still the problem of configuring peripherals, audio and video subsystems, and restoring the previous operating system.

Teaching those students a new and free way of doing multimedia became a
hard, repetitive, and time-consuming activity. After several unsuccessful
attempts, I started to investigate live CDs—CD-ROMs containing a ready-
to-use and self-configuring GNU/Linux, including Knoppix. Unfortunately,
Knoppix has plenty of system administration software, but multimedia
applications are particularly scarce, with a few exceptions for some audio,
graphics, and video tools (more or less 10 applications).

So I decided to learn how to modify the Knoppix live CD-ROM, and used
and exchanged ideas, tips, and tricks with the community that was forming
on the unofficial Knoppix forum (*http://www.knoppix.net*).

Mediainlinux Today

Mediainlinux is a working prototype of a Debian Multimedia Distribution, based on the last version (v3.4) of the Knoppix Linux Live CD. Mediainlinux supports most of the GNU/Linux-compatible graphic, audio, and TV/satellite computer cards on the market. It comes with more than 200 graphical applications and hundreds of command-line tools that cover all the complexity of the multimedia production process: acquisition, conversion, compression, and mastering.

Most of the multimedia applications in the GNU/Linux world are covered, but there are some tools that we don't want to distribute with Mediainlinux either for legal reasons or for the integrity of the code (code covered by copyrights, etc). You can, however, use the Synaptic package installer to install these applications once Mediainlinux itself is installed on the hard disk.

Short-Term Goals

The Mediainlinux project has a number of goals; some have been achieved and some are being currently tested.

Technical goals. Among the technical goals is the creation of a multimedia kernel that is modified to gain more responsiveness from the system with low latency, preemption, and real-time patches, and is focused on support for a variety of graphic and audio subsystems with a better recognition of peripherals. In addition, the kernel is going to be openMosix-enabled to distribute rendering with Blender and Yafray. As always, there is the continuing goal to develop a customized multimedia CD.

Nontechnical goals. One of the main nontechnical goals of Mediainlinux is to include multimedia applications that are not yet a part of the Debian distribution. Speed in the free-software world creates a situation in which hundreds of projects start in a year, but for many projects, it might take two or three years to be included in the major distributions. Part of this goal is the continued support for package maintainers to promote the diffusion of applications that haven't already been packaged by Debian. One of the goals of Mediainlinux is to find economic support for Debian multimedia package maintainers who aren't already sponsored.

Another goal is to increase Mediainlinux use within other organizations. We had contacts with some organizations, like ONU and UNESCO, with Italian (Turin, Padova, Bologna, Siena) and international (Bristol, Oslo, Zlin, Tampere, Georgia) universities, and with some other organizations in the audio and video fields, like FESTPACO and the African Women Media

Center. Mediainlinux was introduced with the goal of collaboration that goes from simple testing and reporting of bugs to requests for new characteristics and development of additional software.

A community of particular interest to Mediainlinux is art academies. Many institutions, like MULTIDAMS of Turin, the school of Art and Media of Tampere, or the Brera Academy of Art in Milan, provide two roles for Mediainlinux: a public place for experimentation (and therefore contamination between technology and art), and the potential for demonstrations and examples of Mediainlinux use by artists and collaborators.

User goals. The look of Mediainlinux is a key aspect of the whole project. One main goal for the end user is to make Mediainlinux a better-looking distribution. The more stylish the distribution is in its design and in its graphic and artistic ideas (from the CD-ROM to the manual, from the web site to an exhibition stand), the more success it gains in the artist community. The project must also continue to surpass the look of proprietary systems. This requires graphics for icons, desktop themes, wallpapers, and screensavers, and audio/video materials (like desktop sounds and video tutorials).

There is a continuing goal to make Mediainlinux simpler. We must provide more integration between different applications (for instance, an Ogg Vorbis file should have a contextual menu to play, edit, record, etc.). This should be done for most of the file formats in the multimedia field, and it is an operation that requires very intensive configuring, programming, experimenting, and daily use. Part of the process to make Mediainlinux simpler is to make better configuration tools. Most of all, we need a good configuration of the automounter to automatically create the icons for peripherals on the desktop.

Another ongoing goal is to improve documentation. We need a manual for the primary applications on the CD (the Mediainlinux documentation page, which is almost done, can be found at *http://www.mediainlinux.org/index. php/mediainlinux/documentation*) and, in turn, we need to translate that document into English, French, Spanish, and German.

To help the end user utilize Mediainlinux to its full potential, one goal is to organize training. We organize many courses on subsystems included in Mediainlinux, ranging from the commonly used (audio and video streaming, 2D and 3D graphics, and musical composition) to the less commonly used (multimedia installations and physical and acoustic simulation). In addition to improved training, we want to continue to improve support. This requires a concrete way to support our users with a mailing list, a forum and a satellite program with tutorials, examples, and demonstrations of creativity.

See Also

- The official Mediainlinux page at *http://www.mediainlinux.com/ez/ mediainlinux*.

—*Marco Ghirlanda*

HACK #83 Educate Yourself with Freeduc

Freeduc is a Knoppix-based distribution with a focus on providing free software to schools. The Freeduc CD boots into an XFCE environment configured with many tools suitable for classroom use.

A Knoppix CD is a fantastic way to demonstrate an entirely free operating system to a free-software newbie. At OFSET (The Organization for Free Software in Education and Teaching, *http://www.ofset.org*), we've found that a customized version of Knoppix is the perfect way to demonstrate to educators and parents what is available for them within the free-software community. To make our demonstrations even more targeted, we decided to produce a customized version of Knoppix, called Freeduc (short for FREe EDUCation). Eventually, UNESCO (United Nations Educational, Scientific and Cultural Organization, *http://www.unesco.org*) decided to support us in the release of Freeduc 1.4. According to UNESCO:

> FREEDUC…is at the disposal of UNESCO to facilitate the use of free software in education and teaching. The gratis distribution of this international version of FREEDUC to teachers will help to promote access to information and communication technologies for education and teaching.

We want Freeduc's users to focus on the free applications and not on the desktop, so we decided to include only one light desktop environment and save CD-ROM space for more applications. We chose XFCE3 because it's light, consistent, and very stable. The XFCE3 application bar has 10 dedicated drawers for launching applications. The drawers organize applications into the following categories:

Basic computer access
Includes killing/destroying a window, formatting a floppy, and opening a terminal

Internet
Includes Mozilla, *gftp*, and *sylpheed*

Mathematics
Includes Dr. Geo, *gnumeric*, and *gtkgraph*

Sciences
Includes *gstar*, *pymol*, *kstars*, and *chemtool*

Audio
> Includes *audacity*, *rosegarden*, and *gmplayer*

Technology
> Includes *dia*, *pcb*, *tkgate*, *qcad*, *tuxpaint*, and the Gimp

Geography
> Includes *xrmap* and *grass*

Languages
> Includes *gnome-dictionary*, *hanzim*, and *collatinus*

Educational games
> Includes *gcompris*, *freeciv*, *xlincity*, and *xboard*

Word processing and help tools
> Includes *OpenOffice.org*, *abiword*, *scribus*, and *tkman*

About 40 applications for education and teaching are available on the CD-ROM (some, such as GCompris and Dr. Geo, we developed ourselves).

Contributing to the Freeduc Project

When we first began working on Freeduc 1.4, several of us were spread out in France. We found a need for a central repository to hold the in-development, unpacked Freeduc. Klaus Knopper graciously offered to host a server at LinuxTag. We were able to synchronize local copies on the developer workstation with the repository using *rsync*.

However, we found we needed to secure the way we were using *rsync* to update our local copy or the repository. We wrote a simple *bash* script to encapsulate the use of *rsync* with the use of a lock file in the repository to prevent upload when another developer was working on it.

Therefore, when a developer wants to start working in Freeduc, she first sets a lock in the repository with the command:

```
knoppix@ttyp0[knoppix]$ fcs lock
```

Her local copy is updated with the repository content, then a simple lock file is set in the repository. That way, the other developers cannot modify the repository until the first developer unlocks it. This tool also handles updates and other syncing issues, and can be downloaded from our CVS repository at *http://sourceforge.net/projects/ofset*.

See Also

- The official Freeduc page at *http://www.ofset.org/freeduc-cd*.

> —*Hilaire Fernandes*

HACK #84 Damn Small Linux

Damn Small Linux is a business-card-sized (50 MB) bootable live CD Linux distribution. Despite its size, it strives to have a functional and easy to use desktop.

The History

Simply put, I'm an efficiency freak, which is why I founded Damn Small Linux (DSL, *http://www.damnsmalllinux.org*). I am also a big Knoppix fan, but running KDE, OpenOffice.org, Mozilla, etc. from a live CD on my older computers is a real chore. I usually grab the lightest applications to use on my home desktop: for email, I use Sylpheed; for browsing, I use Dillo or Links-Hacked.

I wanted a desktop-oriented live CD that was fast and small, so I checked out LNX-BBC (*http://www.lnxbbc.org*) and ByzantineOS (*http://byzgl.sourceforge.net*), the two leading sub-50-MB distributions at the time. They were both very innovative but not really what I was looking for. LNX-BBC is similar to a rescue disk, and ByzantineOS is based on Mozilla (which it uses in very interesting ways). I was on a quest for a Linux distribution that was small enough to fit on a business-card CD, yet had a fully functional desktop.

I read about the reduction efforts to get Knoppix small enough to fit into 80-mm 210-MB CDs. Some of them were quite nice, like Kurumin (*http://guiadohardware.net/kurumin/*) from Brazil, but I wanted something very portable and under 50 MB, like LNX-BBC. I decided to try my hand at remastering Knoppix [Hack #94]. I actually cheated in the beginning and used an already reduced ISO called Model_K (now defunct). In later releases, DSL began as a reduction of Knoppix proper.

Getting a fully functional desktop into 50 MB is not a simple process. Fortunately, all the lightweight applications had already been developed; I just had to be very particular about what was included in DSL. For instance, the X from Knoppix is much too big, so I had to hack a system that uses Keith Packard's Kdrive X servers (*http://freedesktop.org/Software/xserver*).

DSL has evolved a lot over time. Some applications have been dropped and replaced with programs that are a better fit. By the third public release, users started to contribute hacks, which cumulatively improved DSL. In that sense, open source projects are interesting: some people provide a one-time hack, while others continue their involvement and help the project along. For several releases, Peter Sieg (*http://www.petersieg.de*) made contributions that greatly enhanced DSL's functionality.

From about 0.5 and on, Robert Shingledecker (*http://www.shingledecker.org*) has been a major contributor to DSL development. With so many improvements and suggestions, he should be recognized as a coauthor. He's a creative genius, and we are implementing his amazing improvements, including a fully automated application-installation process that we are currently calling "MyDSL Click and Load."

DSL has also picked up many of the Knoppix features that you've already been introduced to in this book. DSL can be easily installed on a hard drive so that it runs as an image, which is similar to the bootfrom cheat code [Hack #5]. There is a restoration process that can grab files from any drive and restore them at boot, which is similar to the persistent settings in "Create Persistent Knoppix Settings" [Hack #21]. It is even possible to do a net install if the user has an old system that doesn't have a CD drive. All these developments have progressed over time as we have tried to make DSL as usable for as many people as possible.

The Present

I believe DSL is a nearly complete desktop. It includes:

A desktop environment
> Containing the FluxBox window manager, and emelFM and Midnight Commander file managers

Office applications
> Containing a spreadsheet; a spellchecker (U.S. English); a word processor (Ted-GTK); a calculator; SQLite, which is used to manage an address book; and four text editors (Beaver, Vim, Zile, and Nano)

Graphics editing and viewing
> Containing Xpaint, Xzgv, and Xpdf

Multimedia applications
> Containing XMMS (MP3, OGG, and MPEG player) and CD-burning capabilities

Internet applications
> Containing Dillo and links-hacked web browsers, Sylpheed email, and Naim (AIM, ICQ, and IRC)

Networking clients
> Containing PPP, PPPoE (ADSL), DHCP, FTP, SSH/SCP, VNCviwer, and Rdesktop

Networking services
> Containing SSH/SCP, web, FTP, and NFS servers

Hardware support
> Containing USB, PCMCIA, generic and GhostScript printer support, and wireless networking

The DSL also includes games and a host of command-line utilities. Getting all of these applications in an ISO that is under 50 MB requires quite a bit of planning, because all the programs need to be light, but also useful and functional.

After putting so much effort and time into DSL, I am uncomfortable calling it a "Knoppix hack." I view DSL as a fine-tuned micro distribution that is built on the base of Knoppix, and utilizes Knoppix's superb hardware detection and compatibility and base operation processes. However, in other aspects, DSL works quite differently from Knoppix. I, along with other contributors, keep a keen eye on size and speed in every application choice, and we have an extendable module system so users can easily add only the applications they want. DSL is highly efficient: it has run successfully on a 486DX2 processor and on only 16 MB of RAM. Because it is a solid framework, several projects have been based on Damn Small; at the time of this writing, there are at least 17 custom-made distributions based on DSL that are listed at *http://www.damnsmalllinux.org/relatives.html*.

See Also

- The Official DSL home page at *http://www.damnsmalllinux.org*.

—John Andrews

HACK #85 INSERT Security Here

INSERT, or the INside SEcurity Rescue Tool, is a small Knoppix-based distribution with a focus on security. It can fit on a bootable business-card CD, but still includes many useful tools for virus scanning, network analysis, computer forensics, and disaster recovery.

INSERT is a specialized live CD and its outstanding feature is size. INSERT is about 50 MB, which makes it ideal for downloading and placing it on a credit-card-sized CD-ROM to be carried on the go.

INSERT is targeted at the Linux professional and system administrators. It carries all (well, most) of the tools the user needs to recover a damaged system from a crash, transfer files, perform network analysis, and assist in computer forensics tasks. See the following table:

Requirement	Purpose
Window manager	FluxBox
File manager	Emelfm, Midnight Commander
Web browser	Links-hacked
FTP client	AxyFTP, ftp
Virus scanner	clamav with avscan frontend
Network analysis	Nmap, tcpdump, smb-nat

Requirement	Purpose
Disk management	Parted, gpart, dd-rescue, testdisk, lilo, grub, cfdisk
Backup	Dvd+rw-tools, cdrecord, partimage, BashBurn, burncenter
Filesystem support	EXT2, EXT3, MINIX, ReiserFS, JFS, XFS, NTFS, FAT, FAT32, NFS, SMBFS, NCPFS, UDF, UFS, HFS, HFS+, software RAID, and LVM.
Basic tools	wget, ssh, tar, etc.

If you're still not convinced that using a Linux desktop, like INSERT, is the way to go, just read what John Andrews, author of Damn Small Linux (DSL), writes:

> Why? Because having a working Linux desktop distro on a 50 MB bootable business card CD is just too cool not to do.

There are currently English and German versions of INSERT. These differ only in the language of the help texts, HTML startup pages, and the default keyboard layout; otherwise, they are identical.

History

In the summer of 2003, I discovered the existence of DSL (which, if you recall, is a Linux desktop distribution on a 50-MB CD), and the idea of INSERT was born. Whereas DSL is targeted at the experienced Linux desktop user, INSERT is a Linux distribution that can be used for all kinds of rescue tasks, is small enough to easily carry, and is downloadable even by people who have access only to low-bandwidth connections.

Additionally, INSERT is used as an eye-catching marketing tool for the company that employs me (which partially funded the development of INSERT). The information material of Inside Security IT Consulting GmbH gracefully resides on the disc for this very reason.

Technical

Technically, INSERT is based heavily on Knoppix with just a few special modifications. One noticeable difference is that unlike most other Knoppix derivatives, INSERT uses its own *namespace*, which means that nearly all occurrences of KNOPPIX have been replaced with INSERT. This was achieved by replacing the strings in all those scripts written by Klaus— indeed, not a very challenging task.

In developing INSERT, one problem arose: the CD didn't unmount at halt time. Knoppix uses a customized version of init. Therefore, INSERT has to contain the correct path /INSERT instead of /KNOPPIX for the loop mount, and it *has to be statically linked* so that it does not depend on the C-library, which resides under /INSERT.

Size

Most of the development effort in INSERT was spent in shrinking the size to under 50 MB, which becomes approximately 120 MB uncompressed. The first task was to remove all unnecessary packages. Due to the many dependencies, this was a time-consuming task. The next task was to remove files from the remaining packages, including most of the documentation from */usr/share/doc*, duplicate binaries (e.g., *mke2fs* and *mkfs.e2fs*), and widely unused binaries (e.g., *xclock*).

Quite a few days and nights were spent removing these packages and files while still maintaining a working system. The Inside Security PDF on the CD was shrunk to nearly half its former size by using the excellent Multivalent PDF tools by Tom Phelps (*http://multivalent.sourceforge.net*). To avoid placing duplicates in the main filesystem, the static *ash* and the kernel modules were copied from the miniroot during boot time to save space. Then the compressed filesystem was created using the --best option to gain an extra 2 MB of space.

Main Additions

For Version 1.2, released at the beginning of February 2004 during a DFN-CERT (Deutsches Forschungsnetz Computer Emergency Response Team) workshop, a major feature was introduced: *captive-ntfs*, which gives full read/write support for NTFS partitions using the native Windows NTFS drivers [Hack #73].

At the same time, the latest version of the open source virus scanner *clamav*, including the signature database, and the Internet update tool *freshclam* were added. The combination of these two new features added the ability to scan and repair NTFS partitions from INSERT. Later, *avscan*, a GUI frontend for *clamav*, was added.

Six months earlier than Knoppix, INSERT booted from *isolinux* rather than from *syslinux*. With *isolinux*, a floppy boot image is no longer necessary and, therefore, more space is now available. There were mainly two reasons why this was done: INSERT needed space for providing *memtest86* (a RAM-checking utility) at boot time, and loop-mounted floppy images were frustrating to work in version 3.4 KNOPPIX also uses this technique, so Klaus was able to nearly double the size of the miniroot, which now includes more SCSI, USB, and FireWire drivers. INSERT v1.2.13 now descends from KNOPPIX 3.4, so it also provides these improvements.

User feedback and open source software development continues to improve INSERT. The next major release (due sometime this year) will probably be based on Linux kernel 2.6.

See Also

- "Collect Forensics Data" [Hack #47]
- "Clone Hard Drives" [Hack #48]

—Matthias Mikule

Download Local Area Security

#86 Similar to the scope of INSERT, Local Area Security Linux (L.A.S. Linux) aims to put many great security tools all on a single mini-CD.

Local Area Security Linux (L.A.S Linux) began as a personal project: to learn more about live CDs and to create a security toolkit. Over two years ago, L.A.S. Linux began as a command-line-only distribution, which was less than 50 MB in size, so it would fit on a business-card CD. My coworkers encouraged me to make it public and release it. At the time, I had owned the domain localareasecurity.com for a few years but had no use for it. I decided to put it to good use by creating a web site to make my Linux distribution available to the public.

The first versions were based on a stripped-down 35-MB version of Knoppix, to which I added a long list of security tools. Within about two months of the initial public release of v0.3, I was receiving hundreds of thousands of hits per month and was Slashdotted for the first time, which made the web site hits skyrocket. During this time, many generous people contributed mirrors of the distribution. These mirrors were sorely needed, because at that time, I was running the site on a shared host in Argentina.

With the increasing popularity of L.A.S. Linux, I made drastic improvements to the distribution over the next few versions and shifted the base to a highly modified version of Damn Small Linux (DSL). The biggest improvement was the addition of the Fluxbox window manager. The addition of many GUI-based security programs, such as Ethereal, Etherape, Nmapfe, and so forth, made the ISO size jump to 185 MB.

One of the rationales for keeping the ISO size limited to 185 MB was to narrow the focus of the distribution. While other distributions had begun using a full-size 700-MB CD for their ISOs, I didn't feel a need to have large desktop environments, games, and full office productivity suites. Each tool was evaluated and weighed for its positives and negatives, which ensured that these high-quality tools wouldn't duplicate the efforts of other tools.

During this time, I added the toram boot option [Hack #5] to allow the entire ISO image to be copied into the physical RAM of the computer. This was a revolutionary addition because it freed up the CD-ROM for burning CDs and other uses. (This addition also speeds up the entire distribution. The distribution is under 185 MB in size, so users with 256 MB of RAM can still use this functionality, whereas a full Knoppix user requires 1 GB of RAM.)

When the web site started receiving close to a million hits a month, I realized there was a need for a dedicated server. I redesigned the entire web site and added a large download section (over 20 GB) to the server with mirrors to *http://wiretapped.net* and other security tools and projects. After adding many more mirror sites all over the world, LocalAreaSecurity.com had officially become a hobby that had gotten way out of hand. With my work schedule expanding and the needs of the site also growing, I felt it was time to find talented people to help contribute to the development of L.A.S. Linux, as well as to the content of the web site. Today, the L.A.S. team has grown to four people, with numerous partnerships with other information security organizations and groups.

To satisfy the requests of our users, we have also created a slightly larger version of L.A.S. Linux to fit on 210-MB mini-CDs. This allows for the addition of the Mozilla Firefox web browser and a handful of additional tools not on the 185-MB version, while still being small enough to fit into 256 MB of RAM using the toram option.

We pride ourselves on our somewhat regular release schedule for new versions. The security tools L.A.S. Linux contains are continuously being improved with new releases, and our users always have an up-to-date version of a tool with the latest signatures (unlike a lot of other security toolkit live CDs, which have come and gone or are updated very seldom).

People have found many interesting uses for L.A.S. Linux. Some of my favorites are:

- One user dropped me an email that informed me how L.A.S. Linux had "saved the day" at his place of employment. It seems that its NT Primary Domain Controller went down. So he booted L.A.S. Linux and used Samba to mount the drives to get the server up and running [Hack #41] until they could rebuild the server.

- In my previous jobs, I have often carried a copy of L.A.S. in my back pocket, so if I am at another site, I can boot to the CD and use VNC tunneled over SSH to connect to my desktop in my office [Hack #37].

- Countless users have informed me of how helpful they find L.A.S. Linux when network troubleshooting in various locations using Ethereal and other tools to ascertain the cause of problems.

- The ability to run *nessusd* from RAM to create a temporary node for network vulnerability assessments [Hack #45].

- The ability to recover files from corrupted hard drives or to use tools such as SleuthKit to perform forensic analysis.

- The ability to set up temporary Snort IDS nodes running off of L.A.S. Linux.

These are just a sampling of the countless uses of L.A.S. Linux. Many times, your imagination is the only stumbling block to the variety of hacks you can use the distribution to perform.

The future holds many new additions to the L.A.S. Linux family. We are currently rebuilding a new version of the distribution from the kernel up, as well as adding a 400 MB+ "Desktop Auditor" version with the help of one of our partners—ISECOM (the Institute for Security and Open Methodologies), makers of the OSSTMM (Open Source Security Testing Methodology Manual).

See Also

- The Local Area Security Linux home page at *http://localareasecrity.com*.
- The Institute for Security and Open Methodologies at *http://isecom.org*.
- Open Source Security Testing Methodology Manual at *http://osstmm.org*.

—Jascha Wanger

HACK #87 Full Protection with Knoppix-STD

Knoppix-STD is a Knoppix-based distribution with a focus on security. This disc includes many useful security tools from packet sniffers to password crackers to honeypots.

Knoppix-STD is a Knoppix variant dedicated to the daily tasks of an information security professional, as well as a learning platform for those interested in exploring information security in a relatively safe and painless environment.

Knoppix-STD got its start from three Linux distributions. Obviously, Knoppix is one, but the other two were information security distributions. Trinux, by Matthew Franz (*http://www.trinux.org*), was the first portable distro I had ever worked with. When I was using it, it was a console-only floppy distribution, and various security tools and hardware drivers could be loaded from other floppies. The other distribution was F.I.R.E. (Forensic and Incident Response Environment) by William Salusky (*http://fire.dmzs.com*). This was the first bootable CD I had ever seen, and although it was mainly limited to Forensic tools, I was fascinated. I'd sometimes boot it just to boot it.

I loved Knoppix for its portability and wealth of day-to-day applications, but I needed Trinux and F.I.R.E. for their respective toolkits. When I read my first HOWTO for customizing Knoppix, I knew exactly what to do. After a couple of months, Knoppix-STD was born.

STD stands for Security Tools Distribution, although I'm well aware of the other meanings of the acronym. Information security tools tend to have questionable names. When you get a bunch of geeks talking about probes, penetration testing, intrusion detection, backdoors, etc., it's no wonder that these tools have such eyebrow-raising names. STD is a nod to those 3 A.M. soda-drinking code crunchers. Keep on typin'!

Knoppix-STD uses FluxBox as its window manager because it's lightweight and powerful enough for STD's needs. The tools available on Knoppix-STD are divided into specific information security disciplines—for instance, encryption, forensics, and vulnerability assessment. These categories are available from FluxBox's application menu. Many of the tools are command-lines and command-line tools are often overlooked, so I also created some specific directories for each category under */usr/bin*, like */usr/bin/forensics*. Covering every tool in STD would take an entire book, but here's a rundown of the security categories in STD and some of the usual suspects found in each.

Authentication Tools

Authentication has been rightly called the foundation of all security. After all, lacking artificial intelligence, authentication is the only method a computer has of telling different users apart. Aside from the standard Linux PAM, */etc/passwd*, and */etc/shadow*, Knoppix-STD also includes FreeRADIUS (*http://www.freeradius.org*), an open source RADIUS server. RADIUS (Remote Authentication Dial-In User Service) is used as a centralized database of users and is supported by many applications and platforms to authenticate users.

Encryption Tools

Encryption is the process of garbling a message so that it can be intercepted without fear of leaking confidential information. The real magic of encryption is the capability of having a special key that ungarbles the message when you need access to the information.

The core encryption library and command-line tool used under Linux for encryption and key generation is *openssl*. Gnu Privacy Guard, *gpg*, is included as the open source replacement for PGP and works in a similar fashion. Super-FreeSWAN is compiled into the custom kernel to provide IPSEC VPN support.

STD also includes multiple *steganography* tools (perhaps better known as *stego* tools). *Stego* tools hide data in other data. *Gifshuffle* hides data in a GIF image, *outguess* does the same using JPEG images, and *mp3encode* hides your data in an MP3 file.

There are also tools to detect and break *stego*ed data; they are aptly named *stegbreak* and *stegdetect*.

Forensics

The original plan for STD was to make it strictly a computer-forensic toolkit in a fashion similar to the F.I.R.E. distribution. The benefit of a live bootable CD for gathering digital evidence can't be measured. You have a reliable operating system with which to boot and investigate a breached machine.

The primary hero of open source forensics is the Autopsy/Sleuthkit combo (*http://www.sleuthkit.org*). Currently maintained by Brian Carrier, Autopsy/Sleuthkit evolved from the original, The Coroners Toolkit **[Hack #47]**. Whether you simply need to recover a deleted file or you need a full case-management system, Autopsy/Sleuthkit provides it all, wrapped in a well-designed web frontend.

Sleuthkit uses a predefined mount point named */mnt/evidence* as its evidence locker under STD. This is where all of its output goes. By mounting anything you want to the mount point, you can carry Sleuthkit output from machine to machine. This mount point might be a local drive or a remote share. I keep mine encrypted on a USB stick.

In addition to the forensic workhorse *dd*, STD provides *dcfldd*, which is the U.S. Department of Defense Computer Forensics Labs extension to the standard *dd*. Among other things, it can automatically produce an MD5 hash as part of a forensic backup. *Foremost* is included and used to search through a forensic backup for specific file types, such as JPG or DIVX files.

ClamAV is a GPL antivirus program. You can boot a suspect machine with STD, mount the local hard drives, and scan for viruses without having to trust the host OS (see also "Scan for Viruses" **[Hack #78]**). The command to scan is *clamscan*. If you have Internet access, you can also update to the most current signature set by running *freshclam*. Similarly, *chkrootkit* looks for your standard root kit infection **[Hack #46]**.

If you are using STD for forensic purposes, you definitely want to boot using the noswap cheat code. Otherwise, STD attempts to use any existing swap files on the system, potentially erasing evidence.

Firewalls

Firewalls are routers that connect two networks together (like your home network to the Internet) and allow only certain types of traffic through. STD has *iptables* like most distributions. To make it a little more accessible for someone new to firewalls, STD includes *firestarter*, which is a wizard to walk you through the process of setting up rules. *Shorewall* is also included as a more advanced firewall package. *Hogwash* is a packet scrubber that automatically blocks packets that match snort IDS rules (see the later section "IDS").

While STD is rather secure in its default state, I make no claims that this is a secure distribution. In fact, some of the services included are vulnerable to many exploits. By design, this is due to time restrictions, but this vulnerability provides the new security admin with not only a machine to attack with, but also a machine to use as a target.

If you use STD and are connected to the Internet in any way, you should hit the key combo Alt-F12. This is a shortcut to run the *blockall* command, a small script that creates a very simple firewall rule for your host. All outbound traffic (yours) is allowed out. All inbound traffic (from that evil hacker out there) is blocked.

Honeypots

Honeypots are used to monitor hacker activity. They give the hacker a target to attack but no valuable data. Honeypots also fishbowl the hacker so that the target can't be used as a hopping point to launch other attacks. In the meantime, the honeypot tracks all activity so that you can learn about new techniques, learn about tools, and get an idea of what kind of threat posture you have.

Honeyd is the main honeypot daemon, but the *labrea* tarpit is also included. Rather than track the hacker, *labrea* holds a hacker's connection open as long as possible and slows it down to a crawl with heavy fragmentation. This slows down automated scanning tools and worms like Code Red.

IDS

IDS, short for intrusion detection system, is an alarm system for your network. Like a security guard watching closed-circuit TV for suspicious activity, an IDS system monitors the network for the same thing. When it sees suspicious activity, it lets you know so you can decide whether you need to respond to the intrusion to minimize the damage it might cause.

Snort reigns supreme in this area. It's mature and widely supported by a huge community of users. STD utilizes MySQL to log the snort data and ACID as a web frontend to monitor and manage alerts.

There's a small bug in starting S/A/M (snort/ACID/MySQL) from the Flux-box menu. In order to get S/A/M to run properly under STD:

1. Right-click on the desktop to get the FluxBox menu.
2. Navigate to IDS → Snort/ACID/MySQL.
3. Run Snort-Init. This copies the necessary files from the CD to RAM to make them read/write.
4. Run Start S/A/M. This launches *snort*, *apache*, *mysqld*, and *barnyard*, and launches Mozilla Firebird to connect to the ACID interface. Initially, you won't see any snort sensors (Sensors: 0).
5. Run Stop S/A/M and then Start S/A/M again. This reinitializes *barnyard* properly.

If you have Internet access, the *snort* rules files can be updated to the most recent versions using *oinkmaster* at the command line.

Network Utilities

Many standard network utilities are included. Samba and Netware tools, like *smbclient* and *ncplogin*, are available, as well as a GUI frontend for Samba that is similar to Microsoft's Network Neighborhood called *LinNeighborhood*.

STD also includes *cheops* for network mapping, monitoring, and management via SNMP. *Ntop*, short for network *top*, is also a great utility for monitoring your network. It is a very robust protocol analyzer and shows you things like top protocols used, top bandwidth utilizers, graphs, matrixes, charts—you name it. It comes with a nice web frontend. Launch *ntop-start* from the Flux-Box menu and then use Firebird to connect to *http://localhost:3000*.

Password Tools

Password-cracking utilities are necessary to access data locked by forgotten passwords, retrieve data left behind by disgruntled ex-employees who changed passwords upon leaving the company, and audit the passwords your users are choosing to verify they are secure.

John the Ripper can be run from */etc/john/*. To see John in action, try this:

1. Drop to a root shell prompt by hitting the key combo Alt-F5.
2. Set a password for the Knoppix user account. I usually use something simple like "buffy" or "Piglet" so I don't have long to wait. The command is:

```
knoppix@ttyp0[knoppix]$ passwd knoppix
```

3. Merge the *passwd* and *shadow* files together with *unshadow*:

   ```
   knoppix@ttyp0[knoppix]$ /etc/john/unshadow /etc/passwd /etc/shadow >
   crackme.txt
   ```

4. Crack the file with *john*:

   ```
   knoppix@ttyp0[knoppix]$ /etc/john/john crackme.txt
   ```

Ciscilia is a distributed cracker that can take advantage of STD's built-in openMOSIX clustering. This allows you to distribute the password-cracking load across multiple machines.

Chntpw combined with STD's NTFS read/write patch allows you to reset the Administrator password on a Microsoft system. Simply mount the NTFS partition read/write, point *chntpw* at the SAM file, and follow the prompts. The *chntpw* utility is covered in "Reset Lost NT Passwords" [Hack #75].

STD also includes a prepopulated dictionary file from CERIAS at Purdue University. It's available at */usr/bin/pwd-tools/allwords2*. It's a 27-MB file of ASCII passwords. If that doesn't crack it, brute force is probably your only hope.

Servers

STD has many servers installed for your convenience, as well as to test your penetration skills. Many of these servers are vulnerable to exploits by now so they should not be used in a production environment. However, when you need a down-and-dirty web or mail server, or maybe a TFTP server, these are very useful.

Packet Sniffers

Packet sniffers allow your network card to see every packet on the wire, not just the ones coming from or to your machine. They are often used to troubleshoot connections and inspect traffic, and are great teaching tools for learning TCP/IP. Start up a sniffer program like *ethereal* and then connect to a web site. Stop your packet capture and see which sorts of packets the HTTP protocol generates.

Ethereal is by far one of the most popular sniffers in the world. It is licensed under the GPL, available for just about every platform out there, and allows more complex analysis with features like the ability to follow a full TCP stream.

Ettercap is the next most popular sniffer. The problem with most sniffers is that they report only what they can see. Most networks utilize switches instead of hubs these days, so sniffers don't see much. *Ettercap* allows you to sniff connections between hosts even across a switch using techniques like ARP poisoning. *Ettercap* also allows you to do a multitude of other tasks, like man-in-the-middle attacks on encryption, that bleed into vulnerability assessment.

Driftnet and *dsniff* are two filtered sniffers. This means they are only looking for very specific data on the network. *Dsniff* looks for any clear text username and password pairs on the wire. Protocols like HTTP, telnet, rlogin, FTP, POP3, etc. pass your username and password unencrypted over the wire. *Dsniff* displays every pair it sees in nice neat columns on the screen. *Driftnet* is looking for any kind of image file passing along the wire. Any JPEG, GIF, PNG file it finds out there is shown on the screen and downloaded to a specific directory. This is excellent for monitoring web-browsing habits.

TCP Tools

The TCP-Tools category is a collection of tools that allow you to access and manipulate the full TCP/IP stack.

Gspoof, *excalibur*, *nested*, and *hping* are all packet assemblers that allow you to custom generate any kind of packet you want and play it out onto the wire. *Tcpreplay* allows you to replay a capture file, which is grabbed via *ethereal* or *tcpdump*, back on the wire.

Arpwatch monitors the IP/MAC pairs on the wire and emails them to the STD root account. This allows you to monitor for ARP poisoning attacks and IP duplicates. *Tcpkill* tears down any TCP session it's pointed at.

Fragroute is a routing and fragmentation tool. In conjunction with *arpspoof*, this can be a very powerful tool for customizing your own ARP poisoning attack.

Tunnels

Tunnels allow you to tunnel data through other protocols. For example, you are at work and you want to *ssh* to your computer at home. Your corporate firewall policy allows only HTTP from the corporate network so you can tunnel SSH through HTTP-looking traffic to bypass the firewall. *Httptunnel* does exactly this. You set up the server (*hts*) at home and direct it to your *ssh* server. At work, you start up the client (*htc*) and *ssh* to it. The *httptunnel* client connects to the server over the HTTP port 80, and it is then redirected to your *ssh* server.

Netcat and *cryptcat* are also included as generic TCP tunnels. *Netcat* is a raw sockets tool and allows you to connect or open listener ports. *Cryptcat* does the same thing but also encrypts the data in the tunnel. Try the following exercise with two STD machines.

On the *cryptcat* server, drop to a root shell (Alt-F5) and run:

```
root@ttyp0[knoppix]# cryptcat -l -p 443 -e /bin/bash
```

This makes *cryptcat* "listen" (-1) on port (-p) 443 and execute (-e) */bin/bash* if someone connects.

On the *cryptcat* client, type:

```
knoppix@ttyp0[knoppix]$ cryptcat ip address of the server 443
```

This returns a *bash* shell prompt from the server. On the wire, this data is encrypted and targets TCP/443. Most security administrators disregard this traffic as HTTPS (if they even catch it at all).

Shadyshell is used to tunnel data over UDP rather than over TCP. UDP port 53 is often used, because it appears to be DNS query traffic and is usually allowed free reign through most firewalls. *Icmpshell* uses ICMP rather than UDP or TCP

Vulnerability Assessment

Vulnerability assessment allows the you to figure out what is at risk on the network, regardless of whether it is a hole in your security policy or a machine that hasn't been patched or configured correctly. Vulnerability assessment helps to define your security policy and allows you to find what's at risk before an attacker does.

Nessus is a vulnerability-assessment tool that has its own scripting language, tiered management, a nice GUI frontend, and multiple report formats, including HTML. It has beaten many commercial vulnerability-assessment tools in "bake-off"-type contests. Even if you have a commercial tool for this job, *nessus* is a free second opinion that should be a part of every security administrator's toolkit. You can update *Nessus*'s exploit plug-ins to the most recent set by running *nessus-update-plugins* if you have Internet access. More information on using *nessus* to perform a network security audit is available in "Audit Network Security" [Hack #45].

Nmap, short for network map, is a host-and-port enumeration tool. One of your first jobs as a security administrator is to inventory your network. You should know every live IP address, the OS behind those addresses, every open port on those addresses, and each piece of software behind every open port. *Nmap* helps you with this task.

Nikto is a CGI-assessment tool that has replaced RFP's *whisker*. This is application-level assessment.

P0f stands for passive OS fingerprinting. It tells you the OS at a particular IP address just by monitoring the wire and seeing which sorts of packets it spits out.

This category also includes many exploits and exploit code (*/usr/bin/vuln-test/src/*) for those that want to see what actual exploits look like and how they work. TESO, ADM, RFP, NMRC, THC, Phenolit, and others are all well represented in this category.

Wireless Tools

Wireless scanning has become a full lifestyle for those with wardriving, war-walking, and warchalking. There are so many wireless access points out there with DHCP and no WEP that you should be able to hop on the Internet from just about anywhere. Orinoco, airo, prism2, hostAP, and airjack drivers are all included. The Orinoco drivers are patched by default, so you are able to get into monitor mode with your Orinoco Gold or Silver with no problems (although some newer models may need a firmware downgrade).

Kismet is the wireless scanner of choice by most system administrators. It simply monitors for access points and lets you know if it finds one. "Wardrive with Knoppix" [Hack #44] discusses how to use *kismet* with Knoppix for wardriving. *Airsnort* and *Wellenreiter* are available for completeness but accomplish much of the same thing.

Gpsdrive is also included and can be very handy if integrated with a GPS device and a map of your hometown. It integrates with *kismet* and marks down the latitude and longitude of each AP found.

Fakeap is a Perl script used in conjunction with the hostAP driver to confound wardrivers by constantly sending out fake access point beacons.

Miscellany

I've included many tools that you might not find in your standard security toolkit. This includes many Internet utilities. Mozilla Firebird is the primary web browser, and all the bookmarks are prepopulated with links to the web sites of the tools and concepts previously mentioned. Sylpheed is used as a mail and news client. Xchat and BitchX are available for IRC. The Tight-VNC client and server are also included. If you don't have DHCP on your network, you can configure your network card from the FluxBox menu. Just click Internet → Connect → netcard config.

Between your 10-hour vulnerability assessment and staring at the ACID alert monitor until all the colors bleed, you'll find that security can get very boring sometimes. To alleviate this boredom, you can listen to your MP3 collection or streaming audio with XMMS. I've also left in some games. Frozen Bubble and Galaga are available for the joystick junkies. Chess and Go are available if you'd rather exercise your mind.

The following table of shortcut key combinations shows how FluxBox is configured:

Key binding	Action
Alt-F1	First workspace
Alt-F2	Second workspace
Alt-F3	Third workspace
Alt-F4	Fourth workspace
Alt-F5	Root shell
Alt-F6	Root file manager
Alt-F7	Mozilla Firebird
Alt-F8	Text editor
Alt-F9	Nmap
Alt-F10	Nessus
Alt-F11	Ethereal
Alt-F12	Block all inbound TCP

Knoppix-STD also allows the use of the toram and tohd cheat codes to free up the CDROM drive after boot [Hack #5].

In closing, I wish to thank all open source security developers out there. Knoppix-STD is simply a patchwork quilt of other people's hard work and energy. White, gray, or black hat, it doesn't matter. Programmers that release source code are not the enemy. It's an odd thing that the art of keeping secrets can't be a secret itself.

See Also

- The Knoppix-STD home page at *http://www.knoppix-std.org*.

—Karl Sigler

Distribute Compiles with distccKNOPPIX

HACK #88

This Damn Small Linux–based distribution is aimed at making it easy to set up a cluster of machines running distccd, which enables the user to leverage multiple machines for compiling.

I was first introduced to *distcc* while compiling Debian unofficial KDE CVS packages. *Distcc* is a program that distributes builds of C, C++, Objective C or Objective C++ code across several machines on a network. I quickly installed *distcc* on my networked Linux systems and was happily using up unused cycles and speeding up my builds a great deal. However, the one Microsoft Windows system sitting idle as my compiles continued gave me an itch to investigate the possibility of using *distcc* on a Windows system. Enter distccKNOPPIX.

distccKNOPPIX is a remastered live CD based on Damn Small Linux (DSL). It runs a *distcc* daemon as its sole task and is as portable as any Knoppix CD. By taking advantage of some of the kernel options of Knoppix, such as toram and tohd **[Hack #5]**, you can have an entire network handle the distributed compile and still be able to reboot the system to its regular settings when finished.

To run distccKNOPPIX, you just need to download the ISO from *http://opendoorsoftware.com*, burn it to CD, insert it in a bootable CD-ROM drive, and reboot. Once booted, confirm that your network is set up correctly as listed in "Connect to the Internet" **[Hack #17]**, and note that your IP is using *ifconfig*. When you are ready to compile a program on the machine running *distccd*, add this IP and any other IPs for *distcc* machines on your network to the DISTCC_HOSTS environment variable:

```
knoppix@ttyp0[knoppix]$ export DISTCC_HOSTS="localhost 192.168.0.1
192.168.0.2'
```

Alternatively, you can run a program like *nmap* from your server to detect new IPs in your subnet. Look for open port number 3632.

```
root@ttyp0[root]# nmap -v -p 3632 192.168.0.0/16
```

This comes in handy if the distccKNOPPIX nodes have no display.

Once DISTCC_HOSTS has your list of machines, you can run *make* with the following command from your source tree:

```
knoppix@ttyp0[code]$ make -j5 CC=distcc
```

Replace 5 with the number of jobs you want *make* to create. A general rule of thumb is to have between one extra job than you have computers and twice the number of computers. This example has three computers, so you should pick between four and six jobs.

DistccKNOPPIX is released under the same licenses as Knoppix and is available from *http://opendoorsoftware.com*. At this writing, v0.8 is DisctccKNOPPIX's available version. Future features include a boot manager to manage some options (such as default-compiler versions), server notification upon boot, and better network detection.

See Also

- The *distcc* home page at *http://distcc.samba.org*.

—*James Michael Greenhalgh*

Distribute the Load with ClusterKnoppix

HACK #89

ClusterKnoppix is a live-CD distribution that takes advantage of the openMosix cluster technology to turn any room full of computers into a makeshift openMosix cluster.

Clusterknoppix (*http://bofh.be/clusterknoppix*) combines the functionality of openMosix with the ease of use of Knoppix. It contains an openMosix kernel and the openMosix userspace utilities, along with various other tools for monitoring and manipulating the cluster, like openMosixview (*http://www.openmosixview.com*). It is meant to be a bootable CD that demos the possibilities of openMosix; hard-disk installation isn't really supported. The CD runs like the normal Knoppix CD. The only difference is that it starts openMosix, the openMosixcollector (from openMosixview), and sshd.

What openMosix Is

The openMosix project (*http://openmosix.sf.net*) describes openMosix as:

> A Linux kernel extension for single-system image clustering. This kernel extension turns a network of ordinary computers into a supercomputer for Linux applications.

The openMosix software makes it easy to create a supercomputer out of your spare machines for heavy number crunching, from brute-forcing encryption cracking to 3D rendering. Details about technologies behind computer clusters and openMosix clusters in particular are outside the scope of this hack. For a more thorough explanation, consult the openMosix project (*http://openmosix.sf.net*).

Set Up a Cluster

To set up a cluster, you need at least two systems networked to each other via a crossover cable or a switch. For small clusters, you can get away with 10 MB, but 100 MB is advised.

There are basically two ways to set up an instant cluster with Clusterknoppix—with a network boot or with multiple CDs. The easiest way is to use network boot (PXE or etherboot). PXE (Preboot eXecution Environment) downloads the bootstrapping code to load an operating system, the Linux kernel in our case, over the network. Most new computers support it look for "Booting from NIC" or PXE in the BIOS. If you don't have a PXE-capable network card, you can get etherboot to do almost the same thing by using a ROM on a floppy to download the bootstrapping code. More information about etherboot can be found at *http://www.etherboot.org*.

If your computer doesn't have a PXE or working Ethernet, you don't want to boot from the network, or you don't know which NICs (Network Interface Cards) are in your computers, simply put a Clusterknoppix CD in each computer.

The Network Boot Method

The first step to set up a cluster that boots from the network is to prepare the master node. With a master node running, you only need a single Clusterknoppix CD.

 openMosix itself doesn't differentiate between master and client—every node is equal by default—but I use the terms master and client nodes to differentiate between the computer with the CD and the computers without it, respectively.

If you have a DHCP server on your network, you should receive an IP address once the master node boots from the CD; otherwise, you must configure the IP manually, as in:

```
knoppix@ttyp0[knoppix]$ su -
root@ttyp0[root]# ifconfig eth0 10.33.1.14 netmask 255.255.255.0
root@ttyp0[root]# route add default gw 10.33.1.254
root@ttyp0[root]# /etc/init.d/openmosix restart
```

Replace *eth0* with your Ethernet card and the IP addresses with the values you want to use for your network.

If you have your own DHCP server on this network segment, you must shut it down for now, because the terminal server you are running starts its own (as mentioned in "Network Boot Knoppix" **[Hack #25]**). Having two DHCP servers on the same network segment creates problems on the network, because you don't know which server answers a client's request for an address.

Configure openMosix

In X, click on K Menu → KNOPPIX → Services → Start KNOPPIX openMosix Terminal Server (see Figure 8-2).

In the dialog that appears, select "setup (re)configure server and (re)start" and press OK.

Next, choose the NIC where your DHCP/TFTP/NFS server is listening and press OK. Now you can add the IP-address range you want to distribute to the client nodes. The default that the wizard uses should be sufficient for most applications.

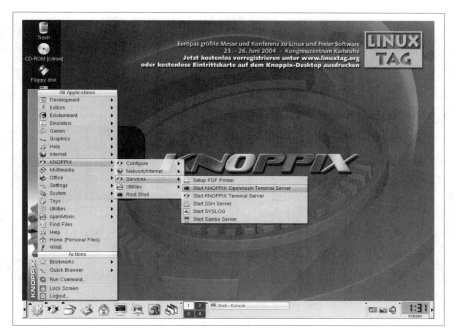

Figure 8-2. Launching an openMosix terminal server

Now you must select the correct network modules. You must select all the modules that your client nodes uses. For example, if you have three clients, each with a different NIC, select those three modules on this screen. They are probed automatically on each client node at boot time. A number of common NIC modules are already checked in this list, so if you aren't sure which module your NIC uses, try the default and skip ahead. Otherwise, you can try booting Knoppix directly on the machine and checking which module it uses for your NIC with the *lsmod* command run from a terminal.

Now select some miscellaneous options:

Secure
> Disables the root access on client systems, which means that the default user *knoppix* won't be able to *su* to root.

Textmode
> Boots the clients in text-mode, thus giving more memory for the migrating processes. Using textmode is the same as specifying 2 as an extra boot option (see "Use Knoppix Cheat Codes" [Hack #3]).

Masq
> Sets the master node as a masquerading/forwarding server so that your clients can connect to the Internet/rest of the network.

DNS
> Sets up a caching nameserver.

Squid
> Sets up a web proxy/cache.

Finally, you get the option to specify any extra Knoppix cheat codes that you want to use on your clients. After the Knoppix cheat codes are chosen, the terminal server starts.

Boot Your Clients

The next step is to boot your clients from the network. This step will be very simple or require a bit of extra work, depending on whether your client supports PXE or requires Etherboot.

PXE. If you are using PXE, this step is easy. Select PXE in your BIOS and then boot the client. If you specified the correct network card driver in the terminal server setup, the client now boots ClusterKnoppix. You can pat yourself on the back now.

Etherboot. Etherboot takes a bit more work. First, go to *http://www.rom-o-matic.net*. Click on production and select your NIC. Next, click on Get ROM to download the ROM to your computer. Then put a formatted floppy in your floppy drive, go to a console, and type:

```
$ dd if=eb-5.2.4-yournic.zdsk of=/dev/fd0
```

Replace *eb-5.2.4-yournic.zdsk* with the path to your downloaded ROM image.

> If you are not sure which NIC you have, you can download an image from *http://drbl.nchc.org.tw/kernel/drbl_nic_detect.img*, then open up a console and type:
>
> ```
> $ dd if=drbl_nic_detect.img of=/dev/fd0
> ```
>
> Boot the client from the floppy, and it will detect your NIC so that you know which ROM image to download.

Put the floppy disk with the corresponding ROM in the client. Make sure the BIOS is set to boot from the floppy first, and once the computer boots, the client is added to your cluster as a node.

The CD-ROM Boot Method

Put a ClusterKnoppix in every CD drive, and then let the computers boot. There you go: instant cluster. Unlike booting from the network, when booting each computer from the CD, openMosixview won't work out of the box, but processes are still migrating. After each node has booted, just run *mosmon* on the master node, and it should show a node for each computer. This *ncurses* tool displays the load, speed, and memory of openMosix nodes as a bar chart in a console.

openMosixview is the X counterpart of *mosmon*, a cluster-management GUI for monitoring and administrating the cluster. To use openMosixview, you must have key-based authentication over SSH working. Key-based authentication uses RSA or DSA encryption for special keys that allow you to log in to other SSH servers without entering a password by hand. This lets openMosixview communicate with all of the nodes securely, without requiring you to enter a password as it logs into each node.

If you use the CD-ROM boot method, you must complete a few extra steps before it works. Here is an example for two nodes. Node1 (IP address 10.33.1.14) is the node where openMosixview is running, and Node2 (IP address 10.33.1.6) represents a regular node on the network.

On Node1, open a shell, *su* to root, enter a password, and remember it:

```
knoppix@ttyp0[knoppix]$ su -
root@ttyp0[root]# passwd
Enter new UNIX password:
Retype new UNIX password:
passwd: password updated successfully
```

Now generate the keys. This DSA key has both a public and private counterpart. The public key exists on any remote machines this machine wants to connect to, and can be used to decrypt packets that this machine creates with the private key:

```
root@ttyp0[root]# ssh-keygen -t dsa -N "" -f /root/.ssh/id_dsa
Generating directory '/root/.ssh'.
Your identification has been saved in /root/.ssh/id_dsa.
Your public key has been saved in /root/.ssh/id_dsa.pub.
The key fingerprint is:
cb:b6:e2:6a:57:ca:c5:1d:42:4d:7a:83:9f:df:ff:22 root@Knoppix
root@ttyp0[root]# cp /root/.ssh/id_dsa.pub /root/.ssh/authorized_keys
root@ttyp0[root]# echo -n "* " >> /root/.ssh/known_hosts
```

On Node2, copy the ssh key from Node1, and place it in the list of authorized keys:

```
knoppix@ttyp0[knoppix]$ sudo mkdir /root/.ssh/
knoppix@ttyp0[knoppix]$ sudo scp root@10.33.1.14:/root/.ssh/authorized_keys
/root/.ssh/
The authenticity of host '10.33.1.14 (10.33.1.14)' can't be established.
RSA key fingerprint is e8:7b:56:eb:02:62:85:bb:93:c8:e7:49:0e:92:0b:f5.
Are you sure you want to continue connecting (yes/no)? yes
Warning: Permanently added '10.33.1.14' (RSA) to the list of known hosts.
Password:
authorized_keys                          100%  668     0.7KB/s   00 00
```

Now go back to Node1, and confirm that the key has been copied correctly:

```
root@ttyp0[root]# ssh 10.33.1.6
The authenticity of host '10.33.1.6 (10.33.1.6)' can't be established.
RSA key fingerprint is 8a:80:b8:2b:fb:cd:a1:90:39:36:ca:03:57:6c:b0:5a.
Are you sure you want to continue connecting (yes/no)? yes

Warning: Permanently added '10.33.1.6' (RSA) to the list of known hosts.
root@0[root]# exit
root@ttyp0[root]# exit
```

Now you are ready to run openMosixview on Node1:

```
knoppix@ttyp0[knoppix]$ sudo openmosixview
```

You can now manage your nodes from the master node using openMosix-view (see Figure 8-3).

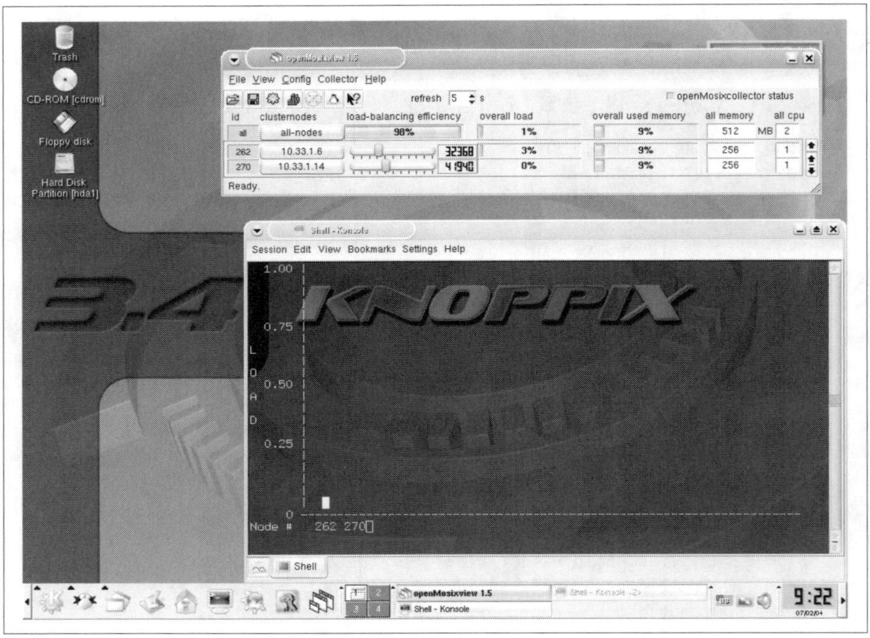

Figure 8-3. openMosixview in action

Test the Cluster

There are a lot of tools to be found on the openMosix web site, from simple programs to stress test suites, but you can simply run the following script to test your cluster. This script creates a nested loop that counts from 0 to 10,000—10,000 times—and is an easy way to fully load your processor.

```
knoppix@ttyp0[knoppix]$ awk 'BEGIN {for(i=0; i<10000; i++) for(j=0; j<10000;
j++);}' &
```

Run this script a number of times so that there are multiple processes for openMosix to distribute among the nodes, then run *mosmon* in another shell, and you should see the load being balanced between each node in your cluster.

See Also

- The official ClusterKnoppix page at *http://bofh.be/clusterknoppix*.
- The official openMosix page at *http://openmosix.sf.net*.

—Wim Vandersmissen

Analyze Quantian
#90

Quantian is an extension of Knoppix and ClusterKnoppix tailored to numerical and quantitative analysis.

The Quantian live DVD distribution (*http://dirk.eddelbuettel.com/quantian.html*) adds a quantitative facet to Knoppix. Based on ClusterKnoppix **[Hack #89]**, Quantian adds software with a quantitative, numerical, and scientific focus: several computer-algebra systems; higher-level matrix languages; data-visualization tools; a variety of scientific, numeric, and engineering applications, as well as many different programming languages and libraries. A particular focal point is the R language and an environment for statistical computing.

With its unique combination of the Knoppix-based ease of use and the additions of both openMosix cluster computing and a very rich set of scientific packages, Quantian can be of immediate use. It can:

- Compute clusters in order to speed up embarrassingly parallel tasks
- Create computer labs by enabling temporary use of a computing environment booted off a DVD and can netboot other machines
- Enable students and coworkers by distributing DVDs that allow everyone to work in identical environments with minimal administration cost
- Provide convenience to users so they do not have to chase down new software releases, and then manually configure and install them
- Provide easier installation of a normal scientific workstation by booting off Quantian and installing that system to hard disk, resulting in 3.6 GB of configured software
- Provide a familiar environment to work in during trips to conferences or other campuses
- Put older hand-me-down machines unable to run the newest and greatest commercial OS to use for Linux

The first two Quantian releases were based directly on Knoppix. Since then, ClusterKnoppix has provided the basic building block, which, similar to Knoppix itself, provides various utilities, games, multimedia applications, a complete KDE environment with its window manager, a browser, an office suite, a development environment and editors, as well as a large number of other general-purpose tools, utilities, and diagnostic applications. Quantian then adds various sets of applications from different areas:

Mathematics
> Computer-algebra systems Maxima, Pari/GP, GAP, GiNaC, YaCaS, and Axion, matrix-oriented languages; Octave (with octave-forge, matwrap, and octave-epstk packages), Yorick and Scilab, and the TeXmacs frontend

Statistics
> GNU R (with numerous packages from CRAN, BioConductor, Rmetrics, and other archives, as well as Ggobi and ESS tools), Xlispstat, Gretl, PSPP, and X12A

Bioinformatics
> BioConductor packages for R, BioPython, and BioPerl, and tools like emboss and blast2

Physics
> CERN tools like Cernlib, Geant, PAW/PAW++, Scientific and Numeric Python, and the GNU GSL libraries

Visualization and graphics
> OpenDX, Mayavi, Gnuplot, Grace, Gri, plotutils, and xfig

Finance
> Software from the Rmetrics and QuantLib projects

Programming languages
> C, C++, Fortran, Java, Perl, Python, PHP, Ruby, Lua, Tcl, Awk, and A+

Editors
> XEmacs, Vim, jed, joe, kate, nedit, and zile

Scientific publishing
> Extended LaTeX support with several frontends (xemacs, kile, and lyx) and numerous extensions and tools for LaTeX and BibTeX

Office software
> OpenOffice.org, KOffice, Gnumeric, and tools like the Gimp

Networking
> Ethereal, portmap, netcat, ethercap, bittorent, nmap, squid, and a host of wireless tools and drivers

General tools
> Apache, MySQL, PHP, and more

Quantian isn't limited to these applications. Quantian also provides instant openMosix clustering with fully automatic configuration (see "Distribute the Load with ClusterKnoppix" **[Hack #89]**), as well as the ability to let other machines boot over the network (in the *openmosixterminalserver* mode) and become additional cluster nodes. Moreover, through the addition of suitable libraries and applications for the *pvm* and *lam/mpich* message-passing interfaces, Quantian also provides Beowulf clustering support. Both open-Mosix and Beowulf styles of distributed computing can be combined—for example, multiple *pvm* or *pvm* node clients can be started on a single host in order to let openMosix spread the load most efficiently across the cluster (see Figure 8-4).

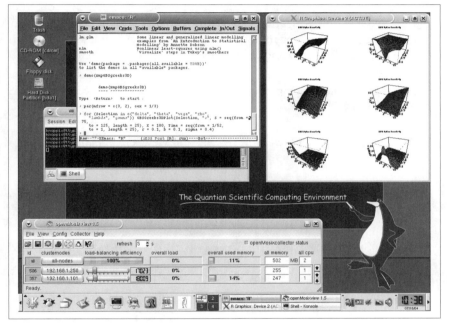

Figure 8-4. Quantian managing a cluster

See Also

- "Distribute the Load with ClusterKnoppix" **[Hack #89]**

—Dirk Eddelbuettel

Find GIS Knoppix on the Map

#91 Cartographers of the world unite! Use GIS Knoppix to view, edit, and create maps using free GIS software.

GIS Knoppix (*http://www.sourcepole.com/sources/software/gis-knoppix/*) from Sourcepole is a Knoppix derivative with a focus on Geographic Information Systems (GIS). On the surface, GIS Knoppix looks and acts like a regular Knoppix disc with many of the same utilities, but GIS Knoppix includes loads of free GIS software, such as:

GRASS
> A raster/vector GIS, image-processing system, and graphics-production system. GRASS was originally developed by the U.S. Army Construction Engineering Research Laboratories (a branch of the U.S. Army Corps of Engineers) for military use, but has since branched out and is also used academically and commercially.

MapServer
> An open source development environment for creating web-based GIS applications.

MapLab
> A suite of web-based Java tools that let you view, create, and edit MapServer files.

MapDesk
> Another Sourcepole project (*http://www.sourcepole.com/sources/software/mapdesk*), MapDesk is a map editor and viewer for MapServer.

TerraView
> A geographic data viewer that can use both vector- and raster-based data.

JUMP
> A GUI workbench for viewing and processing spatial data.

GPS applications
> GPSdrive, GPSman, and support for GPS peripherals.

To get a sense of what GIS Knoppix can do, try one of the demos included on the disk. Click the GIS folder on the desktop, and then click MapLab. In the Mozilla window that appears, click File Menu → Open Map... and select the tutorial (see Figure 8-5).

You can toggle which information MapLab displays from the toolbar on the left, including roads, cities, and national boundaries. You can also use MapLab to create your own map data from scratch. To open the MapLab editor, click the icon that looks like a pencil drawing on the earth, which is in the upper-left corner of the page.

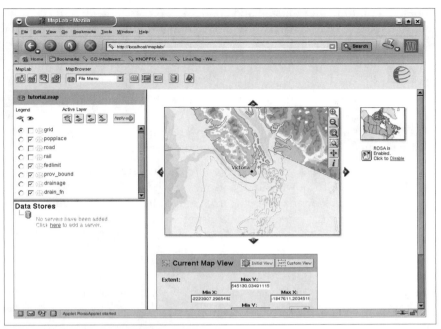

Figure 8-5. MapLab tutorial map

The fact that all of this software is included on a live CD means that you can take your GIS data out to the field with a GPS and a laptop, boot GIS Knoppix, and get to work.

HACK #92 TiVo Your Computer

Use KnoppMyth to quickly turn any computer into a standalone TiVo-like PVR using MythTV.

KnoppMyth (*http://www.mysettopbox.tv/knoppmyth.html*) is a unique Knoppix variant, because its primary function is to install MythTV, not to act as a portable Linux distribution. KnoppMyth uses the excellent hardware auto-configuration of Knoppix, and bundles it with scripts and software to install and configure MythTV automatically.

MythTV (*http://www.mythtv.org*) is an open source PVR project with the goal of being the mythical all-in-one media machine for your home. MythTV allows you to schedule recordings, watch live TV with features such as pausing and rewinding live TV, listen to music, watch recorded video and DVDs, play arcade games, and even check the weather. Think TiVo or Microsoft Media Center on steroids, and you get an idea of what MythTV can do. MythTV is a great project and easy to use once it is running, but many

people find it difficult to install and configure MythTV and all of its components, especially the installation and configuration of the TV Tuner
hardware itself under Linux.

KnoppMyth automates the process of configuring MythTV on a standalone
computer. Desktop environments, like KDE, and the applications most
other Knoppix-based distributions include are absent from KnoppMyth. In
fact, KnoppMyth includes software only to install and configure a MythTV
system. KnoppMyth uses Knoppix's hardware configuration scripts to make
it easy to detect TV Tuners, video cards, and other hardware.

As with MythTV, to use KnoppMyth you need to register with the free Zap2It
DataDirect service to download TV listings for your area. Go to *http://labs.
zap2it.com* and click on the "New User? Sign Up" link to register with the service. As you fill out the survey on the registration page, notice that it asks for a
certificate code. As explained at *http://www.mythtv.org/docs/mythtv-HOWTO-
5.html#ss5.4*, use:

```
ZIYN-DQZO-SBUT
```

Use your login and password in the MythTV setup program after Knopp-
Myth is installed.

When you boot KnoppMyth for the first time, the first thing you see is a no-
frills frontend for the installation script that gives you the following options:

Frontend
    Configures and runs KnoppMyth as a frontend

Auto Install
    Automatically installs to disk

Auto Upgrade
    Attempts to upgrade previous version

Manual Install
    Configures and installs to hard disk

Reboot
    Reboots the machine

Quit
    Exits to console prompt

A KnoppMyth frontend uses the MythTV interface (the frontend) but
accesses a different MythTV server (the backend) for listings, recorded
shows, etc. The Frontend option is the only one that actually uses Knopp-
Myth as a live CD. This option requires another machine on the network that
is configured with MythTV (potentially another KnoppMyth install) with
MySQL   listening   (*http://www.mythtv.org/docs/mythtv-HOWTO-6.html*).
Answer some questions about your MythTV backend server, and then the

MythTV frontend software loads. This can be useful in case you already have MythTV configured on the network recording shows for your TV, but you want to watch them on your computer instead. If you intend on sending the frontend output to a TV, then at the boot prompt, type:

tv

This boots KnoppMyth to an 800×600 resolution suitable for TVs.

The Auto Install option is the main purpose of KnoppMyth. Select this option and answer some very basic questions, such as your name, user-name, and password, and then KnoppMyth automatically partitions your hard drive and installs Debian with MythTV.

> Currently, the auto install works only for /dev/hda (the primary IDE drive on the first bus). There is a roundabout method to install to a different drive listed on the Knopp-Myth site, but if you have such a setup, it is better to go with the manual install.

KnoppMyth reboots once the install finishes, and then boots back into your new Debian install. Enter your root password at the prompt, and then the KnoppMyth install asks some final questions, including your network configuration (DHCP versus manual configuration) and whether to use i586- or i686-optimized modules (i586 for Pentium class processors and i686 for PentiumPro and above and any Athlon processors).

When KnoppMyth's own configuration is done, it launches the MythTV setup program. Use this GUI to tell MythTV about any TV Tuner cards your system has, which channel to default to, which type of TV service you use (broadcast, cable, digital cable, etc.), your Zap2It account information, and so on. Once MythTV is set up the way you want, hit Esc to exit and watch as new television listings are downloaded. This process can take some time, so be patient. Afterwards, the MythTV frontend, the main program you use to watch and record TV, launches. Now you can go through the interface and schedule recordings, and watch live TV.

The Auto Upgrade option is fairly straightforward and simply upgrades the KnoppMyth install that is currently on the machine to the latest version. The Manual Install option is for advanced users and lets you manually partition your hard drive before KnoppMyth installs.

The KnoppMyth project continues to improve as time goes on. There are still rough areas here and there (such as installing only to /dev/hda), but overall, this is a great project that takes out many of the headaches of installing and configuring a standalone MythTV PVR. Visit the official site (http:// mysettopbox.tv) for more tips and hints for getting the most out of this project.

Contribute to Knoppix
Want to give back to the Knoppix community? Here's how.

So you've used Knoppix for a while and love it, and maybe you've even remastered it a few times [Hack #94], and now you want to contribute to the Knoppix project. Even if you don't know how to program, there are still plenty of ways you can contribute to the project: file bug reports, write documentation, share your ideas for improvements, and help others in the forums.

Become a Knoppix Developer

Becoming a Knoppix developer and contributing to the project is an easy process:

- Subscribe to the debian-knoppix mailing list.
- Send a patch to debian-knoppix or Klaus Knopper himself.
- Be very patient.

The debian-knoppix mailing list is the mailing list for Knoppix development-related discussion. You can sign up for the mailing list at *http://mailman. linuxtag.org/mailman/listinfo/debian-knoppix*. Note that since Knoppix is a German project, sometimes threads are in German, although many if not all of the active members on the list also speak English.

A majority of the development in Knoppix involves writing *bash* and *dialog* scripts, and packaging files into *.debs*, so a good background in those areas will help you get up to speed on the project. If you have a patch that you would like to see included, it is recommended that you package it into a *.deb* package. Klaus likes ready-made Debian packages for patches, because they save him the trouble of packaging them himself.

Patience is a virtue. Klaus gets a lot of patches and a lot of emails. Patience and persistence pay off when you have a patch that you would like to see included.

Join the Community

If you don't know how to program, you can still help the Knoppix community. You can file bug reports and general feedback at *http://www.knoppix. net/bugs/*. Provide as much detailed information as you can when filing a bug report, especially if you are having problems with hardware. This ensures that even if a current version of Knoppix might not support your hardware, it can be supported in the future because the developers are now aware of the problem.

All open source projects benefit from people willing to write good documentation. The documentation pages on *http://www.knoppix.net/docs/* run on a *Wiki*, which means that if you join the site, you can help add, edit, and update the documentation with the rest of the community.

Another great way to contribute to Knoppix is to help in the forums and the IRC channel **[Hack #20]**. There are always new users who need help getting started; besides, participating on the community forums is a good way to keep up to date with the latest news and tips.

## CHAPTER NINE

Knoppix Remastered
Hacks 94–100

Were it not for open source software, Knoppix as we know it today would not exist. Almost all of the software on the Knoppix CD, including Klaus's own scripts, uses the GPL or a different OSI-approved license. Because these licenses allow and even encourage the reuse and modification of software, Klaus Knopper was able to piece together software that he wanted to use, and put it on a CD of his own without having to hire an attorney to navigate copyright legalities or pay any licensing fees.

Knoppix itself is an open source project, and, as Chapter 8 shows, many people have taken Knoppix and have further customized it for their own needs. Many Knoppix-based projects have been started simply because someone wanted Knoppix to have an extra piece of software. Other more involved projects have taken the Knoppix base and changed it almost completely. Creating your own customized Knoppix CD isn't that difficult, especially once you get the hang of it. If you have started using Knoppix, but have found that there is a certain piece of software missing that you want or need, this chapter is for you.

Once you start creating your own Knoppix-based distributions, you will discover many more uses for Knoppix than you may have previously thought possible. Many of these uses are of particular interest for a business. As mentioned in "Make a Kiosk" **[Hack #24]**, you could create a custom Knoppix CD that acts as a kiosk for your business. If you are a system administrator who images a lot of systems, you could create your own customized live CD to automate the process. Once the CD boots, it could launch a script you have written that chooses from a series of images stored on a file server and then images the local machine **[Hack #48]**.

Happy remastering! Maybe your CD will be the next big Knoppix-based distribution.

Create a Customized Knoppix

One reason there are so many different Knoppix-based distributions is that they are so easy to create. With these steps, you will be creating your own custom Knoppix CD in no time.

The amount of software that Knoppix is able to fit on a CD is really amazing, but at some point, you might find that one of your favorite programs is missing. You can create your own custom Knoppix CD that includes the programs you want through a process known as remastering. The remastering process looks complex but is pretty simple once you get the hang of it. The basic process is to copy the current Knoppix system to disk, *chroot* into it, change the system to the way you would like it, and then create a new CD image based on the new system.

First, boot from your Knoppix CD. If you plan on installing any new packages on your custom disc, make sure that your Internet connection is up and working. Most of the commands you use to remaster the CD require root privileges; so instead of typing **sudo** in front of everything, click K Menu → Knoppix → Root Shell to launch a terminal with root privileges.

Choose a Partition

Remastering Knoppix requires the use of your hard drive. You do not have to use a completely blank, unformatted partition, but the partition does need to meet a few requirements:

- The partition must be formatted with a Linux filesystem.
- If you plan on using the bootfrom cheat code to boot the *.iso*, make sure that your filesystem is compatible with bootfrom. (Currently, ext2, FAT, FAT32, and NTFS are compatible; XFS and JFS are not.)
- The partition must have at least 3 GB of free space. If you have less than 1 GB of RAM and need to create a swap file on the partition (more on that below), you need an extra gigabyte of free space. On average, I need at least 4.5 GB of free space for my remastering.

If you need to move some partitions to clear up space, click K Menu → System → QTParted **[Hack #56]**. Once you have a partition that meets these requirements, go to your root shell and mount it with read/write permissions:

```
root@ttyp1[knoppix]# mount -o rw /dev/hda1 /mnt/hda1
```

Replace *hda1* with the partition and mount point you are using.

Check Available RAM

Remastering a Knoppix CD requires about one gigabyte of total RAM (physical memory plus swap). You can check the amount of total RAM on your system by adding up the total column for both Mem and Swap rows:

```
root@ttyp1[knoppix]# free
                total        used        free      shared     buffers      cached
Mem:           515264      218832      296432           0        5932      115728
-/+ buffers/cache:          97172      418092
Swap:               0           0           0
```

In my case, I have 515,264 KB (about 503 MB) of physical memory and no swap. I need at least one gigabyte of memory, so I will create a 750-MB swap file. From within the mounted partition, I run the following commands:

```
root@ttyp1[hda1]# dd if=/dev/zero of=swapfile bs=1M count=750
750+0 records in
750+0 records out
786432000 bytes transferred in 27.858599 seconds (28229417 bytes/sec)
root@ttyp1[hda1]# mkswap swapfile
Setting up swapspace version 1, size = 786427 kB
root@ttyp1[hda1]# swapon swapfile
root@ttyp1[hda1]#
```

The *dd* command creates a 750-MB file full of zeros. The *mkswap* command formats that file with the swap filesystem. Finally, the *swapon* command starts using the file for swap.

Prepare the Source Filesystem

To remaster the Knoppix CD, you must copy the complete filesystem to the disk so that you can edit it. To keep things organized, create a *source* directory, and under that, create a *KNOPPIX* directory. Then copy all of the files on the Knoppix filesystem to the *KNOPPIX* directory. Make sure you are in the root of your mounted partition, and then run the following commands:

```
root@ttyp1[hda1]# mkdir source
root@ttyp1[hda1]# mkdir source/KNOPPIX
root@ttyp1[hda1]# cp -Rp /KNOPPIX/* source/KNOPPIX
```

The *cp* command takes some time, as it's copying almost 2 GB of files from a compressed filesystem on your CD-ROM to the hard drive (on my system, it took about 10 minutes). Once the filesystem is copied over, the *source/ KNOPPIX* directory looks like the root filesystem of a Debian Linux install:

```
root@ttyp1[hda1]# ls source/KNOPPIX
bin   cdrom  etc     home    lib   none  proc  sbin  tmp  var
boot  dev    floppy  initrd  mnt   opt   root  sys   usr  vmlinuz
```

Chroot. The next step is to use the *chroot* command to turn the *source/KNOPPIX* directory into the effective root filesystem. This allows you to run commands such as *apt-get* just as though *source/KNOPPIX* were the root directory. Although the network works from within the *chroot* environment, all configuration files that Knoppix creates dynamically when you boot are not copied over in their modified state. This means that to resolve domain names, you must copy your */etc/dhcpdc/resolv.conf* file over to *source/KNOPPIX*:

```
root@ttyp1[hda1]# cp /etc/dhcpc/resolv.conf source/KNOPPIX/etc/dhcpc/resolv.
conf
cp: overwrite `source/KNOPPIX/etc/dhcpc/resolv.conf'? y
```

To use other dynamic configuration files (for instance, */etc/samba/smb.conf* for Samba), you must copy those over as well before you *chroot*.

Now *chroot* into the *source/KNOPPIX* directory and mount the proc filesystem (this provides access to the network and other special interfaces within the kernel):

```
root@ttyp1[hda1]# chroot source/KNOPPIX
root@ttyp1[/]# mount -t proc /proc proc
root@ttyp1[/]#
```

Now you are in a *chrooted* environment. Any command that you run runs as though *source/KNOPPIX* is the root directory.

> If for some reason you forget to copy a file that you need and you have already *chrooted*, press Ctrl-D to exit out of *chroot*, copy the files you need, and then go back to the *chroot* environment. Or, open a second root terminal to gain the same results.

Package management. When you are remastering, you will notice that Knoppix is already very cramped for space. If you want to add new packages, you need to remove some packages to free up space. More specific methods for keeping the size down are discussed in "Trim the Fat" **[Hack #95]**, but in general, simply choose a package that you don't need, and run:

```
root@ttyp1[/]# apt-get --purge remove packagename
```

This command removes the package along with any configuration files it might have created.

Once you have freed up some space for new packages, update the list of packages on the system with:

```
root@ttyp1[/]# apt-get update
```

After you update the list of packages, you can add new packages to the distribution just like with any other Debian install with:

```
root@ttyp1[/]# apt-get install packagename
```

If you are unsure of the name for the package you want to install, use the *apt-cache* program to search for the package name by keywords:

```
root@ttyp1[/]# apt-cache search keyword
```

Once you are ready to create a CD based on your changes, clear out the cache of packages you have downloaded to conserve more space:

```
root@ttyp1[/]# apt-get clean
```

Before you exit the *chroot* environment, remember to unmount the proc filesystem with:

```
root@ttyp1[/]# umount /proc
```

Then press Ctrl-D to exit *chroot*.

Make the Master CD Filesystem

Once you set up the *KNOPPIX* root filesystem, create the actual filesystem that appears on the CD. Put this filesystem in a new directory called *master*, under your mounted partition. Use *rsync* to copy all of the files that appear on the Knoppix CD-ROM (the files in */cdrom*) *except* for the 700-MB *KNOPPIX/KNOPPIX* compressed filesystem. The compressed file isn't necessary, because you create a new version of that file based on your customized filesystem in *source/KNOPPIX*. From the mounted partition, run:

```
root@ttyp1[hda1]# mkdir master
root@ttyp1[hda1]# rsync -a --exclude "/KNOPPIX/KNOPPIX" /cdrom/ master/
```

Now create the *KNOPPIX/KNOPPIX* file. This file is actually a highly compressed filesystem that is created from the *source/KNOPPIX* directory. This (long) command generates an ISO-9660 filesystem like those on CD-ROMs:

```
root@ttyp1[hda1]# mkisofs -R -U -V "Knoppix Hacks filesystem" -P
"Knoppix Hacks" -hide-rr-moved -cache-inodes -no-bak -pad source/KNOPPIX |
nice -5 /usr/bin/create_compressed_fs - 65536 > master/KNOPPIX/KNOPPIX
```

By far, this is the most time-consuming command, because it is not only creating a filesystem, but it is also sending the filesystem through a script that heavily compresses it. On my 1.2-GHz system, it takes approximately 30 minutes to complete. You can ignore the warning it outputs about creating a filesystem that does not conform to ISO-9660.

There are a lot of options used to create the filesystem, and if you are interested in the ISO-9660 spec, then you can reference each of those arguments and which filesystem options they enable by reading the *mkisofs* manpage (type **man mkisofs**). If you want to customize the filesystem, the main two options that might interest you are -V, which specifies the volume ID to use for the filesystem, and -P, which labels the publisher of the CD-ROM.

Once the script completes, and the *master/KNOPPIX/KNOPPIX* file is created, go through the other files in the *master/KNOPPIX* directory, and customize them to your liking. One file of interest is *master/KNOPPIX/ background.jpg*, which is the default background Knoppix uses for your desktop. If you want to change that default, simply copy a new *.jpg* file in its place, such as one from */usr/share/wallpapers*.

After all of the files in the master directory are customized, there is just one step before you create the actual CD image that you burn to a CD. Knoppix uses *md5sums* to check file integrity; you have changed at least one of the major files, *master/KNOPPIX/KNOPPIX*, so you need to regenerate its list of checksums:

```
root@ttyp1[hda1]# cd master
root@ttyp1[master]# rm -f KNOPPIX/md5sums
root@ttyp1[master]# find -type f -not -name md5sums -not -name boot.cat
-exec md5sum {} \; >> KNOPPIX/md5sums
root@ttyp1[master]# cd ..
root@ttyp1[hda1]#
```

Now the CD image is ready to be generated. This requires one final (but relatively quick) *mkisofs* command:

```
root@ttyp1[hda1]# mkisofs -pad -l -r -J -v -V "KNOPPIX" -no-emul-boot
-boot-load-size 4 -boot-info-table -b boot/isolinux/isolinux.bin -c
boot/isolinux/boot.cat -hide-rr-moved -o knoppix.iso master/
```

Once this command is completed, you should see a new *knoppix.iso* file in the root of your partition. You can burn this image to a CD just like any other Knoppix ISO; however make sure that the CD image you have created is small enough to fit on the CD. Even if it doesn't fit, you can still test the image using the bootfrom cheat code. To test the image, reboot the computer and add:

```
knoppix bootfrom=/dev/hda1/knoppix.iso
```

at the boot prompt. Replace *hda1* with your partition. In fact, I would recommend testing your CD images this way just to make sure everything is how you want it before using up CDs.

Trim the Fat

HACK #95

Knoppix has been able to squeeze a lot of useful tools on a single CD image.
When you want to add your tools to the mix, you must use some tricks to
keep the total file size low enough to fit on a CD.

So you've gone through all of the steps, and, finally, your remastered CD is
finished. You are about to reach over for a blank CDR when you notice your
CD image is 740 MB! Welcome to the challenge Klaus Knopper faces with
every release: keeping almost 2 GB of great software compressed under 700
MB. The Knoppix 3.4 release was delayed for some time partially because
some of the popular packages in Knoppix, like KDE and OpenOffice.org,
had continued to increase in size. To get everything to fit, Klaus had to
remove the complete KOffice suite along with TeX and a few other packages.

You might decide to create your own Knoppix CD because there are some
programs that are not included in Knoppix that you want on the CD. To
add those programs, other programs must go, but there are some steps you
can take while you are in the *chroot* environment to make the process easier.

Find Programs to Remove

The first step in slimming down your CD is to find programs you don't need.
Knoppix comes with a lot of software, and depending on how you plan to
use Knoppix, you may be able to do without large parts of the system.

If you are unsure of which software you want to remove, it might help to see
which programs are taking up the most space. The following command lists
all of the packages installed on the system, sorted by size:

```
root@ttyp0[/]# dpkg-query -W --showformat='${Installed-Size} ${Package}\n'
| sort -n
. . .
28684 libwine
30056 kernel-image-2.4.26
31944 mozilla-browser
34662 emacs21-common
45556 kernel-image-2.6.6
243092 openoffice-de-en
```

The file sizes in the output are in kilobytes. As you can see, the largest single package on the system happens to be openoffice-de-en. So, if you want
to free up around 250 MB of uncompressed space on your CD, delete the
openoffice-de-en package by running:

```
root@ttyp0[/]# apt-get --purge remove openoffice-de-en
```

This command not only removes the openoffice-de-en package, but with the --purge option, it also clears the system of any configuration files the package might have used. You will find that every little bit helps when you are trying to make space.

Dependencies

When you remove a package, *apt-get* also removes any packages that depend on that package. For instance, if you remove the emacs21-common package, you see that other packages are also removed, freeing up a total of 42.1 MB. *Apt-get* lists the amount of disk space that will be freed once you remove a package and prompts you to continue, so you can pretend to remove a package just to see how much space will be freed without actually doing any damage. Just make sure to answer "no" when you are prompted to continue.

```
root@ttyp0[/]# apt-get --purge remove emacs21-common
Reading Package Lists... Done
Building Dependency Tree... Done
The following packages will be REMOVED:
  emacs21* emacs21-bin-common* emacs21-common* gettext-el*
0 upgraded, 0 newly installed, 4 to remove and 0 not upgraded.
Need to get 0B of archives.
After unpacking 42.1MB disk space will be freed.
Do you want to continue? [Y/n] n
Abort.
```

Dependencies are also important to consider as you remove programs, because you might inadvertently remove a package you need to keep by removing a package it depends on.

 Be extra aware of which dependencies will be removed when you remove library packages (packages usually starting with lib), because they typically have many other programs that depend on them.

You can also check which packages depend on a certain package with the *apt-cache* command:

```
root@ttyp0[/]# apt-cache rdepends libwine | uniq
libwine
Reverse Depends:
  libwine-twain
  wine-utils
  wine
  libwine-print
```

This example pipes the output through the *uniq* command because the reverse dependencies option in *apt-cache* often generates multiple lines with the same package name, so with the *uniq* command you see only unique packages that depend on this package.

Please Sir, I Want to Remove More

After removing programs that you know you won't need, there still might be ways to trim down the system by removing programs known as *orphans*. Orphans are packages (usually libraries) that have no other packages depending on them. Knoppix includes Debian's tool called *deborphan* for this purpose. To list all of the orphaned libraries on your system sorted by their size, run:

```
root@ttyp0[/]# deborphan -z | sort -n
```

By default, *deborphan* lists only libraries, not other types of packages. The reason for this is that generally a library's purpose is to have other programs use and depend on it. When no programs depend on a library anymore, it has no further use. Many regular programs that you might use don't have any other packages depending on them, yet you generally don't want to remove them. On a default Knoppix install, *deborphan* returns no packages, because Klaus already beat you to removing the orphans. If you have maintained a remastered CD for some time, however, you might find that libraries are orphaned from time to time as packages upgrade and leave behind old libraries they no longer need.

If you want to just quickly remove all orphans from your system, run the following command:

```
root@ttyp0[/]# deborphan | xargs apt-get -y --purge remove
```

Remove the -y option from *apt-get* if you want to be prompted before following through with the command.

Use the Best Possible Compression

When you create the compressed Knoppix filesystem with:

```
root@ttyp1[hda1]# mkisofs -R -U -V "Knoppix Hacks filesystem" -P
"Knoppix Hacks" -hide-rr-moved -cache-inodes -no-bak -pad source/KNOPPIX |
nice -5 /usr/bin/create_compressed_fs - 65536 > master/KNOPPIX/KNOPPIX
```

you can add the --best option after the */usr/bin/create_compressed_fs* command to increase the compression even further. On a 700-MB image, this option can save an extra 20 MB but takes much longer to complete.

Final Tips

If you have tried all of the other methods, and you still need to free up space but aren't sure where, there are still a few other tricks you can try.

Whenever you download new packages using *apt-get*, a copy of the package is cached under */var/cache/apt/archives*. Always make sure to run **apt-get clean** before you create the disk image.

If you are still having trouble figuring out which programs are taking up the most space on the filesystem, try the following command, which will sort all of the directories on your system by how much space they are using:

```
root@ttyp0[/]# du -cb / | sort -n
```

Finally, remember that certain file types compress better than others, which means they are smaller when in the compressed *KNOPPIX* filesystem. So if you have a choice between removing a 5-MB text file and a 5-MB *.mp3* file, remove the *.mp3* file, because the *.mp3* file is already about as compressed as it will go, and the text file will compress much smaller.

HACK #96 — Personalize Knoppix

Customizing Knoppix doesn't just mean changing which packages get installed and what programs run at boot. You can also completely change which the default desktop environment looks and feels like.

So you have created your custom CDs with your custom applications and settings, but when you boot and see the same desktop and themes that vanilla Knoppix comes with, your distribution starts to seem a lot less custom. It's like souping up the engine on your hot rod without giving it a new paint job. With a tweak here and there, you can give your distribution a special look that makes it your own.

I have already covered how to customize the look and feel of your desktop in "Customize the Desktop Look" [Hack #11]. You might have noticed when you started remastering that the */home* directory in the *chroot* environment was empty. This means that customizing the look of your desktop isn't as simple as changing the files in the */home/knoppix* directory and copying them to the *chroot* environment.

Quick Desktop Tweaks

You can take advantage of a custom *knoppix.sh* script like one created with persistent settings [Hack #21] to shortcut many of these more disruptive tweaks and save yourself from the long process of creating a compressed *KNOPPIX* filesystem.

Start with the "Make the Master CD Filesystem" step from "Create a Customized Knoppix" [Hack #94], create the master directory, and then copy all of the files from the CD-ROM, including the compressed *KNOPPIX* filesystem:

```
root@ttyp1[hda1]# mkdir master
root@ttyp1[hda1]# rsync -a /cdrom/ master/
```

Change the desktop to your liking, click K Menu → KNOPPIX → Configure → Save KNOPPIX configuration, and then copy the *knoppix.sh* and *configs.tbz* files the script creates to the *master/KNOPPIX* directory. You can skip the step of creating the compressed *master/KNOPPIX/KNOPPIX* filesystem and go straight to creating the new CD image:

```
root@ttyp1[hda1]# mkisofs -pad -l -r -J -v -V "KNOPPIX" -no-emul-boot
-boot-load-size 4 -boot-info-table -b boot/isolinux/isolinux.bin -c
boot/isolinux/boot.cat -hide-rr-moved -o knoppix.iso master/
```

Once this command is completed, you should see a new *knoppix.iso* file in the root of your partition. When this image boots, Knoppix executes the *knoppix.sh* script you have copied to the CD, and unpacks your settings from *configs.tbz*.

Complete Desktop Tweaks

When Knoppix boots, it runs a script located at */etc/X11/Xsession.d/ 45xsession*. This script not only handles which window manager gets loaded when you boot, but also copies configuration files from the */etc/skel* directory to the */home/knoppix* directory and even tells Knoppix to play the sound you hear when it loads the desktop environment.

To change desktop settings, start the remastering process [Hack #94] and go as far as the *chroot* section, then follow the different guides below to change specific settings. After you are finished making your changes, unmount the proc filesystem with:

```
root@ttyp1[/]# umount /proc
```

Then press Ctrl-D to exit *chroot*. Now you are ready to pick up with the "Make the Master CD Filesystem" section of "Create a Customized Knoppix" [Hack #94].

Change the Default Window Manager

To get a better understanding of how the *45xsession* script works, I will demonstrate how to change which window manager Knoppix uses by default. "Boot Knoppix on a Desktop" [Hack #1] demonstrates how to use cheat codes to change the window manager Knoppix uses, but if you always plan to use a different window manager, you don't want to be bothered with typing in the cheat code every time.

The *45xsession* script controls which window manager Knoppix uses based on the $DESKTOP environment variable. The script runs the */etc/sysconfig/desktop* script if it exists; otherwise, it defaults to using KDE. If you want to default to FluxBox instead of KDE, follow the remastering process to the *chroot* stage, and create an */etc/sysconfig/desktop* file containing the following line:

```
DESKTOP="fluxbox"
```

You can replace fluxbox with icewm, xfce, or any of the other window managers that are on Knoppix.

Change Desktop Environment Settings

If you dig further into the *45xsession* script, you might notice a section full of *rsync* commands similar to the following:

```
# Copy profiles if not already present
rsync -Ha --ignore-existing /etc/skel/{.acrorc,.Xdefaults,.gimp*,.gconf*, .
bashrc,.nessus*,.links,.local,.lynx*,.qt,.xine,tmp} $HOME/ 2>/dev/null
[ "$USER" = "knoppix" ] && rsync -Ha --ignore-existing /usr/share/knoppix/
profile/{.acrorc,.Xdefaults,.bashrc,.nessus*,.links,.lynx*,.qt,.xine,tmp}
$HOME/ 2>/dev/null
[ "$USER" = "knoppix" -a -f /usr/share/knoppix/profile/.fonts.cache-1 ] &&
rsync -H --ignore-existing /usr/share/knoppix/profile/.fonts.cache-1 $HOME/
2>/dev/null
```

These series of commands copy default settings from the */etc/skel* directory to */home/knoppix* if they don't already exist. To change the appearance of KDE, click K Menu → Settings → Control Center and make your changes in the Appearance & Themes section. Once the wallpaper, themes, color scheme, and the desktop itself are arranged to your liking, open a terminal and synchronize your changes with the *source/KNOPPIX* filesystem.

```
knoppix@ttyp0[knoppix]$ sudo rsync -a /home/knoppix/
/mnt/hda1/source/KNOPPIX/etc/skel/
```

If you are using a window manager other than KDE, it is likely that the *45xsession* script does not automatically copy over your settings. This means that you must add a special entry to the *source/KNOPPIX/etc/X11/Xsession.d/ 45xsession* script yourself to manage copying over the settings. For instance, if you use *fluxbox* on the desktop, all of your settings are stored in the *.fluxbox* directory. Reference the startkde function inside the script that Knoppix uses to copy over KDE settings to see how you can do the same for *.fluxbox*:

```
startkde(){
# Play sound
playsound

if [ -z "$DONTCHANGE" ]; then
# No persistent homedir, copy everything
rsync -Ha --ignore-existing /etc/skel/{.kde*,Desktop} $HOME/ 2>/dev/null
```

Find the startfluxbox function in the script that looks something like this:

```
startfluxbox( ){
# Create automatic Desktop icons
mkdesktophdicons

playsound
GDK_USE_XFT=1 exec fluxbox
}
```

Then modify it to look like this:

```
startfluxbox( ){
# Create automatic Desktop icons
mkdesktophdicons

playsound
if [ -z "$DONTCHANGE" ]; then
# No persistent homedir, copy everything
rsync -Ha --ignore-existing /etc/skel/{.fluxbox,Desktop} $HOME/ 2>/dev/null
GDK_USE_XFT=1 exec fluxbox
}
```

Now you can synchronize all of your desktop settings just like with KDE:

```
knoppix@ttyp0[knoppix]$ sudo rsync -a /home/knoppix/
/mnt/hda1/source/KNOPPIX/etc/skel/
```

Of course, if you are using a different window manager, you must find its section in the script and modify the *rsync* command to use its configuration directory instead of *.fluxbox*.

Disable the Startup and Shutdown Sounds

The startup and shutdown sounds that Knoppix makes are useful indicators that the sound card is working. However, if you want your remastered CD to be quiet when it starts up, it is pretty simple to disable the sounds.

First, edit the *source/KNOPPIX/etc/X11/Xsession.d/45xsession* file. Find the startwindowmanager function in the script for your window manager (by default, startkde). To disable the startup sound, simply comment out the *playsound* command for your window manager with a "#" character:

```
startkde( ){
# Play sound
#playsound
```

Disabling the shutdown sound requires that you edit *source/KNOPPIX/etc/init.d/xsession*. Find the section in the script that looks like the following:

```
# Play informational sound if soundcore module present
# (checking /dev/sndstat is unreliable)
OGGPLAY=/usr/bin/ogg123
PLAY=/usr/bin/wavp
```

```
[ -x "$PLAY" ] || PLAY=/usr/bin/play-sample
[ -x "$PLAY" ] || PLAY=/usr/bin/play
if [ -x "$OGGPLAY" -a -f /usr/share/sounds/shutdown.ogg ]; then
case "$(lsmod)" in *sound*) { $OGGPLAY -q -p 64 /usr/share/sounds/shutdown.
ogg \
>/dev/null 2>&1 & } ; sleep 7 ;; esac
elif [ -f /usr/share/sounds/shutdown.wav -a -x "$PLAY" ]; then
case "$(lsmod)" in *sound*) { $PLAY /usr/share/sounds/shutdown.wav >/dev/
null \
2>&1 & } ; sleep 7 ;; esac
fi
```

Then comment out the complete if statement so that the section looks like this:

```
# Play informational sound if soundcore module present
# (checking /dev/sndstat is unreliable)
OGGPLAY=/usr/bin/ogg123
PLAY=/usr/bin/wavp
[ -x "$PLAY" ] || PLAY=/usr/bin/play-sample
[ -x "$PLAY" ] || PLAY=/usr/bin/play
#if [ -x "$OGGPLAY" -a -f /usr/share/sounds/shutdown.ogg ]; then
#case "$(lsmod)" in *sound*) { $OGGPLAY -q -p 64 /usr/share/sounds/shutdown.
ogg \
>/dev/null 2>&1 & } ; sleep 7 ;; esac
#elif [ -f /usr/share/sounds/shutdown.wav -a -x "$PLAY" ]; then
#case "$(lsmod)" in *sound*) { $PLAY /usr/share/sounds/shutdown.wav >/dev/
null \
2>&1 & } ; sleep 7 ;; esac
#fi
```

There are a lot more tweaks you can do once you get experienced with the scripts Knoppix uses to start the desktop environment. Read through the *45xsession* script to find other ways you can tweak your desktop.

HACK
#97

Keep Your Custom Disc Up to Date

After you customize your Knoppix disc, make sure it has the latest and greatest packages.

"Release early and release often" has been the mantra for many open source projects. Debian unstable has over 13,000 packages now, so there's a good chance that every day or two there will be an update to some package you are using on your CD. When the time comes to remaster, it's a good time to also update all of the packages on your system. With Debian, this process is pretty easy.

The first step to updating the packages on your system is to grab the most current list of packages your package repositories have to offer. Inside your remastering *chroot* environment **[Hack #94]**, run:

```
root@ttyp0[/]# apt-get update
```

By default Knoppix uses a mixed repository of Debian stable, testing, and unstable packages. Be sure when you upgrade that you use **apt-get upgrade** and not **apt-get dist-upgrade**, or otherwise, all of the stable packages on the system are upgraded to testing. Also, even if you are running a complete Debian unstable system, **apt-get dist-upgrade** should still be avoided, as it installs all packages that have been held back temporarily, even if installing the packages results in removing other essential files on the system.

As this command runs, you can watch as package lists are downloaded from each repository. If you have trouble connecting to one of the repositories, exit the program with Ctrl-C and rerun the command. If you still have trouble connecting, you might need to wait until the repository is responding before you update. Once the program completes, it's time to upgrade all of the packages on your system:

```
root@ttyp0[/]# apt-get upgrade
Reading Package Lists... Done
Building Dependency Tree... Done
The following packages have been kept back:
. . .
The following packages will be upgraded:
. . .
397 upgraded, 0 newly installed, 0 to remove and 21 not upgraded.
Need to get 275MB of archives.
After unpacking 21.1MB of additional disk space will be used.
Do you want to continue? [Y/n]
```

A good general rule of thumb is to use **apt-get upgrade**, and use **apt-get install** to install individual packages that have been held back. Running **apt-get install** alerts you to the reasons the package is held back (whether it wants to remove an old dependency or possibly install a new one) so that you can decide whether you want to install the package.

When you run this program, you are presented with a full list of packages *apt-get* intends to download and install, told how large the files are, and told how much disk space is used after they install. Pay extra attention to the additional disk space this upgrade uses before you continue. If your CD is already tight on space, you must figure out ways to trim it down after the upgrade **[Hack #95]**. Once you tell *apt-get* that you want to continue, it downloads each new package from its respective repository along with any dependencies it needs, and then, after all of the packages have finished, *apt-get* upgrades each one.

While *apt-get* is downloading, it is safe to stop the program by hitting Ctrl-C. Any partial downloads that result from the program exiting prematurely resume the next time you run *apt-get*. Also, if for some reason a package does not download, or the server doesn't respond, you can simply stop the process and resume a bit later.

After *apt-get* has moved past the downloading phase and is going through the process of upgrading your packages, do not stop the program unless absolutely necessary, as there is a chance that a program might be installed incorrectly if its install is stopped halfway through.

After you update all of the packages, remember to run the following command to delete all the cached packages from the */var/cache/apt/archives* directory:

```
root@ttyp0[/]# apt-get clean
```

As you can see, keeping your system up to date is pretty simple. The challenge comes when trying to fit all of the updates on a single CD. After you are finished making your changes, unmount the */proc* filesystem with:

```
root@ttyp1[/]# umount /proc
```

Then press Ctrl-D to exit *chroot*. Now you are ready to pick up with the "Make the Master CD Filesystem" section of "Create a Customized Knoppix" [Hack #94].

HACK #98 Automate Knoppix Remastering

Automate the remastering process by using one of Klaus's scripts.

After you follow the steps in "Create a Customized Knoppix" [Hack #94] a few times, you might think to yourself, "I type some of the same commands every time. I should put this in a script." A number of people have had the same thought, and you can find quite a few scripts floating around the Internet that help automate much of the process of remastering a Knoppix CD. Klaus and the other Knoppix maintainers don't type the commands in by hand either, and you can actually use the same scripts they use to automate the remastering process. These scripts not only create the compressed filesystem and CD image for you, but they also clean up your distribution, remove excess files, update manpages and locate databases, and perform other timesaving functions.

The first part of the process is the same as in "Create a Customized Knoppix" [Hack #94]. Follow all of those steps in exactly the same way through the *chroot* process, and stop once you reach "Make the Master CD Filesystem."

Make the Master CD Filesystem

At this point, you should have a *source/KNOPPIX* directory on a mounted hard drive that you have *chrooted* into and have changed to suit your needs **[Hacks #95 and #96]**. Now change to the *source/KNOPPIX* directory, download Klaus's scripts from *http://debian/tu-bs.de/knoppix/debian/sarge-live-base/KNOPPIX.build.tar.gz*, and unpack the file in that directory:

```
root@ttyp0[hda1]# cd source/KNOPPIX
root@ttyp0[KNOPPIX]# wget
http://debian.tu-bs.de/knoppix/debian/sarge-live-base/KNOPPIX.build.tar.gz
root@ttyp0[KNOPPIX]# tar xvzf KNOPPIX.build.tar.gz
KNOPPIX.build/
KNOPPIX.build/Knoppix-3.4.mkcompressed
KNOPPIX.build/Knoppix.checklibs
KNOPPIX.build/Knoppix.clean
KNOPPIX.build/Knoppix.hardlinks
KNOPPIX.build/Knoppix.mksortlist
KNOPPIX.build/Knoppix.postupgrade
KNOPPIX.build/Knoppix.removedocs
KNOPPIX.build/mkcomp.diff
KNOPPIX.build/create_compressed_fs
KNOPPIX.build/mkisofs
KNOPPIX.build/mkisofs.timestamp
KNOPPIX.build/mkisofs.sort
```

Now create the master directory to hold the filesystem for your CD-ROM; only this time, create it inside the new *KNOPPIX.build* directory. Then use *rsync* to copy all of the files other than the *KNOPPIX/KNOPPIX* compressed filesystem from the CD-ROM to the master directory:

```
root@ttyp0[KNOPPIX]# mkdir KNOPPIX.build/master
root@ttyp0[KNOPPIX]# rsync -a --exclude "/KNOPPIX/KNOPPIX" /cdrom/
KNOPPIX.build/master/
```

One major difference when you use these scripts is that you run them from within the *chroot* environment. The *chroot* environment is necessary, because the script updates manpages and locate databases and runs other commands that expect the / to be the root of your remastered CD. *Chroot* to your *source/KNOPPIX* directory (if you are still in this directory, you can just use a dot [.] for the directory name) and remount the */proc* filesystem:

```
root@ttyp0[KNOPPIX]# chroot ./
root@ttyp0[/]# mount -t proc /proc proc
```

As you might imagine, Klaus's scripts are customized to suit how he builds his CDs. You won't use many of these features off the bat, and for the purposes of this *chroot* process, you must comment a line in the script to disable remounting the / filesystem read-only, as it fails from within *chroot*. Run the *Knoppix-3.4.mkcompressed* script to finish creating your CD, and then specify the master directory you have created in *KNOPPIX.build* to tell the script where to find the CD filesystem:

```
root@ttyp0[/]# perl -pi -e 's/^(mount -o ro)/#$1/'
/KNOPPIX.build/Knoppix-3.4.mkcompressed
root@ttyp0[/]# /KNOPPIX.build/Knoppix-3.4.mkcompressed /KNOPPIX.build/master
```

This script creates a *master.iso* file under *KNOPPIX.build*, but if you type **/KNOPPIX.build/master/** on the command line instead of **/KNOPPIX.build/master** (notice that there is no trailing /), then the script creates a file called *.iso* under the *KNOPPIX.build/master/* directory. The file still works; it's just in a different place than you expected.

The first thing the script asks is whether you want to update the Knoppix version. This is your opportunity to update the version number to match your distribution versioning scheme:

```
Update KNOPPIX version (3.4 2004-05-17) in file
/KNOPPIX.build/master/KNOPPIX/knoppix-version and /etc/knoppix-version [N/
y]? y
[3.4 2004-05-17] 3.4 Knoppix Hacks
```

For instance, this example changes the version from 3.4 2004-05-07 to 3.4 Knoppix Hacks. You are then asked to update boot files. Say "no" because you do not have the boot file directories the script is looking for. Next, you are asked to recreate the *KNOPPIX* compressed filesystem. Answer "yes" to create the *master/KNOPPIX/KNOPPIX* compressed filesystem image. Then the script asks if you want to sweep and clean the system before you remaster. Answer "yes" for the script to update your Debian package listings, refresh your manpages and locate databases, refresh your font caches, and clean the filesystem of unneeded files.

Now the script creates your compressed filesystem. This process takes the same amount of time as manually entering the *mkisofs* command, so sit back and browse the Web until the command completes. Once it finishes, you are asked:

```
Recreate KNOPPIX-DE isofile '/KNOPPIX.build/master.iso'? y
```

Answer "y," even though it looks like the script is going to create a German version of the CD. Your CD is made from the English version, so all of the files it references are from the English version. After the script creates the CD image, it asks you:

```
Recreate KNOPPIX-EN isofile '/KNOPPIX.build/master-EN.iso'? n
BURN german CD version? n
```

Answer "n" to both questions, because the *master.iso* file is already the English version, and because you are likely booting from a Knoppix CD, your primary CD-ROM drive is not likely free for burning. At this point, your CD image is created and the script ends. Unmount the */proc* filesystem, and then type **exit** or hit Ctrl-D to leave the *chroot* environment:

```
root@ttyp0[/]# umount /proc
root@ttyp0[/]# exit
root@ttyp0[KNOPPIX]#
```

Your new image is *source/KNOPPIX/KNOPPIX.build/master.iso*. To test the image, reboot the computer and type:

```
knoppix bootfrom=/dev/hda1/source/KNOPPIX/KNOPPIX.build/master.iso
```

at the boot prompt, replacing *hda1* with your partition.

HACK #99   Morph Morphix

The modular nature of Morphix that has made it so popular also makes it very easy for a user to create custom discs.

Morphix [Hack #80] is a Knoppix-based distribution that has made many changes to the structure of Knoppix to make it more modular. These modules make it much easier to add and remove software for your own remastering. This hack takes a closer look at how Morphix is built, how it can be changed, and how you can have the modularity of Morphix make your life easier. If you want to skip the details and dive into making your first "morph," jump down to the "Your First Morph" section below.

Structure of a Morphix Live CD

A Morphix live CD has a number of unique directories:

/base
/mainmod
/minimod
/exec
/copy
/deb

One difference in these directories is the file types: the first three (*/base*, */mainmod*, and */minimod*) are compressed filesystems (modules); the last three are provided for extra flexibility. Morphix's modules can be compressed using a number of compression techniques, like *cloop*, *squashfs*, or *zisofs*. Of course, each of these directories has a special purpose, which are described below:

/base

This directory contains the normal boot files, similar to the */KNOPPIX* directory. The *morphix* file in this directory is comparable with the *KNOPPIX* file. It is a lot smaller, however (~30 MB versus ~700 MB), and contains only the bare necessities for getting your live CD up and running. A kernel, kernel modules, and hardware detection reside in the *boot.img* and *morphix* files.

/mainmod

A *mainmodule* is essentially your filesystem after your live CD has booted up. It contains everything, from your command-line tools to your window manager and graphical applications. Typically, most software on a Morphix ISO is kept in the *mainmodule*.

Once *base* has done its work, it attempts to find any files in the */mainmod* directory of your live CD. If there are multiple files, it prompts the user to select one of these *mainmodule*s. If there are none, the user is dropped to a *bash* prompt.

The *mainmodule* that gets selected (automatically or manually) is then mounted. The *base* module scripts link the necessary directories and copy the detected configuration files into the mounted *mainmodule*. The system then *chroots* into the directory of the mounted *mainmodule*. Scripts in the */morphix* directory of this *mainmodule* are then executed too. For example, in a normal Morphix ISO you can run *startx*, and your favorite window manager pops up and you can do business as usual, without even noticing the modular structure of Morphix underneath. An interesting ability of *mainmodule*s is that these don't necessarily have to be Debian-based. Morphix has Slackware, Fedora, and SUSE derivatives, showing the flexibility *mainmodule*s provide.

/minimod

*Minimodule*s are a third type of module. Essentially compressed images with a script inside, *minimodule*s can be as simple or as complex as you want them to be. They are mounted alongside the *mainmodule* at boot time. For demonstration purposes, here are a few examples:

- Morphix Game 0.4–1 has an Enemy Territory *minimodule*. This module seamlessly integrates with Morphix Game 0.4-1, and if a morpher decides he doesn't want to include Enemy Territory, he simply removes its *minimodule*.

- Morphix Gnome and KDE 0.4–1 have a WINE *minimodule*. Likewise, if a morpher doesn't want to include WINE on his live CD, he simply has to remove this file from his live CD image.

There are *minimodules* for console-specific tools, Quake 3 Arena and Unreal Tournament 2003 demos, OpenOffice.org, Speedtouch USB modems, PHP4/Nanoweb/MySQL, and a whole range of others. Morphix offers preliminary scripts to automatically generate these *minimodules* from Debian packages; however, this area is still under quite a lot of discussion and development.

You can also do more down-to-earth changes using *minimodules*. If you want to have different *minimodules* containing different home directories for your live CDs, take a look at *CD-Persistant*, a *minimodule* that even allows you to burn your home directory directly to a running live CD using multisession CD-ROMs, or *Xbroadcast*, which attempts to locate remote XDMCP hosts on your local network.

Needless to say, *minimodules* offer an extreme amount of flexibility, maybe even too much. For this reason, the following three directories for applying changes to your live CD during boot time have become a part of Morphix over the last year. No more do you have to rebuild your compressed images for small changes.

/exec

If you simply want to start a few *bash* scripts at boot time, this directory is the place to put them. Knoppix gives you a single file to be executed at boot time; Morphix gives you a directory.

/copy

Using translucency, the overlay technique in Morphix, you can place files anywhere on the filesystem. This is of course handy for *minimodules* but also for more simple purposes. Place a file in */copy/etc* and it is placed in */etc* of your live CD. Place a file in */copy/usr/local* and it is placed in */usr/local*. Morphers, being a lazy bunch, enjoy using */copy* for quick hacks.

/deb

If your *mainmodule* supports *dpkg* (which means it is Debian-based), put a Debian package in this directory, and the package is installed at boot time. Since this uses *dpkg* directly, you must make sure you handle your own dependencies for any packages you add here. As installing Debian packages does require some RAM, and each package increases the time your live CD takes to boot, make sure you don't put too many packages in here. When you want to install large packages, using *minimodules* or *mainmodules* quickly becomes a better alternative.

Your First Morph

Now that you know how a Morphix live CD can be structured, it is time to make a new live CD. Even if you skimmed over the last section, "morphing" isn't hard to start with. This first example is simple: it changes the default background of a live CD. There are plenty of scripts available to automate most or all of the process, but I won't use them here. Please note that you must be root for some of these commands.

For this morph, you must change the contents of your CD-ROM ISO. So you must make sure you can access the files on it. Make a directory and mount the ISO:

```
# mkdir /tmp/morphlight
# mount -o loop MorphixCombined-LightGUI-0.4-1.iso /tmp/morphlight
```

Alas, you can't directly modify the files on the ISO, so you must copy the files on the ISO to a new directory:

```
# mkdir /tmp/mylivecd
# cp -a /tmp/morphlight/* /tmp/mylivecd
```

The background is located at */morphix/background.png*. Instead of figuring out in which module it is located, use the */copy* directory to copy your new background (located at *~/mybackground.png* for this example) over the original one at boot time:

```
# mkdir /tmp/mylivecd/copy/morphix
# cp ~/mybackground.png /tmp/mylivecd/copy/morphix/background.png
```

Now make a new CD-ROM ISO from the */tmp/mylivecd* directory:

```
# mkisofs -l -v -J -V "My New LiveCD" -r -b base/boot.img -c
  base/boot.cat -hide -rr -moved -o /tmp/mylivecd.iso
  /tmp/mylivecd
```

Well, that's it! You can burn your ISO using your favorite CD-R burning tool, and you're done. One freshly baked live CD with your own background, coming right up:

```
# cdrecord speed=8 dev=0,0,0 /tmp/mylivecd.iso
```

Of course, this was a pretty simple morph. You can do quite amazing things using Morphix without remastering modules directly. For lots of step-by-step recipes and more elaborate documentation, take a look at the HOWTOs on *http://www.morphix.org*.

HACK #100   Auto-Build Morphix Modules

Morphix is already easy to change due to its modular nature, but you can make module creation even easier and more powerful by using Module Maker to automate building Morphix modules.

"Morph Morphix" **[Hack #99]** looks at how you can easily customize an existing Morphix live CD. This hack takes a look at Module Maker, or *MMaker*, a tool for auto-building Morphix modules.

Remastering modules is all fine and good, and you can do this just as you can with a compressed KNOPPIX image. However, laziness is seen as a virtue in Morphix-land: one command is all it should take to (re)build a module.

A Look at a Module Generator

MMaker is a tool under development at the moment, but it is quite simple in nature. Using a so-called template, an XML file with all the information about the module you want to build, you can auto-build a Morphix module:

```
$ mmaker mytemplate.xml mymodule.mod
```

What *MMaker* does when you execute this command is *debootstrap* a new Debian filesystem using the details in the template, set up the necessary *mainmodule* directories, and install all packages specified in the template, using APT to handle any dependencies. Afterwards, it compresses the whole bunch into a fresh new module, ready to be added to a Morphix live CD in the usual manner.

As you might have guessed, the template is the key to all of this. Here is a sample template that is used for Morphix LightGUI:

```xml
<comps>
 <groups>
  <version>0.5</version>
  <id>lightgui</id>
  <name>Morphix LightGUI</name>
  <repositorylist>
   <repository type="debian">ftp://ftp.debian.org/debian</repository>
   <repository type="plain">http://www.morphix.org/debian</repository>
  </repositorylist>
  <description>Morphix LightGUI mainmodule. Includes XFCE4, Firefox,
  Abiword and a host of other goodies</description>
  <type>mainmod</type>
  <suite>sid</suite>
  <packagelist>
   <packagereq>abiword</packagereq>
   <packagereq>xfce4</packagereq>
   <packagereq>mozilla-firefox</packagereq>
   <!-- ... other goodies here ... -->
```

```
    </packagelist>
  </group>
</comps>
```

Seems simple, doesn't it? The actual template for LightGUI is quite a bit longer (it contains more packages in the <packagelist> section and contains a package to start *xfce4* at boot time), but it's very simple to specify which repositories you want to use, which Debian suite you want, which type of Morphix module you want to auto-build, and, naturally, the packages you want. Currently, *MMaker* can build only *base* and *main* modules.

A few tags might need some extra explaining:

<repository>
> With this tag, you define the Debian repository to build your module from. Use the type="plain" attribute when you have a repository without separate suites. (You can verify this by checking the repository. If it has a *Packages* file in the root directory of the repository, we call it "plain.") Normal Debian-style repositories are the default.

<type>
> Mainmod or basemod. *Minimod* templates are in development (a separate *minimodule* generator was constructed before *MMaker*). It would actually be fairly easy to even have a Knoppix type.

<suite>
> Sid, sarge, woody (or unstable, testing, or stable). These are the three branches of Debian that Morphix is derived from.

<arch>
> With this tag, you define the architecture that you are building your module for. Using an architecture different from the host system isn't recommended and can lead to very interesting errors. It defaults to the architecture of your host system, which should be fine most of the time.

There are a few other tags and command-line options for *Mmaker*; consult the documentation for details.

After your module is built (which takes some time without a local Debian mirror), your uncompressed module exists in a directory in your */tmp* directory. *MMaker* outputs details of how to recompress it if necessary. Hopefully, *MMaker* is useful in letting Morphix work for you!

See Also

- The *Mmaker* Wiki page at *http://am.xs4all.nl/phpwiki/index.php/ModuleMaker*.
- MapLab tutorial map

Index

We'd like to hear your suggestions for improving our indexes. Send email to *index@oreilly.com*.

booting (continued)
  from floppy, 3
  from image, 12
  hardware detection, bypassing, 17
  network booting, 80–82
  RAM detection, 18
  troubleshooting, 17
  Windows boot.ini, repair with
       Knoppix, 215–217
boot.ini, 215

C

cabextract, 231
calendar application, 36
Captive NTFS, 219
  configuring, 219
  mounting NTFS partitions, 220
captive-ntfs, 251
CD image generation, 285
CD-ROMs
  booting from, 1
  CD image naming scheme, 5
  CDs, burning, 48
  CDs, writing, 17
  drive, freeing for faster Knoppix
       operation, 11–12
cfdisk, 100
  MBR and, 174
cheat codes, 1, 7–8
  advanced options, 16–19
  alsa, 17
  atapicd, 17
  boot prompt options, 7
  bootfrom, 12
  choosing a window manager, 8
  depth, 13
  dma, 18
  expert, 20
  expert26, 21
  fb, 15, 19
  fromhd, 12
  keyboard, 9
  knoppix2, 8
  knoppix26, 17
  lang, 9
  language cheat codes, 5
  mem, 18
  noapic, 18
  noapm, 18

  noeject and noprompt, 8
  nopcmcia, 20
  nowheelmouse, 15
  pci=irqmask=0x0e98, 20
  reboots and, 8
  screen, 13
  splash, 8
  text file of, 7
  text mode selection, 8
  tohd, 11
  toram, 11
  using, 7
  wheelmouse, 15
  xkeyboard, 9
  xserver and xmodule, 14
  xvrefresh and xhrefresh, 14
checksum, 5
chkrootkit, 150, 256
chntpw, 224, 227, 259
chroot command, 283
chrooted environments, 283
ciscilia, 259
ClamAV, 256
ClusterKnoppix, 265–271
  CD-ROM boot method, 268
  cluster testing, 270
  network boot method, 266
  OpenMosix, 265
  OpenMosix, configuring, 266
  setting up a cluster, 265
  web page, 271
cng_mac, 142
code examples, xix
configs.tbz, 64
console configuration, 15
contact management application, 36
Coroner's Toolkit, 182
cpio, 192
cryptcat, 260
Ctrl-Shift-Tab, 28
Ctrl-Tab, 28
customizing Knoppix, 281–285
  Morphix customization, 298–301
    autobuilding modules, 302–303
    CD structure, 298–300
    mainmodule, 299
    making a new CD, 301
    templates, 302
  personalizing, 289–293

home cheat code, 65–67
home directories, 67
    programs, installation in, 91
    saving, 65–67
honeypots, 257
hotsyncing Palm PDAs and Kontact, 37
httptunnel, 260

I

ide2=0x180 nopcmcia cheat code, 20
IDS (intrusion detection system), 257
init command, 207
    fixing broken init services, 206–209
INSERT (INside SEcurity Rescue
        Tool), 249–252
    captive-ntfs, 251
    history, 250
    Knoppix, compared to, 250
    size, 251
    tools for system recovery, 249
install-mbr, 176
install.sh, 94
instant messaging, 59
Internet
    connecting to, 50–51
        Bluetooth, using, 52–57
    informational resources for
        Knoppix, 61
IRC, 59
    #knoppix channel, 61
ISDN connection configuration, 51
isolinux, 251

J

John the Ripper, 258

K

KDE (K Desktop Environment), 23–29
    customizing, 29–33
        Appearance and Themes, 29–32
        Windows look, mimicing, 32
    K Menu, 24–28
        multimedia applications, 46–51
    K3b, 48
    KAlarm, 36
    KMail, 36
    KNotes, 37
    Konqueror browser, 57

Kontact, 36
    Palm PDA synchronization, 37
language settings, changing, 9
printer configuration, 38–40
saving settings, 68
xawtv, 49
xine, 49
kernels
    copying, 212
    list of parameters, 18
    RAID support, 195
    Version 2.6, 16
    version, checking, 12
Kershaw, Mike, 136
keyboards
    configuration, expert mode, 21
    keyboard mapping, changing, 9
kiosks, 73–79
    configuring Mozilla, 74
    default desktop environment, 75
    JavaScript code, 73
    master disks, creating, 79
    network booting, 79
    saving settings, 78
    startkiosk function, 76
Kismet, 136, 262
    configuration, 138–141
klik, 95
    klik recipes, creating, 96
Knopper, Klaus, xv
Knoppix, xv, 1
    available distributions, 237–279
        ClusterKnoppix, 265–271
        Damn Small Linux, 247–249
        distccKNOPPIX, 263
        Freeduc, 245–246
        GIS Knoppix, 274–275
        Gnoppix, 240–242
        INSERT, 249–252
        Knoppix-STD, 254–263
        KnoppMyth, 275–277
        Local Area Security
          Linux, 252–254
        Mediainlinux, 242–245
        Morphix, 238–240
        Quantian, 271–273
    beta versions, language support, 9
    booting (see booting)
    CD image naming scheme, 5
    contributing, 278

S

Sarge, 99
saveconfig, 63
screen cheat code, 13
SCSI emulation, disabling, 17
security
    auditing, 143–150
    root kits, checking for, 150–152
session files, 68
shadyshell, 261
shorewall, 257
Sid, 99
skins for XMMS, 47
sndconfig, 46
snort, 258
sound cards, 46
sound cards, configuring, 17
sound editing, 47
source code and program
    installation, 92
splash cheat code, 8
spreadsheet application,
    OpenOffice.org, 35
startkiosk function, 76
steganography, 256
<suite> tag, 303
svga video module, 14
symlink farms, 94
system administration, 112
    Knoppix tools for, 112–169
        desktop sharing, 116
        emergency services (see
            emergency services)
        forensics data
            collection, 152–155
        FreeNX, 117–122
        hard drives, cloning, 155–159
        hard drives, wiping, 159
        hardware compatibility,
            testing, 161–167
        krdc, 114
        lisa, 122
        network security
            auditing, 143–150
        NX server (see NX server)
        rdesktop, 115
        RDP, 114
        root kits, checking for, 150–152
        settings, copying to other
            distributions, 167–169

VNC, 113
    wardriving (see wardriving)
    xvncviewer, 113

T

tar, 189–191
    backup, 189
    partitions, backup and
        restoration, 190
    restore, 190
TCP tools, 260
tcpkill, 260
tcpreplay, 260
text mode, booting to, 8
Tivo, using a computer for, 275–277
Todo List, 36
tohd cheat code, 11
toram cheat code, 11
Trinux, 254
tunnels, 260
TV, 49
<type> tag, 303

U

unrm utility, 182–183
update-grub tool, 173
updating custom Knoppix
    discs, 293–295
USB key drives, utility of, 218

V

vesa video module, 14
video conferencing, 59
videos, 49
virus scanning Windows systems, 232
VNC (Virtual Network
    Computing), 113

W

wallpaper, 30
wardriving, 136–143
    connecting to networks, 142
    GPS data, collecting, 138
    Kismet, 136
        configuration, 138–141
    necessary hardware, 137
    session mapping, 141
watch command, 192

Colophon

Our look is the result of reader comments, our own experimentation, and feedback from distribution channels. Distinctive covers complement our distinctive approach to technical topics, breathing personality and life into potentially dry subjects.

The tool on the cover of *Knoppix Hacks* is a pocket knife. Since prehistoric times, knives have been used for hunting, eating, and defense. Frontiersmen, explorers, travelers, and soldiers all found ways of making their knives portable. Some knives were placed in sheaths and attached to belts, or they were slipped into stockings. Knives that were designed to fold into the handle were carried in pockets.

These folding, or pocket, knives were first made in the first century by the Romans for use in exploration and conquest. By the sixteenth century, they had gained popularity in America, because unlike sheathed knives (which were suspicious-looking), pocket knives were easily and safely placed in pockets, invisible to the eyes of potential enemies.

Sarah Sherman was the production editor and the copyeditor for *Knoppix Hacks*, and Matt Hutchinson was the proofreader. Sanders Kleinfeld, Claire Cloutier, and Emily Quill provided quality control. John Bickelhaupt wrote the index.

Hanna Dyer designed the cover of this book, based on a series design by Edie Freedman. The cover image is an original photograph. Clay Fernald produced the cover layout with QuarkXPress 4.1 using Adobe's Helvetica Neue and ITC Garamond fonts. David Futato designed and produced the CD label using Adobe InDesign CS.

David Futato designed the interior layout. This book was converted by Julie Hawks to FrameMaker 5.5.6 with a format conversion tool created by Erik Ray, Jason McIntosh, Neil Walls, and Mike Sierra that uses Perl and XML technologies. The text font is Linotype Birka; the heading font is Adobe Helvetica Neue Condensed; and the code font is LucasFont's TheSans Mono Condensed. The illustrations that appear in the book were produced by Robert Romano and Jessamyn Read using Macromedia FreeHand 9 and Adobe Photoshop 6. This colophon was written by Sarah Sherman.